IN CONVERSATION WITH ELEANOR SHARPSTON

What was behind a legal life lived in the spotlight? In this extended conversation between Professor Adam Łazowski and Dame Eleanor Sharpston KC, one of the most important European lawyers of her generation, two friends lift the curtain on what was happening backstage.

Over nine chapters, they discuss Eleanor's early life, her university years, and her parallel career at the Bar and in academe. They move on to consider her leading cases in the English courts, which included *Brown and Others* (Operation Spanner) and the *Metric Martyr*, before laying out a thoughtful insider's assessment of her time on the bench at the Court of Justice of the European Union in Luxembourg. The closing chapter of the book is dedicated to current events, including the rule of law crisis and the future of European integration. A candid, illuminating and often amusing discussion with a transformative European lawyer.

In Conversation with Eleanor Sharpston

A Life, A Journey

Adam Łazowski
and
Eleanor Sharpston

•HART•
OXFORD • LONDON • NEW YORK • NEW DELHI • SYDNEY

HART PUBLISHING

Bloomsbury Publishing Plc

Kemp House, Chawley Park, Cumnor Hill, Oxford, OX2 9PH, UK

1385 Broadway, New York, NY 10018, USA

Bloomsbury Publishing Ireland Limited, 29 Earlsfort Terrace, Dublin 2, D02 AY28, Ireland

HART PUBLISHING, the Hart/Stag logo, BLOOMSBURY and the Diana logo are trademarks of Bloomsbury Publishing Plc

First published in Great Britain 2026

A catalogue record for this book is available from the British Library.

A catalogue record for this book is available from the Library of Congress.

Library of Congress Control Number: 2026931088

ISBN: HB: 978-1-50999-232-4
ePDF: 978-1-50999-234-8
ePub: 978-1-50999-233-1

Typeset by Compuscript Ltd, Shannon

Preface

This is an extraordinary book about a unique personality.

Lawyers recognise Dame Eleanor Sharpston DCMG KC for her dedication, during nearly 15 years as a member of the EU Court of Justice, to developing European law in line with the high ideals underpinning post-war reconstruction. But to her friends and fans she is simply Leo – Wonder Woman come to life.

Who else but a comic book superhero with a human *alter ego* would appear in so many different roles? Persuaded by friends one evening to apply for the job that was to be her destiny, she discovered that applications had to be in no later than noon the following day. By the time she had put together a written application, it was well past midnight. But that wasn't the problem: she had to be in Cambridge by 9am to teach a two-hour class.

Kitting herself out as a motorcycle courier – one of the many jobs she had taken as a student – Wonder Woman made her way to a government building near Whitehall and woke up the security guard. He reluctantly signed his name halfway down her clipboard of fictitious deliveries.

After a couple of hours' sleep she rode her motorbike to Cambridge and taught the class. Immediately afterwards, having cast aside the demotic persona that disarmed the security guard, she spoke to the government department in the cut-glass tones of Eleanor Sharpston QC and was reassured that her application had reached the required desk.

Months later, the department phoned back. Unfamiliar with her bass speaking voice – though she sings as a tenor – an official addressed her as 'Sir' and demanded to speak to Miss Sharpston. After much prevarication, the official was persuaded to tell her that she was the UK's preferred choice for appointment as an Advocate General in Luxembourg – one of the key figures on whom EU judges rely.

There is much in this book about the important cases on which she advised the Court and the influential Opinions she wrote. But this is also a story of an outsider who excelled at everything she put her mind to.

Sharpston's family roots lie in Lithuania and Ireland. Her Orthodox Jewish father – whose parents simply invented the name Sharpston – had promised his wife-to-be that their children would be brought up as Roman Catholics.

In Brazil – where her father had taken a job and where, inevitably, she learned Portuguese – nine-year-old Eleanor managed to horrify the nuns at her convent school by suggesting that the story of the virgin birth was based on a mistranslation from Hebrew into Greek.

Back in the London suburbs at the age of 12, she was found by her father studying a Hebrew grammar – together with a prayer book and *The Guide for the Perplexed*, written by Maimonides in the 12th century. It was an early sign of Sharpston's relentless autodidacticism.

Three or four years later, when she should have been studying for her A-Levels, Sharpston's parents moved to Austria. Having already progressed from her childhood piano-playing via the mandolin to classical guitar and violin, she duly studied at the *Konservatorium* in Vienna and now plays orchestral viola at concert level – despite a hearing disability. She's also back again as a student at a different specialist music school – the *Conservatoire du Nord* in Ettelbruck – avidly learning the bass *viola da gamba* and resuscitating her mandolin-playing.

And then there are the languages. She has university-level Latin, Greek and Spanish, with conversational Italian and the remnants of her childhood's Brazilian Portuguese. Her musician's German from her schooling in Austria and the total fluency she had acquired in French would have been more than enough to get by in the country where she was to work. But naturally, she taught herself Luxembourgish.

Working in the grand duchy for the British judge Sir Gordon Slynn, she used to take karate lessons at lunchtime. He seemed unconcerned when Sharpston came back with a black eye one afternoon, having failed to block a punch. Back at the Court as an Advocate General, she made up for it by being awarded her black belt.

Sharpston got involved in miscellaneous sports at university team level at Cambridge, where she was awarded a first in economics, eventually getting that elusive Blues recognition in her final term – as a cricketer. Somewhere along the way she qualified as a football referee. Then she moved to Oxford, where she did doctoral research and played squash and messed about in boats. Though no taller than the cox, she rowed for Oxford in the Women's Boat Race in 1980, appearing prominently in a picture of the winning Blue Boat crew that appeared on the front page of *The Times*.

That, though, was how the dean of the Inns of Court School of Law found out that one of his students had been studying full-time, simultaneously, at two academic institutions 50 miles apart – while spending much of her time on the river. Ticking her off for two-timing him, he totally failed to recognise that she was demonstrating the very skills that would bring her success in the law.

But there was tragedy too. When Sharpston met the love of her life, they agreed to try their hand at each other's favourite sports. Naturally, she excelled at his chosen activity, which was scuba diving. He was less keen on skiing, which she had started at the age of 10 and was (and is) seriously addicted to.

'We were best mates as well as husband and wife,' she says, 'and we probably fitted more sheer happiness and slightly unhinged comedy into the eight-and-a-half years of our marriage than many married couples manage over decades.' David Lyon died suddenly of a brain haemorrhage in March 2000.

One last shape-shifting story – this time from her undergraduate days in Cambridge. As editor of the student newspaper, she used to work all night, three nights a week, at the paper's offices not far from her college. She usually made it back to King's shortly before dawn.

'It was not good form to wake the porters,' she recalls. 'After all, you were not meant to be outside college at that time of night.' Fortunately, there was a gap in the railings by the chapel that students could squeeze through.

As she was about to climb in, two police officers leapt from a patrol car and rugby-tackled her roughly to the ground. She was scruffily dressed – though her hair was unusually short for a student – and the paperwork in her bag gave her name as Leo.

'We think we've got him,' they radioed in. 'We think we have the rapist.'

There was, indeed, a sexual predator on the loose. But it was not her. She stood up very straight and stuck her chest out. Realising their mistake, the officers took off her handcuffs and brought her to the college gates.

'Oh, Leo, what have you been up to now, then?' the porter demanded to know.

Asked the same question now, she could simply hand him a copy of this fascinating book.

Joshua Rozenberg

Foreword

Good conversations don't follow a script. Like a good song, they're full of surprises, improvisations, detours. They may be grounded in a specific time and place, reflecting your current state of mind and the current state of the world. But the best conversations also have a timeless quality, taking you back into the realm of memory, propelling you forward toward your hopes and dreams.

(Barack Obama, in Barack Obama and Bruce Springsteen, *Renegades Born in the USA* (Penguin, Random House 2021) XI

Eleanor: Where do we start, Adam?

Adam: Let's start from the beginning, Leo. In a way, we need to travel back to April 2022 when we met again in Budapest after a long Covid-19 break. You were there to preside over the Central and Eastern Europe Moot Competition ('CEEMC'), and I was one of the judges. Over dinner we sat at the same table and talked for hours. The conversation continued over a long midnight walk back to the hotel. As it happened, my bedtime reading at the time was Jeffrey Rosen's *Conversations with Ruth Bader Ginsburg* and the richness of what we talked about made me immediately think that we ought to do such a book.

Eleanor: True, but our acquaintance goes back much further, to the annual seminars in Dubrovnik – lots of threads that are developed in this book stem from there. Partly because we were there together and hung out together after the formal teaching part of the seminar ended every day, we started talking together about a lot of things that were neither law nor what had gone into the most recent AG Sharpston Opinion. Music. Theatre. Languages. *Mitteleuropa* and European history. What really matters about the 'European project'. We became interested in each other's back history. I tell shaggy dog stories from my past occasionally, over a meal after a conference, to amuse my friends. Most of the stories are against myself. But it had never occurred to me to put them together as a connected narrative.

Adam: Well, I have been stuck with this idea in my head since Budapest, however the imposter syndrome kept my fingers away from the 'enter' key on the computer. Then, in December 2023, we met in a small cafe at the back of King's College London to record a short interview from which Catherine Barnard, Daniel Sarmiento, and your humble servant would draw inspiration for the introduction to the *Festschrift* for you. It was Catherine's idea and she was there with us. (Thank you, Catherine!) Then I finally had the guts to ask if such a book would be something that might interest you.

Eleanor: And I was taken aback and honoured in about equal measure. You told me about the RBG book. I had met Ruth Bader Ginsberg briefly when the Court of Justice made an official visit to the US Supreme Court in 2017 and, of course, by that stage she was simply an icon for any aspiring liberal lawyer. I found it breathtaking, extraordinary that you were thinking in terms of doing a similar exploration with me.

Adam: Oh Leo, for many of us you are a role model, not only as a lawyer but – first and foremost – as a human being. As I told you when we were discussing this book, your life story is extraordinary. It is a very European story that should be shared with others. In the words of Lord Anderson of Ipswich: 'Sharpston's life and qualities fully merit that overused epithet, unique.'

Whatever we talked about before, in, and after Budapest would have the law in it. This is inevitable bearing in mind what you have been doing in your professional life. I recall you saying in one of the interviews that one aspect of being in that profession you cherish the most is the ability to engage in a legal analysis. [*Eleanor* (aside): I think that's real professional deformation on my part!] For that to happen one needs to be good at using, as Ruth Bader Ginsberg said, a telescope and a microscope.

Eleanor: I would agree – but I would add, you also need a wide-angle lens. The telescope will enable you to see the far-off objective. The microscope is needed for the close-up detail on which the quality of your analysis will depend. And the wide-angle lens will show you the surrounding landscape into which your decision must fit.

Adam: Absolutely.

Eleanor: To offer a different analogy (one that is perhaps particularly appropriate to EU law, which is very much a work in progress): when you argue or decide a case, you are dealing with one piece in a part-completed mosaic. Some parts of the mosaic are, of course, spectacular and brightly coloured. They're great fun to work on, whether as counsel or as a judge or Advocate General. Other parts – the background stuff in the corners, probably beige or grey – don't draw so much attention to themselves but they too are essential to the final creation. However, you don't have a detailed cartoon showing you exactly what the mosaic is meant to look like when it's finished. And there you are, holding the next small stone cube in your hands. You can see roughly where it's meant to go. But how precisely should it be positioned? You turn it around, trying out this and that option. Whilst doing so, you draw on what's in yourself just as much as you draw on the external elements. How should this fit? Occasionally an individual piece gets positioned incorrectly. Later on, as more of the mosaic gets finished, that becomes apparent; and then the Court has to undo the error, prise out the ill-fitting stone, and re-lay that particular part of the mosaic.

Adam: This is so very true, I'd say not only when it comes to the law but life in general. It is a one big mosaic. To understand any person we ought to use exactly the same three devices as a good lawyer should. Starting with the wide-angle lens. The big picture, someone's background is important to understanding a person: what they have done during the course of a life (including public life) and – above all – *why* they did, said, or wrote that rather than something else. Then we need a telescope and a microscope to understand them better. Just a snippet: if one knows that you come from a mixed Irish and Lithuanian Jewish background, and that your father's family came to the UK as refugees, then what you have written as AG Sharpston in the *Reallocation cases* not only is an exemplar of rich and sound legal analysis but it also has a very profound meaning. It is clear that you wrote from the heart. (And not only the paragraph that I have particularly in mind.)

Eleanor: The story about the men in the boat that found its way into the final section of that Opinion?

Adam: Precisely, that's the one.

Eleanor: That story from the Talmud has been a beacon to my life ever since I first read it aged twelve. I think that there's also an important subtext here. Whatever job you end up doing and however far you go with that job, you should be yourself in that job. You should be who you are, coming from your own background, and that should be your basis and platform for what you then say and do in your career. In order to be an authentic lawyer and get your point across, you don't have to speak as though you have swallowed a dictionary and a thesaurus. On the contrary: forceful advocacy comes from speaking convincingly like a human being. An Israeli violinist, or a Central European violinist, plays with their soul. Exactly the same should be true of a lawyer who is really committed to their work. Whichever side of the case you are arguing as counsel, you are contributing to the rule of law through giving the court well-focused legal analysis. And if you have the chance and the privilege to work as part of the judiciary (broadly defined – obviously, I include being an Advocate General within that term), you should reason with your head but also check with your heart and your soul that what you are proposing rings true.

Adam: Oh yes. I fully subscribe to what you have just said. This is getting very interesting but still we have not answered the question of what we are doing with this book. Why did we sit down and have these conversations together?

Eleanor: Well – I hope *not* to glorify me! To break the mould? To show that you can be a quirky individual from a family background that wasn't full of successful, well-paid establishment lawyers and nevertheless manage to get far enough along the road to make a bit of a difference? To encourage other, younger, unconventional colleagues to back their luck and stick with this particular way of touching other people's lives? To suggest that you can be a committed public servant without having to swallow a poker and be a one-dimensional robot in a grey suit?

Adam: Indeed. I'd definitely add: to show that life can be very rich if only one has a desire to stay away from a daily routine and a blinkered devotion to one's chosen profession. To show that we can nourish our curiosity and engage in 'extracurricular' activities to make our daily existence worthwhile …

Eleanor: … and that we can go on making space for that to happen, not just as a first-year student fresh at Uni, but all the way along our career. That there is more – much more – to life than going to sleep (at the end of a day with at least fourteen billable hours squeezed into it) with a half-read copy of the European Law Review on one's bedside table. However brilliant that latest contribution in the ELRev from a respected colleague undoubtedly is.

Adam: Alright then, the *raison d'être* for this book is getting clearer! Oscar Wilde once said that 'conversation is one of the loveliest of arts.' I have a feeling that our conversations will be as described by Barack Obama: like a good song, full of surprises, improvisations, and detours. They will take us back into the realm of memory, and yet propel us forward in the direction of hopes and dreams. We don't have a script, just a general idea as to the direction of travel. Let's see where it takes us, shall we?

Eleanor: Why not?

Cambridge and London
January 2024–January 2025

Contents

1

The Making of Leo

I came from a family background which was
unashamedly card-carrying intellectual.
The standard way that the family spent time was
talking about things, discussing issues.
We didn't sit down with a TV dinner
and while away the evening.
We tended to start talking about something that was
topical or something that was a philosophical problem.
Inevitably, we took sides, we raised questions.
*This was the air I breathed.**

Adam: A warm spring evening somewhere on the Mediterranean coast, a gentle breeze from the sea. (Dubrovnik will serve beautifully, right?) Or, in the alternative, snow is gently falling, making the world outside look rather idyllic. (Vilnius is particularly picturesque under a blanket of fresh snow, try to disagree!) A group of EU lawyers has gathered and is deep into hours' worth of conversations (formal or more convivial, no difference whatsoever).

Can you picture this?

I can.

Topics fly around, anything from the most recent landmark and groundbreaking judgment of the Court of Justice of the European Union (the 'CJEU') (or, for good measure, an Opinion of one of its eleven Advocates General), through some recent judicial appointments to the Court on the *Kirchberg Plateau*, to a new piece of secondary legislation adopted by EU institutions. I am ready to bet a good bottle of Georgian amber wine (*Rkatsiteli* anyone?) that if, at some point, someone mentions Eleanor Sharpston, all attention will move to her stellar fourteen and a half years on the bench in Luxembourg.

What is your favourite Sharpston Opinion?

Oh, I am passionate about EU citizenship, so surely it is Ruiz Zambrano.

Yes of course. Hmm … these days I am more into rule of law, therefore for me her Opinions in Heinrich or Sturgeon stand out.

C'mon, aren't you at least puzzled why the Court did not follow her in Miles, and declared that the reference for preliminary ruling was not admissible.

Gosh, that Opinion on the Free Trade Agreement with Singapore … what a monster.

Well, do you remember AG Sharpston's Opinion in the Reallocations cases? The last paragraphs about solidarity and that story from the Talmud?

Yes, of course, these last three paragraphs are so powerful, aren't they?

The discussion is likely to focus on the content of the Opinions, the legal argumentation, or – on some occasions – an interesting comparison that AG Sharpston decided to draw to direct readers to a particular phenomenon or to make her audience appreciate better the big picture and the pertinent legal issues at stake. No matter how distinguished the gathering and knowledgeable the conversation is, this is where – most likely – it will end. Many of those in attendance would know Dame Eleanor Sharpston DCMG, KC, *Grand Officier* of the *Ordre de Mérite* of the Grand Duchy of Luxembourg, only from her Opinions and, perhaps, from her academic writing. Some, maybe, would have listened to one, or more, of her engaging conference talks and public lectures. A very few, if anyone at all, in that congregation, would know more about her life and career before becoming an Advocate General. Indeed, as Émile Zola aptly put it, 'We are like books. Most people only see our cover, the minority read only the introduction, many people believe the critics. Few will know our content.'[1] Once someone is familiar with Eleanor's 'content', knows her as a person, appreciates her background and many passions, then the AG Sharpston Opinions prepared for the benefit of the Court and the wider EU law audience, will – perhaps – read differently. They may not only make – even more – perfect sense, but they may also be easier to explain and to understand. Sometimes their meaning will have gained yet another layer or, perhaps, will have become even more powerful. One never knows. This applies in equal measure to the profound and the profane, though. Let me give you two examples, one from each category.

As soon as one learns the story of Eleanor's family on the paternal side, one sees the plea in *Ruiz Zambrano* for EU citizenship to be a meaningful concept, and not just a shop window decoration, in a very different light.[2] This is, of course, AG Sharpston talking but also Eleanor Sharpston, the descendant of the Snipelinsky family, which had been forced to leave their Eastern European homeland in search of a safe haven from persecution. It is also the same Eleanor Sharpston who strongly believes that the European project, despite its imperfections, is worth fighting for as the peace dividend cannot be taken for granted.

This is profound, what about the profane, you may ask. *Et voila*: comparing a tight filtering system for environmental NGOs to gain access to the German administrative courts to a 'Ferrari with its doors locked shut' becomes self-explanatory when Leo takes you for a ride in her little Mazda sports car (just make sure you practice some yoga beforehand, additional flexibility is required to get in and out). And so it goes.

A *cliché*, I know, but still worth repeating. We, as humans, are a sum of parts. We carry our baggage from our early days. We may feel that we are forever eighteen but inevitably, every twelve months we gain another year of experience.

Home (whatever and wherever it may be) is a starting point that often determines who we are and how we navigate our lives. A lucky few are born with a silver spoon in their mouth. Alas, most of us are less fortunate. Yet, no matter where we come from (east, west, north, south, or variations of those) and where we grow up, what the colour of our skin is, what the religion or beliefs are, our goal is to progress forward. As we pass one life goal post after another, we must, in the words of Barack Obama, '[…] honour those who walked so we could run. We must run so our children soar'.[3] Following this desideratum, our conversations start by looking back at early days. We are first introduced to Eleanor's parents and the family home that they created, initially for her older brother Michael, and then – when she arrived a little unexpectedly – also for her. We are also given an insight into the Sharpston family peregrinations. All this, combined with limitless curiosity and her passion for life, shaped Eleanor whom I have had the great honour to get to know better and, just like her other friends, I am permitted to call by her nickname 'Leo'.

First things first, though. Eleanor Sharpston was born on 13 July 1955 in London (as she puts it, 'because the family happened to be there for a bit at the time'). She grew up in Brazil, Switzerland, France, and Austria. Young Eleanor attended schools in Brazil and the UK. From her early days, she excelled academically. She received scholarships to both UK secondary schools (St Paul's Girls' School and Bedales School) that she attended. However, she left formal schooling in the UK at age 16, passed her A levels in 1972 with straight As in Latin, Greek, French, and S level French (merit). Meanwhile she had commenced music studies (classical guitar and violin) at the *Konservatorium der Stadt Wien* (the Vienna Conservatory). Then came the University of Cambridge, with which she would be associated for most of her working life. She entered King's College, Cambridge in 1973 and graduated in 1976. She was admitted to Cambridge in classics (Latin and Greek); studied economics, modern languages (French and Spanish), economics (again) and then a single, fourth year's worth of law. Already, she showed a particular talent for two-, or even three-timing, by pursuing a wide variety of extracurricular activities. On came music, sport, student journalism, and many others. She graduated with her BA with first class honours in economics. The Oxford period of her life was between 1977–1980. At Corpus Christi College she conducted interdisciplinary research in economics and law; lectured in applied statistics for development economics; tutored in economic theory and – but of course – spent time representing the university at squash and, even more comprehensively, at rowing. So, if you associate the name Eleanor Sharpston with only one walk of life, then fasten your seatbelt. This will be quite a ride, both in this chapter and in the ones that follow.

*

Adam: George Bernard Shaw said that 'life isn't about finding yourself, life is about creating yourself'.[4] Leo, you have created a polymath. For the lucky ones who know you, this is not news. I am sure we all, without exception, admire you for your countless talents and seemingly unlimited energy. What you have done could fill many lives, and yet – unless someone has secretly cloned you (and I am not aware of that) – you embarked on all those journeys as one human being. I am very curious how Leo starts a completely new journey and decides to try something different. Does Leo put a lot of thinking into it, or does she just follow her instinct?

Eleanor: I didn't begin the story knowing I wanted to be 'A', 'B' or 'C'. I seemed to be reasonably good as an instrumentalist and I love music. The deceptively easy career path, given that I had managed to get a place at the Conservatory in Vienna to do classical guitar and violin, would have been as a musician. Leo's inner conversation was probably along the lines: 'why don't I see how this plays out' (forgive the pun) 'and whether this is something that I can do'. But in parallel I was doing my academic studies. I started having hearing problems (partial deafness and tinnitus) when I was seventeen. That's not great in the immensely competitive world of classical music. I hasten to add: I might also easily not have been good enough to make a success of a musical career. I'm not putting out the begging bowl for sympathy. Fortunately, it was obvious that I also had a reasonable academic bent. Both my parents had first class honours degrees from the University of Cambridge. There was an expectation that I would go to university; but nothing constraining in terms of, 'when you go to university, you must read this, or you must read that'. Only much, much later did I discover that my father Charles had secretly himself wished to be a barrister, but family circumstances had not made that an available option. He never disclosed that interesting snippet of information whilst I was choosing what I was doing. He never put any pressure on me. Once I had started in practice at the Bar, though, he was obviously so thrilled that his daughter had become a barrister. So, I dug a bit and then I found out. It was, in a sense, very typical of my parents. If there was something I wanted to try, they made sure that it could happen.

There was always a strange mixture of the artistic and the academic. My mother Pauline, when she was at Cambridge studying modern languages, was also in parallel zipping down to London to do ballet classes with the White Russians. She obviously thought that that was something you could combine with the academic world of Cambridge. So, the idea of combining academic, intellectual, and artistic was there. Nobody drew hard and fast lines on the drawing board in my family. No one said that if you are doing 'A', then naturally that excludes doing 'B'. I probably carried over from that the idea that there is no need to put down any dividing lines, any boundaries, on the board at any stage. Maybe you are doing 'A' as a career, but hey, why not give 'B', or even 'C', a try as well?

Adam: I recall you saying that listening to advice provided by your parents' friends, you got the conjunctions wrong and 'or' somewhat miraculously turned into 'and'.

Eleanor: Indeed. My parents' nice friends in Vienna congratulated me very politely on my place at Cambridge (obviously they also congratulated my parents: 'you must be very proud'). Then, with the best intentions in the world, they said:

> *When you are at Cambridge, you must – of course – be serious about your studies. It is important that you come out with a good degree. But you know, dear Eleanor, there are all these other things going on. There is really interesting student life in Cambridge: there is student politics, there is journalism, music, theatre, and various other pursuits. Naturally there is sport and we know you love sports.*

I think that they had intended me to interpolate the conjunction 'or' between those various suggestions, but I do have hearing problems. So I just substituted a different conjunction: 'and' for 'or'. I construed those kind remarks as an invitation to go and play, to go and try whatever was out there that was available.

Adam: It boils down to your character, Leo, because you are an admirably, and perhaps incurably, curious person. Law, music, sailing, rowing, black belt in karate, football referee qualifications, your passion for motorbikes, to name just a few – the list of your interests and passions is way longer. I guess, from what you have already said, it runs in the family. As a saying goes, the apple doesn't fall far from the tree (funny enough we also have equivalents in Polish and in Ukrainian: *'nie daleko spada jabłko od jabłoni'*/*'Яблуко від яблуні недалеко падає'*). Let's then start with your parents, shall we?

Eleanor: My father Charles was a mathematician and economist: a scholarship boy at Corpus Christi College, Cambridge. His family was Litvak Jewish (that is, from Lithuania or Eastern Poland, depending on the vintage of the map that you happen to be consulting). My father's mother was born there, so our arrival in the UK as immigrants is not that far back in the family tree. They moved out in one of the many waves when being Jewish was not flavour of the month. Like all good Jews, they turned up in the East End of London and then – as they became a bit more prosperous – they made their way westward and northward to St John's Wood. They became members of the English establishment – except they never really did, because they remained very, very liberal and very much aware of where they came from and how things had been. They also changed their name because they decided that being called 'Snipelinsky' was not going to help them in identifying as British. So they opted for the name Sharpston, which is a pure invention.

Adam: What about your mother?

Eleanor: My mother Pauline was the most Irish of Irish women that you can possibly imagine. She may have had a cut-glass upper class English accent thanks to her schooling by the 'Girls' Public Day Schools Trust', but she was more Irish than the day is long. Her family was fairly clearly republican Irish, I would say. She got a scholarship to Girton College, Cambridge, to read modern languages

('MML'). This was at a time when the University of Cambridge was not giving women degrees, so she was given a 'title to a degree'. If she had been a man, she would have had her Cambridge BA with first class honours in MML. She finally took her degree after the Second World War and returned much later – when I was already back at Cambridge as an academic – to take part in the festivities to mark fifty years of women (finally) being allowed to be full members of the University. My mother's career – this is obviously at a time when women's careers were subordinate to the husband's career – was a patchwork quilt that encompassed everything from teaching to running a ballet school.

Adam: And then, of course, there was your brother Michael.

Eleanor: My brother Michael was nearly eleven years older than I – my parents had not originally intended to have more than the one child. When people saw Michael and myself together, generally their reaction was, 'Pauline, how could you have done exactly the same thing twice?' We looked ridiculously alike, for a start (we used to joke about 'lateral heredity'); and of course – quite unconsciously – I picked up and imitated a number of his mannerisms. And we were very close emotionally. Most of the time that was a very positive characteristic. During the sad time when Michael was struggling with severe mental illness, it was very negative and in a sense quite dangerous. Before his illness, Michael had had an exceptional career as an economist – as a lecturer at Cambridge, then with the Ford Foundation project in Ghana, after which he joined the World Bank (the International Bank for Reconstruction and Development, to give it its proper title). There he acquired an enviable reputation for being able to think outside the box about big problems. I remember that, in the summer after my first year at Cambridge, my parents and Michael and I were all together in the US. My mother had a few weeks' freelance contract with the UN in New York. My father stayed with her there and I went down to Washington DC to join Michael. I found him utterly immersed in the deep research that led to his brilliant health policy paper, which was an absolute gamechanger for World Bank strategy on health systems in developing countries. Michael had a partial claim on two research assistants but really needed about five. I had just spent a year reading economics, so naturally I stepped very willingly into the gap! It was absolutely fascinating to work with an outstanding professional economist who happened to be my brother. As far as I remember, for a month Michael and I ate, drank, and breathed health policy, stopping occasionally and a bit reluctantly to sleep. I got the chance to see, from the inside, how you began by casting your net over apparently disparate material that no one had looked at properly before or even necessarily thought to be relevant – everything from epidemiology to sociology, via traditional medicine and differing cultural patterns in different parts of the world. And then weaving all those strands together into a new, fully thought-through, coherent whole: such a tour de force! After his illness and his early retirement from the World Bank on medical grounds, Michael turned his analytical engine full-throttle onto the science of photography and – in that totally different field – did some really interesting and creative work. And at that late stage, Michael re-met and married my wonderful Peruvian sister-in-law Inés, herself a fine professional and ex-World Bank staffer, who loved him and looked after him up to his relatively early death in May 2018.

Adam: I suppose the peregrinations during the formative years, as your father pursued various occupations in Brazil, Switzerland, and Austria, must have also nourished your curiosity. How did the travels happen? It must have been quite unusual back then to change countries, or even continents, ever so often.

Eleanor: My parents had the habit of travelling, and they appear also to have made a habit of going somewhere fairly exotic when their child was six, and staying there until their child was 10. That is exactly what they did with my elder brother Michael. When Michael was six, my father got a job with the colonial service in what was then Tanganyika, now Tanzania. So, the family headed off to *Dar es Salaam* and stayed there for four years. When Michael was 10, they came back to the UK. They found that my father didn't really have much in the way of a job when he came back. In fact, I made my appearance at a moment when my father was unemployed. The family was in straitened circumstances, to put it diplomatically. My one grandparent whom I knew, my grandmother on my mother's side, was extremely angry with her son-in-law Charles for being so irresponsible as to add to the family at that particular moment. It really was not the time for another child to show up. But we all survived that, including myself. When I was six, history repeated itself. My father again got the opportunity to go off somewhere exotic. In this instance it was *São Paulo*; and he took with him his wife, his mother-in-law, and his six year old daughter. My brother Michael was about to go up to the University of Cambridge as an undergraduate, so he did not move to Brazil with us, but of course he joined us there during university vacations. We stayed in Brazil for four years. We were definitely a family that was accustomed to the idea of just getting up and travelling.

Adam: I am curious to know, what brought your father to Brazil?

Eleanor: My father set up the subsidiary of the English company for whom he was then working, CAV, which was part of the Lucas group. The backstory is a very simple one. CAV Lucas used to supply fuel injection pumps for diesel engines that went into vehicles made by Volkswagen. At a certain moment, Volkswagen decided to set up its first manufacturing plant outside Europe, in Brazil. They called in all their standard suppliers, the people who supplied light bulbs, brake fittings, gearboxes, and fuel injection pumps. They asked them rhetorically: 'You like being Volkswagen suppliers, don't you?' Of course, everyone said: 'yes,

yes, yes, absolutely, we love being Volkswagen suppliers'. To which Volkswagen said something along the following lines:

> *We are delighted to hear that. In that case, you are going to set up production facilities in Brazil, in São Paulo state, next door to our new plant. That's because we do not intend to run a big production line and be at the mercy of the Brazilian customs as to whether or not a particular component manages to make its way into Brazil in time not to bring the production line to a halt. We are not going to play that game. So you are, all of you, going to set up production facilities in Brazil.*

Everyone said 'yes', of course.

Adam: If I recall correctly, your father Charles was not an engineer. What was the basis for sending him on that mission?

Eleanor: Indeed, he was no kind of an engineer. My dear father was a lovely man and had many qualities. But I promise you, he did not know one end of a fuel injection pump from the other. However, he spoke French.

Adam: Hmm, unless I am losing my marbles, French is not the official language of Brazil, is it?

Eleanor: Of course, French is not the national language of Brazil. That's Portuguese. We never worked out whether (first possibility) CAV Lucas thought that French and Portuguese were the same language; or (second possibility) they thought that if my father spoke French loudly and slowly, the natives – Portuguese speakers – would understand him. There is also a third possibility. They may have said to themselves: 'well, he has already learned one funny foreign language so presumably he can learn another one'.

My father was an intelligent man and a very good linguist. Obviously, as soon as he found out that he was about to be posted to do a job in Brazil, he instantly made a serious effort to learn Portuguese. He ended up speaking very respectable Portuguese, and he was an absolute hit with his colleagues in Brazil. They were so delighted to find an Englishman who was prepared to learn Brazilian Portuguese, and he got all the necessary technical help for setting up the production facility. Actually, he was a great success in terms of doing what he was sent out there to do, despite not being an engineer. And that did mean that I had a wonderful four years of childhood in Brazil.

Adam: The adventure in Brazil came eventually to an end, then it was London – albeit for a relatively short period of time.

Eleanor: When my father came back from Brazil, again he found that he didn't really have a job on his return to the UK. The story is a bit surreal, because it is kind of cyclical. In a very weird way, family history generated an exact mirror, an exact repeat, first for my older brother Michael and then for myself.

On our return to London (when I was 10) we lived initially in a succession of borrowed or rented houses and flats. I lived in about six different places over the course of two years, including a very tiny flat over a record shop on Castelnau, just south of Hammersmith Bridge.

Adam: Can you believe that this is where our families' paths first cross?

Eleanor: Oh?

Adam: My grandmother on the paternal side lived at the upper end of Castelnau, in the vicinity of the Church Road and the Olympic Studios. I spent some lovely childhood moments there. Whenever I cross the river on Hammersmith Bridge and leave Hammersmith behind, I know I am home.

Eleanor: What a small world … we did not live long there, though. We eventually found a rather nice rambling house on Kingston Hill with a big garden. No sooner had we bought that house, however, than my father got a job in Geneva. Then we had hell's delight to sell the house on Kingston Hill. The very features which had made it so attractive to us also made it the kind of house that wasn't very easy to shift on a conventional housing market. (For example: the big garden backed onto a Dr Barnardo's Home!) It took us about two years to sell that house. In the meantime, my father had gone out to Geneva, where he had become the Secretary General of a non-governmental organisation, the International Standards Organisation ('ISO').

Adam: That is a radical change from working for a company making fuel injection pumps for diesel engines.

Eleanor: True, but his experience in Brazil, combined with his general ability as an economist and a mathematician, meant he was very well qualified for that job. Indeed, he loved doing it and he was good at it. However, he had been appointed to the post as the compromise candidate by the supporters of two rival factions. Eventually they buried the hatchet between them, and at that moment, they got rid of my father, who then became unemployed. This was a very curious period because I was at boarding school in the UK. Although I had a scholarship, that was still costing the family significant money, so my father was frantically trying to find a new job. He was now in his mid fifties. Job-hunting wasn't that easy.

Adam: What about your mother?

Eleanor: My mother Pauline started working freelance for the United Nations Office in Geneva ('UNOG'), doing translations and precis-writing (producing the official records for conferences). We were basically working as a family unit: it was all hands to the pump. Whoever was free to do anything, did it for the general collective good of the family. When I was around during the school breaks, I helped with anything I could help with. I remember in particular helping my mother by checking lots of references for a totally impenetrable book on child psychology that she had undertaken to translate from French into English in the evenings on top of her UN work. It was by a lady called Maud Mannoni, and the title was '*L'Enfant, sa 'maladie' et les autres*'.[5] It was virtually incomprehensible in either English or French. It would probably also have been incomprehensible in any other language that you care to name. Anyway, my mother was the translator for the English version.[6] I was put to work, tracking down all the wretched references and occasionally trying to help understand what a particular sentence could conceivably mean. I do think that my French got a significant boost from that work.

Adam: And then came Vienna?

Eleanor: Yes, and it happened like this. My mother was also doing freelance work in Vienna, for the UN Industrial Development Organisation ('UNIDO'). Basically, she was picking up freelance work wherever she could: UNOG, the UN headquarters in New York, meetings of the UN Trade and Development Organisation ('UNCTAD') wherever they happened to be – for example, *Santiago de Chile* – and UNIDO. On one of the occasions when she was in Vienna, my father came over to spend a long weekend. It so happened that it was possible for him to meet the person who was responsible for drawing up the annual budget for UNIDO, an Austrian called Heinz Pichler. My father and Heinz hit it off. Heinz needed a good English speaker who was mathematically very literate to help him with the budget. So, in the end, my father got a new job working for UNIDO. That is how our time in Vienna began. We were there for almost 10 years.

Adam: This explains your passion for Central Europe, this experience must have been transformative.

Eleanor: Effectively my adolescence and early adulthood were spent in *Mitteleuropa*. As a result, when I went up to Cambridge in my turn as an undergraduate, I didn't go there as a British school leaver. I was a very homesick young Viennese girl. As homesick girls sometimes do, when I was feeling particularly low I took refuge in cooking food from home. One evening I was in the gyp room [the communal kitchen] at King's Garden Hostel putting a little something together when a group of fellow first-years came along the corridor. (I found the communal, very English food in the College dining hall rather a challenge.) As they got closer – remember, this was England in the 1970s, where spicy foods were practically unknown and definitely 'furrin' – they caught the scent of my cooking and started sniffing curiously. In they came to the gyp room:

> Leo – *what on earth are you cooking there?*
>
> [Hastily I sniffed back the tears]
>
> *Oh* – I said – *it is just something from my home. I brought the spices with me. Would you – um – like to try some? It is really rather nice. We call it goulasch.*

Adam: This is a very touching story, a very European one. It reminds me of a scene at a Ukrainian restaurant (where – since 2022 – I have been helping out with humanitarian aid): a very international and diverse bunch of volunteers flocking to the kitchen to find out what that wonderful smell coming out of it was. It was borsch cooked by Ukrainians to bring back a bit of their homeland they had to flee and were missing so badly.

But returning to your life … let us travel on the family trajectory further back a bit. Have you ever been to the places where your maternal and paternal families came from?

Eleanor: I went back to Ireland fairly early in the story. Travelling to Ireland was no problem and no issue. Ireland is just across the water, and we took great pleasure as a family in going back to Ireland although we did not go that often. In fact, after my birth we did not go to Ireland until after we came back from Brazil. But then we certainly did go to Ireland – to Dublin, to Cork, to *Cobh* (where my mother's family were from), to *An Ghaeltacht* [the Irish-speaking regions]: the Ring of Kerry, the Dingle peninsula, Galway, the Aran Islands – and we were always very happy to be there.

Adam: Going to Lithuania must have been way more difficult, if not impossible for a long time. At the emotional level it surely was a heavyweight experience.

Eleanor: Lithuania was a different story entirely. When my father's family left to avoid yet another round of persecution – yet another pogrom – their home was, perhaps, better described as being in eastern Poland than in Lithuania. The borders were very fluid at the time. My family was from a very small town called *Vilkomir*, which is now called *Ukmergė*. It is about 80 kilometres from Vilnius. Unfortunately, some family members were still there when the Second World War broke out. By the end of the war, there were no survivors. For years, for decades, nobody in my family ever thought of going to Lithuania. We just did not go back.

Adam: Eventually, though, you did go to visit Lithuania, didn't you?

Eleanor: Indeed. After the collapse of the Soviet Union, when Lithuania applied for EU membership, the European Commission put together a programme called 'TAIEX'. It was designed to prepare candidate countries for accession, in particular by trying to make sure that lawyers were trained in EU law, and that the judges were aware of basic issues of EU law, including the rule of law. I became involved in that programme. Interestingly, I started by doing a training visit for Malta, because the authorities there specifically asked to have an English-speaking common law lawyer on the visiting TAIEX team. The lady who ran the programme on behalf of the European Commission, Christiane Kirchbaum, was very dubious about getting a British person involved, because she assumed on the basis of her previous experience that all Brits were instinctively Eurosceptic. She had heard vaguely there was this person out there called Sharpston, who seemed to be available. Almost under duress she put me on the TAIEX team to give the Maltese their English-speaking common law lawyer.

When she got to know me better, she had the grace (and it's a very rare grace!) to admit that – with the benefit of hindsight – she had been wrong, and to apologise. After that initial engagement she kept me on the team, and I did a lot of work for the European Commission. (We became known as the 'dream team'; and all the central players – Heikki Kanninen, Horst-Peter Kreppel, Caroline Naômé, myself – all of us worked at the Court in Luxembourg in one capacity or another in the succeeding years.)

Adam: So, Malta opened the doors to Lithuania …

Eleanor: At a certain point the opportunity arose to go to Lithuania. I thought very hard about 'going back' to where my father's family came from. It seemed to me that if Lithuania wanted to become an EU Member State, I owed it to my family to do my bit to help. I owed it to those of my family who were victims of a massacre. They were shot in the forest near the village of *Paneriai*. As they died, they fell into the open mass grave that they had previously been required to dig. I also owed it to those of my family who had been taken away in cattle trucks to Auschwitz and had died there in the gas ovens. I owed it to them all to make sure that the Shoah could never happen again; that Lithuania joined the European Union understanding that it had to respect fundamental rights. It was a very simple ethical decision. That was the moment to go back. And so I did go back. Of course, it was very interesting and very moving to be in Lithuania. The story has a good follow-up because I got to know some really nice young Lithuanian lawyers who were working in the Lithuanian Government's European Law team. They were very, very fine young people, so I started hanging out with them a bit. Then I invited them to come and spend some time in my *cabinet* at the Court. What happened evolved into something which was not just 'oh, I can now go back to Lithuania and then tick the box that I have done that'. It turned into something very positive and very rich. It is perhaps a good example of why it's important to follow your instinct. It can turn out very well.

Adam: … and you have been to Lithuania many times since …

Eleanor: Having started going back to Lithuania, I have since regarded it as somewhere that I am always happy to go back to. Lithuania was one of the states that was part of the Big Enlargement 1.0 in 2004. When in early 2024 I got an email from the Ministry of Justice in Vilnius, inviting me to speak at a conference to mark the 20th anniversary of that enlargement, I looked at the conference date and I groaned. The timing was not exactly felicitous. Just before the Vilnius conference I was scheduled to be in Prague to give a keynote speech at another conference, and then to preside over the latest edition of the Central and Eastern Europe Moot Competition. To make things worse, I was already booked to fly back to the UK from Prague. Then I thought: 'no, I can't not get to Lithuania for this conference.' The logistics were not exactly on our side but – with your help, Adam! – we did manage to get me from Prague via Warsaw to Vilnius, and

I did indeed present a closing paper at the 20th anniversary conference. This was lovely, and it also gave me a chance to catch up again with Elzė Matulionytė, one of those nice young Lithuanian lawyers who had worked with me at the Court.

Adam: Leo, thank you. You have explained to me so well why I have been engaged in all matters Ukrainian over the past years, especially since the Russian full-scale invasion started on 24 February 2022. Doing such things is important, isn't it? It is so fundamentally important to help others who are in need but such opportunities give one also that connection with the past and those who are no longer with us. Sometimes it is a journey full of pain but also surprising discoveries, finding the missing bits of a puzzle that we knew existed, but we could not locate them, put them in context or give them a name or a label.

Eleanor: It is very important. It is a way of tackling the past. The past cannot be undone. But instead of lamenting over it, you can try to learn the lessons from the past and transform the underlying forces that made the past what it was into different forces that stand a chance of creating a different future. That is richly worth it.

Adam: The past offers us not only painful and tragic stories, but it also gives us some serendipitous moments or events which change, or could change, the course of our own lives. Sometimes even history repeats itself. In your case, Leo, we have very similar episodes in your grandmother's life and yours. They had something to do with high seas, ships, and being late. Let's start with your grandmother.

Eleanor: My grandmother had American employers who had gone off to the US, and they wished her to join them there. Very courteously, they sent her a ticket. I am sure it was a second, or maybe a third-class ticket, but it was a ticket for the brand new luxury vessel called the *Titanic*. My grandmother was meant to be joining the *Titanic* in *Cherbourg* as she was working in Paris at that time. If you look at the routing for the *Titanic*'s maiden voyage, you will find that she went from the UK to *Cherbourg*, then to Queenstown (*Cobh*) in Ireland, and then met the iceberg. My grandmother was (like her granddaughter after her) incurably optimistic about the number of things that could be fitted into limited space and time. Occasionally (just like her granddaughter!) she miscalculated. On this occasion, famously, that's just what happened. My grandmother missed the train from *Paris* to *Cherbourg*. My grandmother caught the next train. On arrival in *Cherbourg*, she rushed down to the harbour. Because the *Titanic* was so gigantic, she was not moored alongside the quay like a normal passenger ship. She was anchored out in what are called the 'roads', an open area of the harbour. During the boarding process, they had been running a shuttle service with small boats taking passengers from the shore to the *Titanic*. When my grandmother arrived, all of that had long since finished. The *Titanic* was still visibly sitting there at anchor. My grandmother tried to find a boat that would take her out to the ship, but she was told it was by then way too late. They were already getting up steam, they were about to leave. And then the *Titanic* duly sailed. For five days my grandmother was extremely worried. How was she going to explain to her employers in the US that she had (literally) missed the boat? How was she going to pay for a ticket to get herself there? Then, when the news broke on day six, she was (obviously) very relieved that she had been late for the *Titanic*.

Adam: And then history repeated itself …

Eleanor: Yes, we seem to specialise in historical repeats in my family. My story with *MS Herald of Free Enterprise* is very similar. At the time, I was working partly in chambers in Brussels, and partly in London. I was usually to be found moving between these two points on my 250 cc Honda single cylinder motorbike (a red RS 250), via a ferry crossing. These were, of course, the days before the Channel Tunnel and *Le Shuttle*. I had worked out that if I caught the longest overnight sailing from either *Oostende* or *Zeebrugge* to *Dover*, that would give me a chance to get a bit of sleep before I started the next working day. I had settled on *Townsend Thoresen* out of *Zeebrugge* rather than *Sealink* out of *Oostende* because *Townsend Thorensen* were a bit more motorbike friendly. On this particular occasion, I was working in Brussels chambers in the evening. I had splendidly miscalculated how long it would take me to finish a particular piece of work. We had rather exigent Japanese clients at the time and I had to get that text back to them. I couldn't move until I got it finished. Eventually I got it onto the fax machine. Then I looked at my watch and I realised that there was absolutely no way that I was going to manage to get to *Zeebrugge* in time for the overnight sailing. I cursed, because that was my night's sleep gone, and I decided that the best thing I could do was to go back to where I was living in Brussels, have a couple of hours of sleep there, and then get on the motorbike and drive to *Calais*. That meant a longer (4 ½ hour) drive but a much shorter ferry crossing. If I did that, I could somehow retrieve the situation; and I could be in the UK for the following day when I was due to work in London chambers. So I packed up my papers in Brussels chambers, and I went back home. I was staying with an absolutely delightful Belgian family: Monsieur and Madame Seydel. Pierre Seydel opened the door and made wide eyes at me as I was not meant to be there ('*Fille, qu'est-ce que tu fais là?*'). Then they said:

> *Oh Leo, for heaven's sake, so you've screwed up as usual.*
>
> *Never mind, come in, sit down.*
>
> *Let's have a glass of wine together and we'll just watch the late news.*

I sat down with them and we did have that glass of wine together. They flipped the switch on the television – and we stared absolutely transfixed as the pictures came up from *Zeebrugge* with *MS Herald of Free Enterprise* lying on her side. Then they hugged me, and we had a rather emotional moment. We all realised that I had had a very, very narrow escape. I was fond of that particular sailing because I had discovered a really good way of getting a night's sleep without paying for a cabin (which I couldn't afford). Right in the centre of the vessel, three decks down, there were some luggage nets which were hung overhead, about six feet up. Nobody seemed to know that they were there. After all, it wasn't a very obvious place to put luggage nets. So, they were always empty. If you were moderately athletic, you could do a half pull up, half scramble, and get up into them. I had developed a very practical habit of taking a sleeping bag with me on my travels. When I went on board, I would park the motorbike and then I would make my way to the centre of the ship, get up into the luggage nets, and get my head down. I would manage to have about five hours sleep, maybe even five and a half, before I had to get up because we would have docked in Dover. Then I would collect the motorbike, drive off the ferry and make my way up to London.

It was very clear to me that night, watching those pictures, that I would never have got out. There is no way, as the ferry turned on her side and more and more water rushed in through the open bow loading door, that I would have managed to extricate myself from the middle of that ship. I mean, it is not even worth thinking about.

Adam: Thank God you were late.

Eleanor: Being late is sometimes a blessing, thank God.

Adam: Both stories are proof that life can change in an instant. One person will have very diligent guardian angels, someone else will – sadly – have poorly behaved ones and will end up at the wrong place, at the wrong time.

I reckon that the readers already by now get a clear idea that your life has been a continuous peregrination. One thing we could settle from the outset, perhaps, is how you think about yourself. Put differently, where do you belong? You come from a very mixed background, you spent your childhood and adult life in so many different countries. You have already said that when you were doing your undergraduate degree in Cambridge, you felt like a young Viennese girl missing her home. Did it change later? I recall that in the afterword to the book about the British Advocates General at the CJEU you wrote that you never considered yourself to be British but felt European through and through.

Eleanor: I never thought of myself as the 'British Advocate General'. I never thought of myself as a British lawyer working at the Court, or as a British lawyer working for the European Commission TAIEX programme. It may be tricky to explain. Let us go back again to my time in Cambridge as an undergraduate. I was just eighteen when I went up to university. As I've already explained, I spent most of my formative life absolutely not being British. I didn't grow up in the UK. I bailed out of the formal English school system just before I was sixteen. I had been elsewhere, and all my key reference points were non-British reference points. Then I came up to Cambridge and I did the rounds of the students' 'Freshers' Fair'. It's where all the student societies have stalls at the beginning of Michaelmas term. They make a pitch to explain what they are about, and they try to get you interested and signed up with membership. Quite deliberately, I began by visiting the stands that were being run by the reserve forces of the Army, the Navy, and the Air Force. That was not because I am somebody who is naturally military and disciplined and obedient (I don't think that description would fit me or could fit me!), but I do have a spirit of adventure. I also had an underlying feeling that maybe I *should* be trying to see whether there was a way in which, perhaps, I could or would or might identify more as being British. Perhaps there was also a degree of curiosity. So, I visited – in turn – each of those stands. I sniffed around and asked what they were doing and how. I enquired about the opportunities for joining and the activities I could expect to be involved in. Of course, there was a simple limiting fact: I was female. In those far off days there really were not many roles for women in Her Majesty's armed forces. You could be a cook, you could be a nurse, you could be a clerk (an administrative secretary) providing you had shorthand and typing, or you could be a driver/mechanic for an important officer. That was pretty much it. That was true of each of the three services. I collected the information and I came away. I said to myself:

> *You know what?*
>
> *You would not contemplate doing any of those jobs as a job in Civvy Street.*
>
> *Given that, what would be the good reason for using up your free time to do one of those jobs as a reservist in the armed forces?*
>
> *Take your time to think about this one.*
>
> *You cannot think of any good reason – right?*
>
> *So that's it.*

So, there was a moment when I thought, perhaps in a peculiar way, shall I try to identify more with being British? If you are a member of the armed forces, clearly you identify with your country. There is an oath of allegiance, and all that comes with it. That was the moment of asking the question – and that was the answer. That was, really and truly, probably the only point in my life when I tried to move towards being British – and then I moved away. Moving away felt comfortable. I guess that I thought to myself, 'Okay, if you do not have a particular use for me, if there is nothing you can think of, well, fair enough. Here is a woman who speaks a number of other languages, and who can melt into the background as a local but if you cannot think of any way of making use of this woman and her skills, then let it be'. I went back to being European.

Adam: In Cambridge, you read economics, languages, and law, but let us not go there yet and step back a bit. Your first passion as a child was music. It did come down from your parents, didn't it?

Eleanor: Indeed, let's talk a bit more about where the music came from. My mother Pauline was not a musician, in the sense of being a performer with a typical musical instrument. But she was indeed a performer with the most exquisitely beautiful musical instrument of all, which is the human body. She was a fantastic dancer. Of course, you cannot be a fantastic dancer without musicality. She was never a prima ballerina type. For one thing, she wasn't tall enough. But as a character dancer, she was absolutely wicked. It was extraordinary. She could convey character in attitude and expression in something as simple as a slightly different way of using a gesture. She was intensely musical. By the way, she did also play the piano. But she would never have seen herself as being a musician that way. As a dancer, she was a musician.

Adam: How about your father Charles?

Eleanor: My father loved music. He was not bad at all as a pianist; and he was also naturally a good singer. When he got to Vienna, he instantly signed himself up for proper singing lessons. He had a very nice light baritone. Either my mother or I accompanied him on the piano when he was singing; and he accompanied me on the piano for the violin and piano sonatas that I was attempting as a fledgling violinist. My brother was the odd one out. Not that he was a barbarian, nothing would be further from the truth. His engagement with music was passive, not active. He liked good music, but it was not a particularly consuming interest of his. He was much more interested in, and knowledgeable about, the visual arts. But when my parents and I went to live as a family in Vienna, that was like taking drunkards and locking them up in a brewery. My father, apart from the singing lessons, indulged himself by buying a very nice baby grand piano. It was not a *Bösendorfer* – he thought he could not push the boat out quite that far. But he got an *Ehrbar*, which the Viennese cognoscenti considered to be just one down from a *Bösendorfer.* It is a very fine piano indeed. I have it and play it, it is a lovely, lovely beast. So, in Vienna, the music was always just sitting there as part of our lives: concerts, grand operas at the *Staatsoper*, operettas at the *Theater an der Wien* or the *Volksoper* ('there's a new young soprano on this week who's really worth listening to: she's called *Gundula Janowitz*'), or just *Hausmusik* – music-making with friends or family at home in the evenings. I do remember walking downstairs with my father one morning and surprising the *Hauswart* (the concierge) who was in the middle of having a good moan about us to a sympathetic friend. 'Dear God, they are always playing something or singing' ('*Immer singen … immer spielen … ach, du lieber Gott!*') – and then she caught sight of us and hastily changed to a courteous '*Grüß Gott, Herr Doktor Sharpston; Grüß Gott, Fräulein Sharpston*'.

Adam: A Polish tenor Wiesław Ochman (whose painting we used for the cover of your *Festschrift*) said recently in an interview, 'in all stages of life, the music is – perhaps – if not a remedy than at least a very good companion'. I couldn't agree more. Is there any particular musical composition that you associate with home, with your parents and places where you felt safe? A piece of music which gives you comfort as soon as it starts?

Eleanor: It depends which part of my childhood and growing up we are talking about. Brazil obviously goes to the beat of *bossa nova* and *samba*. We were at the carnival in *Rio de Janeiro* on the four hundredth anniversary of Rio's founding, and the city did not stop dancing for two days and two nights. We did not stop very much either. I remember the occasional exhausted nap but basically we were out there dancing.

Adam: Vienna, where you spent your adolescent years, must have been a different kettle of fish.

Eleanor: Vienna is always Vienna. There was a lot of dancing involved, different beats though: waltzes (both *Wienerwältze* and the slower 'old-fashioned' waltzes), polkas, *Ländler* … I am thinking mainly, of course, about *Wienerwältze*. In Austria, the first thing you hear when the New Year comes is *An der schönen blauen Donau* (the Blue Danube Waltz). It's broadcast over the first channel of Austrian radio. By the way, if you are away skiing somewhere near Bolzano, it is brought home to you that the Italian province of *Alto Adige* is culturally really part of Austria and should properly be called the *Süd Tirol*, because you will hear the Blue Danube Waltz just as you would in Vienna as you mark the transition from *Silvesterabend* to the New Year. Of course, there is also the New Year's Day concert of the *Wiener Philharmoniker*. We attended it on one very special occasion. However, both before and after that we always listened to it. We used to have it on, and we used to dance. We would watch the sumptuous broadcast on the television and listen to the sound on the radio (better quality than on the TV!), but we would always have the chairs pushed back. At a certain moment, my mother would look at my father and the next thing we would know, they would be gyrating around the room. Then my mother would sit down, and my father would grab me and we would start dancing. And then I would dance with my mother. It was like breathing – in and out, in and out. We would breathe, so we would waltz. Even now that my parents are no longer with me, I always listen to the New Year's Day concert – and I have been known to grab one of my two beloved dogs and dance with him. My hovawart, Rudy, is so big that when he stands up on his hind paws he's almost tall enough to be my dancing partner.

Adam: Leo, do you associate places or events in your life with particular music?

Eleanor: I associate music with trying to get through particularly difficult moments. For example, I associate being in hospital for major surgery – something that's happened to me on a number of occasions – with Sibelius's *Finlandia* and the *Karelia Suite*. Yes, I specifically associate it with *Finlandia* and using that music – in particular the trumpets – to carry me through, as if they were telling me that it will be alright, that everything will be okay. Music has got me through several very dark places. And because I spent so much formative time in

Mitteleuropa, I would put Smetana's *Die Moldau* (one of six symphonic poems falling under the *Má Vlast* umbrella) straight onto that list. It has a particular place for me.

Adam: The human soul works in mysterious ways. I find it fascinating, but not surprising, that it was *Finlandia*. It is such a profound score in itself but if we add the historical context, it takes it to new levels. After all, Sibelius wrote it in an act of resistance to occupying Russian forces.

Eleanor: I was sure that you would pick up on that, Adam.

Adam: Finlandia says it all, doesn't it. When the trumpets come loud and strong, it is Sibelius making his message and desires clear: 'get out of here, you evil'.

Eleanor: Yes … yes.

Adam: This question came from my own story. I grew up listening to music, but I have always been sandwiched between classical music and rock'n'roll. Classical music is the maternal side of my family. My mum Anna, the music promoter, her brother Adam who is the violinist and Maria, my late Ukrainian grandmother who sang in the Warsaw Philharmonic Choir. My dad Wojtek, on the other hand, is a rock'n'roll type. Funny enough, it is with his mother Barbara, and my grandmother, that I associate a piece of classical music that always gives me comfort – Mozart's Twenty First Piano Concerto. It teleports me back to the opposite end of Castlenau, where you lived as a child, and her home in Barnes. With my parents I associate long evenings in front of the fireplace with music of Vladimir Cosma in the background (and our cat protesting loudly for having been left behind). Whenever I have weak moments, I always go back to that music. Such choices are always very personal.

Eleanor: Do you associate music with historical events?

Adam: I do indeed. Since we will spend quite a bit of time talking about all matters European, I should mention Beethoven's Ninth Symphony, in particular the fourth movement which, at some point, became the anthem of the European Union. I have two favourite recordings of the Ninth. The one that is particularly close to my heart now is a recent Deutsche Grammophon release with the Ukrainian Freedom Orchestra conducted by Keri-Lynn Wilson. The fourth movement is sung – for the very first time in history – in the Ukrainian language. This particular recording gives me strength to go from one day to another as the Russian aggression goes on and I will always associate it with the full-scale invasion of Ukraine. The other favourite recording of the Ninth is from Berlin when orchestras and choirs from all over Europe were conducted by the great Leonard Bernstein. Schiller's lyrics were changed on that occasion to mark one of the biggest events in our contemporary history, the fall of the Berlin Wall. *Ode an die Freude* became *Ode an die Freiheit* for one evening during Christmas of 1989 (and, on the recording, for posterity). I remember the night of 9 November 1989 so vividly as if it were yesterday. I guess it was one of those unforgettable days for you as well.

Eleanor: Absolutely – and I too remember that Berlin recording of Beethoven's Ninth! I had grown up in a Europe that was divided by that wall and by the Iron Curtain. I had grown up in a Europe that seemed to be frozen in time. There seemed to be no particularly strong or reasonable likelihood that it would change during my lifetime. And then it did. I remember that evening, that night of 9 November 1989. I was in Luxembourg, I was working at the Court as a *référendaire* when it happened. Unfortunately, I could not just down tools and go to Berlin. I remember that when the news started to break, the first news reports were very hesitant about putting out the story. They said: 'We are hearing stories, of course they are unconfirmed at the moment, but we are hearing stories about things happening in Berlin'. There are very few nights of my life that I have simply stayed awake all night. I could not *not* be awake for it whilst it was happening. In Luxembourg you are very lucky because you get so many different news channels. So, I was tracking it on the BBC, the French, and the German news outlets; but I also had Italian, Spanish, Portuguese, and Luxembourg channels. I am not normally a TV junkie. But I sat there all night. I switched from one channel to another. As I watched, I was between disbelief and exaltation, pure tears of joy, just watching what was going on. When I had been growing up in Vienna, my family had done little expeditions to Prague or Budapest. We were down in Yugoslavia (the part of it which is modern Croatia) when the Soviet Union invaded Czechoslovakia on 20 August 1968; and the entire Yugoslav army moved to the border within 24 hours. They were worried that Russians would go further, and that they would be next. I was in Prague on the first anniversary of the Russian invasion. I was with young Czech friends in *Václavské náměstí* when the tanks rolled in. In hindsight, I was being very stupid: as a fourteen-year old and a foreigner, I should not have been anywhere near that. Luckily, I had very good Czech friends. We were all very angry, but they made sure that they got me away to safety. The fall of the Berlin Wall was not for me (as I think it was for many people in the UK) a matter of, 'good Lord, look at what is happening over in Europe'. It was intensely personal. This was my Central Europe, my *Mitteleuropa*. Look what is happening, where it is going, and where it might be going. It was like seeing frozen rivers, streams, waterfalls in winter; and then you can hear the water flowing again and bits of ice break off. You think, this is it: winter is losing its grip, spring is coming.

Years later, after one of the TAIEX sessions preparing judges in the Czech Republic for EU accession, I remember walking in the evening across the Charles Bridge in Prague. There was a cellist sitting under one of the statues, just playing for himself – one of the Bach suites for solo cello. I stood and listened and burst into tears.

Adam: This sounds very poetic, indeed. How things have changed … In 2024 we had a long and lovely walk around the old parts of Prague and, at some point,

I took the picture for the cover of this book. Just like that, on the Charles Bridge, on a random Friday afternoon. Your cellist story is like a similar scene I witnessed on an autumnal evening in Tbilisi, one of my favourite cities. It was already dark but there was magic in the air, a slight breeze from the Caucasus, falling leaves, and the city fogged down. I was walking down Ioane Shavteli Street, a narrow pedestrian path sandwiched between old buildings, only modestly lit by streetlamps. And there she was, a young girl playing on an old piano *Comptine d'un autre été: l'Après-midi*, a beautiful theme from the French movie *Amélie*. Just like you, I stood there and tears were going down my cheeks. There I was in this beautiful country, finally free and independent. So European and yet, for centuries, stuck between the big behemoths pushing and pulling it in all possible directions. Even now, as we speak, Georgians are on the streets of Tbilisi as well as other towns and cities fighting to push away the claws of the Russian bear.

Going back to the night the wall fell. I was with my grandfather Karol who was Polish but had been born in what is now Ukraine. If my memory serves me well, my parents were in Yugoslavia on holidays. We were both glued to the TV and to the radio which – funnily enough – played Pink Floyd's 'The Wall'. I always associate this song not with the movie, but with the fall of the Berlin wall. I will never forget when my grandfather Karol, who was a very wise man, looked at me and said:

> *My little laufer, this tide cannot be unturned.*
>
> *This is it.*
>
> *Whatever happens, and I do not know where it is going,*
>
> *but there is no way back.*

Eleanor: Your grandfather Karol was indeed a very wise man.

Adam: A few weeks ago, I was going through some old boxes filled with papers and books. I found a folder, and, to my big surprise, it contained a lot of articles from English newspapers published on 12 September 2001. Back then I deeply felt that it was one of those historical days that would change the world we live in, so as a *memento mori* I kept the newspaper scraps. As I was flicking through them, all the memories were coming back. That was the beginning of what we call the war against terror. It has led to all the things that we've been experiencing in the European Union since 2000. As Matthew Longo put it in his latest book *The Picnic*, 'A whole world ended in 1989; and in 2001, a new one was birthed'.[7] How do you remember 9/11?

Eleanor: I was somewhere unusual when that happened. I was working as a watch leader on board a topsail schooner belonging to what was then the Sail Training Association [now, Sail Training International]. We were going through a set of canals in North Holland when the news started coming through. We did not have any pictures, we got the news flash on the ship's radio. We looked at each other and said: 'what the hell is going on?' You must imagine, it was very difficult to find out what was happening on board an old-fashioned sailing ship.

So I wasn't one of the people who sat doom scrolling on their television, looking again and again at the pictures of the planes flying into the Twin Towers in New York City. But what trickled through on the radio was terrifying enough. You did realise that somehow the entire peaceful and secure world that we were used to, that many of us were rather complacent about, had suddenly been lost forever. Terrorism and terrorist attacks were no longer things that happened at a safe distance, in a far corner of the world: an event that one could somehow compartmentalise as very unfortunate, of course, but somehow not our immediate problem. Suddenly, you realised that the next terrorist attack could be in the marketplace of your hometown or might involve a plane that you had just boarded, as many of us boarded planes every week to go off to a conference somewhere.

Adam: And then came the aftermath …

Eleanor: There are different strands here, of course. In the immediate aftermath of 9/11, there was enormous solidarity with the US, something which I don't remember seeing since before the Vietnam War. Suddenly, at least in Western and Central Europe, that solidarity led to a willingness to be allies with the US in trying to stamp out Al-Qaeda and ISIS and trying to do something about Saddam Hussein. Basically, trying to help the world's policeman to make the world a slightly safer place again.

Adam: In the European Union it was also a very crucial time. We were gearing up for the biggest expansion of the block in history. To begin with, 9/11 happened soon after the entry into force of the Treaty of Amsterdam and incorporation of Schengen *acquis* into EU law. The terrorist attacks and their aftermath have triggered much deeper integration between the Member States in security matters. A good example was the adoption of the legislation on the European Arrest Warrant, which happened rather quickly, at least by EU standards. It unveils the paradox, and we can see parallels even now with the Russian invasion of Ukraine, that such dramatic historical events trigger integration between the Member States.

Eleanor: They do indeed trigger integration, which is very good. At the same time, they should be raising awareness that as you make the world an easier place to move around you may also be helping criminals. For good, law-abiding citizens, removing the border controls is a positive development. As well as making it much easier to transport goods across frontiers, you are making it nice and easy for workers and the self-employed, for families going on holiday, and all that is absolutely great. However, you have also created a perfect barrier-free environment for money launderers, drug smugglers, people traffickers, terrorists – in short, for organised crime in general. You have deliberately abolished the routine checks at frontiers, which previously might have helped to pick up some of what is being done by people whom we would classify as undesirable.

Adam: I have always had a problem explaining this relatively straightforward phenomenon to students here in the UK. They would often look at me and say: 'Well, why would you have cooperation and legal harmonisation in criminal matters? It is such a sensitive area!' I would frequently direct them to the definition of the Internal Market in Article 26 of the Treaty on the Functioning of the European Union (the 'TFEU') and ask them if the free movement of criminals was one of the freedoms of the Internal Market.

Eleanor: Adam, it sounds as though we are using exactly the same teaching technique on that one. Speaking of 9/11 and music, there is a wonderful musical called *Come from Away*, written by two Canadians (David Hein and Irene Sankoff). It follows up on the immediate aftermath of 9/11. It is about the Newfoundland town of Gander, which has an enormous airstrip dating back to the days when propeller planes had to refuel before and after crossing the Atlantic and which became virtually obsolete when jets took over the trans–Atlantic routes. On 9/11 Gander suddenly found itself hosting all the people whose flights were diverted to that convenient unused airstrip that day because the FAA closed the American airspace. I fell across that musical one summer when I was doing a theatre course.

Adam: Leo, a theatre course on top of everything else? But of course, a theatre course. As one does!

Eleanor: Oh yes, I produce these things out of my back pocket for you, Adam! Naturally I do a theatre course during the summer. I go to the Luxembourg European Amateur Theatre Summer School ('LEATSS'). You know, Sinead Cusack once said that 'Acting is the shy person's revenge on the world';[8] to which Dame Judi Dench's gloss is, 'Absolutely true. I couldn't agree more, what a brilliant thing to say. Much easier for a shy person to walk out on stage pretending to be someone else, than to enter a room full of people at a party as themselves'.[9] That absolutely nails it for me.

Adam: And for me. I adore Dame Judi Dench, her acting, wit, and gumption.

Eleanor: I have been going to LEATSS for a few years now and I have done every kind of theatre work in those weeks, from modern works to Shakespeare (of course) to *commedia dell'arte* acting with masks (which was fabulous fun). It is immensely enjoyable. LEATSS is run by a group of committed amateurs who arrange for good professionals from London and elsewhere to come to teach us. About five years ago Graeme du Fresne, who for many years was the course director and taught the music and singing side of things, turned up at summer school with songs from a new musical then running in London, *Come from Away*. He wanted to try them on us. We were absolutely bowled over by them and we organised a trip, as a group from Luxembourg, to go to a performance of *Come from Away* in London. I enjoyed it so much that I sneaked back to see it two more times. You can put it into the *Die Zauberflöte* category, something I could not stay away from. When I drive down to Italy in the campervan with my two beloved dogs, *Boris*-the-samoyed and *Rudy*-the-hovawart, *Come from Away* is always the first thing I put on as I escape to the south. There's a few bars of introduction – just a *bodhrán* beating in quick 2/4 time – and the narrator opens up, speaking over the drumbeat:

> *On the northeast tip of North America, on an island called Newfoundland, there's an airport. It used to be one of the biggest airports in the world, and next to it is a town called Gander.*

And then the company breaks straight into the first big set piece ('Welcome to the Rock: if you've come from away, you'll probably understand about a half of what we say …').

Adam: As you were growing up and exploring all these fascinating things separated by the conjunction 'and', when did the law come into the equation?

Eleanor: Law was always in the equation, in the sense of law in society, and what the absence of law does. The horrible breakdown of civilised law, simultaneously with the imposition to the letter of draconian law, was precisely the downward slide on which the *Third Reich* proceeded. Historically, law for me has always been around. If I had gone to Oxford, I would probably have read law because I didn't think that the Philosophy, Politics, and Economics course ('PPE' for short) was up to much, unless you wished to become a Tory politician, which I did not [*chuckles*]. I went to Cambridge instead; and I offered classics to get in. Because I ended up going to Cambridge rather than Oxford, I did economics, then languages with a bit of classics, then back to economics, graduated in economics and then, eventually, I did go into law. Law in society was always a part of the story, as well as law in Europe and for European integration. I should add fundamental rights to that mix, too. If you had said to me that I could go into law as a career, but that my choice of options would be between family law, property law, and commercial contracts, I would have said 'thanks very much but no thanks, I will find something else to do'. I did not want to do just *any* area of law. I wanted to do a particular type of law. I wanted to do the sort of law which has to do with public policy, with the shaping of what we are doing in society. I won't pretend that, presciently, I chose to do the mixture of subjects that I studied at university with an eye to equipping myself with the ideal background to be an EU lawyer. But the fact that I did those subjects probably unconsciously reflected particular interests. The natural path through was a sequence of conscious choices at key moments. With hindsight, I see that I ended up almost by accident with a really useful background for an EU lawyer. However, my big chance to discover more about EU law had to wait till later. At Cambridge, I just did the 'core' legal subjects that I was going to need for my Bar Part I exemptions (the first stage in qualifying as a barrister). Five out of the (then) six could be fitted into a single (fourth) year; and then I taught myself equity & trusts over the summer – adequately rather than well! – and sat the professional exam in that subject to complete my academic exemptions. So, I never studied EEC law at university as a student. However, when I became a member of one of the four Inns of Court in order to qualify as a barrister, I picked the Middle Temple, which seemed subjectively to be more outgoing, more cosmopolitan, and less dyed-in-the-wool English than the other three Inns. It has a kind of wider background. And – crucially – it was the only one of the four Inns that offered a European law scholarship.

Adam: It is interesting that from the beginning you have travelled on the public service trajectory. This is so commendable but not terribly *en vogue* these days. On my way to Cambridge this afternoon, I spotted at the King's Cross Station a poster of Peter Gabriel's new album titled I/O. 'I' stands for inside, 'O' for out. The song of the same title has the following lyrics: 'stuff coming out, stuff coming in, I am just a part of everything'. As we look around, many people care only about the stuff coming in, not about the stuff coming out, not what they can do for others. What made the public service and doing things *pro bono* appealing to you?

Eleanor: I suspect it was always either in my DNA or in my upbringing. I do not mean the conscious upbringing that my parents gave me, but it was part of their traditions, too. Naturally I took it on board because – for both of them – it was an important thing in their perception of how the world operated. Within the Jewish tradition there is a concept which we call in Hebrew תִקוּן עוֹלָם [*Tikkun olam*] – repairing the world. My father came from an Orthodox Jewish family: a family so observant that when he went up to Cambridge as a scholar, they initially sent him food parcels so he could keep kosher. Over the next few years, he ceased to be a practising Jew, and indeed he married my mother, a Roman Catholic convert. But although my father ceased to be a practising Jew, he did not cease to be a *mensch*. In Yiddish a *mensch* means someone who is a decent and responsible human being. My father was absolutely the definition of a *mensch*. He was upright, honourable, and helped other people. On the maternal side of the family, I vividly remember – from when I was eight or nine, probably not older than that – my mother telling me about her father. He had been an extraordinary amateur sportsman. Then he went off to serve in the First World War and somehow survived that. After the war, there were of course a lot of widows, the wives of his comrades who had been killed. In principle, the British government owed them pensions as war widows. Sadly, most of them had really no idea how to go about claiming those pensions. I recall my mother telling me about all the letters that her father managed to find time to write, outside his day job as a minor civil servant, on behalf of the widows of his comrades, to make sure that they got their pensions. It was not that much money, but it made a big difference to each widow in terms of managing to carry on and carry the family forward, look after the children, and all the rest. What stood between the widow and getting the pension was usually being able to navigate the bureaucracy. You needed to write the right letter and to fill in the right form. I got from those stories a very, very clear picture: if you happened to be fortunate and you had the education, you had the literacy, you had the way with words, there was – I am going to say – an unspoken obligation on you to use all that to help people who were not in the same fortunate position. Put like that, it sounds very much like a sermon being preached. But it was not told to me like that. My mother explained it to me with enthusiasm, with appreciation of her own dear father, as though this was the most natural and obvious thing in the world to do. As I've already indicated, my mother never had a continuous career herself, but she was always ready to give a hand. She was very good with words, and she was always ready to help, very quietly and very understatedly. A letter would get written, or somebody would come round and have coffee and she would listen to them and then say: 'maybe if you were to approach it in this way, you might find that it will unblock the situation'.

So, this approach was literally something that came into me, that flowed into me.

Adam: I suppose your upbringing bore fruit early, didn't it?

Eleanor: Let me travel back in time to when I was 16. All the arrangements for finishing my education in Vienna had fallen over. They were very Edwardian, and they were very improvised, and at a certain moment, the person who was teaching me classics abandoned her career as a fledgling opera singer in Vienna in order to follow her true love to Hong Kong. (Her true love was an earnest student of Chinese lyric poetry.) This produced a domino effect on the rest of my education. So, we looked around and decided that we had probably better rejig everything. The idea was then that I should go over to the UK and stay there for the short period of time necessary to cover the run up to my A levels. After a summer back home in Vienna, I would go back to the UK for the autumn term, to do the extra examination for university entrance to those two bastions of learning, Oxford and Cambridge. That meant that I needed somewhere to stay in London. My parents were concerned for their daughter, her safety, and virtue. That is how I ended up in a hostel run by Italian Missionary Sisters. They had left sunny Italy to go to evangelize the pagan Anglican north, and so there they were running a hostel – St Maria Goretti's Hostel – in the London suburb of Chiswick (pronounced, of course, 'Chi-sa-wi-cka'). I am not quite sure what their original purpose was in founding the hostel, and – obviously – if you were a young Italian girl coming to London to study English, your studies were not going to be greatly advanced by staying in St Maria Goretti's Hostel. Happy calls in Italian floated up and down the stairwell in the hostel. ('Ciao, Maria, can you lend me your hairdryer? We're going out to a party'). Staying there was helpful for my Italian, which was not one of my subjects for A levels, but I don't think it was very good for their English. However, the dear nuns also gave me an early opportunity to develop my social conscience. I have a habit of talking with people, particularly people who are doing things like cleaning rooms or washing down staircases, or who are porters or security guards. I like it because it is a very nice human contact; and generally the people I end up talking with seem to like it too. So naturally I got talking with the very nice Irishwomen – all devout, pious Catholics – who were the cleaning staff at St Maria Goretti's Hostel. In the course of one such conversation I discovered that … well … to say they were being paid peanuts would be an insult to monkeys. They were being paid below peanuts. They were being paid something, you know, obscenely, ridiculously little. There wasn't an official minimum wage in those days, but if there had been, their hourly rate would have been 60% below the minimum wage. This awoke the social conscience in my 16-year-old self, and I said very indignantly, 'This won't do. This won't do at all!' And the nice Irishwoman I was chatting with said: 'ah, sure, you know, it is what the good Reverend Mother pays us'. Hearing 'good Reverend Mother' I kind of saw red, and so I requested a meeting with the aforementioned good Reverend Mother. She gave me an appointment to see her. As I walked in she smiled at me sweetly.

> **Reverend Mother:** *My child, what can I do to help you? Perhaps you are discovering a vocation?*
>
> **Leo:** *No, Reverend Mother. There's something I need to talk to you about. You are exploiting the working class.*
>
> [Reverend Mother looked a little bit puzzled. This was not what she had anticipated when she said I could come and see her. And then I launched, you know, full guns blazing, into the fact that I had become aware that the Hostel was systematically exploiting its workforce by not paying anything plausibly reasonable as an hourly wage. She heard me out a little bit bemused.]
>
> **Reverend Mother:** *But my child, they are working for Holy Mother Church.*
>
> **Leo:** *Yes, Reverend Mother. They are working for Holy Mother Church but if they need to go to the shop and buy a box of cornflakes, the box of cornflakes doesn't cost any less because they are working for Holy Mother Church and you are paying them a shameful pittance instead of a proper wage.*

Adam: Checkmate! I guess it was one of those moments when she either had to throw you out of her office or cave in.

Eleanor: There was a long pause, and then we discussed this a little further. In the end, I managed to get them a wage increase. My Irish friends couldn't believe it. They thought it was the Second Coming. I disabused them – obviously – of that idea. This happened at an impressionable stage of my growing up, and I really was struck by the fact that Reverend Mother – who was not unpleasant, not stupid, and not particularly ill-meaning – had such an enormous blind spot. Since the cleaners were devoting their lives to Holy Mother Church, it was perfectly all right not to pay them very much. I was very hot and strong in what I said to her about workers' rights (St Joseph was a working carpenter, after all). Years later when I found myself in the profession that I ended up exercising, it was not very difficult to go from there to thinking that whilst it is very nice to have the paying work, it is also really important to do work *pro bono* and help those who need it most.

Adam: So, we are talking about Robin Hood wearing a barrister's wig and gown, not the traditional Lincoln green outfit with its trademark feathered hat.

Eleanor: Well, as a self-employed barrister you obviously need the paying work to earn your living, to have a roof over your head, decent food, and so on. In my case, I felt that along with that came an obligation, particularly once I started looking at the ECHR and the rights it guarantees, to work out how to use my training and ability as a barrister to help other people as well. Often those 'other people' who really needed the help did not have the money to pay. So yes, as you said, I ended up playing Robin Hood. I would take the money I received from the paid part of my practice and cross-subsidise. I would buy out my own time in order to make sure that the other cases also got done. I hasten to add that there are quite a few barristers who operate on exactly this principle. I can think of many good friends at the Bar who do precisely this: who take on the *pro bono* work as well as nice fat commercial briefs. It is a good thing, a part of the tradition of the profession. It is *tikkun olam* – repairing the world.

Adam: From what you are saying, Leo, religion and morality matter to you a great deal but, may I dare to ask, which religion?

Eleanor: I have been trying to ask and answer that question all of my life. Because my father was Jewish and my mother was a convert to Roman Catholicism, there was going to be a question mark over what happened to the kids. Now, at that time, the Roman Catholic Church was absolutely strict on this point. If a [Roman] Catholic married a non-Catholic, which encompassed not only people outside the Christian faith but all other Christian denominations too, that marriage would only be blessed by the Church, and could only be celebrated within the Church, if the non-Catholic partner to the marriage gave an undertaking that the children would be brought up Roman Catholic. My father gave that promise. Being an honourable man, he kept it. As a result, I was indeed brought up straightforwardly as a Roman Catholic. I was fed into the machine: I was baptised, I made my first Holy Communion when I was seven, and I was confirmed when I was nine. Between when I was six and when I was ten, I was at a convent school in Brazil (run, a little bizarrely, by earnest and well-meaning nuns from the Midwest of the USA), and I was already a perfect nuisance.

Adam: Why would that be, Leo?

Eleanor: Oh, my natural character was shining through! I kept on asking questions, such as how the Trinity worked, or how on earth anyone could take seriously the idea that if you had not been particularly good today, you should just make sure you included three more Hail Mary's and one more Our Father into your evening prayers, and that would somehow make it okay. I was asking those questions, and many more along the same lines, when I was eight or nine, and the good nuns were disconcerted and horrified. One particular dialogue that I still remember (it happened just after my confirmation, so I would have been about nine and a half, I guess) was along roughly the following lines:

> **Leo**: *Sister, I've been wondering about Mary being a virgin when she conceived Jesus by the intervention of the Holy Spirit. Of course I know that the Church teaches that and we believe that: it was at point [[whatever]] in the catechism that I learnt off by heart for my confirmation. Now, Matthew tells us Mary was a virgin in his Gospel (Matt. 1:22–23), and that Jesus was born like that to fulfil the prophecy in Isaiah ('Behold, a virgin shall conceive and bear a son, and ye shall call his name Immanuel – that is, 'God-with-us') (Is.7:14). I'm really puzzled. I've been reading that Matthew used a Greek translation of Isaiah [the Septuagint] which indeed described Mary as a 'parthenos' [παρθένος] – a virgin. However, the original Hebrew word in the text from Isaiah is 'almah' [עַלְמָה], which seems just to mean a young woman who is able to have children … But on the other hand Immanuel does seem to be correctly translated ['Immanu-el': 'with us – God'] …?*
>
> **Nun:** *(sighs) You always come up with ridiculously complicated questions, my child: just go and look at the answer in the book you were given for your confirmation.*
>
> **Leo:** *Yes, Sister, I have already looked at the answer in the book. I don't find it in the least bit convincing. It doesn't seem to know that texts can exist in different languages and that there can be mistranslations.*

Meanwhile, my father kept his promise. He never – at any stage – gave me any material about Judaism or talked with me about Judaism. What he couldn't do was to stifle my own natural curiosity. And the best illustration was what happened when I was twelve. By this stage I would have been about to become *bat mitzvah* if I had been brought up in the Liberal / Reform Jewish tradition. We were living in the house on Kingston Hill, and my kingdom was at the top of the house. I had two little rooms next to each other in the attic, which had no doubt been the maids' quarters in times gone past. The access to those rooms was via a very old, creaking staircase. So normally, I would hear if somebody was coming up to my lair. That morning, I must have been very absorbed in what I was doing. Suddenly I looked up. There was my father standing at the entrance to my little study. He was staring at me, because I was sitting cross-legged on the floor and around me I had a little collection of books that I had bought with my pocket money. There was a beginner's Hebrew grammar. There was a *Siddur* (a prayer book). I also had Maimonides *The Guide for the Perplexed*. (It was ridiculous to have been trying to read that when I was twelve: I am not sure I am that good at reading it and truly understanding it at sixty-nine.) My father looked at me and I scrambled to my feet. I remember being disconcerted, maybe even a little worried, because he was looking very stern. Then he said to me: 'What on earth are you doing? You have enough books for a *Yeshiva* [a Jewish religious school].'

With that complete absence of tact which at the time characterised me (and possibly still characterises me!), I said: 'Well, you haven't told me anything about Judaism, so I am finding out for myself.' My statement doesn't win a diplomacy prize, but it does win big in the honesty stakes. That was precisely the situation, and it was truly what I was doing.

Adam: Honesty of a curious child, you cannot beat that. What happened next?

Eleanor: There was a long pause. My father looked me up and down and thought about it and said – nothing at all. Then he nodded, turned around, and went back down the stairs. We never, ever, mentioned that conversation again. Coincidentally, my pocket money got increased. I think he knew very well where some of it would be going. So, I started educating myself in Judaism in parallel with being an observant Roman Catholic. In due course, after I went up to Cambridge, I added Anglicanism to the mix. Obviously, having gone to King's College I was going to spend time – lots of time – inside King's College Chapel. Very possibly I was the first practising Roman Catholic to serve as the student sacristan in King's Chapel since the Reformation. Somehow various things run in parallel. For a very, very long time I have kept the high days and holy days of both religions. But then, in a funny way, so did my father. Over time he became a non-practising Jew. However, as I have already said, he was such a *mensch*. He did absolutely everything a good Jew should do in terms of helping other people, of performing *mitzvot* that really mattered. In that sense whether he also went to *shul* [synagogue] or not was completely irrelevant. He used to come along with my mother, my brother (also brought up Roman Catholic), and myself to Midnight Mass on Christmas Day and the services from Maundy Thursday, through Good Friday and Holy Saturday, to Easter Sunday. Somehow we all ran with this, and nobody, including the parish priests (who knew perfectly well that my father was not a baptised Christian, let alone not really a Roman Catholic) behaved as though there was an issue. There wasn't an issue, I suppose, because there was a sufficiently clear sense that everyone was really feeling their way. There was a common central core of belief in God, and belief in what that implied, in terms of the way you ran your life and what you did with it. As I was growing up, that common central core was more important than the detail of the theology (which of course I knew to be – let's say, divergent!). So, over different times in my life, I've been a sort of very Jewish Christian or a rather Christian Jew. It depends which way up you are looking at me. And I dare say, if I were to be cross-examined, my actual belief structure would make the Roman Catholic Church deeply unhappy, and might cause an eyebrow or two to be raised on the Reform Jewish side of the equation – probably, fewer and less worried eyebrows than on the Catholic side, however.

Adam: I bet it would, especially for those not terribly open minded. So, going back to my earlier question: which religion has been your driving force?

Eleanor: I think all I can say is I don't know the answer, and I don't expect to know the answer, at least not in this life, anyway. I am content with the idea that my faith, in the sense of my belief in God, is rock solid; and that has clear implications. The Master of the Universe [*ribbon ha olam*] expects me to live my life according to certain standards and obligations and – to use a very, very old-fashioned phrase – I accept the yoke of Heaven. I try to live by the implications in terms of conduct and service. Sometimes I succeed, and sometimes I fail egregiously (and then I am very grateful for the overwhelming spirituality of *Yom Kippur* [the Day of Atonement]). I have spent so much time as a Christian that the teachings of Jesus are hard-etched into my memory and my conscience as reference points. That said, I feel very comfortable and at home within the parameters of Liberal / Reform Judaism. I would feel extremely uncomfortable within Orthodox Judaism, just as I felt extremely uncomfortable within traditional Roman Catholicism, and was much more comfortable within the Catholic Church in the immediate aftermath of the Second Vatican Council, before the liberal genie let loose by Pope John XXIII started to be pushed back into the bottle by his worried successors. I think that probably tells you that in my religion, as in pretty much everything else, I am basically fairly liberal and fairly left wing: 'Let me in there and let me get on with it. Don't stop me using whatever gifts God gave me within my religion – as I do within my daily life – just because I am a woman'. Both traditional Roman Catholicism and Orthodox Judaism are very good at saying: 'If you are female, it is lovely if you want to come to church / to *shul*, my dear. Could you please just sort out the flower arrangements (or bake *challah*, keep ritual purity, and stay out of sight in the women's gallery)? Above all, don't think of anything that involves a priestly or a leadership role'. I have never accepted that pigeonholing of women's role in my secular life. Why on earth would I buy it in my religious life?

ENDNOTES

[*] Eleanor Sharpston QC, *First 100 Years Biography*, 2019 (available on YouTube).

[1] This quote is widely attributed to Émile Zola, though the exact source is unknown. Still, it is a very apt observation.

[2] Case C-34/09 *Ruiz Zambrano v Office national de l'emploi (ONEm)* ECLI:EU:C:2010:560, Opinion of AG Sharpston.

[3] Remarks of President Barack Obama, Selma, Alabama, 7 March 2015.

[4] Again, a widely attributed quote (this time to George Bernard Shaw) without an exact source. Good point, though!

[5] Maud Mannoni, *L'enfant, sa "maladie" et les autres* (Seuil, 1974).

[6] Maud Mannoni, *The Child, His 'Illness' And the Others* (Penguin, 1973).

[7] Matthew Longo, *The Picnic. An Escape to Freedom and the Collapse of the Iron Curtain* (The Bodley Head, 2024) 259.

[8] David Sterrit, 'Actress tells of life with the Royal Shakespeare Company' (*The Christian Science Monitor*, 1984) https://www.csmonitor.com/1984/1214/121436.html accessed 1 September 2025.

[9] Judi Dench and Brendan O'Hea, *Shakespeare. The Man who pays the Rent* (Michael Joseph, 2023).

2

At the Bar and at the Court of Justice: The Early Years

*I think I always wanted to be a lawyer, and – I think –
I always really wanted to be a barrister.
I say this with some degree of self-deprecation.
I think I would have made a lousy solicitor because I am
not very good at keeping time records, I am not
necessarily good at getting back to the client within half
an hour of the phone call or the email.**

Adam: We are now in the late 1970s. A reminder is fitting that Eleanor Sharpston, having graduated from the University of Cambridge with a degree in economics, moved to Oxford where she enrolled on the MPhil programme, and then went on to prepare a thesis for the DPhil. She also excelled in squash and rowing. And yes, if that were not enough, she also pursued her professional legal studies for admission to the English Bar. In 1980, she successfully took the Bar Finals Part II and was called to the Bar by the Middle Temple in 1980 and given a Jules Thorn Scholarship to help her through pupillage. In 1981, Middle Temple gave her a second scholarship, the Sir Peter Bristow award, which allowed her to spend some very valuable time as a *stagiaire* at the European Commission and at the Court of Justice. It is at that point that her paths serendipitously crossed with two people who later proved instrumental for her career: John Temple Lang at the European Commission and Sir Gordon Slynn at the Court.

Seen from the perspective of 2025, it may come as a shock to the younger generations of readers that, at the turn of 1970s and 1980s, practising law (particularly as a barrister) was not an obvious choice for a woman. To get a taste of the prevalent climate at the time, we do not need to go very far. During her pupillage training in 1980, the middle-aged male barrister taking one of the advocacy exercises told her: 'I suppose if we have got to have you bloody women at the Bar, it is at least easier to listen to one who sounds like a bloke'. She also faced other difficulties. She did not come from a family of lawyers and, as a (negative) bonus, she expressed a desire to practice EEC law. Alas, although the United Kingdom had been a Member State for almost a decade, clients who (knew that they) were in need of EEC law advice were sparse. They were not exactly breaking and entering to jump long queues at the door decorated with a plate saying 'Barrister'. This was the reality that Eleanor had to face, but she is a lioness (or, in her own words, 'impossibly stubborn'), so she picked up the fight. With not much on the horizon in the UK, she commenced her independent practice as a junior barrister at the overseas outpost of the English Bar in Brussels. It obviously helped that she was multilingual and already familiar with the EEC institutions, including the Court of Justice. This time, however, she was a member of teams that were pleading cases in Kirchberg courtrooms. Things were going well until the point where they were not. The circumstances were fraught enough to the point that Eleanor was two-timing between Brussels and London. In 1987, fate and her guardian angels intervened. Having learned from her former mentor at the European Commission that there was a vacancy in the Court's *référendairiat*, she got on her motorbike and rode to Luxembourg via Oxford and London (as one does) to knock on the door of a rather surprised Sir Gordon Slynn. Fast forward, Eleanor joined Gordon as a *référendaire* (judicial assistant) and subsequently became his *chef de cabinet*. Her time with him inside the Court (1987–1990) began whilst Gordon was still the British Advocate General at the Court of Justice; after that first year, she continued with him for a further two years after he transferred across to become the British judge. As a *référendaire*, Eleanor prepared draft Opinions (in English) for AG Slynn, and later draft judgments (in French) for the cases in which he was the *juge rapporteur* (reporting judge). That three-year stint at the Court was critical for Eleanor's later career, in particular the period from 2006 to 2020 when, in her turn, she served as an Advocate General at the Court of Justice of the European Union.

*

Adam: Let us start with this travesty that you lacked motivation, dedication, and self-discipline. Of course, the Dean of the Inns of Court School of Law was profoundly wrong and failed to appreciate that one can successfully juggle plates. Funny to think, years later, that it was rowing that got you into trouble, not your actual performance as a law student.

Eleanor: Rowing got me into bad trouble. I should say, though, that back then I was a bit of a woman in a hurry. In other words, I had a grant to do research in Oxford but that was it. I didn't want to spend a further year doing my Bar finals and I had no funding for a further student year either. So, I decided to telescope. I decided that I could use the third year I was in Oxford to try to write up my PhD, and, simultaneously, I could do my Bar finals in London. Initially, rowing wasn't a part of the equation, except that the Oxford University Women's Boat Club said to me:

> *Come on Leo, you can't leave the job half done.*
>
> *We nearly won last year!*

We need you to run the club and finish the process of turning it around.

We want to win in March!

This would be my seventh year trying to get a winning 'Blue'. (How biblical!) At Cambridge, until my last term I never managed to get my 'Blue' for any of the various sports that I played. Either I had been part of the reserve squad (and / or missed the Varsity match), or the sport in question (for example, women's football) hadn't yet been recognised as a Blues sport by the relevant committee. But I had always won against Oxford. Then in the Easter term of my fourth year I got a 'half Blue' for cricket – as far as I can tell, for being stupid enough to stand like an idiot at 'silly mid-on' very close to the wicket, wearing glasses and hoping to stop balls; and being able to hit two or three 'fours' to the boundary as a batsman before I missed a ball and was got 'out'. I was duly awarded my Cambridge 'half Blue', but we lost the Varsity match. At Oxford, I still didn't have a winning 'Blue'. I had two losing 'full Blue's' from rowing, and also a losing 'Blue' from squash. I had the honour of being an Oxford 'full Blue', but every time, I had lost to Cambridge. So, I allowed myself to be persuaded that Oxford University Women's Boat Club needed my investment, energy, and commitment during 1979/80 as well. As I recall, I also horrified my contemporaries in the club. One day, walking back from the river, we were talking about what we would be in another life. My contribution, when my turn came round, was to say:

> *Well, in my next life, instead of being five foot three and a half, which is too small for a rower, I am going to be at least five foot eight, but I am going to have the same power-output-to-height ratio as I have now.*

There was a moment of horrified silence, as my colleagues looked at each other. Then they said: 'we're getting out of town!'

Adam: … and then came the day of the famous Oxford-Cambridge Women's Boat Race … 23 March 1980 …

Eleanor: It came but it was preceded by months of preparation. I was part of the Oxford University Women's Boat Club, heart and soul, for a period of easily six months. During those six months, I was not just two-timing, I was three-timing – and I managed. It was a bit like a Georges Feydeau farce – it all depended on split second clothes changes and scene changes. For six months, Oxford didn't realise I was in London. London didn't realise I was in Oxford. And neither Oxford nor London realised that a very substantial part of the time I was on the river at Radley, or in the gym, or on the train between Oxford and London.

Adam: Did you sleep at all, Leo?

Eleanor: I did, sometimes. Remember, I was doing all of this because I didn't have a grant or other money to draw on to fund an extra year after Oxford to do my Bar finals course. But I had worked out, being a natural optimist, that

I could probably double it up with my final year in Oxford. Now, in order to do this, I needed to box clever on what was meant to be happening when (and where). Although there is a train line between Oxford and London Paddington Station, it costs money to travel by train, and it also costs time. So I couldn't be yo-yoing up and down between Oxford and London every day. I could make it work if I arranged matters so that, essentially, I would be in London all day on Monday and the first part of Tuesday, and then I would go back to Oxford and not reappear in London until the following Monday (save for occasional court attendances on, from memory, a Wednesday). That was the way it was fixed. That was all fine as far as it went, but it also meant that I needed somewhere to stay overnight in London. Obviously, I was after a place to lay my head that was reasonably priced.

Adam: Which is close to impossible these days and, I guess, it must have been back then, too.

Eleanor: Quite! The price of accommodation in London is (and was) predictably frightening. However, I discovered, having explored a bit, that there was a very curious pricing phenomenon – curious, at least, for an economist – that operated in the immediate vicinity of large railway stations. There were hotels near places like Euston or King's Cross, and they seemed to be pretty rundown. They were seedy, it has to be said. And they seemed to operate a two-tier pricing system. They had an hourly rate (which seemed a bit weird and also quite expensive); and then they had an overnight rate (which was actually, prorata, pretty reasonable). Having discovered this, I worked out what I was going to do to save money when in London. I would come to London with my push bike on the train and be in London all Monday, stay overnight in one of these hotels near King's Cross, go to a class on Tuesday morning, and then travel back to Oxford. The bike accompanied me because I was saving money by cycling in London instead of taking the Underground.

Adam: Oh dear, being a well-brought up Viennese girl, you did not realise what kind of establishments they were ….

Leo: Wait for it! I went along to what looked to me the least flea-ridden of the various hotels on offer. I parked my bike outside, locked it to the railings, and I went inside. I negotiated for a room overnight, money up front (of course those were the days before credit cards, this was cash on the desk). I paid for the room. I was given the key, and I was just turning away when a terrible thought struck me. London is a big and wicked city. Never mind a girl not being safe in London, a self-respecting God-fearing bicycle is also not safe in London. It is at risk of being stolen. Had my bicycle been stolen, that would have been a real catastrophe. It was, by a large margin, my most valuable possession, and it was also the pivot point around which my budgeting – for what I was up to – turned. I had a sudden vision of some evil person cutting the locks and in the morning my bike would not be there. Almost in panic I turned back to the desk to enquire further of the receptionist, a world-weary lady who had truly seen it all over the course of the previous twenty-five years.

> **Leo**: *Would it be okay if I brought my bike in?*
>
> **Receptionist** [Barely looking at me]: *Well darling, whatever turns you on.*

There was a pause while I processed that. I was a very sweet and innocent girl, but eventually I did get the point. And of course, I then blushed to the roots of my hair and started stammering something about the bike … that I did not have a particular relationship with the bike of the kind that she was suggesting. All I was looking for was somewhere downstairs to put my precious bike, where I could lock it securely to something immoveable. I didn't need it in my room so that it could console me in the wee small hours of the morning.

Adam: (laughing) But of course. Did all that juggling of plates work out?

Eleanor: The juggling act somehow always worked well, until the Sunday of the Women's Boat Race. We rowed against Cambridge, and we beat them. Then two things happened: one very good and one that proved to be a little bit more tricky. What was very good (and very touching) was that as we came back to the landing stage at Leander, having beaten that year's Cambridge Blue Boat, and touched land, I was engulfed by a group of lovely contemporaries from Cambridge, all wearing 'Full Blue' light blue scarves. They were my crewmates, whom I had rowed with in the Cambridge reserve crew ('Blondie') in 1976 and 1977, and they came down to the landing stage to congratulate me: the Oxford President. That was so sweet: a very, very wonderful moment. The less good aspect was the press coverage. The photographer for *The Times* newspaper took a fine photo of the Oxford women's boat race crew, sitting victorious in its boat alongside the landing stage. Now, for some reason, the following day there wasn't any significant world news. There hadn't been an earthquake. There hadn't been a plane crash. An influential politician hadn't made a rousing statement on a newsworthy issue. Consequently, *The Times* was a bit short of the usual photo to go on their front page. So, they chose to publish the photo of the Oxford University winning women's boat race crew, with your humble servant – because I was in the 'six' seat of that crew – absolutely centre stage in the photo. I was grinning from one silly ear to the other from sheer delight at finally winning the women's boat race. And I really was centre stage. It's not that I was at the edge of the photo, with only half my face showing, which would have perhaps enabled me to argue, 'No, that isn't really me. No, I know it looks a bit like me, but it's not me'. There I definitely was, right in the middle of the front page. Of course, at the time, in those pre-internet days, *The Times* was the paper of record for the law reports. Every lawyer bought *The Times*. If I had intended to take out a full-page advertisement to explain that I was on the river when I should not have been, I really couldn't have done better. Then of course all hell broke loose. I was called in by the Dean of the Inns of Court School of Law. To say I was 'carpeted' is a very British understatement. I am sure the Dean would have thrown me off the course if he had had the clear evidence of my wrongdoing which he suspected must exist. Of course, the evidence could have existed. He was quite right in suspecting that I must have cut lectures, and that I must not have been attending to my studies with the zeal and devotion which he expected of law students – but he could not prove it. I had made sure that I had attended all the small group teaching where a rota was kept every session. I had scrupulously done all the compulsory court attendances. I had sufficient good friends to ensure that if a random attendance check happened during a lecture, somebody had ticked my name off on the list. During that fateful meeting, I stood to attention and kept my mouth shut. After about 25 minutes, the (very frustrated) Dean threw me out of his office, but fortunately not off the course, saying as a parting shot:

> *I can tell, Sharpston, that you will make nothing of a career at the Bar because you lack the necessary motivation, dedication, and self-discipline.*
>
> *Get out!*

I do remember getting out of his office and checking that my head was still in place on my shoulders. I also recall walking down the corridor thinking:

> *You silly man!*
>
> *How do you think I got through the last six months?*

Adam: I am tempted to bring into this one of the laws of life included in a splendid collection skilfully assembled by Hugh Rawson. Amid all that life wisdom, one can find Sherlock Holmes' second law of life. It is very fitting here: 'It is a capital mistake to theorise before one has the data'.[1] Clearly, the Dean of the Inns of Court School of Law made that mistake. Leo, you not only completed your studies with flying colours, but you were also called to the Bar in 1980. While you successfully made it, it must have been very difficult for a woman to join what back then was predominantly a boys' club. This was the English Bar you were aiming for, after all.

Eleanor: First: it is true that if you look at what I read as an undergraduate, it does look remarkably like somebody who loved being an academic and was determined not to have to make up her mind what she wanted to do for a living. If you come up to university on classics, and then you do economics, and then you do languages, followed by more economics, and then you stay on for a fourth year to read law, that's like a kind of Cook's tour of disciplines. Actually, it is a remarkably useful mixture of disciplines if you are going to specialise as an EU lawyer. As I already mentioned, I didn't plan it. I cannot claim credit for putting it together, mosaic stone by mosaic stone, to come to the right answer. But in fact, it proved very useful. Next: there were some obvious obstacles to trying to go to the Bar. When I joined it, the Bar was still very much a profession which was handed down from father to son. There were families that were Bar families.

Daddy was a high court judge. Your uncle was a very senior solicitor. You knew that some family members in the next generation were probably going to go to the Bar and that the necessary connections would be in place. When you needed a pupillage, somebody picked up the phone and somehow things got sorted out. The Inns of Court were of course aware of this phenomenon, and they were trying to move towards breaking the mould and they were making scholarships available particularly to help people who were not from traditional Bar backgrounds. At the time, I suspect, 'not from a traditional Bar background' tacitly meant that you might not be from a Bar family, but you were probably white British, and often you were male, sometimes you were female. I don't think there was at that stage much awareness of ethnic minorities, people of colour, and so on. Diversity was on the way, but it hadn't gotten that far. There were scholarships, and I was lucky in my Inn of Court, the Middle Temple. I was given two scholarships without which I certainly wouldn't ever have managed to go to the Bar. One was a pupillage award, a Jules Thorn Scholarship. The other was the Inn's European law scholarship, named after Sir Peter Bristow, I think simply because he was known to be vaguely 'European' and / or 'in favour of Europe'. As I mentioned, the Middle Temple was the only one of the four Inns of Court to offer a European law scholarship at that time.

Adam: It sounds like it was a splendid opportunity. What did the European law scholarship entail?

Eleanor: It was a real jewel of a scholarship. It enabled you to go and spend five months as a *stagiaire* inside the Legal Service of the European Commission. In other words, it parachuted you into the Legal Service which – of course – you would never have been able to guarantee as an ordinary entrant in the famous Blue Book system. Then you went on down to what was then the Court of Justice of the *European Communities* (rather than the CJEU) in Luxembourg and spent a couple of months working in the chambers of the British Advocate General there. Really, it was a fabulous scholarship.

Adam: Your application was – of course – successful. Was it challenging to get the scholarship?

Eleanor: The way I got that scholarship did not have much to do with my knowledge of European law; and the story, in its own way, is quite amusing. First: I almost omitted to apply for the scholarship. I had marked down mentally that it existed when I was choosing my Inn of Court, and then I'd forgotten all about it. One evening I went to eat one of my compulsory qualifying dinners at Middle Temple, and there – on the table – was a scrap of paper reminding students that the closing date for the Bristow scholarship was the following day at lunchtime. I looked at it and thought: 'Good Lord, I'd forgotten about that – maybe I should put my hat in the ring'. So, I did, and I was called for interview. However, before presenting myself to the scholarship committee, it did occur to me that it might be wise to have some idea, at least, of what European law – in their eyes – was meant to cover. So, I got hold of a copy of the Treaty of Rome and I had a quick flick through it. Remember, I was a one-year law student. I had never studied academically what was then EEC law. I had merely done the basic 'core subjects' that I needed for my exemptions from Part I of the Bar exams: five subjects in one year at Cambridge – constitutional, criminal, contract, tort, and land law – and then I taught myself the missing one – equity & trusts – over the summer and duly scraped through the additional qualifying exam. That meant that I had what I needed to move on to the vocational stage (Part II of the Bar exams), but I knew nothing officially about EEC law. So, I had a look at the Treaty of Rome before the interview.

Adam: That is always a good starting point, isn't it?

Eleanor: At the interview I got very lucky. On my CV, I had also put – very proudly and accurately – that I had rowed three years for Oxford University as a graduate student, and that I had been the President – for two years running – of the Oxford University Women's Boat Club. My interview panel were absolutely fascinated by that, to the point that for twenty out of the twenty-five minutes of the interview, they asked me questions on what surely would have been my 'Mastermind' specialist subject. How do you run Oxford University Women's Boat Club? What is it like preparing for the Women's Boat Race? Of course, I could answer those questions. I could even speak with great passion, comprehensiveness, and interest on that topic.

Eventually, one of them turned to the other members of the interview panel and said: 'I suppose we should ask her something about the law'. At this point I thought, 'Oh dear, this is where it all goes sadly wrong!'. And then he leant forward and said:

> *Miss Sharpston, is there anything particular about European Economic Community law, EEC law, that interests you or you think is worthy of study, that you would like to tell us about?*

That was the softest of softballs to be bowled. If you cannot do something with that, you really do not deserve to be given scholarship money. And of course, I was an economist by training. So, I happily produced five minutes' worth of (excuse my French) bullshit about the single market, the importance of economic integration, the different mechanisms and Treaty provisions, some of which addressed the actions of the state and others of which were directed at private parties. This was not the height of legal or economic sophistication as an analysis, but it was based on reasonably solid grounds. After all, I had read economics at Cambridge, and I had retained enough from my skim-read of the EEC Treaty to remember that there were provisions about integrating the single market ('frictionless trade' and 'mobility of factors of production', to my economist's mind), about competition law ('level playing field' and 'no abuse of monopoly power'), and about differential taxation. So, I put all these scraps together. The interview panel bought it. They must have bought it because they gave me the scholarship. At the end of the interview the chairman said: 'That's very interesting, Miss Sharpston, thank you so much. It has been fascinating talking with you'. In due course I became Middle Temple's 1981 Bristow Scholar. You might say with justification that at the time I didn't really deserve the scholarship. But I hope I have put it to reasonably good use.

That was one strand of my getting started at the Bar: finding my vocation in terms of what I wanted to specialise in. The other was the financial side. That was pretty much looked after thanks to the generosity of Middle Temple, my Inn of Court. To the extent that it wasn't, I did some work as a motorcycle courier. That brought in additional cash, albeit by a rather dangerous route. Being a freelance motorcycle courier in London is not one of the safer ways of earning money.

Adam: That has proven to be very useful when you applied, years later, for the position of the British Advocate General at the Court of Justice. It is all grist to the mill if you just wait for it to work, but we will come back to it a little later. How did the scholarship time look like, especially, the Brussels episode?

Eleanor: The scholarship was a big springboard because, as I mentioned, it enabled you to go to the European institutions. It was a big deal. First, I went to the European Commission, and I was allocated to an Italian lawyer who was working on state aid. That was pleasant enough, and I did a bit of work for him. But then shortly after arriving, I got acquainted with John Temple Lang, an Irish lawyer who was very well known in EU legal circles. JTL (as he was always known) was a fantastically good lawyer. He was also an extremely nice man. JTL was doing all the big competition law cases for the European Commission. At that particular moment, he was doing the *AM&S* case.

Adam: *AM&S* being the famous legal privilege case (155/79).[2] If my memory serves me well, it was all about legal privilege in competition cases, wasn't it? Years later, it is still an issue that keeps coming back to Luxembourg courtrooms. The big question whether correspondence between in-house lawyers and companies they are employed by is as off limits to the European Commission as letters between independent lawyers and their clients. *AM&S* is one of those interesting cases where we had two opinions of Advocates General: two consecutive British AGs – Sir Jean Pierre Warner[3] and Sir Gordon Slynn.[4] But back then the big question was really whether such a doctrine existed at all at EEC level, correct?

Eleanor: Precisely. During my stint at the European Commission, JTL (who was the Commission's agent in the case) wondered whether the Legal Service *stagiaires* could, perhaps, find time to do a little bit of comparative law research for him on the doctrine of legal professional privilege in the various Member States. Did it exist everywhere? If so, how precisely did it work and what were its limits? So, naturally I did the analysis for the UK; I double-checked the analysis that JTL had already done for Ireland; and – as my Luxembourgish colleague didn't seem too interested in doing extra work outside her official remit – I did the analysis for Luxembourg as well. JTL called me in briefly to discuss that work – that is when I first met him. At that stage, he was still waiting to discover whether his instructions for the hearing from the Commission (that is, from the College of Commissioners) were that he should accept that in principle there *was* a doctrine of legal professional privilege in EEC law but argue as to its limits; or whether he should be submitting that no, such a doctrine did not form part of EEC law. JTL waited … and waited. Literally the day before the hearing in Luxembourg, JTL was hanging around, waiting to be called upstairs to the tenth floor of the Berlaymont building where the gods – I mean, the Commissioners – lived, to be told what they wanted him to say. In the meantime, however, he was meant to be addressing about one hundred *stagiaires* who were due to go on a trip down to the Court to attend that same hearing the following morning. Normally they would be briefed on the case by the Commission's agent, but JTL couldn't do it. So, he called the *stagiaires* office and I got the short message from the fellow-*stagiaire* who took the phone call: 'John Temple Lang wants to see you'.

I shot out of there wondering what it was about (and perhaps, what I'd done wrong!). I scratched on the door of his office and he called me in:

Oh, Eleanor, yes, hello, thanks for coming round so quickly.

Look now, I am in a bit of trouble because I am still waiting for the Commission to tell me what they want me to say tomorrow at the hearing in AM&S, and I should be talking to the stagiaires, to brief them about the case.

Go along and talk in my place, will you?

'Yes, Mr Temple Lang, of course', said the barrister. What else was I going to say?! I had just about five minutes to put my wits together, walking from his office to where the *stagiaires* were all assembled. A hundred people who are my own age, all sitting there waiting for one of the Commission's most senior agents to tell them about the case. Instead of whom, Sharpston walks in and says:

Hello, good afternoon everyone.

I work for John Temple Lang. He sends his apologies because he is still waiting to get his instructions from the Commission.

I am here to brief you about tomorrow's case.

After that, I worked exclusively for JTL for the remaining four months of my *stage* at the Commission. I did some amazing cases with him.

Adam: Any in particular, apart from *AM&S*, that you would like to mention, Leo?

Eleanor: Oh yes. I worked with JTL also on *Musique Diffusion Française (MDF)* and *Pioneer* – an interesting competition case about importers of hi-fi equipment. They had challenged the Decision of the European

Commission so the case eventually ended up at the Court of Justice (Joined Cases 100-103/80).[5] When the cases were being analysed in Luxembourg I was already, as part of the Bristow scholarship, in the chambers of Advocate General Slynn, so of course, I did not do any further work there on that file.

Adam: It sounds like the *stage* at the European Commission was a very good and useful experience. Wasn't it?

Eleanor: Yes, especially working with JTL. I learnt a lot from him about top-quality lawyering. It was very, very useful. Also, because I had my economics background, my input on competition law was even helpful to him from time to time. That was very rewarding.

Adam: Then came your very first stint at the Court of Justice; two months in the chambers of the British Advocate General Sir Gordon Slynn with whom you would end up working as his *référendaire* at the other end of the 1980s. During this first short period in his *cabinet*, were there any interesting cases that you would like to revisit?

Eleanor: To start with, Gordon kindly said at the very beginning that he thought I should work on something that would be useful to me. So, I was spared the staff cases. Obviously, I was not allowed to deal with any case that I would already have worked on with JTL at the European Commission. At the Court I worked on two Opinions for AG Slynn. The first was an unsuccessful challenge to the legality of an EEC ban on the import of mushrooms from Taiwan and South Korea (Case 245/81).[6] This second case may be of more general interest, Adam, as it dealt with an 'action hero', Lord Bethell, who tried to force the European Commission to do something about air fares in Europe (Case 246/81).[7]

Adam: Oh, this sounds interesting, especially for someone who – just like you, Leo – suffers from an incurable condition called *travelitis furiosus* (an unstoppable urge to travel). Do tell, please.

Eleanor: Lord Bethell, as a member of the House of Lords and of the European Parliament, found himself frequently travelling back and forth to Brussels and to Strasbourg. Perhaps, like many of us, he was less than happy about what that was costing him in terms of air fares, and he thought that the European Commission should get on the case and do something about it. This was all happening in the formative days of the common market when there was very little EEC law applicable to air transport, a far cry from the open skies system that we have today. So, he started writing letters to the unit of the European Commission dealing with competition law (DG Competition), poking them in the ribs, encouraging them to do something. Eventually he had received one or two replies that didn't seem to him as though they were taking matters anywhere. He brought a case before the Court of Justice and he tried to frame it in alternative terms: either the Commission had failed to act, which would have been naughty of it and actionable under – what was then – Article 175 EEC (now Article 265 TFEU) or, alternatively, the reply that he had received from the Commission was an implied decision not to act (which would have been a decision he would seek to have annulled under Article 173 EEC (now Article 263 TFEU)). The trouble about this – even though it sounds very logical – is that there is a kind of black hole in between the action for annulment and the action for failure to act. The Commission had very cunningly managed to position its reply in the middle of that black hole. On the one hand, it couldn't be said that they had done nothing at all, therefore the action for failure to act wouldn't work. On the other hand, what they had done wasn't quite enough to amount to a decision that could be challenged under Article 173 EEC. I think it is fair to say that both the AG Gordon Slynn and his temporary, unofficial, extra *référendaire* the Bristow scholar thought that the way that the European Commission was conducting itself was unacceptable. But we didn't think that it was possible to distort the case law and the structure of those two Treaty articles in order to eliminate the black hole in between Articles 173 and 175 EEC.

Adam: The action eventually failed on admissibility grounds but it is clear that Lord Bethell was ahead of his time in terms of the air transport legislation and liberalisation of air transport in the European Union. Now, millions of EU citizens take it for granted that flying is available at the click of a computer mouse and that it can be very cheap indeed.

Eleanor: Not only this, Adam. There is the big picture, too. He was right in thinking that the relations between the European Commission and the general public are weighted in favour of the Commission. In other words, the Commission has lots of discretion as to which balls it picks up and runs with, and which ones it decides to leave quietly lying there in the long grass. There is very, very little that you, as a concerned citizen, can do about it. You cannot force the Commission to take action. It is, of course, entirely right and proper that the Commission should retain an administrative discretion; but sometimes it is very frustrating indeed if getting the Commission to do something looks like the only possible way forward and the Commission is not interested in playing ball. That is partly why the references for preliminary rulings from national courts have played such an enormous part in the evolution of EU law. Those references come through to the Court, and the Court deals with the case as its jurisdiction does not permit it to dine *à la carte*. Whereas if the European Commission doesn't want to go after a Member State which is dragging its feet, nothing happens.

Adam: Yes, there is a very telling passage in the closing paragraph of the Opinion of AG Slynn, where he said: '[…] I see much force in the argument that natural and legal persons should have a wider right of challenge before the Court in regard to the activities of the Commission'.[8] While the action submitted by Lord Bethell was inadmissible, access to Court is a theme that frequently comes up in the academic discourse.

Let's go back to those early days of your career. After the scholarship you returned to London to finish your Bar course.

Eleanor: Indeed, after the scholarship I went back to the UK. The Middle Temple was so considerate and generous that they had put the remainder of my first scholarship – the Jules Thorn scholarship – on 'hold' while I was away doing the Bristow scholarship. In order to understand what I was up to at this point, I need to explain the pupillage requirements. In a nutshell, you had to do six months pupillage before you could accept instructions as a barrister, and you had to do 12 months pupillage in all before you were fully qualified. The Bristow scholarship only counted as three months worth of pupillage. So, having done my earlier pupillage (seven months) and then having held the Bristow scholarship, I still hadn't quite got enough qualifying pupillage to be fully qualified as a barrister. I had served ten months, not twelve. I therefore went and did what was – in theory – a third six months' pupillage. On my return to the UK, I filled in that gap in a set of chambers that did shipping law (4 Essex Court, as a pupil with Nigel Teare [later a High Court judge]).

Adam: Shipping law? That's a turn of events I did not quite expect at this juncture. It is quite an extraordinary change from competition law which you worked on at the European Commission with John Temple Lang.

Eleanor: I appreciate that it may strike you as completely nuts. I mean, how does this fit with anything I was doing before? Part of the answer is that I love the sea and sailing. So, anything to do with water, ships, and what happens to ships was intuitively attractive. I am probably the only pupil barrister who found the Hague-Visby Rules on carriage of goods by sea really interesting. The other half of the answer is that I was convinced that EEC law would sooner or later have to address maritime transport. Overall, I had a very interesting six months as a pupil at those chambers, even though I did no paid work during that period. I managed (finally) to finish qualifying as a practising barrister. I then tried to persuade chambers to take me on as a tenant, doing some shipping work, but also doing some work in other areas of law, particularly EEC law. I failed abysmally as an advocate to persuade them that maritime transport and EEC law were going to meet. It did happen, but I was about 15 years too early.

Adam: In other words, you were ahead of your time as well.

Eleanor: I was ahead of my time. That left me qualified but without a tenancy in the UK. Having spent time at the European Commission and at the Court of Justice, I knew I wanted to do EEC law.

Adam: I guess that in the early 1980s this was not an obvious career choice for a woman wishing to practise law in the United Kingdom.

Eleanor: Back then, if you were a freshly qualified woman barrister and you said you wanted a tenancy to do EEC law, people looked at you as though you had green skin and antennae sticking up from your head and you beeped when you turned corners. You were not taken seriously for at least three minutes (and it was very difficult to get past those initial three minutes). I listened recently to a splendid radio interview with Marin Alsop, the path-breaking American woman conductor. Her narrative, beautifully and wryly recounted, resonated so perfectly with my own recollection of trying to break into an area of law that (a bit like the infamous lodgings for rent with their sign in the window, 'No dogs, no Irish') had an invisible sign up saying 'no women barristers need apply to do this speciality'.[9]

Adam: So what did women barristers do? In which areas could they practise?

Eleanor: Women barristers did family law because it was nice for a distressed female client to have a friendly female shoulder to cry on. They also did criminal law, by which I mean the kind of non-sexy, non-heavyweight cases. They didn't do the difficult commercial frauds or the really juicy murders. They did the lighter stuff. They did common assaults, driving offences, and similar cases.

Adam: And you, Leo, learned it first hand as your first court case was exactly of that kind, wasn't it?

Eleanor: Picture this. Here I am – a keen, eager young lawyer. I am wildly idealistic, committed to justice and the rule of law – and it's my first day going into court as a newly qualified barrister acting for a real client. I had a defence brief to prepare a 'plea in mitigation' for the sentencing hearing for a character who – let's put this politely – was not having his first encounter with the criminal justice system. Everyone, including my instructing solicitor and the client himself, was pretty sure that he was going to 'go inside' this time, the only question being how long a prison sentence he would get. My job, doing the plea in mitigation, was essentially damage limitation. I vastly over-prepared for that hearing.

Adam: I suppose your 'pupil master' had some words of advice and wisdom for you on that day.

Eleanor: Oh yes, of course, but not the kind one would expect. As I was in the middle of looking up everything I could think of checking my supervisor, my 'pupil master', Cyril Newman, popped his head round the door to see how I was getting on and to offer well-meaning reassurance. I asked him if he had any top tips for me doing my first case for real. Without hesitation he replied:

> *Yes … make sure that you have really polished your shoes before you go into court.*

I remember looking at him in utter disbelief. Cyril was a delightful, old-fashioned, English gentleman. Was this an example of the celebrated English sense of humour? Was it designed to get me to relax a bit? Did he conceivably mean it for real as a piece of advice?

Adam: Which one of the three options was it? Perhaps the sense of humour? It does sound very English to me.

Eleanor: I never found out; and since I couldn't be sure that he was joking, yes, I did polish my shoes that evening as well as looking up the law; and then I polished them again just before I went into court.

Adam: Alright then, perhaps he was trying to relax you?

Eleanor: In that case the mission failed. I have to tell you it did not produce a feeling of zen-like relaxation. Rather the reverse. I became even more worried than I was already. Apparently I didn't only have to know all the relevant law: it seemed that I also had to have beautifully polished shoes.

Adam: This leaves us with the very last option: it was a genuine piece of advice, wasn't it?

Eleanor: Actually, when I got to court, the first thing that the magistrates' clerk did was to look sharply, not at my face, but yes, at my shoes. Having satisfied himself that they were polished and gleaming, he looked up from my shoes to me with a pleasant smile.

Adam: Sounds like Cyril Newman's advice was spot on. Your shoes were well noted but did the fact that you diligently followed the words of wisdom coming from your 'pupil master' help you on your first day in court?

Eleanor: The magistrates' clerk was very helpful to me after that throughout that memorable day. His helpfulness really mattered because the one thing I hadn't prepared for – happened. My client didn't turn up for court. When the case was called on for hearing: no client! And the magistrates, who were really not amused, promptly issued a 'bench warrant' for his arrest. That of course meant that he would be in a whole lot more trouble: not just the original charge that he was being sentenced for, but a whole stack of other problems. Thanks to various unobtrusive kind hints from the magistrates' clerk, I did manage to salvage the situation. I got the police not to execute the bench warrant (so the additional problems to which that would have given rise quietly went away). I got the case relisted for hearing at the end of the day. And – I think to everyone's surprise – I did actually keep my client out of prison.

Adam: This sounds like a tough but very promising start to your career as a barrister, Leo. Baptism of fire, huh?

Eleanor: Well, my first encounter with the justice system as a barrister taught me a number of valuable lessons. The one I want to flag up is this: issuing the bench warrant for my client's arrest was simply wrong. The magistrates were annoyed he wasn't there. ('How rude'. 'How disrespectful'. 'We are important people, we are the court – he should be here on time'.) They weren't prepared to consider that they should give him a bit more leeway. Why? Because there might be a perfectly innocent explanation for why he wasn't there precisely on time for the hearing. There was indeed an innocent, even a banal, explanation. He had simply caught the wrong train. He was the kind of guy who catches the wrong train in life. The magistrates took a hasty decision, influenced by their annoyance. That decision was an incorrect use of their powers. There was – in short – a mini rule-of-law issue in this tiny, routine hearing in a minor criminal court. I had to find a way of (politely!) unscrambling the mess and getting my client treated justly. Thanks to those useful hints from the magistrates' clerk, who had liked my nicely polished shoes, that's what happened.

Adam: This is a truly delightful story which in itself has a lot of wisdom to offer. But this was not the kind of case you were dreaming of, was it?

Eleanor: As much as I was delighted to have my first case in court, I had really not gone to the Bar to do that kind of work. I knew exactly what I wanted to do and that was EEC law. As it was, I was an obstinately square peg in a traditional round hole. I would have been a perfect fit in an EEC-law shaped hole, except I couldn't find a tenancy in chambers doing that work.

Adam: You were – again – ahead of your time, Leo. I guess this led to the change of azimuth. Brussels or Luxembourg?

Eleanor: I went back to Brussels. I started working in a law firm called *Community Law Office Belmont* for Stanley Crossick, a very enterprising and flamboyant character. Curiously, Stanley – although a solicitor – did not have a London office; so it was possible for me to work for him without having to request to be voluntarily disbarred. Practising barristers weren't allowed to hobnob with solicitors in those days. If I had been trying to work for *Coward Chance* [now *Clifford Chance*] or any normal law firm, I would necessarily have had to ask to be disbarred. This would have been a shame since I had only just finished qualifying as a barrister. But it was alright for me to associate with Stanley Crossick and *Community Law Office Belmont*. I worked there for six months and I had a number of run-ins with Stanley. Actually, I managed to get a salary increase before I even started, because I told him that what he had thought he was going to pay me was simply ridiculous and he was going to pay me more than that!

Adam: Now, that's what you call gumption! Was working for Stanley Crossick a useful experience?

Eleanor: I truly learnt a great deal that was of immense value later on. I found out what it was like to have the client screaming at the other end of the telephone or the fax machine. This is something to which – as a young barrister – you are simply not exposed. It was very instructive in increasing my understanding of the practice of law. There is another side of this story, too. There was a very interesting symbiosis between Stanley's law firm and the available pool of young lawyers and political scientists in Brussels at the time, who were looking for the next steps in their careers. *Belmont* was an unusual entity – an unusual beast in the Brussels of those days. It was a mixture of law firm and lobbyists firm. Stanley Crossick had some very original ideas in terms of what he was doing and how he ran the place. There were a number of young lawyers around who – perhaps like myself – didn't quite fit the traditional mould. I met some really interesting people at *Belmont*. Above all, in terms of friendships that I made, it was there that I first met Rosa Greaves. Since then, she has had an enormously distinguished academic career in EU law. Rosa is an utterly delightful and charming person, we have remained friends ever since.

Adam: Are there any particularly memorable events from those days?

Eleanor: Well, apart from a few interesting cases, there was the saga of the conference table. One day, Stanley was going to be away all day. So that was obviously the right day to deal with tedious administrative stuff that needed doing. There was an enormous table, which was at the time, if my memory serves me well, on the second floor. Stanley wanted it moved to a big conference room on the sixth floor. He left instructions that this was to be organised during his absence. It proved to be a total nightmare. We did get it up there eventually but it occupied the fee-earning members of *Belmont*, almost every fee-earning member, for a very large proportion of the day. Stanley came back and – of course – he was absolutely furious. He demanded to have a written account, a memorandum explaining what had happened and why. Naturally and inevitably, I was the person who wrote the memorandum. Essentially, I described each step in the process in the most detailed fashion. 'We tried this and this didn't work, so then we tried that, and that didn't work.' I finished with something along the lines of: 'If there is anything more you need to know, Stanley, just come and ask me.' The memo shut him up. He did not peep out of his box again about that and – to our collective surprise – we had no further trouble arising from that wasted, non-fee-earning day. That made my reputation with my colleagues.

Adam: A good way to make someone go quiet and keep schtum! What happened after those first six months in Brussels?

Eleanor: After half a year with Stanley, I was invited by Jeremy Lever QC to join his Brussels chambers. They were the only set of barristers' chambers in Brussels at the time. It was a very small set consisting of Jeremy, Nicholas Forwood (now Sir Nicholas Forwood KC), and Christopher Vajda (now Sir Christopher Vajda KC), and then they added Eleanor Sharpston.

Adam: Woohah! Two future British judges at the Court of Justice of the European Union and a future British Advocate General under one roof. I have to say, not bad for small chambers in Brussels, not bad at all.

Eleanor: All the juniors in the set managed to make 'home runs' to Luxembourg sooner or later, which is probably a record.

Adam: How did your path cross with Jeremy?

Eleanor: I heard, albeit indirectly, that members of Jeremy's chambers in London (Gray's Inn Chambers) later took him to task for offering the junior tenancy spot in his Brussels chambers to a mere woman whom they'd never heard of. Why had he not offered it to one of the nice young men, very promising nice young men, from London chambers? Apparently, Jeremy replied that he had not really wanted to offer me the place but that I came so highly recommended by John Temple Lang that he felt he had to propose 'something'. That proposed 'something' was, as he put it:

> *You can come and join chambers.*
>
> *I won't charge you rent.*
>
> *I can't guarantee you work.*

I said: 'done'. That was not what I was meant to say. I was meant to be a prudent woman, and say: 'That's very kind, but I don't think I can take the gamble'. But that's not what I said, so I joined his chambers in Brussels.

Adam: How did it work out? You stayed there quite a while, didn't you?

Eleanor: I was in practice in Brussels for roughly five years. Initially it went very well, we even did cases at the Court of Justice. The first case where my name appears as a co-counsel alongside Jeremy Lever QC, instructed by Robin Griffith (of (then) Coward Chance), is Case 258/84.[10] We represented a Japanese client *Nippon Seiko KK*, challenging the legality of anti-dumping duties imposed by the Council on imports of certain ball-bearings originating in Japan and Singapore. I did a lot of legwork on that case, I did the initial drafts of the pleadings, and I was also at the hearing at the Court. I have to tell you that anti-dumping cases involving 100 different types of ball bearing in four countries are fairly mind-bendingly difficult and dull. Jeremy wanted to plead the case in a particular way, challenging the calculation of the duties, along the lines: 'had they done 'A' rather than 'B', when they were calculating the reference points for the anti-dumping duty (normal value and export price), that would have resulted in a reduction of the import duty, 'payable ('C') of ('X') per cent'. It was the only time in my life that I've been grateful for a spreadsheet, because I simply could not bear doing this by hand on a handheld calculator. I did the first few rough calculations that way and I thought I would lose the will to live. So, I got hold of some spreadsheet software, and entered all the data (ball bearing type, quantity sold, price, etc.) into the individual cells, with the formula for the duty applied. If you do that, of course, you can then just change one of the underlying assumptions and the spreadsheet will update all the figures for you. I do remember Jeremy looking a little bit surprised, and even quite pleased, when I explained that now that we had the spreadsheet we could – next time he wanted to do one of these wild prophecies – manage to generate the results of the prophecy without spending another eight hours with a handheld calculator. Sadly, we were still not able to persuade the Court of Justice and the action for annulment was dismissed.

Adam: That was not the only anti-dumping case you did at the Court, was it?

Eleanor: No, it was not. After Jeremy left Brussels to return to practice in London, his Brussels chambers mutated and were rechristened as *Charlemagne Chambers*. In parallel with that, my practice stalled and then started to nosedive. There was a senior colleague in *Charlemagne Chambers*, its de facto manager, called Clare Tritton. She was not an EU lawyer but she wanted to get into that area of practice, and she was very good at attracting work. In this instance, she managed to get hold of a dumping case.

Our client was *Gestetner Holdings plc*, an importer of plain paper copiers ('PPCs') originating in Japan. The PPCs were made there by a company called *Mita*, which would sell them to *Gestetner*, which in turn would rebadge them and sell them as their own products. There was a big anti-dumping investigation into PPCs made by various Japanese manufacturers, including *Mita*. *Gestetner* offered a price undertaking to the Commission, which the Commission refused to accept, instead imposing a provisional anti-dumping duty. Subsequently, the Council adopted a regulation imposing a definitive anti-dumping duty on various Japanese PPCs including those manufactured by *Mita*. *Gestetner*'s subsequent challenge to the EU institutions' findings ended up at the Court of Justice as Case 156/87.[11]

Adam: Bearing in mind that the time limit for action for annulment is merely two months, it must have been a rather frantic ordeal.

Eleanor: Quite! Naturally we were finishing the written pleadings right up against the end of the time for lodging the application, not only because the time limit is tight, but also because that is how barristers invariably seem to work. On the last day before lodging the case, we were in London chambers fine-tuning and polishing the application. 'We' (at the time) were: Clare, myself, and Fergus Randolph (now Fergus Randolph KC). It was about 8 pm, the day before we had to lodge the application. Remember, those were the days when you had physically to lodge paper copies of court documents. The plan was that in the morning I would drive on my motorbike to Heathrow Airport, carrying the precious original and certified paper copies of the application, and fly to Luxembourg to lodge them in person at the Registry of the Court. Clare went home. Fergus and I were naturally expected to go on working on the application for however long it took to put it to bed. We both knew perfectly well that we were not going to get any sleep that night. By then we had finished all the big work, but a lot of checking was still needed. As always, that meant a lot of very tedious but very necessary and fiddly work to attend to just before lodging. Everything was in 'hard copy', and we had two 'bundles' – two volumes' worth of material. The first volume was the application. The second volume was the bundle of annexes. We were going to bind the bundles with our client *Gestetner's* beautiful, heat-welded plastic spines to hold the volumes together. This is an important detail! So, we cleaned up the application and we started printing, and then we turned to the annexes. Of course, the first annex was meant to be the Council Regulation imposing the definitive anti-dumping duty whose annulment we were seeking.[12] I picked up a copy of the Council Regulation – but the copy had my graffiti all over it. So I asked Fergus to find a clean copy of the wretched regulation. By now it is 3 am or maybe 4 am. We are on yet another cup of coffee. Clare is at home and long asleep. We are still working. We finally reach the big moment where I sign the original of the pleadings. Then I start to check and sign each copy of the pleadings and certify it as being a true copy. In due course – I haven't quite got there yet – I will do the same for the original volume and each copy volume of the annexes. Suddenly, there is an animal cry of pain from Fergus:

Fergus: *Oh my God!*

[uttered in a very upper class, public school accent, but real anguish behind the accent]

Fergus: [repeats unhappily]

Oh my God! I'm going to have a bibby!

Eleanor: [looks up and enquires mildly]

Fergus, old chap, what's happening?

Fergus: *No, no, I'm going to have a bibby! I'm going to have a bibby!*

I thought I had better go over to investigate. There was Fergus holding one of our beautiful, heat-welded volumes of annexes. Wordlessly he opened it. He pointed to the first document in the prepared bundle. It was not the Council Regulation imposing the definitive anti-dumping duty: the regulation that we were challenging, the 'contested act'. It was the Commission Regulation imposing the provisional anti-dumping duty, which was due to last for three months only, which had since expired, and which at that point had no remaining legal effect.[13] All credit to Fergus: he saw the mistake, even though by that stage we were both absolutely exhausted. I dare not assert that I'm sure I would have spotted it when I started to sign the volumes of annexes. I would probably happily have signed and certified each as a true copy. But Fergus – bless him – spotted the howler. He must inadvertently have picked up the Commission Regulation, of which he did have a clean copy. He had waved it at me, I had said yes, he had made photocopies and put them at the start of the bundle with the other annexes. He had then – very efficiently – heat-welded each one of the bundles into a tightly-bound volume using our client's wonderful, patented equipment.

Adam: I guess that three options were available at that point: to laugh, scream, or cry …

Eleanor: I have to admit that once I realised what had happened, I just lay down on the floor and howled with laughter. Out of the three you mentioned, it was the only conceivable reaction. At that stage we had both gone way beyond the silly point. We were both absolutely exhausted. We somehow had to keep going. The idea that we would have submitted our precious application to the Court of Justice with completely the wrong regulation as 'Annex 1 – The contested Regulation' was actually beyond priceless. It was utterly insane.

Once I was operational again, I fished out my Swiss Army penknife, which was the only tool available. We then spent the next half hour unpicking the heat-welded bindings so that we could – for the original and each copy volume! – extract the offending first annex, replace it with a copy of the correct (Council) Regulation, put everything back carefully into position in the heat-welding machine, and rebind each volume.

Adam: Despite this hiccup, all went according to the plan. You made it to Heathrow and then to Luxembourg. The application was lodged before the expiry of the deadline. As I look at the judgment of the Court I see, however, that you do not appear on the pleadings. Is this because by the time of the *délibéré* you were already at the Court, working as a *référendaire* for AG Slynn?

Eleanor: Well spotted, Adam. I was already working at the Court when this case reached its end (and the action was dismissed). Having worked on the case when in private practice, as a *référendaire* I then obviously had to stay away from it. There was a complete Chinese wall. But other *référendaires*' names were allowed to appear in the case reports in respect of work that they had done before joining the Court's service – for example, as agents for the Commission. So no, that was not the reason.

Adam: It is strange, the judgment says that *Gestetner* was represented by Clare Tritton, K.P.E. Lasok, and Fergus Randolph of *Charlemagne Chambers*.

Eleanor: I think this was part of a much bigger problem which started when Jeremy moved back to London. So did his other two Brussels juniors, who had London homes. Christopher went to *Gray's Inn Chambers* (Jeremy's set) as a tenant. Nicholas returned to his old chambers in London: *4 Pump Court*. I didn't really have a London home. I tried to get a door tenancy somewhere but I didn't have a professional home where I was already known and would be looked after. *Charlemagne Chambers* was Jeremy's initiative. It was an attempt to create a kind of Brussels annex, not for a single set of chambers, but for barristers from various different chambers who were interested in European work. When Jeremy moved back to London, he handed it over to Clare Tritton. She and I fell out, and my practice went into freefall. Until that point I had been doing very well, then my practice stalled and the plane started falling out of the sky. Also, at a personal level it was a very unhappy time. I ended up doing all sorts of very silly things, shuttling back and forth between London and Brussels on my

250 cc motorbike in order to try to pick up the odd bit of work here or there. It was a very strange, vagrant existence. I was stopping at motorway service stations to change out of rough kit, appropriate for driving a motorcycle, into more professional-looking clothes.

Adam: Oh dear.

Eleanor: My Honda 250 cc single cylinder four-stroke motorbike got more than it bargained for. When I say I used it for all my transport, I mean exactly that. I slipped into a pattern, according to which I travelled at very stupid times of the night, the simple reason being cheaper ferry crossings. If you tried crossing in the middle of the day, even with a motorbike, it was quite expensive. But if you were crossing at two o'clock in the morning, the ferry companies would rip you off rather less, because most people are too sensible to want to do that (it's basic supply-and-demand economics). So, I would drive down to Dover from London either late in the evening or early in the morning, depending on which side of midnight you were talking about. Then I would wait for the ferry, drive on board, park the bike, go and crash somewhere for a bit, and then drive off at the other end. At this particular point I was, I think it is fair to say, burning the candle at both ends, and also at – at least – three places in the middle. I was perpetually shattered. On this particular evening I drove my bike down to Dover – as I recall, avoiding a fox on the South Circular. The fox looked at me and said: 'What do you think you're doing out at this time of night?' I politely replied: 'I might ask the same question of you'. Then we went our separate ways. Eventually I got down to Dover and I parked the bike in the lane to wait for the next ferry. I popped the motorbike up onto its centre stand as then the bike is actually fully balanced and very stable (not the side stand, when it is not in balance). I was so damn tired that I literally went to sleep straddling the bike, with my helmeted head resting on the petrol tank. I don't know how long I was asleep, but I was shaken awake by the really nice guy who was the lane supervisor/ticket controller for the ferry. He said:

> *Lad, you shouldn't be driving a bike when you are as tired as that. You'll do yourself a* [expletive deleted] *mischief sooner or later. And it's a cold night. You look perished – here, come along with me.*

The next thing I knew he had shepherded me off the bike and into the little shed, the little cuddy, that the Townsend Thoresen staff had. In there they could make a brew, have a smoke, and stay out of the rain in between patrolling up and down lanes of vehicles. He pushed me in there and he explained the situation succinctly to his mates. Someone put a chair under my bum and shoved me down onto it. A nice mug of really hot and very sweet tea was stuffed into my hands with the instruction: 'now get that down your neck'. From the conversation (naturally, none of this was ever spelled out), it was absolutely clear that the underlying assumption was that I was a young lad who was a motorcycle courier working freelance for one of those robber baron firms in London. They had obviously put me on to doing the cross-Channel stuff and they were equally obviously ripping me off. In their eyes I was one of the many, many poor working-class devils who were being exploited, just like them. There was a lovely solidarity to it. Of course, I did not say anything about either my gender or the fact that I was a young barrister trying to make my way in the world. It didn't seem to be relevant. It was so warm: the solidarity, the concern, the kind of rough humour. Somebody punched me on the shoulder and said: 'You're a bit more awake now, aren't you lad?' With the hot tea inside me (and the amount of sugar that had been put into it) I managed to get up and go back outside, get back on the bike, and drive it safely onto the ferry. Then I found a warm corner and collapsed again for a further hour or so.

Adam: The tea might have been very sweet but the story is both: bitter and sweet in equal measure. As you said, your plane had stalled but – I reckon – it did not crash. How did you stabilise the trajectory on which you travelled and pull up from the nosedive?

Eleanor: Well, this is when JTL comes back into the picture. He kept an eye open for me from the time I served as his *stagiaire*. It was he who told me about the vacancy at the Court, encouraged me to go and be a *référendaire* there. I had 48 hours advance notice on anyone else about that post. JTL met me one evening in a bar (an Irish bar, of course) in Brussels, as we did from time to time, for a chat and a catch-up. He asked how I was doing. The answer was 'actually, John, not so well'. JTL responded by offering me 'a piece of information that could be of interest'. It was not public knowledge yet, but the Council had just voted the additional funds to create an extra third *référendaire* post in the *cabinet* of each Member of the Court. JTL knew that Sir Gordon Slynn had formed a good opinion of me. I thanked JTL profusely, drove my motorbike to Luxembourg, via Oxford and London, and knocked at Gordon's door. The rest, as they say, is history.

Adam: For the next three years you served as a *référendaire* for Sir Gordon Slynn, first when he was an Advocate General and then when he was a judge at the Court of Justice. What was it like to work for Gordon?

Eleanor: To begin with: Gordon was very quick, frighteningly quick. Before he joined the bench in London and became Sir Gordon Slynn, he had been the 'Treasury devil' – the principal barrister taking government cases. There is nothing diabolic about that position, that's how it's called in the English system. The bottom line is – you cannot be the Treasury devil unless you are both fantastically bright *and* fantastically quick. Working for an ex Treasury devil was quite a test for Gordon's *référendaires*. The Court holds a weekly meeting of all the judges and advocates general to process cases: the '*réunion générale*'. Nowadays it takes place on a Tuesday at 5.30pm; back then it was on a Wednesday afternoon. Gordon wanted to be briefed in advance of the meeting on all the cases that were going through later that day. So, the reporting judges were divided up between the three *référendaires*. You had certain judges you followed. If one of those judges put forward a report about a case, you were going to brief Gordon about that case. If 'your' judges were all being productive that week, you might have eight cases that you needed to brief Gordon about. He expected the briefing to be three minutes per file:

> *This is what the case is about;*
>
> *the recommendations are right / wrong (or whatever), for the following reasons;*
>
> *is there anything you want to ask me about the case, Gordon?*

Adam: No pressure then, your foot must have been firmly on the accelerator all the time.

Eleanor: Oh yes. Gordon not only had a thoroughly well-deserved reputation for being super fast, he also had a disconcerting habit of picking, as his moment to talk to you about a case, a moment which might not be exactly when you were expecting to have to perform. One of the most extreme versions of that would be after the working day. Quite often, Gordon would then decide to go to a pizza restaurant called *La Torre* with his *référendaires*. This was his '*siège social*'. You would spend a pleasant evening chatting and eating pizza and of course drinking wine. Then suddenly, at quarter to midnight, Gordon would spin on his chair and say: 'Eleanor, about that case …'. You needed to be straight back on the job and firing on all cylinders. 'What is the wretched case about? Where have we got to in our discussion of it? What are the four things I have already told him about it? Have I anticipated correctly what he is going to think is a weak point?' You would go from 0 to 100 in a nanosecond. So, you developed a technique for doing just that. It was not necessarily a restful way of eating a pizza.

Adam: I had a tiny taste of how Gordon worked at the Central and Eastern Europe Moot Competition over which he was presiding. It must have been 2002, or thereabout, in Plovdiv, Bulgaria. He was firing one question after another at the teams. At some point one student who was pleading got stuck with *Foster v British Gas* (Case C-188/89).[14] I remember Gordon looking at that poor student and asking: 'have you read the Opinion of the Advocate General in that case?'. 'No, my Lord' was the answer. 'You should read the Opinions of the Advocates General, there's some good stuff there', said Gordon. We all burst into laughter (well, um, except for the unfortunate student). In that instance Gordon was referring not to his own Opinion, as he was already a judge in *Foster v British Gas*, but rather to the Opinion of AG van Gerven.

Eleanor: Indeed, I would agree with Gordon that there is good stuff in the Opinions of Advocates General, and Walter van Gerven was very good in that function. Let me give you an example of Gordon operating at high speed. It happened towards the end of my time with Gordon. By now he was a judge; and I left him shortly before his appointment to the House of Lords (this explains why you will find Gordon's name in the Court's decision on interim measures, but not in the final judgment). The Advocate General was Gordon's successor, AG Jacobs. This was a case that the European Commission brought against Germany as it believed that the *Gesetz über Gebühren für die Benutzung von Bundesfernstraßen mit schweren Lastfahrzeugen* (Law on charges for the use of Federal roads and motorways by heavy goods vehicles) of 30 April 1990 was contrary to EU law (Case C-195/90).[15] The Commission took it very seriously and, in parallel with the infringement proceedings, it filed an application for interim relief to stop Germany from bringing the tax into effect. That application was granted by the Court in the order of 12 July 1990.[16] Timing is important here. During the previous days, Gordon had been doing a lot of travelling back and forth to the UK. He was attending Wimbledon, as one does. In his absence, as his *chef de cabinet*, his most senior *référendaire*, I was covering this case. It was an interim relief application, but it was vastly important, interesting, and everyone thought that this was going to be a big issue. It was also a very fresh development. The application arrived on 23 June 1990. The President's *ex parte* order was made on 28 June 1990.[17] Now it was the turn of the Court to confirm or lift the interim measures after an *inter partes* hearing. Belgium, Denmark, France, Luxembourg, and the Netherlands intervened in support of the Commission's claim. The hearing was on Friday, 6 July 1990, just before the final weekend of Wimbledon. Gordon had – perhaps a little reluctantly – come back to sit in it. I read every document I could find, and worked for most of the previous night to get on top of everything and to have it absolutely lined up. It is Friday, 8:45 am. The hearing is due to start at 9:30 am. My office had a communicating door with Gordon's office, so I heard him come in and settle down. John Hambly, his first assistant (and his former judge's clerk in London) brought Gordon his morning cup of tea and *The Times* newspaper. I am twitching slightly: the hearing is just around the corner and it is quite a complicated case to brief him on. At the same time, I also know that before I can do anything, Gordon wants to have his cup of tea, his moment or two glancing at the newspaper. There I am, standing like the greyhound in the slips in Henry V (Act III, scene 1). I am ready to go, and time is running out. Eventually I heard Gordon saying: 'Eleanor', and I shot out of my office and into his, all ready to talk to him. The first thing he said, looking at me very accusingly, was that he couldn't find the *rapport préalable* in his papers. Of course he could not find it! This was an application for interim relief, therefore there was no *rapport préalable*. By now it was already 9:05 am, or perhaps even 9:10 am. Gordon just looked at me and said: 'Oh, you'd better tell me about it then'. Right. I took a deep breath and went in. At some point as I was briefing him, Gordon got up, we left his office, and headed for the courtroom. As we proceeded, I was still briefing him and he was still asking questions. We got to the robing room behind the courtroom. I stopped outside, Gordon went in, put on his robe and went into court.

Adam: I bet he was sharp as a knife at the hearing.

Eleanor: Generically, he was, especially when he felt that one of the parties was being a bit long winded. At this particular hearing I went up into the interpreters' booths. Since I had invested heavily in the case, I wanted to hear what was going on. It so happened that I was in the booth just above where Gordon was sitting (next to Judge Ole Due, the President of the Court). At that particular moment – to my consternation – he was not following the case. He was looking at a draft judgment in another one of my cases. He probably thought that it would be better to move that along simultaneously. However, the next question that he asked the parties was on target, brilliant. I'll leave it to everyone to think about how that was possible.

Adam: It seems that he was – obviously – good at multitasking. Just like you, he could juggle a few plates at the same time. During that very busy time at the Court, did you have the space to pursue your other interests?

Eleanor: Oh yes, sometimes even with funny consequences. As I said, I always had a briefing meeting with Gordon on Wednesdays, preceding the *réunion générale*. Wednesdays were also one of my karate days. I would train during lunch time. On one such Wednesday I was sparring and I failed to block a punch. So, an hour later, I walked in to see Gordon with the world's best black eye just starting. He looked at me, I looked at him, and I kind of dared him to comment on the fact that his female *référendaire* had got a black eye. His only comment was: 'Eleanor, as well as doing your karate at lunchtime, I trust that you had time to prepare for the *réunion générale*'. My reply was: 'Of course, Gordon'. And then we were done with *that* sparring and I started to brief him as usual.

Adam: Who else was in Gordon's cabinet at the time?

Eleanor: When I started, Gordon's *chef de cabinet* was Timothy Millett who had a long and very distinguished career at the Court, ending up as the Deputy Registrar. He was with Gordon during my first year at the Court, when Gordon was the Advocate General. Then Gordon deliberately, as it were, left him for Francis Jacobs coming in, so he became Francis Jacobs' *chef de cabinet*, helping Francis to put his team together. Gordon chose good people to work for him. My contemporaries included, among others, James Flynn (later James Flynn KC), Jean-Yves de Cara, and Jacqueline Minor.

Adam: I guess that already back then the Court of Justice must have been an intriguing intellectual environment. Luxembourg itself is a very picturesque place, which – I suppose – encourages extracurricular activities.

Eleanor: Indeed. One of the very good things about my three year period as a *référendaire* was that there was a group of us who were good mates. Some of us were *référendaires*, others worked in the Research and Documentation Unit. We didn't meet to comply with a formal, scheduled system of mutual education. We met because we were interested in the topics we were working on, and we were interested in discussing them with each other. The meetings had two main contexts.

One context was going for walks over a weekend, nice rambles through the Luxembourg countryside. As you said, Adam, Luxembourg is a very picturesque place, a lovely country for long walks and excursions. We would catch a bus to a departure point and then we would follow one of the marked walking trails. At some stage there would be sustenance and probably some nice local wine. Then we would complete the walk, and catch a different bus back into the city. During those walks, we would be discussing whatever was flavour of the day. For example, directives and the evolving doctrine of direct effect were a major topic of discussion. Sasha Prechal, who later became a long-serving judge at the Court, was a *référendaire* at the time and – of course – was writing academically about directives. Her OUP book, now in its second edition, is a classic.[18] During those walks we were chewing over ideas with her.

Adam: That's a lovely first context to my ears. I wish I were a fly on the wall (or rather on one of those trees in Luxembourg). What about the second context, Leo?

Eleanor: Well, the summer months are traditionally a bit quieter at the Court. If as a *référendaire* you are working during the long summer break, probably your Member isn't anywhere near. Normally Members will have disappeared off to their respective Member States. They may be doing very important things back home or just having a bit of down time. The bottom line is, they are not in Luxembourg breathing down your neck. In the meantime, you are getting on with all the preparatory drafting that you haven't had time for during the frantic scramble in July to get as many judgments and opinions out as possible. But although you are at the Court and you are working, the rhythm of life is significantly calmer. Very often, at about five o'clock, a little bit of telephone tag would be played: 'Have you got any plans for this evening? How about going down to the Moselle?' We had a favourite restaurant – the *Caves [now Pavillon] Saint Martin* – about three kilometers north of *Remich*. They used to have as their speciality *friture de la Moselle*: little whitebait, small fried fresh fish straight from the water, with salad and chips, and – of course – wine. There are vineyards all along 'the coast', so you are spoiled for choice when it comes to white wine ('tonight, rather than wine from *Remich*, why don't we have wine from *Schengen*, or from *Wormeldange Haut*? Well, why not?'). I just spoke of 'the coast', because that's how we Luxembourgers tend to think of it. Of course it is not a proper coast: it's the *Moselle* riverbank. That is where the Luxembourgish seaside spirit lives. You can't beat that.

Adam: Sounds to me like a συμπόσιον – a symposium in ancient Greece, long conversations over wine after a good meal. Life was tough, huh?

Eleanor: Very! Life was and is tough. As you can imagine, Adam, so much by way of good, useful discussion happened in a completely non-organised, non-formal, and non-structured way. So many good ideas got chewed over and explored.

Might there be a problem with this?

Wait a minute, in my legal system, we have a sort of way of doing this, which is ....

Oh, that sounds interesting.

I wonder how we would turn that into a European law idea.

It was a fabulous way of taking the thinking forward. It really confirmed to me the idea that the best thinking is done in very loose form when nobody is insisting on holding the floor, nobody is being hierarchical. Everyone is giving respectful and attentive listening time and space to other people in the group. If there was somebody who had not talked yet, you would deliberately bring them in. You would turn across and you say:

Well, hang on a minute – Jackie, what do you think about that?

Does this have legs?

Could this go somewhere?

Everyone was in that discussion.

Adam: This sounds lovely, Leo. As you were describing it, I could easily picture the wonderful environment you were sitting in and endless discussions. It immediately took me back to seminars in Dubrovnik we both have been attending for years. We will come back to them a little later. For now, I should like to go back to Sir Gordon Slynn. During your three years in his *cabinet* you saw and worked with him acting in two different capacities. Was there a difference between working for him when he was the Advocate General and when he was the judge?

Eleanor: Working for Gordon when he was an Advocate General was a lot of fun. It was like going hunting in the jungle with your panther. You stayed behind the jaws, of course, but it was really exciting. Watching your panther hunt is special. He is so sleek, so powerful, a fantastic beast of prey.

Adam: Being an Advocate General surely gave Gordon a lot of intellectual freedom. This must have completely changed when he became a judge. With no dissenting opinions available to the judges of the European Court of Justice he must have felt a bit like a prisoner in paradise. How did the panther take to his new role?

Eleanor: Not well by any stretch of imagination. But first of all, we should address the question of why he became a judge. The answer is that he made an entirely correct and pragmatic calculation. The English legal system doesn't know what an Advocate General is. It does know what judges are. Gordon wanted, when he finished in Luxembourg, to go straight into the House of Lords. He didn't want to go back and be put in the Court of Appeal. He had already been the President of the Employment Appeal Tribunal before his appointment to the bench in Luxembourg. He wanted the House of Lords, and he knew that his chance of getting the House of Lords would be a lot better if he were the British judge. So when Lord Mackenzie Stuart, the previous British judge at the European Court of Justice, retired in 1988, Gordon talked to people and became the British judge. At the same time, Francis Jacobs came in as the Advocate General. A wonderful choice.

Adam: So the panther did not enjoy his new, though temporary, habitat in Luxembourg.

Eleanor: Gordon found life as a judge incredibly frustrating. It was bad for his blood pressure; it was very bad for his temper. That was partly the fault of President Due, who (uncharacteristically) failed to be his normal, perceptive self about human character and temperament, and who put together, in a chamber of three, Gordon, René Joliet, and Gil Carlos Rodríguez Iglesias. It became known as the chamber from hell. Putting Joliet and Gordon together was catastrophic because of their different backgrounds. Joliet was very clever but also very much a pure academic. Gordon was different, he would say: 'I am the judge. I know about being a judge from the UK context. I have a lot of experience unlike these academics. What are they up to?' Both Rodríguez Iglesias and Joliet were academics. It was terrible. When Gordon was coming back from the *délibéré* I would wait for him as his *chef de cabinet*. First, I would hear a stomping noise down the corridor and Gordon growling 'bloody academics, arrggg'. We kept a bottle of whisky in chambers for such occasions. So, I would pour a decent measure into a glass and have it ready for him. He would come in through the door and he would throw his papers down onto the nearest flat surface. I would hand him the whisky and the conversation would look something like this:

> **Eleanor:** *Gordon, I gather it wasn't a bed of roses …*
>
> **Gordon:** *Bloody academics! If I could write a dissenting judgment, I would tear them to shreds.*
>
> **Eleanor:** *Unfortunately, that's not an option. Gordon, do you feel like telling me a bit more about what has happened?*
>
> **Gordon:** *ok* [growls], *I suppose so …*

I needed to know what happened at the *délibéré*, because if Gordon was the reporting judge, we would have put the draft judgment together – the draft that had gone into the *délibéré*. So, I needed to know what happened in order, in the next reiteration of the draft, to reflect what his dear colleagues had decided and therefore wanted to see happen. Trying to debrief him was a delicate business. From going hunting with your panther in the jungle, which was the mode when he had been the Advocate General, we were down to being together in a small cage at London Zoo. I was locked up inside the cage with an extremely unhappy panther. The panther would walk up and down lashing its tail. Just occasionally out of sheer frustration one of those big paws would be raised, the claws would come out, and the panther would take a swipe at you – probably, for no better reason than that you were in its path. It was not really the panther's fault. It just did not appreciate being caged.

Gordon liked being a judge, but he hated being a judge in a collegiate court when his colleagues got it wrong. They were in the majority, and he could not express his dissent. There was a perfectly good and objective explanation why he hated that. But he knew that he had to put up with it for long enough to secure his return ticket to the UK. He did indeed duly manage to secure that return ticket and entered the House of Lords. That was a good outcome, because Gordon had the intellectual ability in spades, and he also brought a liberal note into the House of Lords. He was in some respects very, very liberal.

Adam: His dissenting opinion in *Brown and others* is a very good example of that, isn't it?[19] But before we talk about that case, let's stay in Luxembourg for a little longer. Are there any particular cases where Gordon served as the Advocate General, or as the judge, that you should like to return to?

Eleanor: Let's start with two cases that I did literally as I started at the Court. The hearing was probably within a few days of my arrival in Luxembourg. These were two references for preliminary ruling from Dutch courts, *Mulder* and *von Deetzen* (Case 120/86 and Case 170/86, respectively).[20]

Adam: So, you were thrown into really deep water straight away.

Eleanor: Absolutely! You were not given a gentle slope as you settled in. You arrived, you hit the ground, and your legs already had to be in running mode. That was required, or you would have fallen straight onto your nose.

As to the substance of both cases, we need to go back to the time of milk lakes. The background reality was a continuing problem with overproduction of milk. Dairy farmers were very good at flooding the EU market with milk and the European Commission was at its wits' end as to what to do about it. It kept trying different schemes. One earlier scheme they invented consisted of non-marketing undertakings. The deal was that you, as the dairy farmer, signed an undertaking that for five years you would withdraw from the market in milk. You wouldn't produce milk, and in return for not producing milk you would be paid compensation. There was also a separate and different scheme, which was 'conversion'. Under that scheme, you agreed to leave the market permanently. What we are talking about here, however, are the five-year non-marketing undertakings. The Commission tried out its new scheme. Unfortunately, the milk lake continued to be a milk lake. Then, the Commission had another bright new idea: the supplementary levy on milk (known by the ugly acronym of 'SLOM'). SLOM was a very messy system – to be honest, not a terribly bright idea after all. Not surprisingly then, there was a lot of SLOM litigation. The way SLOM worked was that a year was selected as the 'reference year'. As I recall, Member

States had a choice between two or three options, but anyway they had to select a single reference year. A farmer's production in that year, after applying a slight reduction factor, was his reference quantity. The farmer could produce that quantity of milk without penalty. However, if he produced more milk than the reference quantity, he was subject to a swingeing levy. This was all meant to suppress excess milk production.

Here's the problem. During the reference year, a number of farmers would not be in the market at all. Why? Because they would have signed a non-marketing undertaking. So, artificially, they were not in the market that year. But of course, they had every thought and expectation, having only left the market temporarily, that they would go back into the market after five years and resume being dairy farmers. When their five year non-marketing undertakings came to an end, they applied for reference quantities because without them they couldn't return to milk production. The national authorities duly allocated them reference quantities of zero, because they had no production in the reference year. The applicants in these two cases were good Dutch farmers and they said some very blunt Dutch words to describe the SLOM system. They persuaded national courts to make references for a preliminary ruling to the European Court of Justice, so the two test cases bore their names, *Mulder* and *von Deetzen*.

Adam: Right, one should never mess with angry farmers, that does not end well. I bet a good milk chocolate bar that quite a few Dutch farmers expressed their interest in the proceedings in Luxembourg.

Eleanor: Absolutely. Coach loads of Dutch dairy farmers turned up at the Court for the hearing. We need to understand that this was a big deal. The Netherlands is a big dairy producing Member State and the Dutch farmers were absolutely up in arms, whether on their own behalf or out of solidarity. SLOM was very much not okay. The case was meant to be heard by the Full Court but of course the actual physical space was completely inadequate to deal with the coach loads of milk farmers who were showing up on the forecourt. The hearing was slightly delayed while the Court organised for the proceedings to be video-streamed through to several extra conference rooms. In the meantime, muggins here was sent out to keep the farmers happy. I was a brand new *référendaire* who had just arrived at the Court, and almost the first thing I did was to put on my jacket and trot out to talk to all these Dutch farmers. I told them how pleased the Court was to see such an interest in the case. It was a straight lie but it was a necessary lie. I continued by assuring them that things were getting sorted out logistically; and that whilst that was happening, I would tell them a bit more about what they would see and hear, about how the procedure worked. I was the warm-up act before the hearing and my job was to keep these guys quiet, or at least reasonably quiet and content, while the Court got everything straight so that people could indeed follow the proceedings. Once I was tipped off that the arrangements were in place, I told them that the hearing would be starting shortly, bade them farewell, and shot round to the courtroom to take my seat – for the very first time – at the *référendaires*' table.

Adam: Gordon was the Advocate General in both cases, wasn't he?

Eleanor: Indeed, he was. The interesting thing about these two cases was they restored your faith that lawyers have a shared belief in justice. I remember discussing the cases with a French *référendaire* colleague and a German *référendaire* colleague. Of course, we came from different legal traditions but we all had the same feeling about the legal issues in play. Approaching it from an English law perspective, I was thinking in terms of equity and estoppel, that the administration would be estopped from taking this measure in respect of these farmers, because they had relied on assurances given to them that their exit from the market was temporary. My French colleague spoke about '*Le principe de protection de la confiance légitime*'. Here are people who have dealings with the administration, they are entitled to have a legitimate expectation that the administration will behave honourably and correctly towards them and not stab them in the back. Then my German colleague said: '*na ja, bitte, das ist Vertrauensverschutz*'. It is a lovely German portmanteau word, and it stands for protection of the trust that one has placed in the administration. So, here we had three colleagues from different legal traditions talking about the case. We were doing this at *référendaire* level, and later the judges were doing the same thing at judge-level. We all felt that what the European Commission had come up with in devising SLOM was absolutely not acceptable. You couldn't entice people to leave the market with non-marketing undertakings and then slam the door in their faces when they tried to come back in. To use a different picture for it, it would be as though, having bought a return ticket, you got onto a train from London to Cambridge, and when you arrived at the barrier in Cambridge the ticket collector had taken your tickets and torn up the return half. You would not be pleased, would you Adam?

Adam: Not in a million years, Leo. Since I am planning to travel back from Cambridge to London tonight, I certainly would not be pleased if my return ticket were torn apart. I would have felt that it were neither fair nor acceptable to be treated like that. Leaving my return journey aside, what did Gordon make of it?

Eleanor: I needed to begin by persuading Gordon and we had a very interesting discussion. The way Gordon used his *référendaires* was that he would deliberately challenge whatever position you adopted, and he would then play devil's advocate. Effectively I was there as a kind of substitute barrister for the farmers explaining why this scheme was absolutely unconscionable and not okay. Gordon was also interested in the economic reasoning behind my stance. My starting point was that this was a managed market. For a managed market to function effectively, the operators in the market have to trust the administration. If the administration were allowed to get away with something like this in this case, it would become much more difficult to run the market in the future. Any sensible operator would be very wary indeed of trusting anything that the administration said about a new scheme for subsidies, or whatever it might be. They would always have in mind what had happened to the others, and they would not be prepared to play along. I don't know whether it was my legal arguments or my economic arguments that convinced Gordon, but he was convinced. We hunted around a bit for which heading to put the argument under, and we settled on legitimate expectations. I remember Gordon saying:

> *Well, I know I am prepared to do the Opinion that way around.*
>
> *I don't know if the Court will follow me, but I don't care.*
>
> *I am satisfied this is the right thing to be saying.*[21]

The Court did follow him. Possibly Gordon was also influenced by the fact that – at the hearing – he had asked the European Commission how many farmers were affected by the challenged scheme. That was a perfectly sensible question from an English common law judge. Believe it or not, the Commission representative didn't know the answer. But then the Commission tried to have its cake and eat it. It tried to say, simultaneously, that – on the one hand – maybe not very many farmers were affected, so it didn't really matter. But, on the other hand, if there were a lot of farmers in that category, it would be impossibly disruptive to the market to try to accommodate them – therefore the Court could not (or at least should not) annul the scheme. In other words, the Commission pleaded that either way round, the Court shouldn't interfere with what the institutions had done. This was really pulling Gordon's tail. I don't know precisely how that played with some of the other members of the bench. I do know that Gordon came out of the hearing quite ready to tear the institutions limb from limb.

Adam: As you said, the Court followed Gordon in this case and annulled the contested scheme. But that was not the end of the SLOM saga, was it?

Eleanor: Oh no. The institutions amended the regulation but they opted for a rather grudging half fix. So the Dutch farmers came back to the Court, and the Court again struck down what had been adopted. Later the farmers also submitted an action for damages against the institutions.

Adam: At your end, Leo, there was also an academic offspring of the SLOM ordeal.

Eleanor: Indeed. My contribution to the *Festschrift* for Sir Gordon Slynn focused on his Opinion in the case and, more broadly, on the story itself.[22]

Adam: One of the biggest cases you did with Gordon when he was a judge was *Foster v British Gas*.[23] It later came back to haunt you when the reference in *Farrell II* (Case C-413/15) arrived in the Court's docket, and you were called as the Advocate General to provide the Court with an Opinion.[24]

Eleanor: *Foster* absolutely haunted me! And I knew it was going to haunt me from the moment we signed off on a very dubious English translation of the key passage in the judgment. *Foster v British Gas* was decided when the Court had only very recently developed the doctrine of vertical direct effect of directives, allowing individuals to bring claims in national courts based on clear, precise and unconditional provisions in non-transposed or poorly transposed directives. But, while the Court endorsed vertical direct effect (where the underlying claim was against the Member State itself), it set its face against horizontal direct effect (where the claim was against another individual or enterprise). So, it became of crucial importance to know what exactly was meant by the Member State or an 'emanation of the state' for the purposes of determining whether you were allowed to rely on a clear, precise, and unconditional provision of a directive against that defendant. That was, in a nutshell, the legal issue in *Foster v British Gas*.

Adam: It sounds so simple, in principle. However, when one digs deeper and takes into account that we are operating in a multilingual Europe with so many different legal cultures, troubles are inevitable. This case is a very good example.

Eleanor: Here, the trouble was that the *délibéré* was (of course) in French. At some stage during the deliberations, someone – presumably the French judge but maybe a different colleague, I have no idea who exactly put this forward – came up with an idea borrowed from well-known French administrative law case law as a way of shaping the new definition in EU law of what was an 'emanation of the state'. Of course, people were very happy to buy into it: 'Oh, good. We don't need to reinvent the wheel, here is a nice definition, let's use it'. For the proposer, who knew French administrative law, the definition had – I am sure – an extremely clear and precise meaning. The problem was we were transplanting that definition from French administrative law into EU administrative law, where there were no equivalent reference points to latch onto. The question then became how on earth to explain this (new) concept in a way that would be comprehensible to everyone who was going to have to read it from now onwards, and of course, in all the EU languages. We always have to remember when dealing with the CJEU that it prepares its judgments in French, but the resulting case law has got to work in all the languages of the EU. *Foster v British Gas* was – as the name implies – a British case. It was a reference made by the House of Lords (with John Laws [later Sir John Laws] and David Pannick [now Lord Pannick KC], both highly respected counsel, representing the UK government). Inevitably, the English version of the judgment was going to matter because it was going to be applied by the referring court. At the time, the practice was that the translation into the language of procedure was given to the judge from that Member State and was signed off by her/him as being correct. So, the draft translation (inevitably) landed on Gordon's desk. We had somehow to find an appropriate English translation for the passage in the judgment which says:

> *20. Il résulte de ce qui précède que figure en tout cas au nombre des entités qui peuvent se voir opposer les dispositions d' une directive susceptibles d' avoir des effets directs un organisme qui, quelle que soit sa forme juridique, a été chargé en vertu d' un acte de l' autorité publique d' accomplir, sous le contrôle de cette dernière, un service d' intérêt public et qui dispose, à cet effet, de pouvoirs exorbitants par rapport aux règles applicables dans les relations entre particuliers.*

This is what we ended up with in English:

> *20. It follows from the foregoing that a body, whatever its legal form, which has been made responsible, pursuant to a measure adopted by the State, for providing a public service under the control of the State and has for that purpose special powers beyond those which result from the normal rules applicable in relations between individuals is included in any event among the bodies against which the provisions of a directive capable of having direct effect may be relied upon.*

Apart from the fact that that sentence is a complete mouthful, and that it's not an exhaustive definition (the words 'in any event' necessarily imply that), you are left asking: 'what on earth do you mean by "has for that purpose special powers beyond those which result from the normal rules applicable in relations between individuals"'?

The French for 'special powers' is '*pouvoirs exorbitants*' and, as I've said, that concept does have a meaning in French administrative law. We couldn't write a treatise on French administrative law. We had to find an equivalent phrase in English. Angus McKay, who I think I remember was the then head of English translation, requested a meeting with Sir Gordon Slynn, the British judge, in order to discuss the draft translation. Angus had looked at it, his colleague who was doing the translation had laboured over it. It was obvious that this was the key paragraph in the judgment. However it was far from obvious how to translate it. Gordon had excellent French, Angus had superlative French, my French is pretty reasonable. The three of us sat there and stared at the wretched French text. What on earth were we going to say? We tried out one or two different formulations and we ended up with the translation that appears in the English version of the judgment. We could not find anything better, and we could not write a detailed footnote explaining what 'special powers' was going to mean. But at the same time we gave 'special powers' our imprimatur and said that the English version could go out, it was abundantly clear to us that there would be further references, certainly from English speaking courts. They would be asking the very reasonable question, 'what is meant by "special powers"?' That question was obviously initially asked by the academics who had fun writing learned case note after learned case note on *Foster v British Gas*, dissecting and belittling this wretched phrase. But, as you said, the phrase came back to haunt me as the Advocate General in *Farrell II* a quarter of a century later – a case we will talk about later on.

Adam: The other two cases from your time as *référendaire* which you picked out for us today are *Dekker* and *Hertz* (cases C-177/88 and C-179/88).[25] Both dealt with pregnancy-related discrimination.

Eleanor: Let me start by saying that these were the draft judgments that Gordon was going through during the hearing in *Commission v Germany* that we have already spoken about. These two cases indeed 'bookended' the process of being pregnant. *Dekker* was about refusing to give a job to a woman who, as she explained at her job interview, was in fact already pregnant. *Hertz* was about dismissing a woman who was unable to return to her job after her pregnancy and giving birth due to a pregnancy related illness. Legally, how did you deal with those two cases? Did you treat them in the same way on the basis that both were pregnancy related problems, so it was unlawful in both cases to discriminate against the woman? Or did you say that the refusal to hire in *Dekker* was clearly pregnancy-related as only women can become pregnant, so that was direct discrimination on grounds of sex; whereas in *Hertz* the lady happened to be off work sick for a pregnancy-related reason, but anyone – male or female – can get sick. If a man had been sick for some other reason, would he have been treated in the same way? Answer: yes, he too would have been dismissed. The two cases were conceptually interesting and they were also very early cases on how the CJEU should handle the phenomenon of pregnancy. In a couple of paragraphs in his Opinion, AG Darmon waxed rather lyrical about the condition of pregnancy.[26] It wasn't perhaps the most useful part of his Opinion but it was very flowery and very beautiful. It is best consumed if possible in the original French, it doesn't come across quite as well in the English translation:

> *22. Pendant longtemps, la vie économique, domaine réservé des hommes, n' a pas eu à prendre en considération les différences physiologiques entre les deux sexes. Ce n' est plus le cas aujourd' hui. Dès lors, il faut opérer la difficile conciliation des exigences de la vie professionnelle avec la maternité.*
>
> *23. Poser le problème, c'est parfois y répondre. Y a-t-il un événement qui soit plus lié à la spécificité même de la femme? Accorder l' égalité de traitement aux travailleurs féminins avec leurs homologues masculins peut-il se concevoir sans prendre en considération la maternité?*
>
> *22. Being a male preserve, economic life could long afford to take no account of the physiological differences between the sexes. That is no longer so today. It is therefore necessary to undertake the difficult task of reconciling the demands of professional life with motherhood.*
>
> *23. Defining the question sometimes supplies the answer to it. Is there any event more closely connected to the specific nature of womanhood? Is it conceivable to treat female workers on an equal footing with their male counterparts without taking account of motherhood?*

It is one of those 'purple passages' where you say (a little impatiently) 'yes, yes, yes' and skip forward to find where the Advocate General is going to get on to the legal issue. I remember reading the Opinion and thinking 'well, I'm so delighted that you think that pregnancy is a great arrangement, but we need more than that to help us to decide the case!'

Dekker was one of those 'smoking gun' cases. The bottom line was that the foundation who would have hired Ms Dekker wouldn't have been able to get money from the social insurance (the *Risicofonds*) to pay somebody to fill in for Ms Decker while she in her turn was away on maternity leave. That was one of the considerations that had weighed heavily with them. But the future non-employer had written Ms Dekker a letter which started in a very friendly and informal way 'Beste Els' (first name terms). The letter openly and apologetically admitted that she had been the best candidate, but explained that they couldn't give her the job as they would not get reimbursed. It was a true smoking gun letter! I find it a little surprising that people write those letters, but sometimes they really do.

Adam: I guess you have seen quite a few of those in your practice.

Eleanor: Yes, for example in *Bougnaoui* (Case C-188/15): my first case as an Advocate General about the Islamic hijab.[27] There we had a letter from the employer to Ms Bougnaoui, whom they were dismissing. They made it clear that they were really sad about her leaving, because she was an excellent software engineer and therefore they had been hoping for a long collaboration.

Adam: Leo, this looks to me like cruising for bruising, in other words, an invitation to sue.

Eleanor: Indeed, Adam. From the perspective of a lawyer, it is not an intelligent letter to write.

Adam: When you finished your three-year stint as a *référendaire* in the chambers of Sir Gordon Slynn you opted to go back to the United Kingdom. Why not stay at the Court? It is quite acceptable for a *référendaire* to move from one cabinet to another when their Advocate General or judge retires.

Eleanor: Gordon made it clear to me from the beginning that he regarded three years (plus or minus a bit) as the length of time that somebody should spend being a *référendaire*. He was very against something which is indeed, I would say, a feature of the Court of Justice. There is a hardcore of quasi-permanent *référendaires* there who are extremely experienced because they have effectively made careers as *référendaires*. They are passed on like precious jewels from one Member of the CJEU to another. I hadn't been long enough in Gordon's chambers to make the transition across. The other part of it was – and here you have the barrister speaking – that I had watched so many people turn up and plead cases badly. The palms of my hands were starting to itch. I would sit at hearings and listen to lawyers making a complete hash of their submissions, and think 'why don't you just make your four best points which are 1, 2, 3, and 4'. If you are a barrister and you are getting that feeling watching others plead, you should try to get back on your hind legs. Your question, Adam, is a very fair one, but – as much as I loved being at the Court – I never really envisaged for myself a full career as a *référendaire* there. I wanted to go back to practice, and that's what I did.

Adam: How did that happen? If I recall properly, the transition was rather immediate. You did not take a break.

Eleanor: My first bid was unsuccessful. I applied for a fellowship at Wadham College in Oxford, linked to a University lectureship. I was shortlisted, they were absolutely lovely to me but I did not get the job. It was University College London ('UCL') that offered me a home for a couple of years. How I returned to legal practice was more curious. It was no accident that Sean Overend and Julian Picton (now Julian Picton KC) came and talked to me for two hours after Gordon had chatted with them for about five minutes at the start of their visit to Luxembourg. As I later discovered, Gordon had deliberately pushed them in my direction, having ascertained from them that they were on a scouting expedition. He must have said something like: 'I think you should talk to my *chef de cabinet*. She is a barrister and she is about to finish as a *référendaire* and move on from here.' Effectively, what I thought was a perfectly standard talk with visitors, answering their intelligent and curious inquiries about how we ran procedure at the Court, was in fact my tenancy interview. That is how I returned to the Bar and to academia.

Adam: And, around that time a big change in your personal life took place. You met your husband, David Lyon.

Eleanor: I met David Lyon, a distinguished maritime historian who was my senior by some thirteen years, on a converted Baltic trader called *Queen Galadriel*. As far as I knew, this was just going to be one of my excursions in traditional sail over a long weekend. I probably shouldn't have gone – I had a heavy cold – but I wasn't going to miss out on the little reward I had promised myself after some very heavy weeks at the Court. David wasn't a member of *Mariners International*, which had arranged the charter of the vessel, but his mates at the National Maritime Museum, where he held court in the 'lion's den' as Director of Enquiries, had told him that there was a spare berth going begging. At the instant of our first meeting, he mistook me for the cabin boy / third hand and fended me off asking him to help with unmooring (admittedly, at 04h00) with a ferocious glare. He later realised that the third hand was tall, male, and a man of colour; and that I must be that extra female who was joining (on the edge of being late, as usual) from Luxembourg. We discovered that we had both been to King's College Cambridge, which broke the ice nicely. At the end of the voyage, we exchanged addresses. Uncharacteristically for both of us, we followed up on that with a weekend together in Belgium. At the end of that weekend, he asked me to marry him. I demurred: I said I thought he ought to get to know me better, in case on reflection he found he didn't like me as much as all that after all. But he was pretty single-minded and went on asking. I returned to work in the UK in September 1990 and David moved into my little flat on the Isle of Dogs (chastely, into the tiny spare bedroom that we instantly christened the 'kennel'). Having conducted a long-distance courtship (London – Luxembourg), we needed to run some field trials to see whether we could really live together. Eventually I said 'yes' to his umpteenth proposal of marriage – and sat on the floor of the flat in stunned silence for a good 25 minutes as I contemplated what I had done. David, meanwhile, just gently stroked my hand.

It was the best decision that I could possibly have made. David was sufficiently older and well-established in his own field (amongst other things, as an international authority on the ships of Great Britain's 'sailing navy') that he didn't regard having a clever wife as any kind of a threat. He was ridiculously proud of me, ridiculously supportive. He always had my back. We were best mates as well as husband and wife; and we probably fitted more sheer happiness and slightly unhinged comedy into the eight and a half years of our marriage than many married couples manage over decades. We had remarkably few arguments and, when we did disagree, it was generically my fault: it meant that I had forgotten to switch off being a barrister as I walked in through the front door. We wanted a family and had a lot of fun trying for one, but had not yet succeeded when we went off to the Caribbean in late February 2000 on a working trip for David as a guest lecturer: a voyage on the beautiful *Sea Cloud* (a four masted bijou little square-rigged yachtette, some 360 feet long, with 32,000 square feet of sail, built for the American cereals millionairess Marjorie Merriweather Post). I had been invited courteously as David's wife to accompany him. Actually, they got two for the price of one. I managed to wangle myself onto the crew muster, rated able seaman, for a symbolic dollar's pay, so that I could work with the Filipino crew in the rigging; and I gave a couple of guest lectures myself about the mechanics of rigging – that apparent cat's cradle of ropes is all very logical – and how you sail big sailing vessels. After disembarking, David and I went to spend a few days with an old college friend of my mother's in Tortola on the British Virgin Islands. Then, on 1 March 2000, a few hours before we were due to fly back to London, David suffered a brain haemorrhage. I got him into hospital, first in Tortola, then in the US Virgin Islands, where they had a scanner and could see the real extent of the damage. We medevac'd him to Miami, where he underwent surgery. At first it looked as though he was going to make it back safely to being himself. Who cared if he could reel off the names of US presidents when his recollection of core historical facts that mattered to him was unshaken? ('David, these doctors want to ask some questions to see how you're doing. Can you tell me what happened to *HMS Hood*?' 'Which *Hood*?' 'World War Two *Hood*.' 'She sank'. ES to doctors: 'he's fine, he's just fine!') But then suddenly everything plummeted. Soon he became brain dead. I wrestled in anguish with the moral decisions that were facing me about switching off life-support machines. But David did me a final favour. He signed himself out. He died on 13 March 2000.

ENDNOTES

[*] Eleanor Sharpston QC, *First 100 Years Biography*, 2019 (available on YouTube).

[1] Hugh Rawson, *The Unwritten Laws of Life* (Carbolic Smoke Ball, 2008) 136.

[2] Case 155/79 AM & S *Europe Limited v Commission of the European Communities* ECLI:EU:C:1982:157.

[3] Case 155/79 AM & S *Europe Limited v Commission of the European Communities* ECLI:EU:C:1981:9, Opinion of AG Warner.

[4] Case 155/79 AM & S *Europe Limited v Commission of the European Communities* ECLI:EU:C:1982:17, Opinion of AG Slynn.

[5] Joined Cases 100-103/80 *SA Musique Diffusion française and others v Commission of the European Communities* ECLI:EU:C:1983:158.

[6] Case 245/81 *Edeka Zentrale AG v Federal Republic of Germany* ECLI:EU:C:1982:210, Opinion of AG Slynn.

[7] Case 246/81 *Nicholas William, Lord Bethell, v Commission of the European Communities* ECLI:EU:C:1982:148, Opinion of AG Slynn.

[8] Ibid, page 2299.

[9] This cultural life (BBC Podcast) <https://www.bbc.co.uk/programmes/m00274xz> accessed 1 September 2025.

[10] Case 258/84 *Nippon Seiko KK v Council of the European Communities* ECLI:EU:C:1987:205.

[11] Case 156/87 *Gestetner Holdings plc v Council and Commission of the European Communities* ECLI:EU:C:1990:116.

[12] Council Regulation (EEC) No 535/87 of 23 February 1987 imposing a definitive anti-dumping duty on imports of plain paper photocopiers originating in Japan [1987] OJ L 54/1.

[13] Commission Regulation (EEC) No 2640/86 of 21 August 1986 imposing a provisional anti-dumping duty on imports of plain paper photocopiers originating in Japan [1986] OJ L 239/5.

[14] Case C-188/89 *A. Foster and others v British Gas plc* ECLI:EU:C:1990:313.

[15] Case C-195/90 *Commission of the European Communities v Federal Republic of* Germany ECLI:EU:C:1992:219.

[16] Case C-195/90 R *Commission of the European Communities v Federal Republic of Germany* ECLI:EU:C:1990:314.

[17] Case C-195/90 R *Commission of the European Communities v Federal Republic of Germany* ECLI:EU:C:1990:271.

[18] Sacha Prechal, *Directives in EC Law* (2nd ed, OUP 2005).

[19] *R v Brown* [1993] UKHL 19.

[20] Case 120/86 *J. Mulder v Minister van Landbouw en Visserij* ECLI:EU:C:1988:213 and Case 170/86 *Georg von Deetzen v Hauptzollamt Hamburg-Jonas* ECLI:EU:C:1988:214.

[21] Case 120/86 *J. Mulder v Minister van Landbouw en Visserij* ECLI:EU:C:1988:1 Opinion of AG Slynn; Case 170/86 *Georg von Deetzen v Hauptzollamt Hamburg-Jonas* ECLI:EU:C:1988:3, Opinion of AG Slynn.

[22] Eleanor Sharpston, 'Milk Lakes, SLOMs, and Legitimate Expectations – a Paradigm in Judicial Review' in David O'Keeffe, Antonio Bavasso (eds), *Judicial Review in European Union Law. Liber Amicorum in Honour of Lord Slynn of Hadley* (Kluwer Law International, 2000).

[23] See above endnote 14.

[24] Case C-413/15 *Elaine Farrell v Alan Whitty and Others* ECLI:EU:C:2017:492.

[25] Case C-177/88 *Elisabeth Johanna Pacifica Dekker v Stichting Vormingscentrum voor Jong Volwassenen (VJV-Centrum) Plus* ECLI:EU:C:1990:383; Case C-179/88 *Handels- og Kontorfunktionaerernes Forbund i Danmark v Dansk Arbejdsgiverforening* ECLI:EU:C:1990:384.

[26] Case C-177/88 *Elisabeth Johanna Pacifica Dekker v Stichting Vormingscentrum voor Jong Volwassenen (VJV-Centrum) Plus* ECLI:EU:C:1989:424, Opinion of AG Darmon.

[27] Case C-188/15 *Asma Bougnaoui and Association de défense des droits de l'homme (ADDH) v Micropole SA* ECLI:EU:C:2016:553, Opinion of AG Sharpston.

3

Return to the Bar: The Big Cases and Other Pro Bono *Work*

*I always wanted to do EU law and the Human Rights Convention. And people looked at me as though I had horns and green skin. A woman, doing those very intellectual areas of law? She can't be serious, she's a freak.**

Adam: Coming back and restarting a career after a long absence from the market is akin to reinventing the wheel. That often translates into starting from the dark. When Eleanor Sharpston returned in 1990 to the United Kingdom, after almost a decade of working in Brussels and Luxembourg, it was both of these: she started from scratch and had to reinvent the wheel. Her 'European' experience was not necessarily in her favour. Those were not yet the days of Brexit; but anything that had to do with the European Communities (as they were back then) was not exactly the flavour of the month. This, apart from her passion for academic work, was one of the reasons why for the next fifteen years Eleanor would travel on two parallel trajectories. To make ends meet, she held a series of academic jobs whilst simultaneously practising at the English Bar. Two parallel professional careers covered the entire period from 1990 to 2006. For anyone who has ever held more than one job at a time, the key word is 'perseverance'. Eleanor Sharpston had it in large quantities. To begin with, she was a member of the English and the Irish Bar (she had been called to the latter in 1986). In 1999, Eleanor took silk: she became a Queen's Counsel. Her practice had two main strands. The first was paid work. One of her specialities was representing the United Kingdom in cases pending at the CJEU. The second strand, perhaps even closer to her heart, was *pro bono* work. Her first big case came early on in the timeline. Her tenth time on her feet as a barrister found Eleanor in the House of Lords, the then highest court of the United Kingdom, where she, together with four QCs and four other junior barristers, represented a group of homosexual sadomasochists prosecuted for consensual sex. On that occasion, her expertise in the European Convention for Human Rights was what got her the brief. Much later in her career, Eleanor Sharpston had the prosecution brief in

Thoburn v City of Sunderland, a case well known to any law student or public law *afficionado* in the United Kingdom. Admittedly, it was not a case she would have chosen to prosecute had a choice been on offer – she would have had a lot more fun with the defence brief. But under the Bar's cab-rank rule, she did not have that luxury of choice. *Au contraire*, she had to take the brief. And so she prosecuted (or, as the tabloids put it, 'persecuted') the Metric Martyr. The case became a darling of Brexiteers ('How dare they prosecute a good fella who sold bananas in imperial measurement by the pound!') and of public law lawyers ('Lord Justice Laws proclaimed that some Acts of Parliament are more important than others, we call them constitutional statutes. How extraordinary and interesting'). If one were to ask Eleanor to pick a highlight from the array of cases she did during her time at the English and Irish Bar, she would – in all likelihood – opt for *SS Storaa*. Not only was it a very honourable case to take on *pro bono* but also it was very close to Eleanor's passion as a sailor and to the professional interests of her husband David.

*

Adam: Once done at the Court of Justice you returned to the UK and started two parallel lives. On the one hand, you restarted your career at the Bar. On the other hand, you entered the world of academia. As we already know, two jobs were lined up when you arrived in Dover and rode your motorbike to London. Having said that, re-establishing your practice was not easy. At least, you finally had your tenancy.

Eleanor: Yes, finally it was a real tenancy. *4 Paper Buildings* said to me, with total frankness, that they did not have any EU law work coming into chambers. But they thought it was an interesting and promising area of law, which is why they wanted to recruit me. Their clerks had never clerked any EU law work, but they were up for having a go. The arrangement I was offered was that chambers made me very welcome and promised to do their absolute best to help. To get me going, they would not charge me any chambers' rent for the first year. My reply was short and sweet: 'done'. I had spent ten years trying to attain the Holy Grail, a full tenancy in London chambers, and for ten years I had failed. This was a gamble I could afford to take. I had put aside some savings from my time at the Court and – in parallel with re-starting my practice – I would have the academic post at UCL to keep me going.

Adam: In the early days you worked as a junior barrister but then, in 1999, you took silk.

Eleanor: That I applied for silk at that point was entirely the fault of my dear husband David! Look: for a practising barrister, deciding to apply for silk is a big deal. Let's say that you have built up a reasonably successful practice as an ordinary barrister, as a 'junior'. Your solicitors like you and they send you a reliable stream of work. Getting to that point occupied me from 1990, when I returned to the Bar, to 1999 – and bear in mind that throughout that time I was juggling practice and my academic commitments, first at UCL and later at Cambridge. Now: if you apply for silk, you are staking everything on that throw of the dice. If you are successful, you won't be able to go on doing the same work that you did as a junior – you will no longer receive those instructions. You (and your clerk!) hope that there will be sufficient *new* well-remunerated work for you, from existing or other solicitors, in your new incarnation (if you get silk and you *don't* get that new work, you can't turn around and become a junior again). If you are unsuccessful, you will be demoralised and you will start to doubt yourself and your abilities: 'they' don't think that I have the necessary judgment and skills to be worth those magic letters 'QC' after my name. Though we barristers don't always like to admit it, there are close parallels between the Bar and the theatre. Just like an actor going on stage, you have to believe in yourself completely, including after those days in court that happen to all of us, when an irate unfriendly judge chews you up and spits you out.

David believed in me, simply and unconditionally. He was sure that I should put in for silk then. He brushed aside my wails that I wasn't yet well-enough established; that although I might be reasonably well-known and perhaps even respected over at the Court of Justice in Luxembourg I didn't have many members of the English judiciary who knew me from Eve; that I was so far from the quarter-of-a-million pounds turnover in professional fees which the Bar in those days regarded as the bare minimum benchmark from which to launch an application for silk, my turnover was still in five figures. (I wasn't practising full-time anyway; and often up to a third of my practice was *pro bono*.) David was utterly convinced in his bones that of course it would all turn out splendidly. He stood over me kindly whilst I agonised over how, precisely, to fill in the wretched form and sell myself as the best thing since sliced bread. He hand-delivered the completed paperwork to its destination. He made reassuring noises through the long, long wait (in those days, the process was both labyrinthine and totally non-transparent). And he just smiled at me when, utterly disbelieving, I opened the envelope on Maundy Thursday that told me that my first application had been successful and that it was proposed to grant me letters patent as 'one of Her Majesty's counsel learned in the law'.

Adam: Bless! As we will find out a little later, your practice was largely based on your work representing the UK government at the Court of Justice, however you also had a number of big cases in front of the British courts. The first one was *Brown and others*, wasn't it?

Eleanor: Well, the first case of mine that people are likely to have heard of was certainly *Brown and others*.[1] How I got involved is a really classic Bar story. It is almost too good to be true, but it is true nevertheless. I was at an advocacy training weekend being run by the Middle Temple (my Inn of Court), in which I was participating as a (very inexperienced) trainer for pupil barristers. This was just after I had returned from working in Luxembourg for Sir Gordon Slynn. The training took place at Cumberland Lodge in Windsor Great Park. On Saturday evening, a very pleasant senior colleague – a very experienced criminal practitioner, Anna Worrall QC – came up to me in the bar and said: 'Eleanor, can I pick your brains? Let me buy you a pint'. (This is a standard Bar technique. You buy someone a drink and see in exchange what they think about a particular idea you would like to bounce off them.) So, she bought me a beer and then she started to tell me about a criminal appeal that she was doing. The appeal involved a group of homosexual sadomasochists. They had been convicted in the Crown Court. However, the conviction had not been under the sexual offences legislation (as you might have supposed), because that legislation didn't cover what they had been up to. Rather, they had been convicted of assaulting each other, and of aiding and abetting assaults upon themselves, under the Offences Against the Person Act 1861 (the 'OAPA 1861'). To put it mildly, that was a little weird. The OAPA 1861 is normally used to prosecute punch-ups outside pubs after closing time. It is not normally used to sanction consensual sex. I probably spluttered a little into my beer as Anna went into the more graphic details of what had been going on. Then she looked inquiringly at me. My response was: 'well, there isn't an EEC law point in there, but there are enormous points under the European Convention of Human Rights (the 'ECHR')'. In fact, there were two ECHR points. The main point was Article 8 of the ECHR – the right to respect for private and family life – because your sexual personality is part of your private life, and there was already case law protecting homosexuals (*Dudgeon v United Kingdom*, for example).[2] Then there was a subsidiary point under Article 7 of the ECHR, because criminal law is meant to be foreseeable for the ordinary citizen and it didn't look immediately foreseeable that the law on criminal assault would be used to prosecute consensual sex. I outlined those two points to Anna and she looked interested. She asked me to do some 'devilling' for her, so I did a bit of research work, and she ran the ECHR arguments in the Court of Appeal. There, they sank like a lead balloon. The defendants then appealed to the House of Lords. A week before the case opened in the Lords, the defence team (there were five defendants and already eight barristers – four silks and four juniors – were involved) remembered that they had put a passage into the petition of appeal arguing that the convictions were contrary to Articles 7 and 8 of the ECHR. But none of them had ECHR expertise and (to be blunt) they had not much idea how to plead the ECHR point. They convened a counsel-only consultation and Anna invited me to come along and brief everyone about it. When I had finished, they looked at each other and said: 'we need you on board'. So, they wrote a quick opinion for the Legal Aid Board. I regret to say that they did slightly confuse the Luxembourg and Strasbourg legal frameworks in the course of that opinion, but never mind. They clearly and convincingly explained to the Legal Aid Board that it would be good to get specialist 'European Law' counsel involved. The legal aid certificate was duly extended to the benefit of the clients, to cover my official involvement. At that point I still believed that I was going to be there to pass notes and provide detailed material, because naturally (naturally!) one of the silks would be standing up arguing the ECHR point to the Law Lords. That was until Friday evening, when they broke it to me that I would be on my feet pleading the ECHR part of the case in the UK's highest court. I spent most of the weekend with my long-suffering husband David inside the Squire Law Library in Cambridge, frantically making photocopies of ECHR authorities. Fortunately, as a newly appointed University Lecturer I had a passkey to the Squire because I don't know what I'd have done otherwise. The case duly opened on Monday in the House of Lords. Up till then, I had of course been involved in some interesting cases. But I had been involved as a backroom girl, because I am a reasonably good researcher. So, I had been sitting in court as junior counsel listening to leading counsel plead. And I had done some tiny magistrates court stuff myself as a second-six pupil barrister. This was – literally – my tenth time ever on my hind legs in court conducting legal argument. I was in the House of Lords.

Adam: That must have been petrifying and interesting in equal measure. Not only were you pleading a case which was legally intriguing and spicy on the facts, but also at least some members on the bench must have had conservative inclinations.

Eleanor: Indeed. Let's start with the design of the committee room, where the judicial branch of the House of Lords operated. That design made you feel like a bull in a bullpit. The committee members sat around you in their business suits (not robed) in a sort of a semicircle, and counsel's lectern was in the middle. You were isolated, and nobody could really help you, or easily pass notes to you. As the chairman of the panel, I had Lord Templeman. I think it is fair to say that he found it very difficult to understand, still less have any sympathy for, this particular form of sexual gratification. In the back of the courtroom, we had – it may not have been wise – a number of supporters, as it were, of the defendants. There were people wearing dog collars (leather, not clerical), and there was some clanking of chains, which didn't really go down well with Lord Templeman.

Adam: I guess the rest of the bench was not amused either, huh?

Eleanor: I think it may have amused Lord Mustill and Lord Slynn but I doubt it really played well with the three who ended up being the majority (Lord Templeman, Lord Jauncey, and Lord Lowry). At a certain point I recall Lord Templeman, almost frothing at the mouth, glowering at me and saying:

> *Miss Sharpston, you cannot possibly be suggesting that these vile and disgusting acts – I say again, these vile and disgusting acts – had anything to do with love!*

I remember wrapping my gown around me in the vain hope that it would serve as a flak jacket, swallowing, then looking Lord Templeman straight between the eyes and saying: 'Yes, my Lord, that is precisely my submission'.

Adam: May I dare ask what his reaction was?

Eleanor: Well, let's say that I knew that I didn't have him on board. At the end of the day, three members of the House of Lords Judicial Committee dismissed the appeal. They were also the three older judges and the three public school boys. The two dissenting judges were Lord Mustill and Lord Slynn: younger than the majority judges, and the two grammar school boys.

Adam: How was your interaction with Lord Slynn? It must have been awkward, bordering on surreal, bearing in mind that you had worked for him at the Court of Justice just two years earlier.

Eleanor: Lord Templeman's reaction to my submission about love put a slight smile on Gordon's face. Yes, Gordon had gone straight from the Luxembourg bench to the House of Lords. To plead in front of him in the Lords was very surreal. Actually, though, the interaction with Gordon was precisely the same as the exchanges that we had so often had when I was working in his chambers as his senior *référendaire*, save that I was calling him 'my Lord' and he was calling me 'Miss Sharpston'. It was, quintessentially, the same sort of discussion and give and take that we had had any day in Luxembourg. 'What do you say about this?' 'Well [delete the word 'Gordon' and insert 'my Lord'], my submission would be …' and then I was straight into what I would have said as a *référendaire*. To that extent, I think I was fortunate. Given the hostility, the relentless assault, the artillery fire from Lord Templeman in the chair, it was nice to be able to have a civilised, intellectually rigorous discussion with one of the members of the panel. And Lord Mustill was obviously very interested, asked very good questions, and was very courteous.

Adam: This is not how the story ended, did it? *Brown and others* landed at the European Court of Human Rights in Strasbourg.[3]

Eleanor: It did. The case was legally aided in the House of Lords. A fighting fund was put together to help take the case on to the European Court of Human Rights but – well, I reckoned that the unfortunate clients needed that money more than I did. They had all served prison terms and their lives had been destroyed by the prosecutions, so I did the case *pro bono* in Strasbourg. I remember the surprise, actually the straightforward bewilderment, of my client Colin Laskey, at finding himself imprisoned because his sexual preferences put him on the wrong side of the criminal law. He was a nice, quiet, unassuming Welshman who was a rugby referee in his spare time. I remember him saying to me with a gentle Welsh lilt in his voice:

> *But Eleanor, you know, when we'd finished having a session we would all sit down, and we would have a nice cup of tea together. I don't understand all of this because we weren't hurting anyone.*

If you back off a bit, and you think about the meaning of the verbs 'to hurt' or 'to harm', actually he had a perfectly fair point. Hurting or harming somebody implies doing something to them that they don't want to have happen. But this was all about consensual sex. Much care of one's partner, much affection – obviously – underpinned everything that had been going on. And the scenes had strict limits. The group had a stop word, 'butterfly'. You could ask somebody to stop beating you and that would just be part of the scene. But if you said 'butterfly', that meant: stop there! And as far as one can tell, the group operated within its self-appointed rules. The stop word was respected. And everyone involved really was taking pleasure and getting sexual satisfaction from what was going on.

In the course of a full practising career, you take on a lot of cases, and (obviously!) unless you are incredibly lucky, you also lose a number of cases. In most of those cases, you say to yourself: 'well, okay, I gave it a good try, but we lost'. I have always felt very strongly about 'Operation Spanner' (as *Brown and others* was colloquially known), that the result and the reasoning of the majority judgment were unjust. It was not the proper business of the State to prosecute, and indeed to punish with very significant jail terms, private and consensual sexual conduct that was not expressly identified and prohibited in the sexual offences legislation. That was not a civilised or a just result.

Adam: Another case in which you were involved as a barrister is *Thoburn v Sunderland City Council*, usually referred to as 'the Metric Martyr' case.[4] It could not have been further away from *Brown and others*. The issue it addressed keeps on coming back. Only a few weeks ago it was all over the British media when the government abandoned the plan to switch back to imperial measurements. I was slightly disappointed that buying wine by the suitcase, a brand new measurement unit introduced by the Downing Street staff during Covid-19 lockdowns, did not get onto the statute book. Jokes aside, *Thoburn v Sunderland City Council* was surely one of your big cases. Not to mention that Lord Justice Laws suggested in his judgment there that we do have constitutional statutes in the United Kingdom. For years now this has put UK constitutional lawyers in a state of frenzy.

Eleanor: Well, that is definitely the other big case of mine which most English law students have come across. My claim to fame with that constituency does indeed rest upon being defence counsel in *Brown and others* and having – as the popular press put it – persecuted the Metric Martyr. That was, by the way, the only prosecution brief I have ever had. To the extent that I did criminal law, I always did defence work. My junior in that case was Philip Moser (now Philip Moser KC).

Adam: In the autumn of 2012, in an interview you gave to *Competition Law Insight*, you said that it was the low spot in your career. As you put it there: 'I had the dubious pleasure under the Bar's cab-rank rule of prosecuting the Metric Martyr. […] It's always been assumed that I deliberately chose to prosecute, to persecute, the Metric Martyr but actually I was just following the rules of my profession. It was, though, a very uncomfortable case to do'.[5]

Eleanor: The reason that it came to me was, I think, that I had previously been asked for some EU law advice by the nationwide association of trading standards officers from local government councils. That is not its official name, but that's the description of what it was. I had been asked to advise, as an EU lawyer, upon certain EU directives on measurements and labelling. *Thoburn v Sunderland City Council* was, in fact, an early precursor of UKIP (the United Kingdom Independence Party) and of course Brexit. A number of traders up and down the country were still selling in imperial measures. The trading standards officers were making noises at them that they needed to sell in metric. Then UKIP would get in there and encourage the traders to trade in imperial measures, like true Englishmen – to stand up for their rights.

Adam: Against evil Brussels?

Eleanor: Oh yes, against the wicked Brussels bureaucrats. Steve Thoburn was a grocer in Sunderland. Had I lived in Sunderland, I am sure that I would very happily have bought my fruit and vegetables from Steve. He was a fine and honest man. He wasn't perhaps the sharpest knife in the block, but he was a thoroughly decent trader. He bought good quality produce wholesale and he sold it on for a fair price to his customers. The trouble was that he had a set of scales that weighed only in imperial measures. At a certain moment the trading standards officers visited his stall and noticed this. They defaced the 'approved' stamp on the scales (so that they were no longer fit for use for trade) and they said: 'Steve, get it sorted please, all you need to do is to get scales that weigh in both imperial and metric, and that will be fine'. And Steve told them that he was just going on holiday, but he would get it sorted out when he came back. That was all fine and the trading standards officers left him alone for three months. Then they went back to check up. Unfortunately, in the interim UKIP had got to Steve Thoburn and encouraged him to strike a blow for freedom and to be a hero to his country. When the trading standards officers came back, he told them to eff off. The City of Sunderland hesitated about what to do. But then UKIP got bolder. They wrote to all the councils up and down the country and said: 'either one of you prosecutes somebody for trading using only imperial measures, so that this issue can be brought out into the open and ruled upon in court, or we will select a council at random and we will bring judicial review proceedings and ask why that council is not enforcing the law'. From a technical legal perspective that would have been extremely difficult to defend. I mean, imagine being counsel for the local authority whose trading standards officers are not enforcing the law. You are asked by the judge hearing the judicial review:

> **Judge:** *Miss Sharpston, why are your clients not enforcing the law?*
>
> **ES:** *Well, of course we say the law is valid my Lord, but we say we have a discretion …*
>
> **Judge:** *Miss Sharpston, your clients can't possibly be entitled to exercise their discretion in a way that means that they never prosecute.*

How do you explain that? That would not have been a good place to start from in presenting legal argument in such a judicial review. The City of Sunderland bit the bullet. They brought a prosecution against Steve Thoburn, having made a test purchase of a bunch of bananas on the famous imperial-only scales. 'Making an unlawful sale based on a weight calculated on a pair of scales whose 'approved for use' stamp had earlier been defaced by the local trading standards officers': this was surely the world's most technical prosecution. I prosecuted Steve Thoburn with velvet gloves because the whole thing was politically as hot as it comes. I made it abundantly clear that there was no allegation of any kind that would have a negative impact on his character, trustworthiness or probity. Nobody was suggesting for a moment that he was selling short measure, or that he was deceiving his customers. His scales would measure only in imperial measures. For that reason, the stamp authenticating the scales for trade had been defaced by the trading standards officer. But the trader had nevertheless made a sale to a customer using those scales. The case lasted for five days in front of the Sunderland stipendiary magistrate. At the end of the five days, Steve Thoburn was convicted. I realised at that moment that nobody had explained to him that there was a very reasonable chance that would happen. Poor Steve Thoburn! He looked rather like a stunned, bewildered ox when he was told that he was being convicted. That was very shocking. Of course he should have been warned by those advising him to stand up and strike a blow for English freedom and imperial weights and measures of the risk that, if he traded with those scales, he was likely to end up with a criminal conviction. As far as I remember, the scales were confiscated and he was fined around £800. He wasn't clapped in jail. This was a minor offence. But he got a criminal record.

Adam: Did he appeal the judgment?

Eleanor: He might have left matters there, certainly his wife wanted him to leave matters there. But UKIP urged him on. He did appeal and the case went up to the Divisional Court with Lord Justice Laws from the Court of Appeal sitting as the lead judge with Mr Justice Crane as his wingman. Lord Justice Laws produced an extremely interesting, heavyweight constitutional law judgment. He held that English constitutional law has normal statutes and then it also has a limited number of super statutes – statutes on steroids, one might say – which can only be repealed if Parliament says expressly that that is what it is doing. This is fascinating for constitutional lawyers. He based his ruling on four authorities (three of which had been decided by Laws J when he was a *puisne* judge) which neither my opponent nor I had cited to him because we didn't think they had anything to do with the case. When the defence sought leave to appeal to the House of Lords, I found myself in the curious position of being obliged, as an honourable member of the Bar, to agree with my opponent that those four authorities had indeed not been mentioned, still less debated, in front of the court below. I went on to argue (on instructions from my anxious client, the City of Sunderland) that there was nevertheless no need for the House of Lords to review the resulting decision, which was a slightly interesting line to have to take. The House of Lords didn't want to touch the case with the proverbial barge-pole. The City of Sunderland Council was immensely relieved. They had already blown most of their legal budget for the entire year on a case that they had never wanted to run. I will add that I would have been delighted to have taken the defence brief on behalf of Steve Thoburn in that case, had I been offered it.

Adam: Let us imagine that you had been offered it. What would have been your line of defence?

Eleanor: If the defence had been run on the basis of EU law, I think that there would have been a very reasonable chance that Steve Thoburn would have been acquitted, albeit probably after a trip to the CJEU in Luxembourg. He was selling bananas loose from bulk at an inland market in a Member State. The domestic rules in question were based upon a chain of EU directives. Somebody in Brussels had been tidying up loose ends; and they had put into the final directive in that chain that goods sold from bulk would also be covered by the rules on metrication. If I had had the brief for the defence, I would have argued that was ridiculous. The EU directives were single market measures, aimed at liberalising the free movement of goods and thus avoiding a negative effect on trade between Member States. But this type of retail sale – taking a subset of goods held in bulk and selling them to customers at an inland market – had nothing to do with the free movement of goods. The goods had already travelled. They were now in the Member State of destination. They were not pre-packaged, so there was no issue about labelling. They were being sold from bulk. The public was not being misled. The public was perfectly well aware which measurement system was being used and what they were getting for their money. I would have argued: 'this particular provision in the directive is unlawful *under EU law* because it makes improper use of the legal base chosen under the Treaty; it also violates the principles of subsidiarity and proportionality. I want a reference, please, to the CJEU in Luxembourg!'

I am tolerably certain that a national judge would gratefully have seized the opportunity to make a reference. The case was politically very hot. Shunting it onto some other judges' desks would have been very attractive. I think that there was also a real sporting chance that in Luxembourg, in front of the Court, that particular provision in the directive would have been struck down. If you remember the Working Time Directive case, which I had the honour of being involved in [Case C-84/94],[6] the Court struck down the provision in that Directive which said that in principle the weekly rest period should include a Sunday.[7] It did so because Sunday rest is purely cultural. There was no empirical evidence that rest on a Sunday was more beneficial (in health terms) than rest on another day of the week. So, the Court had already shown that it was prepared to strike down part of an EU measure if the legislator failed to show sufficient justification for it. I would have cited that case, and I would have invited the Court to strike down the article in the metrication directive which said that even if you are selling from bulk and the goods are not going to move across any further frontiers, those goods must nevertheless be sold in metric measure.

Adam: *Thoburn* is one of those cases that never made it to Luxembourg, although it potentially should have.

Eleanor: I think the obvious reason why Steve Thoburn's defence was not argued in that way, and why the case didn't make it to Luxembourg, was because UKIP did not want that to happen. UKIP wanted a stand-up fight in the English courts about Parliamentary sovereignty, with the opportunity to complain vociferously if (applying the principle of the supremacy of EU law over domestic law) the EU measure – the metrication directive – were upheld over an Act of Parliament that was purely a consolidation act. Please note: a consolidation act does exactly what it says on the tin. It consolidates messy existing law. It does not change the law in any way. But this particular consolidation act, the Weights and Measures Act 1986, post-dated the European Communities Act 1972. And UKIP were after a fight on sovereignty.

Adam: Your European credentials, so to speak, must have added fuel to the fire.

Eleanor: Worse, Adam, much worse! My junior, as I've said, was Philip Moser who is half Austrian. I, of course, grew up in Austria. So, the Metric Martyr team fostered the impression that we were filthy foreigners (and crypto-Krauts, to boot), doing down a true-blooded Englishman. Having said that, there was a lovely moment worth recalling. On day three of our case, Philip and I were having lunch in the break between the morning and afternoon court sessions. Remember, we were in Sunderland and (I mean no disrespect here) at the time the number of places to have a swift but decent lunch was possibly a little limited. Philip and I had found a very unpretentious workmen's cafe, which did really good fish and chips. Freshly caught fish in a classic beer-based batter, properly deep-fried so it was nice and crispy, with decent chips, mushy peas, and a nice cup of tea. And all very reasonably priced. This wasn't fancy cooking. This was an excellent local cafe with proper, decent British grub. We had just got there and ordered our fish and chips, when in came some members of the opposition team: the British Weights and Measures Association, and the men from UKIP. I cannot describe the look of appalled surprise – the sheer horror on their faces – at finding these filthy continentals polluting their nice British cafe. They were even more confused when they saw what we were eating. The sheer cheek of it! Bloody foreigners adding insult to injury by choosing to order a classic British lunch.

Adam: (laughing) Did they stay for lunch or run out screaming as if they had just seen a ghost or a devil, or both?

Eleanor: They did stay. They looked at us and said rather stiffly, 'oh yes ... hello'. It was a rather small cafe and they went and sat as far from us as was physically possible. Then there was a pause whilst they worked out what they were going to have. There was some internal struggle going on. Given that we – the filthy foreigners – had ordered the fish and chips, could they also have fish and chips? If my memory serves me well, they did end up having fish and chips. It smelt so nice and fresh and – well, it was by a mile the best offer on the menu.

Adam: The third case that you have particular affection for is *SS Storaa*.[8] In the same interview for *Competition Law Insight*, you called it 'the high spot of your career'. That was your last case before you moved to Luxembourg to serve as an Advocate General.

Eleanor: It was my last case, and fittingly, it was a case I did *pro bono*. It was a very idealistic case. It had nothing to do with commercial matters, or indeed with money at all. It was about the respect that we should show for the last resting place of people who gave their lives during the Second World War fighting for the freedom of Europe.

Adam: It is a coincidence – but a very appropriate coincidence – that we are talking about it on 6 June 2024 – the eightieth anniversary of D-Day.

Eleanor: That wasn't pre-planned, but it is a very striking and fitting coincidence nevertheless. I watched the ceremonies yesterday evening and again this morning, and listened to the dwindling band of veterans, recalling what they felt at the time and recording – almost to their surprise – that 80 years later, they are still here and so many people that they went into that landing with are not because they didn't make it past the first few days of the invasion. So yes, it is a very interesting coincidence, Adam.

Adam: I find such stories, especially such war stories, extremely humbling. They show our daily challenges and pressures in a completely different light and put everything into perspective. Returning to *SS Storaa*, *prima facie* it is hard to imagine how a case dealing with a ship that was torpedoed and sank in late 1943 could have reached the UK courtrooms in the 2000s. What is the story behind it?

Eleanor: To begin with, we've been talking about '*SS Storaa*' but the full name of the case is *Fogg & Anor, R (on the application of) v The Secretary Of State For Defence & Anor*. *SS Storaa* was a Danish merchant ship of 1,980 gross registered tonnage. After a very curious and elaborate career, under several flags, she ended up as part of a convoy going down-Channel towards Cardiff. *SS Storaa* was sailing under military orders, because she was part of a convoy. Her crew included serving Royal Navy personnel on detachment (amongst them Petty Officer James Varndell, the father of mesdames Fogg and Ledgard) and gunners from the Maritime Royal Artillery Regiment (a wartime part of the Royal Artillery). She had guns and ammunition supplied by the Ministry of Defence, with the government broad arrow symbol on them. Her cargo was tank- and aircraft parts. Her captain was sailing under naval discipline. Because *SS Storaa* was an armed merchantman, rather than just a cargo-carrying vessel, she was part of the defence force for the convoy, and she had already been involved firing her guns to beat off one attack by German E-boats. Sadly, the E-boats came back a little later for a second try. They had obviously identified *SS Storaa* as being a danger (because she was armed), and they took her out. She was torpedoed and sank on a cold winter night in the Channel, on 3 November 1943. Twenty-one men died. There were a few survivors. When the archaeologists were piecing together the available information about *SS Storaa*, they had, for example, the record of an official interview with her surviving third mate, listing what cargo had been on board and describing the attack.

Adam: This is a very sad story though – I guess – quite a common one. At that time, many merchant ships were helping out with the war effort. How did you get involved in the case and why was judicial review required at all?

Eleanor: As you know, my late husband David was a respected maritime historian, and he was a trustee of the Maritime Museum in Hastings. I used to go down to Hastings with David to meetings of the Trust, and there I met Dr Peter Marsden who is a well-known archaeologist. David and Peter used to talk about *SS Storaa*. The wreck is about five miles off Hastings and it lies at a depth of 120 feet of water. So she is within diving depth for amateur scuba divers. The wreck is more or less complete, so it is a very attractive dive. Also, because *SS Storaa* went down to the north of the present traffic lanes in the Channel, it is possible to dive on the wreck. Obviously, if she had sunk further out – further south – the wreck would be protected by the fact that there would be supertankers going by overhead all the time. But she lies coastwards of the northern traffic lane, so she is in water that you can dive safely. People had been diving on *SS Storaa* because – for divers – she is a really nice site to dive. And some of them had been taking souvenirs.

Adam: Gosh, that's horrible, bearing in mind that it is a graveyard for the crew members who did not survive the E-boat attack.

Eleanor: Here we arrive at the essence of the case. Petty Officer James Varndell's two daughters, Rosemary Fogg and Valerie Ledgard, were extremely upset that souvenir hunters were diving on their father's grave. They contacted Dr Peter Marsden. Somehow the idea got rolling that it would be good to try to get the wreck of *SS Storaa* designated under the Protection of Military Remains Act 1986.

Adam: Now it makes perfect sense, Leo. Bearing in mind that it ended in court, though, the official winds cannot have been very favourable.

Eleanor: It took about five years of research to put together the file on *SS Storaa*. The wreck at that particular location had to be identified, to be matched reliably with that particular vessel. Then we needed all the available details about the voyage, the cargo and so on, and pieced everything together. Once all that had been done, Dr Peter Marsden formally approached the Ministry of Defence ('MoD' for short) and asked it to consider designating *SS Storaa* as a protected site. I should say that such designation does not involve any expense. Designation involves the Minister making an order that the site is protected. It is then marked as a protected site on maritime charts, and you are not meant to take anything from the site. The idea is that one can dive, one can look, but one is prohibited from touching or taking anything. The MoD decision was negative. According to the MoD, the Secretary of State didn't even need to consider whether to designate *SS Storaa*. Their view was that she didn't qualify for designation under the Protection of Military Remains Act 1986 because she was not 'in service with, or being used for the purposes of, the armed forces'. Had the E-boat that attacked her sunk, the E-boat would have qualified for designation. But not *SS Storaa*.

Adam: The logic of it escapes me. I guess this had something to do with the fact that despite all links to the Royal Navy, it was *par excellence* a merchant ship. Still, something does not feel quite right.

Eleanor: Precisely! Dr Peter Marsden came and talked to me about the refusal. In turn, I persuaded a splendid campaigning solicitor called Richard Buxton, who is based in Cambridge, to act as my instructing solicitor. Remember, as a barrister, I cannot act without instructions. Richard Buxton normally does environmental law cases (he'd used me as counsel before in a few of them) so this wasn't his standard area of practice. However, he listened to the story of *SS Storaa* and he felt that this was a bad show. Being the nice man he is, he decided he was prepared to act. We put contingency fee arrangements in place for Richard and for my junior barrister, whom I obviously needed. Over the course of the case, I had both a bright young – Angela Patrick – and an old friend – Peter Gibbs – in there as juniors. I was acting *pro bono*. Richard wrote an official solicitor's letter to the Ministry of Defence, suggesting politely that they might want to think hard about reconsidering their decision. Since they said they weren't disposed to do so, we applied for judicial review. We also needed to protect our two claimants, Rosemary and Valerie, because – although we were acting for them either for free or on a contingency fee basis – they would be liable for the MoD's legal costs if we lost. They were two very nice middle-aged ladies of modest means. Exposing them to that risk was unthinkable. We applied for a protective costs order, relying on the *Corner House* decision. It is accepted wisdom at the Bar that it is close to impossible to get a protective costs order for such litigation. Yet, very much against the odds, we were not only given permission to proceed for judicial review, we were also granted the vital protective costs order that made it possible to proceed.

Adam: I know it was just the beginning of the litigation but still, what an achievement and a promising start. It must have been rather emotional, bearing in mind the history of *SS Storaa* and the way her crew perished on that cold November night.

Eleanor: I went along to plead that case, and it was the honour of my life to have that opportunity. When I stood up to plead, I had sitting in court behind me on the public benches two rows of elderly gentlemen – all wearing blue blazers, polished shoes, very carefully turned out – sitting very quietly, very respectfully, listening very intently. These were merchant seamen who had served in convoys in the Second World War. They were in court to listen to their case: finally, the opportunity to have their service and the service of their lost comrades recognised.

We finished the first day's hearing. The judge, Mr Justice Newman, rose and went out; and I turned around to ask them how they felt it had gone. One of them said to me:

> *Well, it is clear that the Ministry of Defence has absolutely no idea what it was really like to be in a convoy.*

At this point, I smelt a potential witness. I had no idea that these gentlemen would come to the court. Obviously, in theory, I knew they existed, but I had had no contact with them before the case. I met them for the first time because they were sitting in the hearing. The gentleman who made that comment had served in the Merchant Navy through the war. He had obviously had an extremely effective guardian angel. He had been torpedoed three times before reaching his 18th birthday, and yet somehow he had been fished out of the water in time, on all three occasions, and he had survived the war. Since he was willing to talk, Richard Buxton and I took him back to my chambers. We gave him tea and chambers' very best chocolate biscuits, which we reserved for special clients. Then Richard and I sat down with him, and we took down an affidavit (a written proof of evidence). He told us what it was like being in convoy, how everything was very much controlled by the Admiralty. Even if you thought what they were asking you to do was completely bizarre, nevertheless, obviously you obeyed Admiralty orders. He gave us a first-person account: a window into history.

Adam: Leo, you sharing all of this gives me flashbacks of long conversations with my late step-grandfather Robert about their *sorties* on RAF Avro Lancasters into Germany and occupied territories, and back. I shall never forget that. What interests me now is if you were able to use any of this evidence in the court?

Eleanor: Believe it or not, Adam, the answer is yes. The following morning, I stood up and I applied to put in that affidavit. I said to the judge:

> ES: *My Lord, I have a very unusual application to make.*
>
> *I say at once that I do recognise it is extremely unusual but I respectfully suggest that this is a very unusual case. Your Lordship will perhaps have noticed a group of mature gentlemen in court yesterday …*

Newman J: *Yes, Miss Sharpston, I saw your fan club.*

ES: *My Lord, yes … After court, my Lord, I became aware of the existence of evidence – first-hand evidence – that would shed light on the type of event that we have been presenting to your Lordship as history that happened over sixty years ago. Neither my instructing solicitor nor I were aware, or could reasonably have been aware, that that evidence existed. Before your Lordship sat this morning, I have of course made my learned friend aware of the content of the evidence in question.*

I have no idea, my Lord, if your Lordship will find it useful and informative, or whether your Lordship will wish to look at it in detail or not. But I should like to apply – exceptionally – for permission to put it in.

My opponent, obviously, then got up and said all the things you would expect him to say: that it was completely outrageous, that the rules say that all affidavit evidence must go in 'X' weeks before the hearing, etc, etc, etc.

Adam: What was the reaction on the bench?

Eleanor: Mr Justice Newman sat for a while and looked thoughtful. Then he said:

Well, Miss Sharpston, as you have said, this is a very unusual application. However, as you also said, this is a very unusual case. I have no idea whether this affidavit will assist me in understanding the case, but I am minded to let it in, because it is the nearest I shall have to actual evidence of what was going on.

My response was simple: 'My Lord, I am most grateful'. As to my opponent, I am not sure if he actually put his head in his hands, but it was very clear what he thought of the judge's decision.

We were very lucky in Mr Justice Newman. We got a judge who was prepared to think through what were (and importantly, what were *not*) the implications of the case. For example, the Ministry of Defence tried running a floodgates argument: if you let this one through, we will have to look at every case. That was just ridiculous. I said as much, because it had taken five years of work to put the file together. Floodgates it would certainly not be!

Adam: What was the judgment then? There are obvious limits to what judicial review in the English system can deliver.

Eleanor: The judgment was in our favour. The judge found that the Secretary of State had directed himself wrongly as a matter of law, and that he was required to consider designating *SS Storaa*. So – entirely correctly – the order was not 'you must designate *SS Storaa*' but rather 'you are not entitled to say that you won't even think about it'. The important conclusion was that the vessel did fall within the criteria laid down by the Protection of Military Remains Act 1986. It was then for the MoD to go away and decide whether to designate or not.

Adam: I guess that was not the outcome the Ministry of Defence was hoping for. Did they appeal?

Eleanor: They most certainly wished to do so! All this was happening just before I was due to leave for Luxembourg to be sworn in as the new British Advocate General at the Court. The judgment came out on 13 December 2005 and I was sworn in on 10 January 2006. Obviously, I could not continue with the case. I had an urgent talk with my co-head of Hailsham Chambers, Michael Pooles QC, another hero of this story. Michael is an extremely fine advocate. His normal area of practice is professional negligence, but he immediately said to me:

> *Well, you've carried the baton for the first lap.*
>
> *I will obviously, with pleasure, do the second lap.*
>
> *If we can get me paid, that would be nice, and if we can't, I will do it for free.*
>
> *That's not a problem.*

In fact, we managed to convince Mr Justice Newman that the MoD should be given permission to appeal conditional upon paying both sides' costs. The judge told them:

> *You know, this has been very fully argued once already, before me. It is a matter of public interest, so I understand that you want to appeal, but the appeal – both sides of the appeal – should be paid for by yourselves.*

The case went up to the Court of Appeal. Meanwhile, I'd gone to Luxembourg. I was like a cat on hot bricks. This was my last case, and I cared passionately about it. I had been so happy that we had won, but what was going to happen now? Reports of the hearing were relayed to me from London. Sir Anthony Clark, the Master of the Rolls, was sitting as presiding judge, with two wingmen who knew about admiralty law. The MoD was represented by Nigel Teare QC (my former 'pupil master' from my earlier incarnation when I had been doing a third six-months' pupillage in shipping law with the hope of combining that with EU law). Apparently, there was a kind of pivot point in the appeal hearing, when the Master of the Rolls said to counsel for the MoD:

> *Let me be sure that I understand your case.*
>
> *You are saying that this vessel with this armament and this crew and this cargo, sailing in convoy towards Cardiff Docks is not covered by the Act. But had she been torpedoed as she left Cardiff Docks for Alexandria, she would have been covered by the Act, because she would have been sailing to support the Eighth Army fighting in the desert.*

Nigel Teare QC, acting on instructions, said: 'Yes, My Lord, that is the Minister's submission'. Apparently at that point the Master of the Rolls put his pen down. The Court of Appeal upheld the judgment of Newman J.[9] The MoD then thought about going to the House of Lords.

Adam: Hadn't they had enough? I find it hard to understand why they were like a dog in the manger about this. It just does not add up.

Eleanor: It was very bizarre. They really weren't getting good publicity out of this (including from Conservative papers like the *Daily Telegraph*) and there was also no cost to enforcement. The only explanation I can think of is that when the MoD conceived the Protection of Military Remains Act 1986, the civil servants involved in the drafting had thought about its scope and what would be covered by it. They had not included merchant vessels, although fleet auxiliaries (like the *Sir Galahad* in the Falklands War) were covered. Anyway, the MoD took their time and eventually decided against going to the House of Lords. I think that if they had asked the Lords for permission, they would have been turned down. I am not sure about that, of course.

Adam: How did this story end? The court ordered the Ministry of Defence to reconsider. It didn't tell them that they had to designate *SS Storaa*. The ball, so to speak, was back in the MoD's court.

Eleanor: About two, maybe three years later, I received in Luxembourg a letter from Dr Peter Marsden to tell me that the Secretary of State had just designated *SS Storaa* as a protected wreck. A little later, to my very great surprise and pleasure, I was made an honorary Vice Master of the Honourable Company of Master Mariners in recognition of my work on behalf of the Merchant Navy in fighting for *SS Storaa* to be designated.

The *Storaa* case was terribly important to the Merchant Navy. It was so symbolic, so emblematic. The Merchant Navy had suffered appalling losses during the Second World War. Their casualty rates were much worse than those of the three armed services. The survival rate on the convoys – notably both the Atlantic convoys and the Arctic convoys – was horrifically low. Yet for decades the merchant seamen had no recognition. There is just the memorial to the Merchant Navy on Tower Hill, opposite the Tower of London, but that's about it – the only real commemoration of their sacrifice. By the way, *SS Storaa's* name is on that memorial, along with so many, many others. It was such an honour to do that case.

Adam: There is another piece of *pro bono* work that you were engaged in just before moving to Luxembourg. It was not a court case, this time. Was it?

Eleanor: No, not litigation in a good cause this time. It was work that occupied me on and off for about two years of my life (and of course it was *pro bono*). South London Citizens, which claims to be 'the second oldest Citizens UK Chapter' had decided that the way in which Lunar House, the big Immigration and Nationality Directorate ('IND') of the Home Office based in Croydon, operated was a matter of concern. Every day there were long, long queues of people standing outside Lunar House for hours in the cold, in the rain, waiting their turn to get inside and ask what had happened to their application. There was a spillover effect into the community. If you were a South London citizen and you had eyes to see, you could quickly figure out that this official government administrative process was not operating very well. So, South

London Citizens decided that they wanted to set up a 'Citizens Enquiry'. We all know about public enquiries, right? Well, this was going to be the first-ever Citizens Enquiry: a 'Citizens' Enquiry into Service Provision at Lunar House', with a direct mandate from ordinary citizens. South London Citizens contacted a number of people: a Roman Catholic bishop, a nonconformist pastor, a few other liberal-minded lawyers – people like me. They asked us if we would serve for free as Commissioners to hold the enquiry. In return, they offered a small support team to help review written evidence and produce a first draft of the final report. The whole thing was voluntary, and it was run on a shoestring. But Lunar House badly needed to be looked into and so I agreed to serve. The Commissioners chose Bishop Charles Henderson and myself to act as co-chairs. Then we needed to work out how we were going to conduct the enquiry. The basic premise was that we were going to do this strictly and correctly and we would be scrupulous about being absolutely fair to the Home Office. We would hold public meetings and collect evidence. Then we would put that evidence to the Home Office. We would ask to be allowed to visit Lunar House and look at the premises. We tried to set it up so that our procedure resembled – as closely as possible – that of a normal enquiry, including safeguards for all those involved. We wanted to be very respectful of everyone. What was really interesting was watching the dynamic change over time. To start with, the Home Office was, frankly, fairly dismissive (as in, 'who are these lunatics?'). But when they saw that we were going to play very straight, and we had held some meetings, asked non-biased questions, the Home Office changed its attitude. We asked to be allowed to visit Lunar House and IND agreed and showed us around.

Adam: How did the situation on site look like? I take it that the Lunar House was not exactly the lobby of the Savoy or the Ritz.

Eleanor: Let me give you a flavour. In the main reception area, where there was a long line of numbered counters, all the chairs were screwed down to the floor. I asked why. Was it tidiness? Or was it (perhaps) to guard against the possibility that people might pick up a chair and move it somewhere – or perhaps even use it as a weapon? The blunt answer was: 'Yes, there might be a risk that a chair would be used in that way'. (Were people really that frustrated?) Then I queried accessibility for people in wheelchairs. Could people with such a disability get through in between the screwed-down chairs to a counter? Well, if one was good at steering a wheelchair, one might perhaps be able to get to the final counter on the far right (I wondered a bit about that!), but no, one wouldn't be able to get to any of the other counters. Then I tried out one of those chairs screwed to the floor placed in front of a counter. All the counters had protective screens, and the IND official would be sitting behind that screen. I sat down in the chair. I made as though to talk to the official on the other side of the screen. It quickly became apparent that in order to talk to the official and for the official to be able to hear what I was saying, I would need to lean forward at an angle of about 45 degrees. This is not a very normal or natural position from which to have an exchange between a citizen and an official about an administrative matter. Literally, you were leaning forward in a position of supplication. If IND needed to screw down the chair to the floor, that was one thing, but it didn't seem justified to screw the chair to the floor at that distance from the counter. Then we continued our tour. We discovered (for example) that the only toilet facilities were on the top floor, and there was no lift. So if you were a mother with a baby, you were schlepping with them all the way up. The IND staff working at Lunar House were incredibly stressed. They were really not supported. They had an impossible workload and very bad working conditions. It became apparent that the Citizens Enquiry was going to be making recommendations about how to look after applicants, but that we would also be addressing how to look after the IND staff better. (I should emphasise that we were very, very careful not to address the substantive requirements of the immigration rules and how they were applied. We were talking exclusively about how to make the processing slightly more humane.) IND then realised both that we were clearly fiercely independent, and that we were going to be prepared to make recommendations which the Home Office would find extremely useful in the context of its perennial battle to get an increased budget from the Treasury. From that point onwards we got a lot of cooperation from the Home Office. We had a final open public meeting, at which the Citizens' Enquiry Report was presented to South London Citizens. The Deputy Under Secretary responsible for IND came along to the meeting. The Commissioners were all given garlands of flowers, and there was a garland of flowers for her too. And it was a very lovely public event. What was interesting was how far positions had shifted during the enquiry. From a first contact where, if not exactly antagonistic, we had been seen as a potential enemy, and certainly as a time-consuming nuisance, we had travelled a long way to 'what you have done is to shine a valuable light on things that weren't good; your report will help us to get the money to fix them, you were nice to our staff, and actually, thank you very much for your work'.

Adam: So, it turned into a very rewarding experience for all concerned, even the Home Office.

Eleanor: Indeed. I should make it absolutely clear that this was a team effort. There was a secretariat of three who did the initial reviewing and writing for us, and then we revised and approved the draft. A lot of really important heavy lifting was done by that secretariat team, who were three representatives of South London Citizens. The Commissioners couldn't have got the job done without their unstinting support.

ENDNOTES

* Heledd Pritchard, 'A woman doing intellectual areas of law? She can't be serious' (*Luxembourg Times*, September 2019) 25.

[1] *R v Brown* [1993] UKHL 19.

[2] *Dudgeon v United Kingdom* App 7525/76 (ECHR, 21 October 1981).

[3] *Laskey and Others v the United Kingdom* App. 21627/93; 21628/93; 21974/93 (ECtHR, 19 February 1997).

[4] *Thoburn v Sunderland City Council* [2002] EWHC 195 (Admin).

[5] Interview with Eleanor Sharpston (*Competition Law Insight*, 16 October 2012) <https://www.competitionlawinsight.com/Interview/eleanor-sharpston-interview-2-59752.htm> accessed 1 September 2025.

[6] Case C-84/94 *United Kingdom of Great Britain and Northern Ireland v Council of the European Union* ECLI:EU:C:1996:431.

[7] Council Directive 93/104/EC of 23 November 1993 concerning certain aspects of the organization of working time [1993] OJ L 307/18.

[8] *Fogg & Anor, R (on the application of) v The Secretary Of State For Defence* [2005] EWHC 2888 (Admin).

[9] *The Queen on the Application of Rosemary Fogg and Valerie Ledgard v The Secretary of State for Defence* [2006] EWCA Civ 1270.

4

All Roads Lead Back to Luxembourg

After I got the news that I was being put forward by the UK for appointment as an Advocate General, I put down the phone and in a total daze
I wandered out into the courtyard of my little house on a hillside in Wales.
I burst into tears, and said:
'I'm going home.
*I don't believe it, but I am going home'.**

Adam: The commercial part of Eleanor Sharpston's practice centred around representing the United Kingdom before the CJEU and – on two occasions – also before the European Free Trade Association (EFTA) Court. To readers who are not *au courant* with the procedure at the CJEU (and, for that matter, the EFTA Court) we owe, as the point of departure, a short explanation. Irrespective of how the case reaches a Kirchberg courtroom, whether it is a reference for a preliminary ruling from a national court, an infringement case brought by the European Commission, or an action for annulment submitted by an applicant that enjoys the necessary *locus standi*, all Member States have the right to intervene and submit written and – should there be a hearing (which is for the Court to decide) – also oral pleadings before both the General Court and the Court of Justice. The most common way for a Member State to proceed is by appointing government agents who, as their main task, are involved in both parts of the procedure (sometimes supported by wingmen coming from the Bar). When the United Kingdom was a Member State of the European Union, it operated in a different way. Treasury Solicitors ('TSol') would coordinate the case internally within government with the relevant ministries and government departments. TSol would then instruct counsel – a barrister – to plead on behalf of Her Majesty's Government. Eleanor Sharpston QC was one of those who were frequently instructed to plead in that capacity in the Luxembourg courtrooms. Such instructions naturally came with strings attached. Treasury counsel, whether they find the *raison d'être* for the intervention and its substance plausible or not, have to present the UK government's position before the Court. That is so even if – deep down – counsel know that the line of argument insisted upon by Whitehall stands little or no chance of succeeding before the Court. Despite those limitations, this part of Eleanor's practice had at least three advantages. Firstly, she was returning regularly to the Court of Justice. Thus, as she explains in this chapter, in a way she never really left the Court after her three years in Sir Gordon Slynn's *cabinet* ended. Secondly, since these assignments were remunerated at standard Government rates (less than commercial rates, but still respectably paid), they allowed her elsewhere to play Robin Hood in a barrister's gown. Eleanor could cross-subsidise from her paying practice and take *pro bono* cases, like the ones we talked about in the previous chapter. Thirdly, recurring appearances at Kirchberg came with the dividend of valuable experience that would prove to be extremely useful when, in 2006, she became the fourth (and sadly the last) British Advocate General at the Court of Justice.

Looking back at Eleanor's career at the Bar, one can effortlessly see the trajectory on which she travelled. Like a pilot navigating a plane through ever-changing weather conditions, and yet progressing from one beacon of navigation to another *en route* to the destination airport, Eleanor headed to Luxembourg. After years of intervening on behalf of the UK government, when Sir Francis Jacobs retired from the bench on the Kirchberg, she applied for the position of Advocate General. It is worth mentioning, though, that jobs on the bench of the Court of Justice are not easily available. Firstly, there are only limited options and vacancies are rarely available to be grabbed. Secondly, appointments are made by the Member States after a candidate is selected in a national procedure. (These days, the nominees have also to survive being grilled by the Article 255 Committee.)

The CJEU has two categories of Members. To begin with, there are the judges. At the General Court (formerly known as the Court of First Instance) there are two judges per Member State. This, however, dates only as of 2016 when the General Court underwent a major reform. Before that, the General Court, just like the Court of Justice, had only one judge per Member State. At the Court of Justice, apart from the number of judges (which equals the number of Member States), we also have Advocates General – eleven at present. (When Eleanor became an Advocate General, there were eight AGs at the Court). How are these few AG positions distributed between the Member States, you may ask. Well, some Member States (now, after Brexit, five: France, Germany, Italy, Poland, and Spain) always have the right to nominate an Advocate General, while others are subject to a one term only rotation system (in the alphabetical order of the Member States). For judges, the six-year fixed term of appointment is always renewable, while for AGs the appointment is only renewable for those Member States with the right to a 'permanent' Advocate General. Since the United Kingdom belonged to the latter group, during its forty-seven years of EU membership it continuously had Advocates General on the bench in Luxembourg (Sir Jean-Pierre Warner [1973–1981], Sir Gordon Slynn [1981–1988], Sir Francis Jacobs [1988–2006], and Dame Eleanor Sharpston [2006–2020]). All four were, unquestionably, AGs *extraordinaire*. As argued in the book about the UK Advocates General, these four exceptional lawyers left a firm mark on EU law.[1]

In this chapter, our conversation focuses on the days when Eleanor Sharpston was representing the United Kingdom as counsel before the Court of Justice and how, in 2006, she became the British Advocate General.

*

Adam: During your time at the English Bar, you were not always playing Robin Hood. To be able to do that, you had to make a living from other work. In fact, you were a frequent visitor to the Kirchberg courtrooms. Seemingly, in your case Leo, as the title of this chapter suggests, all roads led to Luxembourg. How did that happen?

Eleanor: My 'Luxembourg practice' started with *Exportur SA v LOR SA and Confiserie du Tech SA* (Case C-3/91).[2] I moved back to the UK in September 1990. In November 1990, that case was referred to the Court of Justice by the *Cour d'appel de Montpellier* and the UK government needed to decide whether to put in written observations. At this moment, fate intervened. A friend of mine, Catherine Crisham, a very bright government lawyer who had been on secondment to the Court of Justice from the Government Legal Service and had worked for AG Francis Jacobs, had also already moved back to the UK. She worked for the Ministry of Agriculture, Fisheries and Food ('MAFF'). Treasury Solicitor was, of course, the instructing solicitor; but the lead department for *Exportur* was MAFF, because the case involved a food product ('*Turrónes de Alicante*' and '*Turrónes de Jijona*'). Catherine said to her colleagues at MAFF that she had met somebody called Eleanor Sharpston at the Court, who had just returned to practice, and that she would like to try me out as Treasury counsel in Luxembourg. So MAFF told TSol that they would like to instruct me and I settled the written observations for them. This was the first real case that I did having returned to the Bar. (My VAT return for my first quarter back in practice had shown fees received of £250 plus VAT.) I was literally starting again from scratch, which is why it was so vitally important to have in parallel the academic post at University College London ('UCL'). Otherwise, I would have had nothing to live on.

Adam: *Exportur SA v LOR SA and Confiserie du Tech SA* looks like an interesting case. Was it a good baby case or did it turn out as being yet another baptism of fire for you?

Eleanor: The latter, Adam. *'Turrónes de Alicante' and 'Turrónes de Jijona'* are rather delicious types of confectionery. They benefit from protected designations of origin. Two French companies, *LOR* and *Confiserie du Tech*, produced and sold similar confectionery in Perpignan (France), respectively as '*touron Alicante*', '*touron Jijona*' and '*touron catalan type Alicante*', '*touron catalan type Jijona*'. Obviously, the producers of authentic Spanish *'Turrónes de Alicante' and 'Turrónes de Jijona'* were not pleased about this.

At stake (as well as EEC law on intellectual property rights) was the bilateral convention between France and Spain on the protection of designations of origin, indications of provenance, and names of certain products.[3] That convention reserved exclusively to products made in Spain the right to sell in France under the nomenclature '*Turrón de Alicante*' and '*Turrón de Jijona*'. It was my first case and I chewed my fingernails because it didn't seem to *me* like a very easy baby case to start me off. I thought it was rather difficult. But of course, I kept my mouth shut and I went on with my written observations. Then, the Court of Justice sent the case to the Full Court, not to a chamber. That rang more alarm bells in my head but I kept my misgivings to myself. Then, on 23 January 1992, came the hearing in Luxembourg. Judge René Joliet was completely impossible. He machine-gunned me with questions. For instance:

> *Well, Miss Sharpston: for example, you make a lot of cutlery in Sheffield. Solingen in Germany is also well-known for its cutlery. So, is Solingen allowed to say that they're making Sheffield cutlery and in Sheffield are you allowed to say that you are making a Solingen knife?*
>
> [I was on my feet but, of course, I had no instructions on any of this stuff. I could hear MAFF and TSol quietly having a heart attack behind me. So, in sheer desperation, I started to improvise and I invented the Solingen sausage. I said:]
>
> *My Lord, perhaps if we can return to agricultural products, let me take the example of the Solingen sausage. Now, let's first suppose that the Solingen sausage tastes the way it does because the pigs in Solingen eat grains and acorns and herbs which grow in that particular area. The result is that when the pigs become pork, and then the meat is minced up to make sausages, that meat gives a particular flavour to the sausage. That would be a true Solingen sausage and it would rightly be protected by a designation of origin. If, however, a Solingen sausage is really just a recipe for a certain amount of minced pork, combined with certain spices or herbs that get added to it, we say that that is merely a recipe for making a product and that it can be used elsewhere. Any problem about origin is perfectly, adequately, and proportionately addressed by appropriate labelling. You label the product and you say, 'this is a sausage made in Sheffield, to the Solingen recipe'.*
>
> *I hope I have answered your Lordship's question.*

Judge Joliet went on in that vein for what seemed like an eternity. The rest of the Court, who knew that until very recently I had been a *référendaire* with Sir Gordon Slynn, sat back and enjoyed the show. It was good free entertainment. After the Q&A finished I did a short reply and turned away to go back to my seat. Then I half-heard President Due saying something to me, so I swung back instantly towards the lectern. 'My Lord?'. President Due smiled broadly: 'No, no, no. I was just saying thank you, Miss Sharpston'. To which I replied, really without thinking: 'My Lord, I am so sorry. I thought that Judge Joliet might have a further question for me'. Of course, the entire Court laughed.

Adam: I bet! Have you managed to find out what happened on that day to Judge Joliet? I hope this was not personal. Of course, we remember that he had been in the same chamber with Sir Gordon Slynn and they had not been exactly spraying red hearts in the corridors at Kirchberg.

Eleanor: I went to find Judge Joliet after the hearing and apologised, saying that I had not intended to be impertinent. He replied very graciously that he thought that some of his questions had perhaps been a little impertinent. A little later that day, I went off to have coffee with a friend and found out the true background to what had happened. I think I said to my friend something along the lines of, 'I just had a hearing before the Full Court. My God, what bit Joliet today? What was his problem?' And the reply was:

> *Oh, YOU got him this year, did you? Every year, we get a visiting group from the University of Liège, where Joliet was (and still is) a Professor. Every time that visiting group comes to the Court, Joliet shows off to them. Therefore, whoever the poor bastard is who is pleading a case in front of Joliet when that visiting group is there, they get it in the neck. Joliet was just showing off how clever he is. Although it sounds as though – this particular time – it may have been a two-way exchange of fire.*

Adam: Right, a true baptism of fire it was indeed (and again, for you, Leo). This was just the beginning. In the *Festschrift* for you, Professor Graham Butler provided readers with a very useful list of 55 cases in which you pleaded on behalf of the UK government before the Court of Justice.[4] And, I must say, it is an impressive list: free movement of goods, direct effect of directives and of international agreements, interim measures in national courts, the Working Time Directive, and many others.[5] Are there any cases you, perhaps, regret taking?

Eleanor: Well, I was traditionally wearing a black hat, because – actually, without exception – I was arguing the case on behalf of the United Kingdom (I had no private client work before the Court). And what I was saying on instructions on behalf of Her Majesty's Government may not always have coincided with my own view of where EU law was going or should go, and what the texts at issue meant.

Adam: I could clearly see that going through your cases on the direct effect of international agreements and then juxtaposing them with Leo's academic writing on the topic. But I behaved and did not elaborate on that nuance in my own contribution to your *Festschrift*.[6]

Eleanor: People were kind enough not to throw my academic writings back in my teeth in open court, and I was and am grateful for that courtesy! But you asked me whether I ever regretted the arguments that I found myself advancing on behalf of the UK government. I can think of one or two examples.

I remember walking into a big lecture hall in Cambridge on the day on which judgment was delivered in the UK's challenge to the Working Time Directive (the

'WTD') (Case C-84/94).[7] I was junior counsel in that case, being led by Michael J. Beloff QC. The UK had argued that the WTD was invalidly based upon the EC Treaty provision (then, Article 118 EC Treaty) that promoted health and safety at work. The (Conservative) Government said that the WTD was really a wicked socialist measure, and that it should have been based on the Treaty legal basis that promoted social policy. Such a treaty base would have required unanimity in the Council, and the UK could and would have blocked it, whereas the health and safety legal base requires qualified majority voting ('QMV') and the UK did not manage to muster a blocking minority. So, we went along and argued that the Working Time Directive had nothing at all to do with health and safety. We searched around and found a professor willing to write an expert report for us. Even he couldn't bring himself to say there was no link between health and safety and working time; but he tried to say that there wasn't really sufficient material to establish a cast-iron link, and that all the relevant material hadn't been referred to in the Commission's explanatory memorandum accompanying the proposal for a directive. He then found out he had been sent to Coventry by all his academic colleagues. When we got around to drafting our reply to the Council's defence, our professor went missing. He was not prepared to produce further evidence for us. As to the substance of the case: there was one slight problem that we had overlooked. One of the very first sets of empirical data that connected excessive working time with health and safety problems were the studies of munitions workers carried out in the United Kingdom during the First World War. At the time there was, obviously, enormous demand from the Western Front for vast quantities of munitions. Workers were being encouraged to put in extra-long shifts and do their bit for Britain. Consequently, very tired people were handling explosive ingredients. Occasionally, when they were just too tired, they mixed the wrong powders together, or in the wrong proportions. Then there was a very big bang and, sadly, numerous casualties. The study was commissioned by the war government in the UK, not with any particular desire to be nice to workers, but out of concern that occasionally blowing up munitions factories was not good for the war effort. Those munitions studies undermined our central argument for annulment. On the day of the judgment, I walked into that lecture hall in Cambridge with a big fat grin on my face. By then the students kind of knew me and someone called out, commenting that I looked particularly cheerful that morning and asking if I had any news. 'Yes', I said, 'I do have news. I regret to inform you that the United Kingdom has just lost its challenge to the legality of the Working Time Directive'. There was a general howl of laughter in the lecture hall.

Adam: It was not your only encounter with the Working Time Directive, was it?

Eleanor: No, there was also *BECTU* (Broadcasting, Entertainment, Cinematographic and Theatre Union) (Case C-173/99).[8] At the time, a lot of jobs in the entertainment industry were based on 12-week contracts. The reason was that the government of the day had decided to implement the Working Time Directive in such a way that you only acquired your entitlement to annual leave after you had served a 'qualifying period' of 13 weeks. You might think that that was a bit strange, because Article 7 of the Working Time Directive begins with the words 'every worker' shall be entitled to a particular amount of leave. True, Article 7 ends with the words 'in accordance with the conditions laid down by national law', but it begins with 'Every worker …'. *BECTU* brought proceedings for judicial review in the High Court which, in turn, made a reference for a preliminary ruling to the European Court of Justice. I became involved after the reference had already been made. (It often happened that I was brought in to do the Luxembourg bit of a case, not having been instructed earlier in the national proceedings.) So, I bowled up in Luxembourg to argue that on closer inspection the words 'every worker' in Article 7 of the WTD do not actually mean 'every' worker. They mean that only that (smaller) subset of workers whom the UK has decided fulfil certain qualifying conditions imposed by national law shall be entitled to annual leave. That is a slightly counterintuitive argument, and (unsurprisingly!) I got a lot of questions from the Court. After the hearing, I went off to the Court canteen to have a bite of lunch. I had collected my food and picked up my tray, and I was sitting quietly at my table, when I became aware that at the table just behind me there was a group of judges who were also having their lunch.

Adam: It does not sound terribly serendipitous; I think I know where this is going …

Eleanor: Three of them were judges from the hearing I had just been in and they were regaling their colleagues with a description of the morning's proceedings. And they were saying something along the lines:

> **Judge 1:** *Do you remember that woman who used to work for Gordon Slynn?*
>
> **Others:** *Oh yes, Eleanor Sharpston. She was here as Gordon's référendaire for three years.*
>
> **Judge 1**: *Well, she turned up this morning to argue on behalf of the UK Government that the words 'every worker' do not mean every worker.*
>
> **Others:** *Ho-ho, ha-ha.*

Meanwhile, I am hastily finishing my lunch, and wondering if there is a way of getting out of the canteen invisibly – perhaps, by crawling discreetly under the tables towards the exit! As often happens, the judges were chewing the fat about that morning's hearing, and it was so obvious what they thought of the argument (not only those sitting in the case, but their colleagues too). Indeed, it had been obvious to me – when I got the brief – that the argument was not going to fly and indeed it did not.

Adam: Years ago I was fortunate to have many conversations with the late Professor Norbert Reich. We were both engaged in training the Estonian judiciary after EU accession and we spent tons of time together, in the classroom and in the Irish Vilde pub, in Tartu (a charming university town where the Estonian

Supreme Court is based). Somehow, one evening we ended up talking about *Cassis de Dijon* (Case 120/78).[9] I recall asking him who on earth would argue, as the German Government had in that case, that having stronger alcohol is actually pro-health. It simply did not make much sense to me back then, and decades later, it still does not. It turned out that Norbert knew the person who had pleaded, obviously without much conviction, in Luxembourg. His reply was: 'I had to say something, that was the brief.'

Eleanor: Thank you for that. I have also wondered who on earth could have thought that a national rule which says that you have to ensure a minimum alcohol content in a beverage is a rule that promotes public health (and can therefore be used to derogate from the principle of free movement of goods). That is, indeed, very like my 'every worker' brief in *BECTU*.

Adam: The European Court of Justice was not the only European court where you represented the United Kingdom. You were the first English barrister to plead in front of the newly established EFTA Court, in one of the first cases ever heard by that Court, and definitely the first in which the UK decided to intervene. That must have been an interesting experience.

Eleanor: It was certainly a voyage into the unknown. We had really no idea what the dynamic of that Court would be, or how serious they would be in terms of using the hearing to probe the quality of the arguments being advanced. The EFTA Court was a very young court with only a small number of judgments under its belt. Back then it was still based in Geneva: later, it moved to Luxembourg. The two cases (E-2/95 and E-3/95)[10] were on a topic – the Acquired Rights Directive – about which the UK at the time felt particularly strongly. I think the UK's position is easiest to understand by looking at the way in which that directive was implemented in national law: via the *Transfer of Undertakings (Protection of Employment) Regulations 1981*. Now, you might have thought that the focus ought to have been the other way around, because the Acquired Rights Directive is all about protecting employees in the event of a transfer of the undertaking for which they are working. So, if you had been reflecting that focus, you might perhaps have called the regulations the *Protection of Employees (Transfer of Undertakings) Regulations 1981*. Anyway, these two cases before the EFTA Court raised issues that were different slants of the emerging case law about the Acquired Rights Directive, and the UK wished to leave no stone unturned in constraining and limiting employees' rights. When they realised that those cases were being brought before the EFTA Court, they decided that they had to be there. Since I had already done some of the relevant cases before the Court of Justice, I was instructed.

Adam: It also gave you an opportunity to go back to Geneva, a city that meant a lot for your family.

Eleanor: It was a rather emotional moment. I had always thought of Geneva, the city where some of my childhood had been spent, in terms of going back home to see the family and being off duty. Suddenly there I was, very much on duty, as counsel for the UK.

Adam: As you were gearing up for the hearing, did you prepare like you always did before pleading in Luxembourg or was it something different?

Eleanor: Because I had no idea what was going to happen, I prepared everything (everything!) that I could possibly think of preparing. To quote a very dear friend of mine at the Bar, Bernard Richmond KC, the best advice for any barrister before going into court is 'be prepared, be very prepared' (which is, of course, a different 'take' on the Scouts' well-known motto). I have never been so pleased in my life to have over-prepared a case as I was for those cases in front of the EFTA Court. The three judges on the EFTA Court bench were absolutely into those cases (Bjorn Haug, Thor Vilhjâlmsson, and Carl Baudenbacher). They were deeply interested and they were like terriers. All three had clearly been through the file marking it up with highlighter pens and a red pencil. They must have scrawled various questions to ask in the margins of our written observations. I was delighted. It gave me the real opportunity to argue the cases properly, rather than come out of the hearing thinking: 'I wonder why they didn't ask about 'X' because, in their place, I would certainly have asked about it'. From my personal perspective as an advocate, they were really, really satisfying hearings. I am not sure the UK felt quite so satisfied because the arguments that we were putting forward were given a good old prod and a poke! But for me as an advocate, it was a really interesting experience; and the quality of the judgment that the EFTA Court delivered was also very good.

Adam: How did the courtroom look like? I guess it was not a proper one.

Eleanor: Basically, it was a meeting room that had been hastily converted into a courtroom. I mean, it was not a courtroom in the usual sense of that word: not a 'bespoke' courtroom.

Adam: What about the attire? Were the requirements similar to the European Court of Justice?

Eleanor: I remember that I went along sporting the full kit of an English barrister including the wig and, of course, wearing neatly polished shoes. I was somewhat disconcerted to find that counsel for Norway was wearing a gown over jeans and sneakers.

Adam: If my memory serves me well, Leo, these were the only two cases you did before the EFTA Court?

Eleanor: That's correct, Adam. Although I prepared the written pleadings for the UK in case E-3/05, I never got a further chance to plead a case orally before the EFTA Court.[11] During my time as an Advocate General at the CJEU, I had very good friends at the EFTA Court. I knew the judges. They tended to organise one-day conferences, to which I was always invited. I also referred to the jurisprudence of the EFTA Court in my Opinions. Relations were very, very cordial.

Adam: Talking about hearings and pleading in front of courts, I really adore the story of a boring hearing in a technical VAT case in which you represented the UK government at the European Court of Justice. In 2023, I had the pleasure of dining in Copenhagen with a group of lawyers, one of whom happened to have represented another Member State in that case. He remembered vividly how you were the first lawyer to plead after the lunch break (which is definitely the 'graveyard slot' for a pleader) and your acting skills proved to be quite useful. If I recall correctly, you approached the lectern and said something along the lines: 'my Lords, I have nothing to add to what my colleagues have pleaded, thank you'. You turned around and started going back to your seat, then, suddenly, turned around again, came back to the lectern and said: 'However, there is one point I should like to focus on'. Brilliant move, if I may say so. That must have woken up those on the bench. Where did that come from?

Eleanor: I think I was feeling mischievous that day. Sometimes you can be cheeky, right? Sometimes, of course, it can backfire horribly, but sometimes you should be cheeky. But you should be cheeky in a way that plays well in a multilingual and multicultural environment. For instance, you cannot do something that is dependent on making the joke in one language and hoping it can work before the CJEU.

Adam: Leo, this is a very valuable point for those who are pleading in Luxembourg these days and who will do so in the future.

Eleanor: One of my abiding memories, which is perhaps worth retelling to show how things may backfire spectacularly on the Kirchberg, goes back to my time as a *référendaire* at the Court – so, not a case that I was pleading. My judge, Sir Gordon Slynn, was the reporting judge. It was a case concerning dairy farmers, a reference for a preliminary ruling from the High Court in London. We got to question time, and Gordon was asking questions of counsel for the dairy farmer. I swear they had both forgotten that they were sitting in a courtroom in Luxembourg; mentally, they were back in the High Court in London. Gordon was asking the sort of questions that a high court judge would ask, and counsel was responding. Gordon asked a question, and there was a response from counsel; another question, and another response. Gordon asked a final question. Counsel answered the question. Then, he thought he would be clever and round off his reply neatly. So he said:

> *Indeed, my Lord: one might say, my Lord, that what is sauce for the goose is sauce for the gander, my Lord.*

Gordon smiled, and counsel smiled back, the way counsel always smile when they see that they have managed to say something that has pleased the judge. Everyone else was sitting there, holding the earpiece to their ear very patiently, waiting for the interpreters to explain what was the last thing that counsel had said. All the interpretation channels went silent. The interpreters were looking wildly at each other. What on earth did that mean and what do I say? Frankly, I don't blame them. Although it felt like an eternity, the silence did not last for that long. It was broken by the French interpreter. (French is – unofficially of course – the 'lead' language at the Court.) She was a very senior interpreter, and she was definitely not amused. She leant forward. She punched the button on her microphone with a certain viciousness; and in a voice so cold that it was about 30 degrees below absolute zero, she said: '*Il vient de raconter une blague sur la volaille*' ('He has just made a joke about poultry'). It was absolutely priceless, and she saved the day. Her colleagues gratefully translated exactly what she had said.

Adam: If we apply 'what they say, what they mean' principles here, she basically said: 'This was a joke, you were supposed to laugh!'

Eleanor: More likely: 'He has just made a really stupid joke about poultry. You should laugh now!' All the judges and the AG smiled as the message came through from their respective interpreters. Counsel smiled too, probably because he thought: 'well, it took a moment or two, but they got the point'. Actually, we were all laughing at him. What a total muppet. How could you possibly have thought that was a clever way to end your submissions in a multilingual court? My French is reasonably good, but I would not like to be put on the spot as to how you should translate that very English idiom 'what is sauce for the goose is sauce for the gander'. I seem to remember that one fowl is *l'oie* and the other fowl is *le jars*, but I would not necessarily remember that under pressure doing simultaneous interpretation. And in any case, if you translated it literally, what would it mean?

Adam: Such a trick would only work if you did a bit of research and figured out what the equivalents are, if any, in a few other languages. Even if so, one ought to give a fair warning to interpreters. Years ago the former Polish President Lech Wałęsa, during a state visit to Japan, compared Polish communists to radishes, red on the outside and white on the inside. His interpreter, having intelligently realised that Japanese radishes are all white, quickly changed radishes to shrimps.

Eleanor: That is something that you can do fairly readily as a translator of written pleadings, if you have time and leisure, if you are really curious, and if you want to try to convey exactly what is being said. There is almost no way that a simultaneous interpreter can do that, so all credit to that particular interpreter! The French interpreter in my story saved the day, but she was fuming. I think there was a kind of collective feeling on the Court side of the equation that she had every right to be so annoyed. What counsel had just done was ridiculous.

Adam: We are talking here about a particular member of the English Bar. Having said that, it is a well-known fact that common law lawyers, including the British and Irish judges as well as Advocates General at the Court of Justice, brought a bit of fresh air to the courtrooms in Luxembourg. Surely, they have introduced some sense of humour. Professor Laurence Gormley in his contribution to the book about the British Advocates General shared a story of AG Slynn showing his lighter side at the hearing in the famous *Conegate* case (Case 121/85).[12] The defendant in the UK proceedings was pleading a breach of free movement of goods when an imported consignment of pornographic materials was seized on public morality grounds by the UK customs authorities. The agent for the British government stated in open court that it was the first time he had seen such goods in his life. AG Slynn commented, somewhat *en passant*, that one should be careful what one says in the courtroom.

Eleanor: That sounds like just the sort of thing that Gordon would say. It is possible to liven up proceedings as an advocate. I remember doing one hearing for the UK brandishing a chunk of fruitcake. The case was about labelling, and we were saying: 'providing you label in a way that is clear to the consumer, that will solve the problem'. I had acquired the fruitcake at a French motorway service station, and it featured prominently at the hearing. I said to the Court: 'as you can see, this cake has got a big Union Jack flag on the packaging, and it is described as 'English fruitcake', but the label also in fact clearly says that this fruitcake was made in France. We can perhaps discuss the respective sizes of the various pieces of information on the label, but there is a clear indication that this cake was not made in the UK'. You can do things like that at a hearing and make your point effectively. But you cannot tell a joke in which the reference points are so country-specific that it won't go across.

There is also a more general point to be made here. Advocates who have English as their mother tongue, or who are pleading in English, are so lucky. They have such an advantage! If Finnish is your mother tongue, unless the Finnish judge happens to be sitting, nobody is going to be listening to you in the original. Whereas, if you have English as your mother tongue, if you plead clearly and attractively, there are two big bonus points. First, the percentage of what you say that the interpreters will get and will interpret correctly will go up from, perhaps, 75% to 98%. Second, because many members of the Court speak English, if you are really clear in what you are saying, a number of them will listen to you in English rather than listening to the interpretation. However good the interpreter may be (and there are some fabulously good interpreters who work for the Court) – as an advocate, I would like you to listen to me, please. I want you to have my voice in your ear, not the voice of the interpreter.

Adam: Sometimes when I teach overseas and I do know that I will use idioms, I check with interpreters beforehand, asking if they have equivalents in the language they will interpret my words into. Otherwise, one can easily get into trouble. Of course, delivering a lecture is one thing; it is quite another to plead where every single word matters. Luckily, in Europe it is no longer a matter of life and death, yet being lost in translation is never a desired state.

Eleanor: Making friends with the interpreters by treating them decently is very important. Of course, you should do that anyway out of respect for a fellow professional. But at a purely mercenary level, the interpreters will be so pleased if you treat them respectfully and check in with them before you get going. You are working in partnership with them. If I am in Lithuania giving a conference speech to an audience that is mainly not fluent in English, I am entirely dependent on the interpreters to get across whatever my message may be. It makes sense at every level, from the strictly practical to the more, perhaps, moral and idealistic, to behave decently to the interpreters.

Adam: These are very insightful words of advice, Leo. You have obviously spent a lot of time and in various capacities in the courtrooms at Kirchberg plateau. In hindsight, it is quite clear that the azimuth was Luxembourg. Looking back at the early days when you were a *référendaire*, and later when you were representing the UK, was there any point where you thought that you could return to the Court and join the bench?

Eleanor: In a way, I never really left the Court. I never fell out of touch with the Court, because I was always coming back to do new cases.

Did I ever think that I could go back for good and become a Member of the Court? Let's go back in time to the day in early September 1990 when I finished working as a *référendaire* for Sir Gordon Slynn. I am sitting on a very overloaded motorbike, my main mode of transport. I have tied all my worldly possessions that haven't already gone into the removals van onto the motorbike. I have been working for Gordon up to the very last minute, getting stuff finished and all loose ends tied down. It is late evening. I am just about to drive overnight from Luxembourg to London so that I am available to start teaching at 9 am the following morning at UCL, my new workplace. I remember coming out of the Court, stopping the motorbike, looking back a little wistfully at the Court building, and engaging in an inner dialogue between Leo-the-dreamer and Leo-the-realist:

> **Leo-the-dreamer:** *It would be so amazing if I ever got the opportunity to come back here as an Advocate General …*
>
> **Leo-the-realist:** *Oh Leo, stop being stupid! Come on, this is NOT the moment for daydreaming!*
>
> **Leo-the-dreamer:** *I said it would be so amazing if I could come back as … one day … one day.*
>
> **Leo-the-realist:** *Don't be a total idiot. You are just daydreaming, that's not going to happen. Come on! You now need to get back to the UK, start your academic career,*

> *somehow restart your practice at the Bar. Come on! Pigs don't fly! You're not going to come back, now get on with it.*

I really did have that moment. Note, I said 'come back as an Advocate General'. I didn't say 'Gosh, I would like to come back as the British judge'.

Adam: Years passed since that day but in 2005 the opportunity arose when AG Francis Jacobs announced his intention to retire from the Court.

Eleanor: When Francis announced that he was retiring, and the post of the British Advocate General was advertised in *The Times* newspaper, I thought it was too early for me. I thought I didn't stand a chance. I was not well enough known in the UK, I was a woman, and – perhaps – I was too young. I also knew that it was going to be so painful. They would pick somebody, and then whoever they picked would stay in post for years and years, just like Francis. Initially I wasn't going to apply. Then I got kicked into it by two good female friends.

Adam: And the rest, as they say, is history. Do you remember what you put in your motivation letter when you eventually decided to apply?

Eleanor: Fortunately, perhaps, I didn't have too long to think about that. I decided to apply very much at the last moment, at about eight o'clock in the evening on the day before the deadline for applications at noon. That doesn't give you limitless leisure to suck your electronic pen and wonder what you are going to put into the application. The first thing was, of course, to dig out a CV. Naturally I did not have anything like an up-to-date CV to hand. By the time I hunted down an old one on my computer, added to it, polished it, and made it sound more impressive than it really was, there was not all that much time left. So, I wrote a very short covering letter saying that the job of Advocate General was important because you were there to try to assist the Court in hard cases; and that I had seen it from the position of *référendaire* to Sir Gordon Slynn. Hence, I had some idea what the post of Advocate General involved; and it would be a very great honour to be considered for the job in the front office. I filled a page. I didn't say anything that was very inspired. I think, if I had been marking my letter for advocacy, I would have described it as competent, no more. Then I had to get my application in. By the time I had the CV and the cover letter ready, it was well past midnight. Fortunately, I was physically in London; but I was due to teach the following morning at 9 am in Cambridge.

Adam: This sounds very tight indeed. I guess back then in 2005 you did not submit such an application online, it had to be a hard copy that had to be lodged physically in a designated place. Since you had to teach at 9 am in Cambridge and in London courier services are not exactly easily available in the middle of the night, I guess Leo had to multitask.

Eleanor: Remember that in my early years at the Bar I too worked as a motorcycle courier. So I knew some of the tricks of the trade. If you are couriering a document during the night to a large law firm or a government department, there is always some unfortunate soul who is the nightwatchman. The building is never actually fully closed. If you have something to deliver out of hours, you can in fact always deliver it and get it signed for. Of course, you won't exactly be popular with the nightwatchman because you are going to wake her or him up. On the plus side, though, you will be able to get a signature showing that the document was duly delivered. Having the benefit of insider knowledge, I organised myself very correctly and carefully. I had a clipboard and, clipped to it, there was a list with a number of (imaginary) jobs that had already been signed off for. Then there was the 'next job', namely delivering this particular letter to a government building right by the Admiralty Arch. And then there were more jobs for later in my shift. I put on my helmet and my leather jacket; and I got onto my bike. Naturally I needed to carry a bag which (presumably) had in it the other envelopes and small parcels that I would be delivering later. I slung a suitable bag over my shoulder – I think I padded it out with a pullover to make it look as though it were full – and I drove to my destination address. I parked the bike right outside on the double yellow line (as any motorcycle courier would!), went up to the deliveries door, and rang the bell. To be more accurate, I put my thumb on the bell and I left it there. I could hear the bell ringing inside. Eventually, of course, the nightwatchman came out, swearing at me because I had indeed woken him up. I learned some new words! And then I got down to business:

> **Leo-the-courier:** *Yeah, look, I'm sorry mate.*
>
> *You know how it is.*
>
> *There's always some f***ing idiot who thinks he needs to have something delivered overnight and we get it as a rush job.*
>
> *Like I said, sorry mate.*
>
> *Here's the sodding letter I'm meant to deliver.*
>
> *Just sign for it here, would you?*
>
> [So the nightwatchman duly scribbled on the clipboard.]
>
> **Leo-the-courier:** *Cheers, mate.*
>
> *You go back to sleep.*
>
> *Take care now.*

I got back on my motorbike and drove away. Job done. The motorcycle courier went back home and had – probably – a couple of hours of sleep. Then I drove the motorbike up to Cambridge and taught my 9–11 am LLM class. At 11.05am I telephoned the government department. At that stage of course I was no longer a motorcycle courier, I was Eleanor Sharpston QC, with a very upper-class professional accent:

> **Eleanor Sharpston QC:** *Hello, good morning.*
>
> **Government department:** *Oh yes, hello. How can I help you?*
>
> **Eleanor Sharpston QC:** *I wonder if I could just check something with you please?*
>
> *I've decided to put my hat in the ring for the job in Luxembourg that's been advertised. I had to arrange for my application form to be brought around to you out of hours. The courier company tells me that it was signed for; but I should like just to check with you that you have received it safely. Perhaps you could look for me?*
>
> *Thank you so much.*
>
> [after a pause]
>
> **Government department:** *Yes, Miss Sharpston. I can confirm that it has been delivered.*

Knowing that my application had been safely received before the deadline, I thanked them prettily and hung up.

Adam: That was the easy bit, wasn't it? Then came the interview.

Eleanor: Before that happened, they had to sift the applications down, first to a long shortlist, then to a short shortlist of six people. I was, by that stage, getting more and more gloomy about my prospects. All of us who were the candidates thought we knew that although the job had been advertised, it was in fact earmarked for one particular person who was one of the shortlist of six, and who would indeed have been a perfectly obvious candidate to pick. The rest of us wondered a little whether this was a real competition or whether it was what the French call a *concours bidon*. Since I was the only woman and a rather young candidate, I became more and more convinced that I really was there just to make up the numbers, to make sure there was appropriate gender diversity. I felt I stood no chance at all. And I remember thinking to myself:

> *It is really going to hurt if they call you for an interview. And then of course, they're going to tell you you haven't got the job.*

I knew that my only chance lay in doing the interview of my life.

Adam: Then the day of the interview arrived. It must have gone really well, it was the interview of your life, wasn't it?

Eleanor: Earlier that morning, shortly before the interview, I had coffee with one of my law students from King's. She had recently done her Bar exams and she was going for a pupillage interview that same morning. She and I were really a pair. I am not sure which of us was the more downbeat about our chances. We swapped negative vibes over coffee and then we went our separate ways.

The Foreign and Commonwealth Office was not particularly well organised about conducting the interview. We were, of course, not meant to know who the other people on the shortlist were. Yet they parked us in an open hall area where the candidates could see each other as we went in and out. The candidate before me coming out, I knew. The candidate behind me who was waiting, I knew. We smiled at each other and we courteously wished each other 'good luck'.

Adam: Do you remember who was on the panel?

Eleanor: The interview panel was chaired by a member of the House of Lords. It had a couple of senior civil servants from each of the main ministries involved: the Ministry of Justice because this was a judicial appointment, and the Foreign and Commonwealth Office because it was a 'foreign' job. In addition, there was a very pleasant woman who was there to represent civil society. Unlike the other members of the panel, she was not a lawyer. She was the CEO of a very large NHS hospital trust.

Adam: If she were not a lawyer, what was her role in the proceedings?

Eleanor: Her function really was to be there to see what was going on, but also – if she felt like it – to ask different questions. In fact, the only question I really remember clearly from that interview was her question to me. Obviously, there were lots of the usual questions about EU law, but the only question that has stayed in my memory is hers.

Adam: Interesting! What did she ask?

Eleanor: She leant forward, looked at me with a very charming smile, and said:

> *Miss Sharpston, if you were to get this job, you would have a small team working with you at the Court. What do you think would be important?*

I could have hugged her. I looked at her and I said:

> *Thank you so much for that question. It seems to me that the answer is actually a simple one.*
>
> *I would need to create a working environment within that team that meant that any member of the team, however junior, could tell me that I was wrong. Because that team would be for me – as an Advocate General – the only safety net, my only bulwark against making a complete fool of myself by missing some important precedent, or trying to argue that water runs uphill when actually it doesn't.*
>
> *So what would matter above all things would be to make sure that within the team, people knew that they were completely free to speak up, that they were expected to speak up, and that there would be no reward for saying:*
>
> *'Advocate General, the sun rises in the west? Advocate General – that is an astonishingly brilliant discovery. We had not previously realised that the sun rises in the west; but of course now that you have pointed it out, it must be so.'*

She looked at me, smiled, and said:

> *'Thank you, I don't have any further questions'.*

I came away from that interview knowing that I had left everything out there on the field. I had given everything that I had. I did not know if it was good enough, but I knew that I had tried my absolute best.

Adam: Then the horrible suspense, they never tell you whether you got the job or not at the interview or immediately thereafter.

Eleanor: Then there was silence. Complete silence. We overshot the deadline that had been announced. The waiting went on, for weeks after the deadline. Meanwhile, the various candidates kept on bumping into each other. After all, we were all in the same profession – worse, in the same specialist area of the profession. I met my academic colleagues at conferences, I met my practitioner colleagues going in and out of the Royal Courts of Justice. We would greet each other. Then we would sidle across and have a swift, discreet chat:

> *Have you heard anything?*
>
> *No, not a word. You?*
>
> *Same.*
>
> *Very strange, isn't it?*
>
> *Very strange.*
>
> *Oh, well, very nice to see you.*

Then we would go our separate ways thinking: 'I wonder if he/she is lying to me. I wonder if she/he knows something'. That was a very, very uncomfortable time.

Adam: They did put you out of your misery at some point, but it took a while, didn't it?

Eleanor: We were meant to know the outcome by mid-June. We went all the way through July without news. The decision finally came through in mid-August. I was away from London by then. I was up at my home in Wales. I was in the courtyard of the house, tinkering with a petrol strimmer that was misbehaving. It was a lovely morning and I was swearing at the strimmer. I had grease all over my hands when the phone rang. I rubbed my hands down a bit on my jeans, went inside, and picked up the call. On the phone I discovered that I had the female equivalent of Sir Humphrey, a very senior female civil servant. She had phoned my chambers in London and stated that she wished to speak to me. Since obviously I was not there, my senior clerk had given her my contact phone number in Wales. The next five minutes were hysterical.

> **Civil servant:** *Excuse me Sir, I need to speak to Eleanor Sharpston QC.*
>
> **Eleanor Sharpston QC:** *Absolutely no problem, you are speaking to her.*
>
> **Civil servant:** *No, Sir. I must speak directly to Eleanor Sharpston QC.*

I tried (initially, unsuccessfully) several ways of explaining to her that she had Eleanor Sharpston QC on the other end of the telephone line; and would she please tell me what she wanted to talk to me about. Those were the days before video phone calls on mobiles and Skype was young. I am not sure what would have happened if we had been using a video link, because I looked pretty scruffy and much like a workman trying to fix a strimmer. I nearly rang off. Anyway, slightly to my surprise, I did eventually manage to convince her that there was not an alternative Eleanor Sharpston QC to whom she could speak. She then produced the most wonderful, Sir Humphreyesque sentence:

> *I am directed to inform you that the Lord Chancellor* [pause for genuflection] *and the Foreign Secretary* [pause for further genuflection] *have indicated that – subject to the following conditions* [she listed 10 or 12 conditions] *– they are minded to recommend to the Prime Minister that you be considered favourably for nomination as the United Kingdom's candidate to serve as an Advocate General at the European Court of Justice in Luxembourg.*

By the time she was about halfway through that sentence, I was no longer breathing. I was just hanging on wondering whether by any extraordinary chance it was going to end the way I hoped it was. Obviously, I gave her at once some of the additional material that she wanted, and I promised her that I would send her the other material required to prove that I had never been convicted of a crime and that I did not regularly commit frauds. I remember putting down the phone at the end of the conversation, and going back to the garden. You already know what happened next: tears of joy that I was going back home to the Court and to Luxembourg.

Adam: You mentioned earlier that you and four other candidates felt that the remaining candidate was, so to speak, in pole position. Yet at the end of the day, you were chosen. Do you have any insights as to what happened, what were the decisive factors?

Eleanor: Sir David Edward, a former British judge at the CJEU who has been for many years both a friend and a mentor, phoned me up shortly afterwards. We both knew that my nomination would probably ruffle a few feathers. For the very first time, the UK was nominating a woman and I wasn't the obvious candidate. David told me that there were a couple of things that I should know. First, I had indeed not been the preferred candidate going into the interviews, but I got the nomination at the interview. That's what turned it around. Second, the recommendation from the interview panel was a unanimous recommendation. David wanted me to know that, in case people started scratching at me. That was immensely kind of him.

ENDNOTES

[*] Cambridge, January 2024.

[1] Graham Butler and Adam Łazowski (eds), *Shaping EU Law the British Way. UK Advocates General at the Court of Justice of the European Union* (Hart, 2022).

[2] Case C-3/91 *Exportur SA v LOR SA and Confiserie du Tech SA* ECLI:EU:C:1992:420.

[3] *Convention pour la protection les appellations d'origine, des indications de provenance et des dénominations de certains produits*, Journal Officiel de la République Française, 18.04.1975, p. 4011.

[4] Graham Butler, 'An Advocate before Advocate General: Eleanor Sharpston at the European Courts' in Catherine Barnard, Adam Łazowski, Daniel Sarmiento (eds), *Pursuit of Legal Harmony in a Turbulent Europe. Essays in Honour of Eleanor Sharpston* (Hart, 2024).

[5] Council Directive 93/104/EC of 23 November 1993 concerning certain aspects of the organization of working time [1993] OJ L 307/18.

[6] Adam Łazowski, 'Throwing the Cat among the Pigeons: from Pabst and Kupferberger to Prohibition of Direct Effect of EU Neighbourhood Agreements' in Catherine Barnard, Adam Łazowski, Daniel Sarmiento (eds), *Pursuit of Legal Harmony in a Turbulent Europe. Essays in Honour of Eleanor Sharpston* (Hart, 2024).

[7] Case C-84/94 *United Kingdom of Great Britain and Northern Ireland v Council of the European Union* ECLI:EU:C:1996:431.

[8] Case C-173/99 *The Queen v Secretary of State for Trade and Industry, ex parte Broadcasting, Entertainment, Cinematographic and Theatre Union (BECTU)* ECLI:EU:C:2001:356.

[9] Case 120/78 *Rewe-Zentral AG v Bundesmonopolverwaltung für Branntwein* ECLI:EU:C:1979:42.

[10] Case E-2/95 *Ellert Eidesund v Stavanger Catering A/S* [1995-1996] EFTA Court Report 1 and Case E-3/95 *Torgeir Langeland v Norske Fabricom A/S* [1995-1996] EFTA Court Report 38.

[11] Case E-3/05 *EFTA Surveillance Authority v Kingdom of Norway* [2006] EFTA Court Report 104.

[12] Case 121/85 *Conegate Limited v HM Customs & Excise* ECLI:EU:C:1986:114.

5

Advocate General Sharpston

Being an AG at the Court is
the best job on the planet for an EU lawyer.
Despite the pressures and imperfections [...]
that remains emphatically the case.
I was lucky enough to have that dream job,
into which I could put my heart and my soul
*and all my energy, for 14 and a half years.**

Adam: 'So, you are the British Advocate General, jolly good, jolly good. In which regiment do you serve, eh?' This is not a quote from one of the comedy shows on the BBC but rather an actual question that Eleanor Sharpston was asked by an elderly gentleman who happened to be attending the same social function as she was. As funny as it sounds to anyone *au courant* with EU law, it is hardly surprising, unless someone comes from one of those rare jurisdictions where Advocates General have a role to play in the judicial process. As far as EU law is concerned, the origins of AGs can be traced to the French *commissaire de gouvernement*, who is a person providing independent opinions to the benefit of the *Conseil d'Etat*. The EU equivalent is not exactly a carbon copy of the French system, however many similarities remain. So, who is then an Advocate General at the Court of Justice? Well, the AG is neither an advocate, nor a general. An Advocate General is a Member of the Court with the same status as the judges, whose task is to provide an independent Opinion in a difficult pending case. Strictly speaking, the opinions are there to help the judges who are sitting in a given case come up with a well-reasoned judgment. Opinions are not binding, so the judges do not have to follow what the Advocate General has proposed. Knowing this basic, yet important fact, one should be excused for asking a fundamental question: why bother then? Why have Advocates General altogether if their Opinions are merely advisory?

There are a number of reasons why having Advocates General is a very good idea indeed. To begin with, there is a much broader audience for Opinions of Advocates General than just the judges sitting in a case. Thanks to the fact that Opinions are made available to the public (and as a bonus, in all official languages of the European Union), the 'consumers' of AGs' work are more numerous than one would initially anticipate. To begin with, there is the CJEU itself. The Opinion that an Advocate General presents in one case may well radiate further. For instance, it may well be that an AG is ahead of her/his time and an Opinion that was not followed in the case in which it was presented may rise like a phoenix from the ashes at a later point. An Opinion may also persuade or inspire other Advocates General or judges working on other cases. Then there are the worlds of legal practice and academia, which both benefit from the work of Advocates General. It does not require a vivid imagination to picture lawyers using arguments and reasoning borrowed from Opinions of AGs, or academics employing the work of AGs in their teaching, conference speeches or publications.

For Eleanor Sharpston, being an Advocate General was – in her own words – her 'dream job'. She was finally dealing with her beloved EU law in a full time capacity and at the institution she knew so well, and towards which she felt such affection and loyalty. She was home.

*

Adam: The UK government's nomination decision was taken in late summer of 2005. However, it would take another six months before you were sworn in. Back in 2005, that is before the Treaty of Lisbon, the selection of judges and Advocates General was largely in the hands of the individual Member States. Nominations would be put on the table of the Council which, in turn, would take unanimous decisions on appointments. The latter, though, would be a *fait accompli*. Back then there was no Article 255 Committee to grill the candidates (and in some instances, shish-kebab them). Still, your investiture had to wait until early January 2006. What happened in the meantime?

Eleanor: Well, I had to start putting *cabinet Sharpston* together. I knew for a fact that one of the other possible candidates for the job had made it known publicly that if he were successful, he would make a clean sweep. He wouldn't keep any people from Francis Jacob's *cabinet* because he didn't want his predecessor's 'leftovers'. I had diametrically the opposite approach. Francis obviously had a very good, well-balanced and well-organised team that knew the job of how to write good Opinions inside out. I had been at the Court before but now I was going to be coming in and learning how to do the job in the front office.

Adam: That is a very interesting point, Leo. Unlike many others before or after you, you had a particular advantage at the start line. You had worked at the Court of Justice before. In a way, history had repeated itself as Francis Jacobs had been a *référendaire* with the first British Advocate General, Jean-Pierre Warner, and then he became an Advocate General himself. Did your experience as a *référendaire* to Sir Gordon Slynn prepare you for your time as an Advocate General? Did it actually make it easier for you to get going from day one?

Eleanor: Certainly having been a *référendaire* made it much easier, because I knew how the Court worked, although obviously it had changed, grown, and developed in the intervening years. Furthermore, I had never been out of touch with the Court, because – as we've already discussed – I kept coming back to plead cases before the Court. Whenever I returned to do a case, I did *not* catch the lunchtime flight back to the United Kingdom. I deliberately stayed on until the evening. I wandered around and saw old friends. I wanted to keep my finger on the pulse: to hear what people were talking about, what was going on. So, I never actually lost contact with the Court between when I finished as a *référendaire* and when I went back as an Advocate General. Obviously, knowing how the Court works, and having served with an Advocate General in the past were very useful. Still, working in the front office was going to be a different kettle of fish to being a *référendaire*.

Adam: So, at the end of the day, did you manage to keep Francis's team?

Eleanor: I did. I badly wanted the whole team to stay on for me. I was worried that because the whole nomination process in the UK had dragged on and on, I was likely to lose some of the members. Very understandably, not knowing what was happening, they were likely to start looking after themselves and hunt for alternative employment.

Adam: Wouldn't a quick call to Francis and a meeting with his team be an option? That would have been the easiest fix, wouldn't it?

Eleanor: In theory, sure. That would have been the most natural thing to do. The problem was that Francis had been told who his successor was, but he had also been sworn to secrecy. He couldn't contact me. And I had been told that I couldn't contact Francis unless I happened to bump into him.

Adam: Oh, that surely made matters more complicated. Having said that, serendipitous 'bumpings into' are not unheard of.

Eleanor: I managed to get around that problem by turning up in Luxembourg for a farewell party for one of Gordon's former assistants. So I organised 'bumping into' Francis in Luxembourg, the way I sometimes do organise 'bumping into' people. Once I was inside his office, we could speak:

> **Eleanor:** *Hello Francis! I know you had a phone conversation with a senior civil servant called Martin. I know he told you some things. And (conspiratorially) I know that you know that I know.*
>
> [Poor Francis, he was so embarrassed. He got up at once and came around his desk.]
>
> **Francis:** *Eleanor, I'm so sorry. I wanted to phone you at once to congratulate you but I was told I couldn't contact you unless we happened to bump into each other.*
>
> **Eleanor:** *Yes Francis, that's why I am in your office now. Please, say to everyone in your team that you have spoken with your successor, and that your successor has made it clear that they absolutely want everyone in the team to stay on. Please tell them that they have no need to start thinking about other jobs as you know that your successor wants them!*

I was really worried. I needed and wanted a fully operational team that knew how the job was done. A team that knew all the stuff inside the Court, a team that knew how to get high quality Opinions out through the door in the right way. I didn't care if they were Francis's team – on the contrary. They had obviously done such good work with Francis. I was sure they were professional enough that they would be prepared to give me a chance and to work with me. They were excellent.

Adam: On 10 January 2006, a very solemn ceremony took place at the Court of Justice: an '*audience solonnelle*' at which, in accordance with well-established custom, you were sworn in as an Advocate General. As we have seen in the previous chapter, you had come a long way from 1990 and that moment of daydreaming on the motorbike as you left the Court, to the appointment to the bench on the *Plateau de Kirchberg*. How did the first days in your dream job look like? Was it a smooth introduction or did it look like your first days as *référendaire* for Sir Gordon Slynn, running at full speed from the moment you entered the Court building?

Eleanor: History repeated itself, Adam. In fact, my work began before my first official day at the office because the Court had stockpiled Francis's cases. The first weeks at the Court really passed in a blur. I took over all the cases that Francis had in his docket. There were a number of cases which were (frankly) overdue to be heard, but where Francis obviously would not have had time to sit in a hearing and then write up an Opinion before he retired. I was sworn in on Tuesday 10 January 2006 at 6 pm, and I sat in my first hearing as an Advocate General on Thursday 12 January 2006 at 9:30 am. Fortunately, Francis had quietly given me a copy file with all the documents in that case. Otherwise, it would have been impossible to have been on top of the case in time for the hearing. So, I came into work on the morning of Wednesday 11 January 2006 having already read the papers. I grabbed the *référendaire* whose case it was and we got straight down to business:

> *Please can we talk through everything and what's happened so far?*
>
> *How far have you got with preliminary ideas … with initial drafting?*
>
> *Can you tell me something about each of the judges who are sitting in this chamber, especially the reporting judge?*
>
> *Tell me, tell me, tell me.*
>
> *Please give me the necessary information so that I don't look as green as I'm going to feel when I walk into court tomorrow morning.*

Now you understand fully how important it was to keep Francis's team. They were efficient and sensible people. They had taken every case as far forward as they could. That meant – thank God! – that when we had each hearing (and it really was one hearing, sometimes two hearings, a week for the first six weeks),

I had in place all that I needed to get all those cases launched again and back on track. My *référendaires* were wonderful. They had got everything tee'd up and ready.

Adam: So, you operated on full throttle from day one, even before that. Not to mention that you had really big shoes to fill. AG Francis Jacobs had been an excellent and long-serving Advocate General, everyone knew him and his work. That, in itself, must have been intimidating.

Eleanor: Let me put it this way. I still had to find a house to live in. I was staying in a little studio bedsit, a bit like the room that you have as a first-year student in college. Symbolically, that was entirely appropriate. I felt very new, very inexperienced. Yes, I knew the Court from being a *référendaire*; but it is very different coming back and being a Member. I was running flat out to try to get on top of everything. It wasn't a soft landing. And of course, I was acutely conscious of the fact that AG Francis Jacobs had an immense reputation as an Advocate General – and I was there as his successor.

Adam: I recall that in your afterword to the book about the British Advocates General you shared a story about a diplomatic reception you attended in Luxembourg in mid 2006.

Eleanor: Ah yes … I was introduced to a group of lawyers at that reception as 'the British Advocate General at the Court'. Their unanimous response was 'You can't be – that's Francis Jacobs'.

Adam: When you joined the Court, the British judge had (until recently) been Sir David Edward. Knowing David, how kind and professional he is, he must have offered a helping hand and words of wisdom during your first months at the Court.

Eleanor: Absolutely and I am forever grateful for that. David supported me all the way through, including when I got the nomination to go to Luxembourg. He gave me direct and very useful advice on how to assist the Court as an Advocate General: essentially, 'Get in there and help! Dissect the problem, lay out the options, and explain why you are recommending one solution rather than another'. Some of the advice was, of course, spiced with David's typical sense of humour. I recall him briefly explaining the difference between the Advocates General and the judges: 'the Advocates General bark, we judges bite!' And I was lucky enough already to know Sir Konrad Schiemann, who was the British judge when I arrived at the Court in 2006. He too was kindness itself in helping me to settle in.

Adam: So the starting point for Advocate General Sharpston was hectic but your prior experience, combined with friendly faces around, made it slightly easier than it would have been otherwise. But let me ask you this. While your prior experience in Luxembourg was helpful, the Court had evolved in the meantime.

Was it a completely different animal in 2006 compared to the turn of 1980s and 1990s?

Eleanor: Well, it was and it wasn't; that is what was so surreal. Obviously it was a different animal in the sense that it was a much bigger animal. When I was at the Court as a *référendaire*, the entire personnel of the Court probably numbered about 600 people. When I went back to the Court, it was not far short of 2000 people. That's already a big difference.

Adam: Indeed. This was already after the 2004 Big Bang enlargement and a series of major reforms of the EU founding treaties that were approved and entered into force in the meantime. So, the calibre of cases was completely different.

Eleanor: The obvious illustration is that when I was at the Court as a *référendaire*, there were lots of internal market cases: free movement of goods, or freedom of establishment, or free movement of workers. By the time I went back to the Court, very few cases had anything to do with the single market, whereas a lot of cases involved the Area of Freedom, Security and Justice ('AFSJ'). Much of the AFSJ legislation was, typically, put together after a late-night compromise by a group of representatives of Member States who had all arrived in Brussels with red lines in their briefcases. The final text adopted had usually moved on a long way from the Commission's original draft, which may indeed have respected the official drafting guidelines. The Member States' different red lines frequently affected the process of negotiations and the way the legislation was agreed. The trouble is that you do not change legislation for the better if you knock off all the sharp edges in the draft (sometimes, entire corners were excised too!) because they give offence to somebody. So, you might well be left with a text which typically had preambular recitals proclaiming contradictory objectives, and substantive provisions which didn't have key definitions. Such legislation begs to be tested at national level by enterprising lawyers seeking to advance their clients' cause, and a national judge looking at a text that is – frankly – a bit of a mess will often, wisely, make a reference for a preliminary ruling.

Adam: One of those areas was EU criminal law and, in the early days, the expertise at the Court in this particular area of law was scarce, wasn't it?

Eleanor: That's an understatement. The long-serving Danish judge Lars Bay Larsen (we joined the Court on the same day; and he was later the Court's Vice-President) and my late lamented colleague Advocate General Yves Bot both had a genuine criminal law background. To my embarrassment, I also got classified as somebody who knew a bit about criminal law, on the strength of nothing more than the fact that I had done a few criminal law cases as a baby barrister, that I had defended in *Brown and others*, and had prosecuted the 'Metric Martyr' in *Thoburn v Sunderland*. As we discussed earlier, these were both big and widely reported UK cases, so the assumption was that – obviously – I must have done a significant amount of criminal law in the course of my practice at the Bar. Honestly, that was stretching the truth. But yes, you are right. The arrival of criminal law has added a rather new flavour to the Court of Justice and its work.

Adam: As someone once said, everything is constant except change. We will come back to the areas of EU law covered in your Opinions a little later. For now, let us not travel too fast and stay a bit longer in your early months at the Court as an Advocate General. We know by now that you were not phased in gently into the new role. Still, I should like to ask you if, when writing your first Opinions, you spent a lot of time thinking how to express yourself. Unlike judges, Advocates General have a fair amount of freedom to write anything they wish and how they wish.

Eleanor: Funnily enough no, this is not what I did. Remember, I had been in practice at the Bar and I had been writing opinions in an English context for twenty-five years. I had drafted Opinions for Gordon when he was an Advocate General; and I had read a lot of Francis's Opinions. In the English context, I have always admired Lord Denning for the beautiful directness of his prose. I don't necessarily agree with everything that Lord Denning said in his later judicial career, but I have always thought that his judgments were a wonderful illustration of how to explain to somebody reading your text what a case is all about.

Your question, Adam, touches upon something very important. Being an Advocate General gives you immense freedom. That is a real privilege and an advantage but it also carries with it serious responsibility. You are the sole author. The Court writes judgments by committee. The *juge rapporteur* (the reporting judge) is trying to generate a text that (s)he can get through the *délibéré* by consensus. Obviously, to do that you make compromises. There will be ambiguities. There will be passages that are not as clear as they might be, because that was the price of agreement in the *délibéré*. An Advocate General should never be ambiguous. The only person who has to make up their mind about what to say is the author of the Opinion: the Advocate General. You can discuss, indeed you should discuss, the text with your *référendaire* but, at the end of the day, you are going to make up your mind and say what you want to say. Whatever you say should be absolutely crystal clear. Unlike judges, you don't have to negotiate – but there is also no hiding place.

One thing was certain. I wanted to make sure that I sounded like myself. Obviously, I couldn't write sounding like Francis because I am not Francis. Sounding like myself involves changes of pace, short sentences; sometimes it involves metaphors, images, analogies. And it involves a sense of humour.

Adam: These sound like essential ingredients of a good Opinion of an Advocate General, though implementing them in some very technical cases may be a challenge. One also needs to avoid getting lost in translation. We have already spoken about this a little. What works in one official language of the European Union may not necessarily work in another.

Eleanor: I remember one of my early cases, *Commission v Greece* (Case C-251/04),[1] which arose because Greek law limited being the captain of a seagoing tug to Greek nationals. For some reason, which was and still is entirely unclear to me, the European Commission had pleaded the case against Greece exclusively under the maritime transport regulation. They could, and I think should, have pleaded it – in the alternative – under the Treaty itself. What was happening was, unquestionably, blatant discrimination on grounds of nationality. But the Commission had chosen to plead only breach of the maritime transport regulation. So, was the service provided by a seagoing tug a maritime transport service? If so, the regulation applied and the Greek rules were unlawful. In my Opinion, I argued that seagoing tugs do not provide a transportation service and, therefore, the regulation did not apply. The Court agreed. To make my point stronger, and because of the way that I think about problems, I decided to give an example. I imagined a tanker carrying a cargo of oil that lost engine power somewhere to the south of the Lizard Point in Cornwall. With words I drew a vivid picture of the helpless vessel and its captain on the radio, pleading for help. I carefully organised the scene so that the swell, the set of the tide and the prevailing wind were all pushing this unfortunate vessel towards inevitable shipwreck on the Lizard. I warned of the consequences should she hit the Lizard: possibly loss of life, certainly an environmental disaster. The key question was: if a seagoing tug arrives and rescues the tanker by towing her away from the Lizard, is that tug (as such) providing transportation services? These were the relevant points of the Opinion:

> *45. Towage does not generally entail straightforward carriage of goods or passengers by sea. Rather, it involves assisting the movement of a vessel, rig, platform or buoy. […] As a general rule, the purpose served by towage services is different from that served by the forms of maritime cabotage expressly listed and defined in Article 2(1).*
>
> *46. An illustration will serve to make the point more clearly. Imagine an oil tanker with engine failure lying five nautical miles southwest of the Lizard [..] with a southerly force 4 wind, a sou'westerly swell and the tide setting up-Channel. The tanker's captain would, unquestionably, radio requesting towage services from at least one seagoing tug as a matter of urgency so as to avoid risking the lives of her crew, the loss of her cargo, damage to her hull and any consequent environmental harm. Such towage would certainly be necessary to enable the vessel to complete her voyage safely and transport her cargo of oil to its destination. It would not normally, however, be regarded as 'transport' either of the oil or of the tanker. A towing vessel that is assisting another vessel to manoeuvre, or supplementing that vessel's own propulsive machinery, or substituting for it in cases of failure or breakdown, is assisting the vessel by which the passengers or goods are transported. It is not itself the transporting vessel.*

Two takeaways from that story. First of all, my senior *référendaire* Alan Bailey demurred a little with me about putting in that illustration. He said he had been fascinated by the image, but had temporarily lost the thread of what we were really talking about because he was wondering what was going to happen to the tanker! The other aspect of the story, which takes us back to translation, is that when I got the draft French translation back to check, I realised that the translator did not have, as one says in French, '*le pied marin*'. He was not somebody who knew about the sea, and (inadvertently) he had turned the wind around. Although I had arranged for the tide, the swell and the wind all to be conspiring to push the vessel towards the Lizard, the draft French translation had magicked up a nice strong wind that was blowing – very helpfully! – in the opposite direction. I did correct the draft so that the text in French and in English produced the same effect. I confess, I also had a good laugh at that one.

Adam: Well, it has certainly made me laugh now. I shall make sure that from now on it is part of my lectures about the Court of Justice. I have also noted that you were checking the French version against your original English. This takes me to an important aspect of the Advocate General's work. While the Court's judgments are drafted in French and the *délibéré* is conducted in French, AGs can write in the official EU language of their choice.

Eleanor: French is indeed the working language of the Court. Having said that, you have reminded me of a surreal experience from my very early days back at the Court. Inside the Court building you expect that you will hear the various languages of the European Union. Most frequently, you will be hearing 'Court French' – however badly pronounced, structured, and grammatically glued together. The default value, if you go to a meeting, or if you walk into a room or a lift, is that people will be speaking French. On one of those early days, I walked into a lift and, as the doors closed behind me, I realised that I had entered a sealed bubble which was … a Russian-speaking zone! The reason was very simple. In the lift when I entered were three judges from recently joined Central European states. They were all gentlemen of a certain age. It is virtually certain that, at some stage, they had all done part of their legal studies in Moscow. Given their age and where they came from, for each of them their second language was obviously Russian. It would have been much easier for them to chat together in Russian than in Court French. When I entered the lift there was a kind of gear change, and very politely they all switched to French and greeted their newly arrived colleague. It was an extraordinary moment. As you remember, I grew up in Vienna, right next door to the Iron Curtain that divided the European continent. If someone had said to me then: 'Later in your career, you will join the Court of Justice of the European Union as an Advocate General, and you will walk into a lift and find people speaking Russian because it will be full of colleagues from Central and Eastern Europe', I would have looked at them and said: 'What planet are you living on? Haven't you noticed the Cold War, the Iron

Curtain, the division of Europe?' Never in my teens would I have imagined that happening.

Adam: That is a surreal story indeed. Similar things happened at the European Parliament with MEPs, especially in the 2004–2009 term. This, though, is a thing of the past. Unlike the judges, you – as an Advocate General – could choose the official language of the EU in which to write. Was it English? French? Perhaps both?

Eleanor: Both, Adam. We normally wrote in English. However, for the PPU – the special fast-track procedure for urgent references involving the AFSJ – we always wrote in French.[2] There wasn't time to write in English and have the text translated into French in time for the judges' *délibéré*. That meant that later we had to try to make sure that the English translation of the Opinion (which would be done subsequently: often, a long way subsequently because by then – of course – it wasn't urgent at all) somehow sounded like me in English. But when we were writing, we weren't thinking in English: we were thinking in French.

In the last months of my time as an Advocate General, in what we might call the Brexit war zone, we were writing anything in anything. One member of my team was a bit more comfortable writing in French than in English, so I wrote with him in French. There was one case we dealt with at that time where it would have been insane to write the Opinion in English. It was part of the *Dieselgate* saga (Case C-693/18).[3] The reference came from a French court, and it arrived with the French expert's report dealing, in full gory detail, with the technical aspects of cheat devices in diesel cars. There was no way, working against the clock, that we were going ourselves to translate that expert report into technical English so as then to write the Opinion in English, thank you very much. My *référendaire* Matthias and I wrote our Opinion in French, and – rather unkindly, perhaps – we left the difficulty of putting all the technical details into technically correct English to be addressed by the Court's highly competent translators at rather greater leisure. I should probably say at this point that the language I am writing in really does have an impact on how I write. I simply think differently in English and French.

Adam: And then you also wrote three Opinions in Spanish. How did that happen, Leo?

Eleanor: There is a very tragic story behind it, Adam. I took these cases over from AG Dámaso Ruiz-Jarabo Colomer after he suddenly passed away. I spoke to him in the corridor in the Court the evening before at about 8pm and we wished each other good night. The following morning his *chauffeur* went round to collect him and found him dead. We were all immensely shocked, as you can imagine, at the death of a very nice colleague. As sad as it was, though, the show had to go on. In particular Vassilios Skouris, the then President of the Court, was adamant that he did not want Dámaso's cases to sit there while Spain selected his successor. So, there was a reallocation amongst the seven remaining Advocates General of anything that was live and about to come up for a hearing. I took over four of Dámaso's cases. Since my own team was already working flat out on my own cases, for each of those cases I borrowed the *référendaire* from Dámaso's *cabinet* who was working on that file with him. This meant that I did two cases with Daniel Sarmiento, and one each with two of his very nice colleagues: Antonio Perez van Kappel and Dimitry Berberoff. Three of the four Opinions (for Case C-28/08P, Case C-263/08 and Case C-350/08) already existed as very preliminary drafts and (naturally) those drafts were in Spanish.[4] Since Spanish is my third language, it would have been silly to insist that we changed languages just because I had taken over these cases. So there are three Sharpston Opinions where the first footnote says '*lengua original: español*' ('original language: Spanish').

Adam: This is, indeed, a very sad background story. I guess, on those three occasions you had three different language versions to check against each other.

Eleanor: We had to align not just two texts, English and French, but three texts: English, French, and the original Spanish. I thought that when I was writing those cases, I had removed most of the beautiful fancy flourishes that Spanish likes. Really flowery, elegant Spanish is a bit like a baroque church: you find cherubs all over the place; there are curlicues, drapes, and foliage. Obviously, the ornamentation was already in the preliminary draft Spanish text of those three Opinions which I inherited. Each time, I said gently to my borrowed *référendaire*: 'well, you know, it is all very well, Dámaso wrote like that but I can't write like that. I am a very plain-speaking English speaker. So I'm afraid that we are going to take out things that are purely ornamental'. They looked at me, I looked at them. I said, 'I know it's brutal, but it won't sound anything like me if you keep all the curlicues in there'. Almost with tears in their eyes, they complied and took some of the ornaments out.

Adam: Did it do the trick? Did the three Opinions written in Spanish sound like Advocate General Sharpston?

Eleanor: Eventually yes, but here's the point. When I got back the draft English translation of my Spanish text – which, by the way, did sound very authentically like me in Spanish – I looked at it and said: 'What is wrong with this woman? She sounds as though she is being evasive'. The draft English text didn't sound like me in English! I spent literally a week on each of those three Opinions trying to align sufficiently the Spanish, the French, and the English versions. I was the author and I was the Advocate General. Fortunately, that meant that I had the necessary authority to say 'I don't care if there is a very slight divergence between these three texts. That divergence has to exist in order for the text to work and to sound like me in each of the three languages'. In doing so, I necessarily overrode some of the standard instructions that the lawyer-linguists in the Court's translation service would themselves have had to follow; but I did so to end up with three texts that did say the same thing in three different languages, all sounding like AG Sharpston. But it took me a week per text.

Adam: This is very interesting indeed, and multilingualism seems to be a recurring theme in our conversations. For now, I should like to return to another recurring theme. Already at your 'job interview' Leo, you spoke about the importance of having a good team. How you fought to keep Francis's team shows how much you meant it. So, how did *cabinet Sharpston* operate? Were all *référendaires* involved in writing each and every Opinion?

Eleanor: Every Opinion was the product of team work. I would co-write an Opinion with one of the *référendaires* but the rest of the team would be involved as well. At the beginning, we followed exactly the same procedure that Francis had developed. It was a tried and tested model for producing very good Opinions. That procedure meant that every single draft, once it had been put into something approximating to reasonable shape, was then distributed for comment to every lawyer within the *cabinet*. That's to say, the other three *référendaires*, plus any *stagiaire*/intern and any visitor. As the pressure of work crept relentlessly upwards, we had to think about whether that was still the right procedure to follow. In my latter years at the Court, we started doing a kind of triage. If a case was at the bottom end of the scale in terms of having needed an Opinion, we asked one other *référendaire* to read the draft. If it was a middle-level case, it got a two-*référendaire* review. If it was a blockbuster case, of course, it got reviewed by the other three *référendaires*. We would also ask *stagiaires* and visitors to read every draft as it became available.

Adam: Blockbuster cases in the sense of Grand Chamber cases, or rather the ones that you, and your team, thought were important, raising interesting and pertinent issues of EU law?

Eleanor: That is a truly excellent question. The answer is, 'blockbuster cases in the collective estimation of *cabinet Sharpston*'. That might, of course, coincide with the Court sending the case to the Grand Chamber but it wouldn't necessarily always mean that. I can think of cases which got all four *référendaires* involved (one drafting, three reviewing) but which were handled by a chamber of five judges because, for whatever reason, that had seemed to the Court to be a good way to proceed. For example, the Court may not wish to signal that a particular case is a really important one, so the case may be 'kept down' in a chamber of five judges even though, objectively, it should have been a Grand Chamber case.

Adam: I suppose your Opinion on the Free Trade Agreement with Singapore (Opinion 2/15) would easily tick the box of being a blockbuster.[5]

Eleanor: Jaysus, Mary and Joseph – and the wee donkey! If ever there was a blockbuster, that was it. Surely it was the longest thing I ever wrote at the Court. I guess the only good thing about having left my dream job is that I shall now never be asked to write a longer Opinion than that. It was a six-month, multi-draftsman nightmare.

Adam: 570 paragraphs of the main text, and 131 paragraphs in the Annex. It is a monster, indeed. It is not as long as AG Pitruzzella's parting shot before he abruptly retired from the Court in November 2023. His Opinion in *Lithuania and others v European Parliament and Council* (Joined Cases C-541/20 to C-555/20) has 1167 paragraphs and 638 footnotes.[6]

Eleanor: Respect for stamina, but you don't want to be doing that. The Opinion on the Singapore FTA required us to go through every single chapter of the Free Trade Agreement and analyse it to decide whether it involved matters that were EU exclusive competence, mixed competence (the EU and the Member States), or something that was still exclusively a Member State competence. There were no shortcuts. Having set out the parameters and the criteria for the analysis, you had to do it chunk by chunk, chapter by chapter, every single one of the chapters in the Agreement. That is why it was such a long process.

Adam: You were treading on very thin ice because it was the first such huge case after the Lisbon reform. It was all about contrapuntal tendencies in EU external relations. On the one hand, the Lisbon Treaty expanded the scope of the common commercial policy and thus gave extra thrust to the exclusive competences. On the other hand, since the entry into force of the Lisbon Treaty, the Member States have been forcing the European Union to conclude many agreements still as mixed agreements, as if nothing had happened. The clash point came with the request to check *ex ante* whether the Free Trade Agreement with Singapore *in toto*, or which of its parts, fell under exclusive or mixed competences. It looked like the Commission had had enough and called the Court to the rescue.

Eleanor: I think that from a purely practical negotiation point of view, somebody had to try to explain what fell on which side of the line. The Court and I were not in complete agreement, but I think the simple fact was that that analysis had to be done.[7] The guidance had to come from the Court because what had resulted from the Treaty, frankly, was not clear.

Adam: I remember reading your Opinion and the Opinion of the Court, and thinking that for the very first time, probably, the UK government was happy that the decision of the Court was so generous in terms of exclusive competences. Effectively, that made the conclusion of the post-Brexit EU-UK Trade and Cooperation Agreement ('TCA') a few years later possible.[8] Given the time constraints, that had to be an exclusive competence agreement and Opinion 2/15 had made that possible.

Eleanor: That is a lovely observation, Adam. Yes, I hate to think what it would have been like trying to get the EU-UK TCA to happen if it had also needed to be signed off by all the Member States. I don't think we want to go there.

Adam: Certainly not, that would have surely resulted in a spectacular fall from the cliffs of Dover. Opinion 2/15, being such a monster, was of course a team effort by your cabinet. I cannot stop myself from asking, though, if there were any cases where, for one reason or another, you wrote Opinions pretty much by yourself?

Eleanor: *Farrell II* (Case C-413/15)[9] on refining the scope of the vertical direct effect of directives is one of the very few examples of that. I wrote the draft and the entire team Sharpston provided the critique of my text.

Adam: Was that because, as a *référendaire*, you had written with Sir Gordon Slynn the judgment in *Foster v British Gas* (Case C-188/89)[10] and now the same fundamental issue of EU law had landed on your desk again?

Eleanor: It was partly that. The other reason was that *Farrell II* arrived at a time which was very difficult for us within *cabinet Sharpston*. There were too many other cases already on the blocks. There was no *référendaire* available with 'spare capacity' who could take on *Farrell II* in addition to their existing workload. It was just a horrible mess. In general terms, it is much more efficient to have a *référendaire* write the first draft and free up the Advocate General to review and revise their text. But we were so deeply in over our heads in terms of how much we had to do that I said to the team: 'Look, can you do some background research for me, please, and I will write *Farrell II* myself'. Different members of the team researched different bits of the topic and fed the results across to me. By an accident of history, as a *référendaire* for Sir Gordon Slynn I had worked on *Foster v British Gas*, which was at the root of the problem that we then had to solve in *Farrell II*. That made me uniquely placed to write it and I had a fairly clear idea of what I wanted to say. It just took much, much longer than I wanted to get it down on paper: to say it properly and clearly. So, we had the inverse of the normal situation. In *Farrell II* the AG wrote the draft, and the team critiqued.

That is, maybe, not a bad illustration of the general degree of democracy within team Sharpston. It mattered desperately that people should feel free *not* to be reverential towards me as the Advocate General. I needed them to say whether something worked or not. Perhaps it wasn't clear enough, perhaps it didn't convince them. So somebody might read a draft and say:

> *I am with you on the answers to questions one and two.*
>
> *Frankly, I don't think you have yet nailed down question three.*
>
> *I am not convinced.*

The *référendaire* drafting with me and I would take that absolutely seriously and we would go back and rewrite the answer to question three. The standard procedure was that the *référendaire* in charge of the case would get back the comments from the colleagues who were doing the review. They would decide which comments to take on board, which ones could be disregarded. They would then produce a revised draft that they would give to me, together with all the comments that they had received and an explanation as to why any particular comment had not resulted in a change to the draft. Ultimately, therefore, I had all the material. I read all the comments and I looked at what my *référendaire* had done with them. I would also pick up anything else that I thought needed to be picked up, and would indicate if material needed to be added or rewritten. It was very much a collaborative process.

To return to *Farrell II*: that Opinion took a long time to finish and we failed to comply with the Court's *échéancier* (the internal timetable for completing any given Opinion or judgment). Yes, it was a difficult Opinion; but the main problem was that it was out of sequence and I was writing it on my own. I also needed, of course, to review and revise all the other Opinions that we were working on at the same time. That inevitably meant that anytime there was another Opinion that was ready for me to look at, I had to put down what I was doing on *Farrell II* and make sure that the other Opinion got processed normally. The reality is that the Court's current working methods are not designed to allow any Advocate General to write any Opinion on their own, doing most of the drafting. If you try to do that – as I had to do with *Farrell II* – it slows everything down and also risks putting other work onto a slower track than should be the case. And you nearly kill the Advocate General because they have to manage to find time to do top-notch drafting between two and four in the morning, when they might otherwise prefer to be asleep. Eventually I did get *Farrell II* finished. I hope and believe that, actually, it is a good Opinion. But I am sure that the length of time that it took me to get it out did not make me popular either with the President or with the judges in that particular Grand Chamber.

Adam: For a happy consumer of AG Sharpston Opinions, this is most fascinating, Leo. I wish I were a fly on the wall. Frequently when I read something or listen to a good recording, I have this feeling that I really want to know what was behind it. Often a bit of background story is very enriching; I think it takes the experience to the next level. I will give you a good example later in our conversations. Sometimes the truth may be quite disappointing, sometimes it is the opposite. Of course, the latter is the case here and I know that there is much more to be said. We know by now how you and your *cabinet* worked. It is also clear how much you enjoyed being an Advocate General. You were reappointed twice. Did you ever consider following in the footsteps of Sir Gordon Slynn and becoming a judge at the Court of Justice?

Eleanor: Good question, Adam. At the beginning of 2012, when Sir Konrad Schiemann was retiring as the British judge, a number of people asked me if I were going to move across onto his post. I started thinking about it. I got hold of the official information pack. Having read through it, I decided that the only way I was really going to know what I wanted to do was to start the process and see what I had to say. So, I started drafting what would, hypothetically, be my *lettre de motivation*. I thought – naturally – that I would find that I had set out the usual stuff. You know: 'this is why I am the best thing since sliced bread and this is why you should appoint me'. Then I looked at the first paragraphs that I had written and I roared with laughter. I had opened my pitch for appointment as the new judge by saying how greatly I enjoyed my job as an Advocate General and how very happy indeed I was to be doing that job. Then I said to myself: 'OK, if that is the first thing you write down, what does that tell you, Leo? You've always said that being an AG was your dream job. What does it tell you about yourself?' Then I started thinking back to Gordon. In some respects – not in every respect, but in some respects – Gordon and I were uncomfortably like each other in terms of character. And I had seen how somebody who was truly a great person to work for as an Advocate General became a rather grumpy person to work for as a judge in a collegiate court.

Adam: You have just said what I did not dare to say!

Eleanor: Well, I was looking for words that wouldn't be disloyal to Gordon, but I don't think that what I have just said is disloyal. It is an objective statement. Sir Gordon Slynn gave me the chance to spend three years working at the Court and I am very grateful for that, not least because I had such a good time working for him whilst he was an Advocate General. Until I returned to the Court as a Member, the three years that I spent with Gordon as a *référendaire* were the highlight of my professional career – in some ways, even better than being in silk. I started thinking back and remembered what had happened to Gordon when he moved across. I had such a clear picture of a strongly independent-minded person who found themselves having to submit to the discipline of a consensus judgement, to less-than-ideal compromises, to the wilful mutilation of good drafting in order to arrive at a text which would garner sufficient support to get through the *délibéré*. I looked at myself in the mirror. Then I tore up my draft *lettre de motivation*. I said to myself: 'You know what? You are going to put everything you have into trying to be better as an Advocate General. You're not going to apply to be the judge'.

Adam: Amen to that! I think it is time to move to something slightly more general, yet very much linked to the Court and the role of Advocates General. When you joined the Court in January 2006, the reforms introduced by the Treaty of Nice were already in force. So, unlike the position for the first two British Advocates General (Sir Jean-Pierre Warner and Sir Gordon Slynn), and for parts of the term of your immediate predecessor Sir Francis Jacobs, Opinions of

Advocates General were no longer compulsory. So, for every case the Court has to take a decision at the *réunion générale* as to whether or not to ask the AG for an Opinion. This creates a false picture that Advocates General only work on a case if they produce an Opinion. This is slightly brutal and it does not reflect all the preliminary work that would have been done to reach a decision, one way or another, at the *réunion générale*.

Eleanor: First, it is really important to emphasise that every single case has an Advocate General, not just the cases that have Opinions. As you said, there is a common misconception that Advocates General only work on cases with Opinions. That is simply untrue. Advocates General look carefully at every case that is allocated to them. When I joined the Court, there were eight AGs, so my docket held one-eighth of the Court's entire caseload. Second, for a long time there was a charming gentlemens' agreement, named the '*règle Cunha Rodriguez*' after the Portuguese judge who was its proponent. The informal agreement was that if either the *juge rapporteur* or the Advocate General thought there should be an Opinion, then there was an Opinion. It was a rather good working rule, but later it fell into disfavour. The difficulty then was that if the reporting judge wanted an Opinion, that was fine as you were always happy as AG to write one for her/him. If the *juge rapporteur* didn't want an Opinion but you felt that the case needed one, you then had – at the *réunion générale* – to argue your corner why there should be an Opinion. You didn't normally just roll over and say: 'well, if you don't want an Opinion, fair enough'. At that stage, although you would have done some preliminary work on the case and were very sure that it needed an Opinion, naturally you hadn't finished thinking about all the issues and their implications. So, you then had to convince your judge colleagues and the other Advocates General around the table *without* having a fully-formed idea of exactly what you would put into the Opinion, were you to write it. At some point, the judges started to use a slightly condescending and deeply unhelpful formula to fend off an 'unwanted' Opinion:

> *Nous savons tous que les conclusions sont toujours utiles, mais est-ce qu'en l'espèce elles sont nécessaires?*
>
> *(We all know that an Opinion is always useful; but is an Opinion necessary in this case?).*

Of course, there was sometimes *Schadenfreude*. You would meet your judge colleagues in the corridor looking distraught, having just emerged from a fruitless *délibéré*. You would say to them solicitously, 'you don't look very upbeat this morning'. They would clutch their heads and mutter, 'we should have asked you for an Opinion in that damn case'. Whenever that happened to me, I would just smile sweetly.

Adam: Ah, the sweet joy of 'I told you so!'. How about the Court turning back the clock? Cases can travel, can't they? From the top of my head, *Commission v Italy* about trailers to mopeds and a ban on use of goods (Case C-110/05)[11] was bounced back by the chamber of five to the *réunion générale*. Then it was re-allocated to the Grand Chamber, the oral procedure was reopened, and an additional Opinion by the Advocate General followed.[12] A full Rolls-Royce treatment.

Eleanor: Very occasionally, the Court is prepared to go back round the procedural loop. I remember a case of mine that was initially allocated to a chamber of three, with the idea that it needed neither a hearing nor an Opinion. And then the chamber of three fell out amongst themselves as to the outcome. It was two against one, except that the one in the minority happened to be both the President of chamber and the *juge rapporteur*. So, they came back to the *réunion générale* and said:

> [cough cough]
>
> *We would like the Advocate General back in the case and we would like this case to be sent to a chamber of five.*

At that point, with a sweet smile on my face, I joined the conversation:

> *Of course I am happy to step back in and write an Opinion, no problem. However, I would also like a hearing. I don't know why you couldn't agree and you are not going to tell me, because of the 'secret du délibéré'. It is very clear to me that there is more digging to be done. So, I should like us to hold a hearing, please.*

I had my way. During the hearing, I gave the case a prod and a poke from every conceivable direction. As I asked my questions, I listened to the answers but I also watched the judges to see how they were reacting to what I was asking. That told me a great deal about what the problem had been. And then I duly wrote them an Opinion.

Adam: By the looks of it, going back round the loop proved useful for that case. What about having an additional Opinion of the Advocate General on top of the one that has already been provided to the Court? Have you had one of those in your docket, Leo?

Eleanor: That happened in one of the early cases that I took over from Francis. He had already written an Opinion for a chamber of five in a case with no hearing. Studying the file, Francis had uncovered a really serious problem and he set it out four-square in his Opinion. The chamber had taken fright and brought the case back to the *réunion générale*, asking for the Grand Chamber, a hearing, and a further AG's Opinion. In the meantime, there was the changeover from Francis to myself, so I wrote the second Opinion in that case.

Adam: So, history repeated itself. The same, in terms of Opinions by British Advocates General, happened in *AM&S* (Case 155/79).[13] First, we had an Opinion by AG Warner, and then a follow-up Opinion by AG Slynn.[14] Figuratively, your path also crossed that case: you had been involved in *AM&S* working for John Temple Lang during your Bristow Scholarship at the European Commission.

Eleanor: How interesting that lightning struck twice! Going back to the question of whether or not to have an Opinion, the answer often depends on how strong the reporting judge is. If your reporting judge is strong and both of you are on the same page (either that an Opinion is needed or that it is not), it is much easier to steer the case smoothly through the *réunion générale* on list B, that is without discussion. The problem can become acute, however, if the reporting judge is not really on top of the file. I had one case, which I am *not* going to identify further, where the draft *rapport préalable* that we received for comments from the *juge rapporteur* bore remarkably little resemblance to the contents of the case file. My team and I completely rewrote that *rapport préalable*. After the expenditure of much diplomacy, we got the reporting judge to accept our rewritten version of the *rapport préalable*. Then I wrestled with my conscience as to whether I should say that there should be an Opinion. The case was not one that on any normal view needed or deserved an Opinion. Eventually, I looked carefully at who were the two other judges in the proposed chamber of three to decide the case, and I said to myself: 'I think they can keep it on the straight and narrow. So I think we probably don't need an Opinion'. I kept my fingers crossed and fortunately the case made it through to judgment without any untoward incidents. Obviously, it's very rare to have a situation like that.

Adam: We also have cases which, *prima facie*, are not exciting by any stretch of the imagination; the monetary value may be low and a case seemingly irrelevant. And yet, in the great scheme of things, such cases may prove important. This happened with one of your early cases called *Brzeziński* (Case C-313/05).[15] It was a fairly straightforward tax discrimination case that in EU law textbooks appears only in footnotes (if at all). However, it was the first reference for a preliminary ruling from a Polish court, and hundreds of similar cases were pending all around the country. They were all suspended awaiting the judgment of the Court of Justice. This was a real test case, checking the ability of Polish courts to apply EU law and the principles of direct effect and primacy.

Eleanor: True, you do get quite a lot of technical problems to decide: cases about something that is important in its context, but the monetary value of that individual case is low and/or the substance of the case is not headline-grabbing blockbuster material. *Brzeziński* was one such case. On a slightly funny note, I once wrote an Opinion about one dead cow.

Adam: Oh dear, I did not quite expect a dead cow to make an appearance in our conversations.

Eleanor: The problem was with an export declaration. If my memory serves me well, the export declaration had been made out in respect of 31 bovine animals leaving the farm, but one cow then died *en route* before the consignment left the territory of the European Union. The exporter was erroneously given his export refund in respect of 31 animals. The discrepancy was only discovered some time after the money had been paid over. So, the technical question was about 'post clearance recovery of an export refund'. The amount of money at stake was under 600 €; but the problem occupied the attention of a chamber of five, with an Opinion by AG Sharpston.[16] A bit later, the same referring court came back with a follow-up question about three other consignments of beef.[17] So that case became known in my chambers as the 'zombie cow'.

Adam: That is the beauty and the curse of preliminary rulings. The Court cannot act like the supreme courts of many Member States and just say: 'well, that's not interesting, it doesn't disclose any interesting new points of law, so no, thank you very much indeed'. The Court does not operate *à la carte* and it proceeds under the presumption of admissibility. At the same time, to mitigate this general lack of control over its docket, it may decide to ignore questions sent by national courts that do not seem to be relevant. What is your take on that practice, Leo?

Eleanor: It is true that the Court sometimes takes shortcuts. I have in mind a case concerning the rights and status of Palestinian refugees in which three questions were referred by *Fővárosi Bíróság*, a Hungarian court. The case was called *Bolbol* (Case C-31/09);[18] it was a Grand Chamber case, and I wrote an Opinion.[19] The Court took the short route home. It answered the first question and – having done so – held that there was no need to answer questions two and three. A couple of months later, we got an extremely disgruntled second reference from the same national judge in the same Hungarian court in Budapest. He referred three cases linked together, of which the first was called *El Kott* (Case C-364/11).[20] The gist of the referring judge's message to the Court was not really very diplomatic:

> *I submitted a reference in Bolbol with three questions.*
>
> *That is because I have a number of cases in my docket which are waiting on the outcome.*
>
> *You only gave me an answer to question one in Bolbol. I also need the answers to questions two and three.*
>
> *I am therefore referring these three cases. On the facts of the cases that I have selected to refer, you will not be able to wriggle away from it this time and not answer my questions.*
>
> *My two questions in this reference are verbatim the same questions as questions two and three in Bolbol.*

Predictably, *El Kott* also went to the Grand Chamber. There was another hearing and another Opinion by AG Sharpston.[21] The Court eventually answered questions two and three from *Bolbol*, aka questions one and two from *El Kott*.

Adam: Right, so here we have proof that taking such shortcuts may backfire spectacularly. I have also noted that we now have another 'efficiency' driven practice, whereby the Court of Justice asks its Advocates General to focus only on selected aspects of a case. I recently read the Opinion of AG Richard de la Tour in *Getin Noble Bank* (Case C-118/23)[22] and it did strike me that he twice emphasised that, following the request of the Court, he was going to focus only on selected questions referred by the national court. It did sound like: 'do not blame me if things go wrong and we miss something'.

Eleanor: The practice always used to be that if you wrote an Opinion, you wrote an Opinion about the whole case. Alternatively, you didn't write an Opinion. You never (ever) wrote an Opinion about only part of a case. Indeed, it was almost a matter of honour for an Advocate General that when you wrote an Opinion, you looked carefully at everything, even if you suspected that probably the Court wasn't going to go there. For example, you might be able to make a shrewd guess that the Court would probably answer questions one and two a particular way, and therefore wouldn't need to answer question three. Nevertheless, you would produce a brief answer to question three. Even if the Court didn't touch it, you would nevertheless be putting down a kind of marker for the future as to what you thought about question three. Sometimes that provided real value added for academics and practitioners, because it represented quotable thinking by a Member of the Court on that point. Then, the Court got onto the idea that a particular case might have aspects already covered by settled case law; but, at the same time, there might be one question, or some sub-part of the case, which was novel and which merited an Advocate's General Opinion. So the Court changed its practice. Some cases still got full Opinions. But in other cases, the *réunion générale* would decide that a partial Opinion was needed, confined to certain aspects of the case. That would be a binding decision, taken by the Court, limiting the scope of the Advocate's General Opinion.

Adam: Alright then, expediency prevails but this can really backfire …

Eleanor: From the perspective of the Advocate General, it can be quite uncomfortable. As you are writing the partial Opinion, you are probably also thinking about the other questions that you're not answering. Left to your own devices, you would have written answers to those questions as well. You may have even gone through a particular intellectual process in first answering the unwanted questions before you got on to the questions that the Court wanted you to deal with. Truth be told, starting writing about a question that only arises later in a sequence is a little bit bizarre intellectually. It is like saying to a playwright:

> *We all know what is going to happen in Acts I, II, and III. So, could you please pick it up in Act IV where Clytemnestra suddenly realises that her son has returned?*
>
> [And the playwright might well feel]
>
> *But, wait a minute, what about the events that happen between Clytemnestra and Agamemnon? How am I meant to pick it up when Orestes confronts Clytemnestra without having told the audience the story so far, with the important nuances that I see in those central characters?*

So, what you mentioned, Adam, is perhaps almost like a point made in self-defence. The Advocate General may say: 'I have been asked to confine my Opinion to these points'. Obviously, one is polite and there is *le devoir de délicatesse*. As an AG, you are not going to say publicly that you think that the *réunion générale* may have made a mistake in limiting you to writing about only a part of the case. From the Court's perspective this is again one of those resource saving exercises. If the AG only deals with selected aspects of the case, the resulting Opinion is going to be shorter. Well, that is objectively true; and the Opinion will take correspondingly less time and resources to be translated. Behind that may be another assumption: that the Opinion will, therefore, take the AG (much) much less time to write. If so, that assumption is only half true, I am afraid.

Adam: Why is that so?

Eleanor: It is indubitably true that, if you are only writing about question 4, you won't spend time checking and refining pages of careful drafting that describe your thinking on questions 1, 2, and 3. At the same time, you won't be able to get to the starting point for dealing with question 4 without – inside your head – spending the necessary time on questions 1, 2, and 3 and being really sure what you think about them, down to the nuances. So, at the end of the day, you will have to deal (to some extent, at least) with questions 1, 2 and 3 anyway. And you may need to say, 'In approaching question 4, I am starting from the following premises'.

Adam: I get the point about the efficiency but as we already agreed, a good lawyer should use a microscope, a telescope, and a wide-angle lens. We should see the wood for the trees.

Eleanor: True, Adam. But the Court has made an absolutely deliberate, strategic decision to make use of partial Opinions. It is a measure to try to make sure that (scarce) resources are spread more efficiently and used exactly where they should be. It is a halfway house between saying:

> *Okay, let's have an Opinion … oh dear, that means we are also going to be told that two and two make four but never mind.*
>
> or saying:
>
> *We don't want to be told that two and two make four so we will make do without an Opinion, even though an Opinion would have been useful for the final aspects of the case.*

To the extent that having partial Opinions is a way of avoiding making a bad decision not to have an Opinion at all in a case where the first bit of the analysis is obvious, maybe it is a good way forward. But, at the same time, it is an intellectual and functional distortion.

Adam: It is also quite risky. If we go back to *Bolbol*, there the Court was selective in its judgment, to begin with, and received another reference exactly because it had opted for shortcuts the first time around. Having said that, you did not take or suggest shortcuts, hence your Opinion covered all questions raised by the Hungarian court.

Eleanor: Yes, but remember that my Opinion was not the judgment of the Court. It was just an Opinion of the Advocate General. For practical reasons, my sympathy lies with the Hungarian judge in *El Kott*, who got the judgment in *Bolbol*. He probably thought: 'For heaven's sake! I asked three questions and I wanted answers to all three of them'. Having said that, when writing my Opinion in *El Kott* I took the opportunity to correct a detail that I had got slightly wrong in *Bolbol*.

Adam: In a way, the end result in such cases is similar to the Court delivering a judgment that lacks proper reasoning. Many years ago, I presented a paper in Cambridge where I argued that in such cases, in particular in Grand Chamber cases, assistance of Advocates General starts to border on substitution. This is neither healthy, nor what Advocates General are designed to do under the EU Treaties. I remember that I tested your temperature on my ideas, Leo, during one of our meetings in Dubrovnik. It took me quite a while to fight down a nasty attack of imposter syndrome, but when I finally got the ideas off my chest, and used *Ruiz Zambrano* as an example, you started your answer by saying:

> *Adam, the Advocate General is telling you that she has no clue whether she was really followed or not by the Court in Ruiz Zambrano.*

Ruiz Zambrano (Case C-34/09)[23] is, of course, an extreme case where we have a very robust Opinion by the Advocate General and an appalling seven paragraphs by the Court.

Eleanor: All these years later, Adam, and having read and reread the seven paragraphs of the Court's judgment, I have to say that I am still not very much the wiser. Sometimes you write an Opinion as an AG, the Court meticulously mirrors all your reasoning but then, at the end, it arrives at a different conclusion. That may happen because your reasoning had fifteen steps in it, and the Court followed you in steps one through fourteen; but then, at step fifteen, you turned left, and the Court turned right. When that happens, the Court reaches a different answer, but it is very clear that, intellectually, they have followed the same path as the Advocate General. You cannot say that about *Ruiz Zambrano*. That is probably on my shortlist of the three cases that I spent the most time chewing over as an AG. I was very lucky to be able to work on it with Daniel Sarmiento.

Ruiz Zambrano wasn't originally my case. As First Advocate General, I had allocated it to my colleague and friend AG Dámaso Ruiz-Jarabo Colomer. I did that deliberately because I had myself just written an Opinion about citizens' rights in the context of the Flemish health insurance scheme (Case C-212/06).[24] The Court by then was fairly well-informed about what AG Sharpston thought about such things. I knew that Dámaso would look at the problem critically and carefully with a sympathetic eye for the difficulties of the case. I also thought I should not keep this plum to myself! So I gave it to him. When Dámaso died so suddenly, *Ruiz Zambrano* had not progressed as far as the other three cases of his that I took over. Inevitably, there were going to be different perspectives on how to handle that case. Was it a purely internal situation? If so, it could be disposed of by an order adopted by a three judge chamber, without a hearing or an AG's Opinion. Or were you going to look harder at it? If so, it was unquestionably a Grand Chamber case. *Ruiz Zambrano* was, indeed, allocated to the Grand Chamber, but very little drafting had been done by the time Dámaso sadly died. Daniel Sarmiento, among his many talents, is extremely good in English, so we decided that we would write in the language of Shakespeare. In hindsight, that Opinion gave us such trouble! I think we rewrote it four times. We knew what we were trying to say but we were also aware that where we were going was so revolutionary that we wanted to try to get it across in little incremental bytes.

Adam: Oh yes. I remember reading your Opinion on the day it was published and uttering at regular intervals Al Pacino's 'Hoo-ah!' (from the movie *Scent of a Woman*). It is a truly blockbuster Opinion, Leo.

Eleanor: The Opinion in *Ruiz Zambrano* is the joint product of this particular common lawyer and Daniel Sarmiento, a very good Spanish constitutional lawyer who had also studied in the USA. It was that particular intellectual blend which generated the Opinion. Would it have been different if I had written it with one of my usual team of *référendaires*? The answer and the recommendation would have been the same; but the Opinion would not have been written in the same way.

Adam: Even on a first reading, it is very clear that that Opinion was deeply thought through and it received a lot of care and attention. I guess it must have taken a while to put it together.

Eleanor: Oh yes, we made ourselves deeply (I mean: really deeply) unpopular with President Skouris. The process of writing and then going back to the drawing board and partly rewriting inevitably took time. Eventually President Skouris sent round his *chef de cabinet* to insist that I commit to a firm date for the Opinion. So, I gave him a date. The unfortunate *chef de cabinet* turned white and said: 'I can't possibly tell President Skouris that: he will kill me'. My rather unsympathetic answer was: 'You insisted that you had to have a firm date. So I have given you a date that I know that I can stick to, but – for that reason – it is not going to be an earlier date. Now, if you'll excuse me, I do need to get on with my work'.

President Skouris had a reason for getting antsy: he was committed to getting as many cases as possible through the system as fast as possible. But the Opinion in *Ruiz Zambrano* was not one that you could write in a hurry, with a gun at your head.

Adam: Just looking at the dates, it is obvious that the Grand Chamber also needed time. The cynical part of me says: hang on a minute, nearly half a year for seven paragraphs? We will never know what exactly happened at the *délibéré* but I guess the judges struggled with the reasoning.

Eleanor: Very possibly; but let's first look a little more closely at that timeline, Adam. The hearing was on 26 January 2010. I delivered the Opinion on 30 September 2010. That is why President Skouris was so unhappy. The Opinion (and we need to remember that it was a long one) must have gone to translation, at the latest, in early August 2010. *That* is when it would have been shared with the judges. It would have gone onto what is called the *site des présidents* (an internal server accessible only by the judges and their teams). That was the moment at which the *juge rapporteur* would have had sight of it and the point from which time would run for him, under the Court's *échéancier* (the internal timetabling requirements), to start producing either a *note de tour de table* saying 'I don't agree with the Advocate General so we need to talk about this, and here are the issues', or a short email saying 'I agree with the Advocate General and attached is the *projet de motifs*, my first draft of the judgment'. As to the *délibéré*, one can only hypothesise. As the Advocate General, I merely waited like everyone else to find out what was happening.

Let's go back to your point, Adam, about the judges struggling in *Ruiz Zambrano*. It may well have been the case that at an earlier stage, the draft judgment was much longer. Perhaps the judges chewed over the case in the *délibéré* and they agreed where they were going to end up, but found it much more difficult to agree on the precise reasoning that would get them there. It is an observable scientific fact that it is much easier to take text out of a draft than to agree on replacement text to go in its place. Without knowing the actual facts, what I suspect probably happened to *Ruiz Zambrano* is that it began as a much much longer text that gradually got whittled down to a bare fig leaf, which brought us to a rather bald statement: 'these are the facts, here is the question from the national court, and here is the answer'.

Adam: This was not terribly helpful for the referring court or for courts all around the European Union which had similar cases in their dockets. At that time one of my colleagues at Westminster Law School was an immigration judge who frequently sat in such cases. Every time we passed each other in the corridors he would always look up and say: arggggg, *Ruiz Zambrano*! (As if it were my fault!) Anyway, it was one of the really rare cases where the judges were extremely economical with their reasoning. And we still do not know if you were followed or not, Leo. This is often hard to detect anyway, as the judges will never openly say whether they agree or not with the Advocate General. What we are likely to get are cryptic references along the lines: 'as the Advocate General noted in paragraph [...] of their Opinion'. Have we ever had a case where the Court just said: 'We agree with the Opinion of the Advocate General so there is no need to repeat the reasoning, just look it up, would you?'

Eleanor: To my knowledge that has happened only in *Hauptzollamt Hamburg-St Annen v Ebbe Sönnichsen GmbH* (Case C-59/92)[25] where Sir David Edward was the *juge rapporteur*. That was one of the shortest CJEU judgments ever. The Court ruled:

> *4 For the reasons indicated in the Advocate-General's Opinion of 31 March 1993, the reply to the question put by the national court must be that the second sentence of Article 4 of the aforementioned Regulation No 1495/80, as amended by the aforementioned Regulation No 1580/81, is to be interpreted as meaning that in the event of a deterioration of goods which reduces their customs value no distinction is to be made according to whether it occurred before or after the risk passed to the buyer.*

That caused a stir. It has never been repeated for a case that is being examined seriously by the Court. Yet now, curiously, a not dissimilar procedure is followed for orders in trademark cases that are going to be declared manifestly inadmissible and/or manifestly ill founded. In such cases, the order adopted by the chamber of three fits like a shell around the Advocate's General mini-Opinion which provides all the reasoning. The order merely records procedurally what has happened, and then it hands over to the Opinion. When that procedure was introduced, there was a certain amount of discussion and some concerns were raised, as it looked like a distortion of the role of the Advocate General. Fundamentally: if the chamber isn't really looking at the case at all, the Advocate General is deciding the case. If the judges in the chamber *are* looking properly at the case, it is a real waste of an AG's time to write a mini-Opinion about an appeal where the correct answer is 'manifestly' obvious.

Adam: Which goes back to my point about quietly changing the role of Advocates General from providing assistance to substitution. Having said that, such cases are the extreme. What we are more likely to see on a daily basis are cases where the Court, without being vocal about it, agrees or not with an Advocate General. Leo, of course, you had a good share of both. We have over 350 cases to select from, so I should like to take the liberty of suggesting we take a closer look at *Heinrich* and *Sturgeon* (respectively, Case C-345/06 and Joined Cases C-402/07 & C-432/07).[26] For two people who, as we have already established, have incurable *travelitis furiosus*, these cases seem to be perfect examples to dwell on as they dealt with different aspects of travelling by air. Yet, behind perhaps fairly pedestrian sets of facts, they – first and foremost – touched upon the rule of law, something that is very close to your heart and mine.

Eleanor: Dr Heinrich was, at least at the time, a keen tennis player who had booked to fly from Vienna to somewhere in Turkey for a week's tennis holiday. He turned up with his wife at *Schwechat* Airport, checked in his hold luggage, and enquired about the contents of his hand luggage, which of course contained his tennis racket. Apparently, some doubts were raised whether he could take it on board or not (the facts as recorded in the order for reference were a bit murky at that point); but the next thing we know is that he boarded the plane with his tennis racket and asked about stowing it in the overhead locker. Then all hell broke loose. A heavily armed airport security squad turned up and removed him from the plane on the grounds that he was about to fly with an offensive weapon – a tennis racket – in his hand luggage. Putting it mildly, Dr. Heinrich was very unamused. His wife had the keys to the apartment; she remained on the flight; and if memory serves me well, he had to get his daughter to come into Vienna with a spare set of keys so that he could get back into his home. Dr. Heinrich asked, by what right had he been forcibly removed from the plane? He was told 'EU law' and was given references to a European Parliament & Council regulation and a Commission regulation. However, the European Parliament & Council regulation did not list 'tennis rackets' as an offensive weapon that may not be taken on board a plane.[27] The Commission regulation (the latest in a sequence of similar regulations) said very little in the main text.[28] It had an annex with detailed information about security procedures at the airports. However, the annex was described as 'confidential' and was therefore not published in the Official Journal of the European Union.

Adam: I doubt anyone would be amused in such circumstances. Yet, at the same time, perhaps a reminder is fitting that all of this happened not long after 9/11. We were in the midst of the war on terror when many laws were drafted and adopted in anger. Never a good idea, some say.

Eleanor: I could readily have understood the need for secrecy in relation, for example, to technical information about how security scanning machines work. It would have been entirely right and proper not to make that information public. But (procedurally) you would not annex such information to a regulation. You would have taken a decision which would then have been notified confidentially to the Member States. The Commission could then resist any request to make that information public under one of the derogations provided for in the Access to Documents Regulation.[29] However, that is not what the Commission chose to do. Curiously, at the same time, there was a Commission press release that was very much in the public domain which purported to address the question of what you could take onto an aircraft in your hand luggage.[30] It was published in three languages only: English, French, and German. That, in itself, was not terribly handy. More importantly, it didn't mention tennis rackets.

Adam: What a mess ….

Eleanor: The existence of that press release created an impossible position for the Commission to defend. If it needed to keep that information secret, then it shouldn't have published a press release. If, on the contrary, the Commission thought it would be a good idea for passengers to know what they may or may not bring onto an aircraft as hand luggage, then – obviously – it should have published the information in the annex to the regulation in all the official languages of the European Union. The judgment of the Court in *Skoma-Lux*

(Case C-161/06)[31] unequivocally says that for legislation to be enforceable *vis-à-vis* individuals, it has to be published in all official languages. What was perhaps even more bizarre was that throughout the procedure, the Court was never shown the annex. I never saw the annex, the judges never saw the annex. It was never produced! As the Advocate General, I did not know whether – in fact – tennis rackets were listed in the annex. If that unfortunate press release was anything to go by, they were not.

Adam: All of this must have pulled your tail, so to speak.

Eleanor: *Heinrich* was one of my earlier Opinions, which I wrote with a very bright Belgian lawyer: Geert de Baere, back then my *référendaire*, now a judge of the General Court. We went nuclear. We said that what the Commission had done was a complete affront to the rule of law. The offending regulation should not merely be held to be unenforceable *vis-à-vis* individuals: it should be declared non-existent. The Grand Chamber was more restrained: the Court ruled that the regulation and its annex could not apply to Dr. Heinrich as long as it was not published fully in the Official Journal.[32] In the meantime, the European Commission took the hint from my Opinion and they split the information that was – I suppose – in the annex into confidential and non-confidential material. The end result was that the travelling public began to be informed about what they could take on board an aircraft.

Adam: This was one of those bizarre cases where the Court decided not to go nuclear even though there was no reason why they should not follow you. By the time the judgment was rendered, the Commission – as you said, Leo – had published the regulation including (some of) the information originally well hidden in the annex. In the great scheme of things, this turned into a Shakespearean much ado about nothing. Since the Commission had already published the relevant parts of the annex, it would have done no major harm to have ruled that the non-published legislation did not exist. But there's something that I find interesting, and that takes us back to our early conversations, where you said that you feel very European, not necessarily very British. In your Opinion in *Heinrich* you were indeed very European. In legal terms, you followed the German standards, not the quirky Hansard whereby, in the United Kingdom, we don't have a proper promulgation gazette.

Eleanor: In this instance, I was being very continental, very Germanic, very loyal to the principles of the *Rechtsstaat*. If you have a legal system where you publish all laws in an Official Journal, then what is binding upon the citizen is what you publish and make available in that medium. *Au contraire*, you can't have something that is binding and not publish it. To that extent, the Court and I said the same thing. I really wanted to drive the point home that this was unacceptable. What made it worse in my eyes was that this was recidivist behaviour by the European Commission. There was a whole chain of these wretched regulations, each with its invisible annex. It seemed to me that unless somebody stood up and shouted at them, they would continue using that defective procedure. That is, of course, something you can do as the Advocate General. You can say things which you know the Court is not going to put into the judgment but which, nevertheless, bear saying. It is one of the great privileges of being an Advocate General.

Adam: Another privilege is, I guess, to send the Court warning signs as to the direction of travel that one suspects the judges may choose. Leo, you did fire such a warning shot in *Sturgeon*, didn't you?

Eleanor: *Sturgeon* was one of those occasions where the Advocate General wrote what she thought was a short and innocuous sentence that acted like a red rag to a bull. The problem in *Sturgeon* was that the Air Passengers Regulation didn't explain whether, if your flight was delayed rather than cancelled, you had an entitlement to compensation.[33] It gave you an entitlement to be looked after: the possibility of making a phone call, or getting something to eat and drink. But there was no specific provision that gave you the right to financial compensation if your flight was delayed. If your flight was cancelled, you clearly did have such a right.

Adam: Oh yes, at that point flights were hardly ever cancelled, they would just be delayed for hours on end. I remember being stuck at a tiny non-Schengen transit zone at Budapest airport for twelve hours. Every hour, Malev staff would announce a further delay until the next scheduled flight to Tirana was due to depart. At some point closer to the departure time, I magically received a new boarding pass with a new flight number. When the lawyer in me kicked in, the only reply I got from the ground staff was: 'Aren't you tired enough after twelve hours of waiting here?'… Then came the *Sturgeon* case.

Eleanor: The Opinion in *Sturgeon* was again written with Geert de Baere. We came to the conclusion that the regulation didn't really work very well because it could readily lead to discrimination. It seemed very strange that you would get compensation if your flight was cancelled, and you were put on a new flight. But if your flight was merely delayed, and you arrived at your destination later than the equivalent passenger who had been put on a new flight, you wouldn't get any compensation. That just did not add up. So, in the Opinion, we pointed out the problem of discrimination. We invited the Court to reopen the proceedings in order to hear arguments about it. This was our way of saying: 'look, the legislator has to fix this'. There was enough in the Opinion to indicate that the Court should have reopened this procedure and given the legislator time to go in there and fix it. We warned the Court that it should not step in and 'pick a number': that is, select a number of hours of delay after which compensation would become payable. A legislator can do that because any number is, in a sense, arbitrary. So, the legislator can select a number that they considers to be appropriate and then defend it. Then that fatal short sentence: 'The Court cannot'. I think the judges regarded that as a challenge. Clearly, they were up for it because they duly created in their judgment in *Sturgeon* some pure judge-made law.[34] They created the right to compensation if your flight was delayed for more than three hours.

Adam: I am sure that many air passengers have since then been extremely grateful to the Court, including your humble servant who has done robust empirical research on compensation for flight delays. Having said that, I have always been torn about this case. On the one hand, as a frequent flyer I obviously appreciate the perks it confers. On the other hand, as a lawyer I feel a great unease. The point you made in the Opinion about the division of tasks between the legislator and the judiciary keeps ringing in my ears. It was not the Court's job to fix the problem created by the legislator. The *Sturgeon* case has the rule of law and separation of powers written all over it.

Eleanor: I couldn't agree more. It was not the Court's job to create a right to payment for delayed flights and fix the bar at three hours. As often happens in such cases where the Court is being creative (or when it fails to provide proper reasoning), the Court then got lots of follow-up references. In this instance, among others, the *TUI* case stands out (Joined Cases C-581/10 and C-629/10). That was a reference from the High Court in London and the gist of it was: 'were you out to lunch when you wrote *Sturgeon*?' I recused myself from writing the Opinion as I felt that I should not be involved further. The case went to my nice French colleague, Advocate General Yves Bot, who did a splendid job of explaining why it was perfectly all right that the Court had decided *Sturgeon* as it did.[35] The Grand Chamber followed the AG and made it clear to the High Court in London that *Sturgeon* was there to stay and that it was now the task of national courts to apply it.[36]

Adam: I guess at this point the judges were immediately removed from the Christmas card lists of CEOs of major European airlines!

Eleanor: I suspect that many passengers who should perhaps have been sending Christmas cards to the same judges never actually realised how much they owed to the Court.

Adam: I bet. To change the topic, albeit slightly: I guess you have also had your share of cases where the multilingualism of the EU legal order came to the fore. Wasn't *Rinau* (Case C-195/08 PPU)[37] the first PPU case where the Member States were pleading during the hearing and it sounded like they were pleading about different pieces of legislation, while in fact it was the same Brussels IIa Regulation?[38]

Eleanor: That is a good illustration but issues arising out of multilingualism are not confined to the Brussels IIa Regulation. I had another case involving *Emirates Airlines* and passengers' right to claim compensation if their flight was delayed (Case C-173/07).[39] The need for interpretation arose because the German version of the Air Passengers Regulation was out of step with other versions of the same text. The applicant in that case – Dr. Schenkel – had booked a return flight from Düsseldorf to Manila via Dubai. There had been a severe delay on the return journey. Emirates Airlines, as the name indicates, is not a European Union carrier. The regulation covers all carriers flying *out* of an EU airport, but only EU carriers flying *into* the EU from third countries. So, as Dr. Schenkel was flying back into the EU on a non-EU carrier, you would have thought that the regulation didn't cover him. His argument, however, was that he had bought a return ticket. He had started his journey from a German airport and, he said, the return leg of his round trip should be regarded as part and parcel of the same journey. Since he had started off in the EU, covered by the regulation, the return leg should also have been covered by the regulation. The *Oberlandesgericht Frankfurt am Main*, the referring court, working from the German text of the regulation, thought that he was probably right. As a precaution, however, they decided to make a reference for a preliminary ruling. This time, the Court and I were on the same page: we both said that one could not read the regulation like that. To reach our conclusion, we had to analyse the various different linguistic versions of the regulation. The others proved to be closer to each other than they were to the German text. We also had to look at the preamble and the objectives of the regulation. Once you did that, the meaning was indeed not in Dr. Schenkel's favour. Having said that, if one looked at the German text in isolation, his argument was far from groundless.

Adam: In this instance, you and the Court looked at different language versions of the same legal act. How about using the wide-angle lens that we spoke about, and venturing into other jurisdictions, however close or distant they may be. For instance, when preparing Opinions, did you look into what the EFTA Court was doing?

Eleanor: Yes, naturally I looked at the EFTA Court's case law if they had issued a judgment on a point about which I had been asked to opine. I have always taken the approach that, if another judicial mind has already grappled with the problem that I am trying to tackle, it is both informative and respectful to have a look at how they approached it, what they thought did and didn't matter in analysing the problem, and the conclusion that they arrived at. Whether you end up agreeing with them or not, looking at what happens when a judicial mind meets a problem is always informative.

Adam: This is particularly relevant in the context of the European Economic Area where both sides, that is the EU and the EFTA countries, apply the same rules.

Eleanor: You are looking at what a close cousin has done with the sort of problem that you have. So, if the EFTA Court had issued a judgment that was relevant to a case that was in my docket, naturally I would cite their judgment in my

Opinion. I never really knew how it worked on the judges' side of the equation, because I did not participate in the *délibéré*. Collectively, by general agreement, we didn't look at national court decisions interpreting EU law. Reaching an authoritative interpretation of that was our business, rather than theirs. I have been asked sometimes: suppose that there was a Supreme Court decision in the UK on the exact point of EU law that we were looking at, would we take it into account? The blunt answer to that question is 'no'. Why would we?

Adam: I have noticed that you refer to the EFTA Court as a 'close cousin'. Sometimes people refer to it as a 'younger brother' or something like that, as if it were a less important court than the Court of Justice.

Eleanor: That is disrespectful to the EFTA Court. Calling the EFTA Court a 'younger brother' implies that the quality of the EFTA Court's output will somehow automatically be inferior to that of the CJEU. I don't buy into that at all, not least because of my experience as an advocate before that Court. As I already told you, the judges there put me through my paces to a far greater extent than normally happened to me in front of the Court of Justice. You can obviously say that the EFTA Court has fewer cases to deal with, whereas the Court of Justice has an ever-increasing workload. Of course that is entirely true. But nevertheless, just looking at the amount of judicial analysis and attention being applied, I would find it very difficult to say that the EFTA Court is the younger brother. The quality of the legal discussion that I experienced as counsel leads me to take that Court very seriously.

Adam: What about the views of national courts as included in their references for a preliminary ruling? The Court is encouraging domestic judges to share how they think the questions should be answered. That, of course, is a different matter, nevertheless it is very interesting and it also takes us back to Sir Francis Jacobs who was a strong supporter of adding a few paragraphs to the Recommendations of the Court of Justice for national courts on making references for a preliminary ruling.[40]

Eleanor: This was, in fact, Francis's idea and it has been referred to as a 'green light procedure'. It is, of course, a slightly different point from the one I have just made about the use of national case law by the Court of Justice. Here, we are not talking about a domestic court having a go at EU law but rather about a referring court divulging to the Court of Justice what it itself feels should be the answer in the case that it is referring to the CJEU. There is, by the way, a lovely historical example: the Court of Appeal of England and Wales in *Polydor v. Harlequin* on the interpretation of the EEC-Portugal Association Agreement[41] (Case 270/80).[42] If my memory serves me correctly, the Court of Appeal in its order for reference, having looked at the case law on what were then Articles 30 and 36 EEC, gave a rather clear indication as to what it thought was the correct answer. Nevertheless, out of prudence the Court of Appeal decided to make a reference. It is just as well that it did so, because the Court of Justice came to the opposite conclusion. In so doing, it explained in some detail that the way that you interpret the Treaty and the way that you interpret an association agreement between the EU and a third country are not necessarily the same.

Note that the wording in the Court's Recommendations to national courts is very careful. To paraphrase what is written there: 'If it is okay in terms of your own national procedural law, and you feel like telling us what your views are as to what you think the answer should be to the questions that you are referring, please do so. We would be really interested to know'. The reason that it is framed in those terms is that, as I understand it, there are some Member States where if the judge is making an order for reference, it is deemed procedurally improper for the judge nevertheless to express a view as to what he or she thinks the answer to the questions referred should be. The rationale behind that is that, if a judge knows the answer, why is (s)he making a reference? So the recommendation is phrased in a way that says, if your national procedural law allows you to do this, we would very much like to know what you think the answer should be. On the other hand, if your national procedural law doesn't allow you to do that, that's okay. We completely understand.

Adam: This is very interesting indeed. Now, I would like to ask about something else related to the time when you were an Advocate General. I recall that when we spoke about *El Kott*, you mentioned that it gave you an opportunity to clarify something that you had missed in *Bolbol*. With the benefit of hindsight, are there any Opinions that you feel you should have written or pitched differently?

Eleanor: It probably sounds very arrogant to say this – but no, I don't think so. I always focused very intensely on an Opinion when I was doing it. I have a very clear memory of some Opinions because they took a particular investment of time and effort. I wrote what I thought was right at the time. Even if the Court didn't follow me, I still think (or hope … or believe …) that what I wrote was probably of use or value in highlighting the problem. I am going to illustrate that point with a couple of Grand Chamber cases, which arose in the middle of the refugee crisis. At the time, about three quarters of a million refugees were using the Western Balkans route to flee the inferno that was Syria. In legal terms, the problem was that the Dublin Regulation[43] was never designed with such a situation in mind. The first two cases, in which I gave a single Opinion, were *A.S. v Slovenia* and *Jafari* (respectively, Case C-490/16 and Case C-646/16).[44] A later case was *Tsegezab Mengesteab v Germany* (Case C-670/16).[45]

The Opinion in *A.S and Jafari* started with the map of Europe and an explanation of the problem, because I wanted people to understand the human dimension before going into the law. It is, in places, a very passionate Opinion. I have never been afraid of being passionate if I felt passionate. In these cases, I more or less said to the Court: 'what on earth was Croatia meant to do?' You had all these refugees showing up! If Croatia had shut the frontier, there would have been refugee encampments along the lines of the frontier and winter was coming. What were the Croatian authorities meant to do? They opened the frontier. In my Opinion, I said that I thought that was not an 'irregular frontier crossing' within the meaning of Article 13 of the Dublin Regulation. Because to me, there is a degree of official *imprimatur* to crossing a frontier that is open with frontier guards waving people through, giving them bottles of water, and putting them onto coaches. To me that official connivance (if you want to call it that) was inconsistent with the idea of an 'irregular' crossing. As far as I am concerned, an irregular crossing is people putting a ladder across a fence at dead of night. The Court disagreed.[46] It ruled that this was an irregular crossing and that Croatia was, in consequence, required to process those people's claims for international protection.

Adam: The underlying problem seems to be, and this is not only *spécialité de la maison* of the European Union or, more generally European states, that there are natural limits to the imagination of law makers. When an unexpected crisis hits, we are often caught off guard as our laws are not prepared for what is happening. The refugee crisis was a stark reminder of that, then came Covid-19. But going back to these cases from your docket, Leo: what was *Mengesteab* about?

Eleanor: Here, the legal issue was the length of time a Member State has to process an asylum application. Again, the Court and I counted the amount of time in a different way. I thought that Germany still had time to request another Member State to take over processing the applications for international protection under the Dublin Regulation. The Court said no, Germany had run out of time and therefore it should have been looking after those particular applicants.[47] Probably – and this is absolutely unprovable! – if you look at the global number of people involved after *A.S and Jafari* and *Mengesteab*, the Court and the Advocate General may very roughly have ended up with a similar number of people in the various Member States. The Court and I, in those two cases, came to different conclusions. The truth, however, is that in neither *A.S. and Jafari* nor *Mengesteab* was there a good answer to give. Whatever answer you gave couldn't really address the underlying problem: namely, that the Dublin Regulation was not intended to deal with such a challenge – it required a completely different set of rules.

Adam: Indeed, and years later we see that the European Union is still engaged in a whack-a-mole exercise, struggling to find good solutions that will be effective, human rights compliant, and acceptable to all Member States. This takes us to the *Reallocation* cases in which the European Commission took Poland, the Czech Republic, and Hungary to the Court of Justice for failure to comply with EU Council decisions (Joined Cases C-715/17, C-718/17, and C-719/17).[48] Leo, for me this was one of the finest Opinions you wrote as an Advocate General.[49] You delivered your Opinion on 31 October 2019, which was one of the possible 'Brexit dates'. To borrow from the title of a very moving Julian Barnes book, your Opinion had 'the sense of an ending' written all over it. One may read those last three paragraphs as if Leo was saying: 'I might be on my way out from the

Court, however, here is the message I have for you'. And, if you ask me, we are going back here to your upbringing. *Tikkun ha olam* – repairing the world.

Eleanor: That was one of four Opinions I delivered on 31 October 2019. We had a kind of moving target as to when I was going to leave the Court. We didn't know when Brexit Day would be because of all the shenanigans at Westminster. So, we went on trying to get Opinions through the system. The really ironic aspect is that for the next six months, whilst a number of things were going very bad indeed, Koen Lenaerts (the President of the Court of Justice) was quoting that Opinion and those three paragraphs everywhere. Those cases gave AG Sharpston a chance to stand up and say what she thought about the duty of cooperation, and very specifically about solidarity. But this is partly the difference between the function of the Advocate General and the function of the Court. There are times when the Advocate General has the liberty to say something that matters, knowing that the Court in its judgment may think the same way but will probably say nothing. And if the Court does say something, it will say it in clunky prose because that is the only drafting style the Court knows. Whereas, as the Advocate General you get a chance – you have the inestimable freedom – to say it a bit better.

Adam: The three closing paragraphs are so powerful, Leo. I remember reading this Opinion for the very first time. I was at home, at my desk, looking at the text with my graffiti already all over it, and just bowed my head. You have managed to share so much wisdom in literally three paragraphs of a very long Advocate's General Opinion. I don't think anyone who is passionate about European integration can skip these paragraphs without taking a step back. I just refuse to accept that these first two paragraphs can leave one indifferent:

> 253. *Solidarity is the lifeblood of the European project. Through their participation in that project and their citizenship of the (European) Union, Member States and their nationals have obligations as well as benefits, duties as well as rights. Sharing in the European 'demos' is not a matter of looking through the Treaties and the secondary legislation to see what one can claim. It also requires one to shoulder collective responsibilities and (yes) burdens to further the common good.*
>
> 254. *Respecting the 'rules of the club' and playing one's proper part in solidarity with fellow Europeans cannot be based on a penny-pinching cost-benefit analysis along the lines (familiar, alas, from Brexiteer rhetoric) of 'what precisely does the EU cost me per week and what exactly do I personally get out of it?' Such self-centredness is a betrayal of the founding fathers' vision for a peaceful and prosperous continent. It is the antithesis of being a loyal Member State and being worthy, as an individual, of shared European citizenship. If the European project is to prosper and go forward, we must all do better than that.*

It was so poignant back then in 2019 when you wrote it. For me, it received even deeper meaning on 24 February 2022, when Russia invaded Ukraine and, soon afterwards, Ukraine applied for EU membership. The overwhelming support for Ukraine and its citizens in the months and years that followed has shown that – despite being united in diversity and, at times, very much divided – Europeans can show solidarity. Then your Opinion ends with the story from the Talmud.

Eleanor: Indeed, but for someone with my background, that was the most natural thing to include. The final section was also the part of the Opinion where I wrote every word myself. I said to my team:

> *Listen, I am going to write this next bit. I know what I want to say. I don't want to explain it to you, and then you go away and you try to write it. I know you will give me your honest best endeavour of what it was you thought I was trying to say. But it will be quicker if I write it up and you tell me if it works (and if it doesn't work, why it doesn't work). And if it doesn't work, then I will revise my own work and I will change it.*

Usually when I drafted something, the members of my *cabinet* would come back with editorial suggestions, with corrections. I don't remember any being offered for that particular passage. This Opinion also gave me the opportunity, which I think is unique in the history of the Court, to quote a *midrash* – a teaching story – from the *Talmud* in the final paragraph of the three that you mentioned. As I said at the very beginning of our conversations, this particular story has been a beacon to my life ever since I read it aged twelve:

> *255. A group of men are travelling together in a boat. Suddenly, one of them takes out an auger and starts to bore a hole in the hull beneath himself. His companions remonstrate with him. 'Why are you doing that?' they cry. 'What are you complaining about?' says he. 'Am I not drilling the hole under my own seat?' 'Yes', they reply, 'but the water will come in and flood the boat for all of us'.*

ENDNOTES

* Eleanor Sharpston, ''Can't Those European Judges Think for Themselves?' An Afterword on Why the Court (Still) Needs its Advocates General' in Graham Butler and Adam Łazowski (eds), *Shaping EU Law the British Way. UK Advocates General at the Court of Justice of the European Union* (Hart, 2022) 591, 603.

[1] Case C-251/04 *Commission of the European Communities v Hellenic Republic* ECLI:EU:C:2006:565, Opinion of AG Sharpston.

[2] This procedure is known universally, even to English speakers, by its French acronym, the 'PPU' (*procédure préjudicielle d'urgence*). Try pronouncing the English language acronym for 'urgent preliminary ruling procedure' ('UPRP') and you'll understand why.

[3] Case C-693/18 *CLCV and Others (Defeat device on diesel engines)* ECLI:EU:C:2020:323, Opinion of AG Sharpston.

[4] Case C-28/08P *European Commission v The Bavarian Lager Co. Ltd* ECLI:EU:C:2009:624, Opinion of AG Sharpston; Case C-263/08 *Djurgården-Lilla Värtans Miljöskyddsförening v Stockholms kommun genom dess marknämnd* ECLI:EU:C:2009:421, Opinion of AG Sharpston; and Case C-350/08 *European Commission v Republic of Lithuania* ECLI:EU:C:2010:214, Opinion of AG Sharpston.

[5] *Opinion 2/15 (Free Trade Agreement with Singapore)* ECLI:EU:C:2016:992, Opinion of AG Sharpston.

[6] Joined Cases C-541/20 to C-555/20 *Lithuania and others v European Parliament and Council* ECLI:EU:C:2023:866, Opinion of AG Pitruzzella.

[7] *Opinion 2/15 (Free Trade Agreement with Singapore)* ECLI:EU:C:2017:376.

[8] Trade and Cooperation Agreement between the European Union and the European Atomic Energy Community, of the one part, and the United Kingdom of Great Britain and Northern Ireland, of the other part [2021] OJ L 149/10.

[9] Case C-413/15 *Elaine Farrell v Alan Whitty and Others* ECLI:EU:C:2017:492, Opinion of AG Sharpston.

[10] Case C-188/89 *A. Foster and others v British Gas plc* ECLI:EU:C:1990:313.

[11] Case C-110/05 *Commission of the European Communities v Italian Republic* ECLI:EU:C:2009:66.

[12] Case C-110/05 *Commission of the European Communities v Italian Republic* ECLI:EU:C:2006:646, Opinion of AG Léger; Case C-110/05 *Commission of the European Communities v Italian Republic* ECLI:EU:C:2006:646, Opinion of AG Bot.

[13] Case 155/79 *AM & S Europe Limited v Commission of the European Communities* ECLI:EU:C:1982:157.

[14] Case 155/79 *AM & S Europe Limited v Commission of the European Communities* ECLI:EU:C:1981:9, Opinion of AG Warner; Case 155/79 *AM & S Europe Limited v Commission of the European Communities* ECLI:EU:C:1982:17, Opinion of AG Slynn.

[15] Case C-313/05 *Maciej Brzeziński v Dyrektor Izby Celnej w Warszawie* ECLI:EU:C:2007:33; Case C-313/05 *Maciej Brzeziński v Dyrektor Izby Celnej w Warszawie* ECLI:EU:C:2006:598, Opinion of AG Sharpston.

[16] Case C-281/07 *Hauptzollamt Hamburg-Jonas v Bayerische Hypotheken-und Vereinsbank AG* ECLI:EU:C:2008:522, Opinion of AG Sharpston.

[17] Joined cases C-278/07 to C-280/07 *Hauptzollamt Hamburg-Jonas v Josef Vosding Schlacht-, Kühl- und Zerlegebetrieb GmbH & Co. (C-278/07), Vion Trading GmbH (C-279/07) and Ze Fu Fleischhandel GmbH (C-280/07)* ECLI:EU:C:2008:521, Opinion of AG Sharpston.

[18] Case C-31/09 *Nawras Bolbol v Bevándorlási és Állampolgársági Hivatal* ECLI:EU:C:2010:351.

[19] Case C-31/09 *Nawras Bolbol v Bevándorlási és Állampolgársági Hivatal* ECLI:EU:C:2010:119, Opinion of AG Sharpston.

[20] Case C-364/11 *Mostafa Abed El Karem El Kott and Others v Bevándorlási és Állampolgársági Hivatal* ECLI:EU:C:2012:826.

[21] Case C-364/11 *Mostafa Abed El Karem El Kott and Others v Bevándorlási és Állampolgársági Hivatal* ECLI:EU:C:2012:569, Opinion of AG Sharpston.

[22] Case C-118/23 *Getin Holding and Others* ECLI:EU:C:2024:511, Opinion of AG de la Tour.

[23] Case C-34/09 *Gerardo Ruiz Zambrano v Office national de l'emploi (ONEm)* ECLI:EU:C:2011:124; Case C-34/09 *Gerardo Ruiz Zambrano v Office national de l'emploi (ONEm)* ECLI:EU:C:2010:560, Opinion of AG Sharpston.

[24] Case C-212/06 *Government of the French Community and Walloon Government v Flemish Government* ECLI:EU:C:2007:398, Opinion of AG Sharpston.

[25] Case C-59/92 *Hauptzollamt Hamburg-St. Annen v Ebbe Sönnichsen GmbH* ECLI:EU:C:1993:167.

[26] Case C-345/06 *Gottfried Heinrich* ECLI:EU:C:2008:212, Opinion of AG Sharpston; Joined Cases C-402/07 & C-432/07 *Christopher Sturgeon, Gabriel Sturgeon and Alana Sturgeon v Condor Flugdienst GmbH (C-402/07) and Stefan Böck and Cornelia Lepuschitz v Air France SA (C-432/07)* ECLI:EU:C:2009:416, Opinion of AG Sharpston.

[27] Regulation (EC) No 2320/2002 of the European Parliament and of the Council of 16 December 2002 establishing common rules in the field of civil aviation security [2002] OJ L 355/1.

[28] Commission Regulation (EC) No 622/2003 of 4 April 2003 laying down measures for the implementation of the common basic standards on aviation security [2003] OJ L 89/9.

[29] Regulation (EC) No 1049/2001 of the European Parliament and of the Council of 30 May 2001 regarding public access to European Parliament, Council and Commission documents [2001] OJ L 145/43.

[30] European Commission, 'Air security: Commission draws up EU-wide list of prohibited articles on passenger aircraft' (16 January 2004) <https://ec.europa.eu/commission/presscorner/detail/en/ip_04_59> accessed 1 September 2025.

[31] Case C-161/06 *Skoma-Lux sro v Celní ředitelství Olomouc* ECLI:EU:C:2007:773.

[32] Case C-345/06 *Gottfried Heinrich* ECLI:EU:C:2009:140.

[33] Regulation 261/2004 of the European Parliament and of the Council of 11 February 2004 establishing common rules on compensation and assistance to passengers in the event of denied boarding and of cancellation or long delay of flights, and repealing Regulation (EEC) No 295/91 [2004] OJ L 46/1.

[34] Joined Cases C-402/07 & C-432/07 *Christopher Sturgeon, Gabriel Sturgeon and Alana Sturgeon v Condor Flugdienst GmbH (C-402/07) and Stefan Böck and Cornelia Lepuschitz v Air France SA (C-432/07)* ECLI:EU:C:2009:716.

[35] Joined Cases C-581/10 and C-629/10 *Emeka Nelson and Others v Deutsche Lufthansa AG and TUI Travel plc and Others v Civil Aviation Authority* ECLI:EU:C:2012:295, Opinion of AG Bot.

[36] Joined Cases C-581/10 and C-629/10 *Emeka Nelson and Others v Deutsche Lufthansa AG and TUI Travel plc and Others v Civil Aviation Authority* ECLI:EU:C:2012:657.

[37] Case C-195/08 *Inga Rinau* ECLI:EU:C:2008:406; Case C-195/08 *Inga Rinau* ECLI:EU:C:2008:377, View of AG Sharpston.

[38] Council Regulation (EC) No 2201/2003 of 27 November 2003 concerning jurisdiction and the recognition and enforcement of judgments in matrimonial matters and the matters of parental responsibility, repealing Regulation (EC) No 1347/2000 [2003] OJ L 338/1.

[39] Case C-173/07 *Emirates Airlines – Direktion für Deutschland v Diether Schenkel* ECLI:EU:C:2008:145, Opinion of AG Sharpston.

[40] Recommendations to national courts and tribunals in relation to the initiation of preliminary ruling proceedings OJ C, C/2024/6008, 9.10.2024.

[41] Agreement concluded on 22 July 1972 between the European Economic Community and the Portuguese Republic [1972] OJ L 301/16.

[42] Case 270/80 *Polydor Limited and RSO Records Inc. v Harlequin Records Shops Limited and Simons Records Limited* ECLI:EU:C:1982:43.

[43] Regulation (EU) No 604/2013 of the European Parliament and of the Council of 26 June 2013 establishing the criteria and mechanisms for determining the Member State responsible for examining an application for international protection lodged in one of the Member States by a third-country national or a stateless person [2013] OJ L 180/31.

[44] Case C-490/16 *A.S. v Republic of Slovenia* and Case C-646/16 *Jafari* ECLI:EU:C:2017:443, Opinion of AG Sharpston.

[45] Case C-670/16 *Tsegezab Mengesteab v Bundesrepublik Deutschland* ECLI:EU:C:2017:480, Opinion of AG Sharpston.

[46] Case C-490/16 *A.S. v Republic of Slovenia* ECLI:EU:C:2017:585 and Case C-646/16 *Proceedings brought by Khadija Jafari and Zainab Jafari* ECLI:EU:C:2017:586.

[47] Case C-670/16 *Tsegezab Mengesteab v Bundesrepublik Deutschland* ECLI:EU:C:2017:587.

[48] Joined Cases C-715/17, C-718/17, and C-719/17 *European Commission v Republic of Poland and Others* ECLI:EU:C:2020:257.

[49] Joined Cases C-715/17, C-718/17, and C-719/17 *European Commission v Republic of Poland and Others* ECLI:EU:C:2019:917, Opinion of AG Sharpston.

6

The Court on the Kirchberg Plateau

*One of the richnesses of the Court is precisely that it has people who come from different legal traditions. We are all reading the same text against our different backgrounds and trying to construe it, trying to make it coherent and intelligent – and yes, trying to come up with an answer which is a just and correct answer.**

Adam: The CJEU has travelled a long way from the early days when it was small and resided in *Villa Vauban*, located in the *Parc de la Ville* in Luxembourg city. Just like the European Union itself (including its earlier reincarnations) and other EU institutions, the Court has had to evolve to remain fit for purpose and, as Article 19 TEU requires, to fulfil its unenviable mandate of ensuring that 'in the application of the Treaty the law is observed'. Like other courts in different corners of the democratic world, the CJEU faces a constant challenge: how to reconcile the ever-increasing number of cases arriving in its docket with the *desideratum* to proceed efficiently and in a timely fashion. However, when it comes to the CJEU, the situation is particularly complex due to its legal character and position among other EU institutions. To begin with, for several decades now we have had two courts – the General Court and the Court of Justice, which together comprise the Court of Justice of the European Union. As the quote from Eleanor at the beginning of this chapter tells us, the CJEU is a very international court with all the richness that entails. It has Members on the bench from all twenty-seven Member States. It operates in all twenty-four official languages of the European Union (though the unofficial, internal working language is French). It is a true jazz jamboree of legal cultures and traditions. As the Member States are united in diversity, all these factors have to be taken into account, not only in the everyday functioning of the Court but also when reforms are being designed on the drawing board. There is one more basic premise that one needs to have in mind. The big decisions are often not for the CJEU to make autonomously. Whilst the Court is free to propose the reforms it deems necessary, those reforms frequently require the involvement of the Member States. Thus, whatever the CJEU puts on the table will have to take the shape of – *par excellence* – a political decision. An obvious example is the increase in the number of judges at the General Court in 2016. The CJEU originally asked for a handful of additional Members on the bench. However, the Member States could not agree as to which countries would have one judge and which would have two. Eventually, the political decision was taken to double the number of judges, so that all Member States would have two judges in the General Court. This in itself has proven to be both a blessing and a curse. Sometimes less is more, as opposed to the more the merrier.

During her time at the Court, AG Eleanor Sharpston contributed to several reforms of the Statute and the Rules of Procedure of the Court of Justice. In this chapter we discuss, for instance, how the Urgent Preliminary Ruling Procedure ('PPU') for the Area of Freedom, Security and Justice came about; and how the Court tested the waters with the first cases handled under this ultra-fast-track procedure. We also look into the most recent transfer, from the Court of Justice to the General Court, of jurisdiction to deal with references for preliminary ruling in six selected areas of EU law. Some further ideas as to the potential future reforms of the CJEU are also discussed.

*

Adam: Let us continue the conversation about the Court. I should like to start by asking about one aspect of your work which is largely unknown outside of the Kirchberg bubble: the invisible contribution of AG Sharpston to the functioning of the Court. You served on the Rules of Procedure Committee and thus had a role in shaping several internal reforms.

Eleanor: From the day I joined till the day I was ejected from the Court, I sat on the Rules of Procedure Committee. That Committee had previously been chaired by AG Francis Jacobs. When Francis retired and I joined the Court as his successor, I went straight onto that Committee. I think the reasoning was that for balance the Rules of Procedure Committee needed another Advocate General and it also needed a common law lawyer. It was fairly obvious where that took you.

Adam: One of the reforms that you contributed to was the creation of the PPU, the Urgent Preliminary Ruling Procedure for the Area of Freedom, Security, and Justice. We have already touched upon it in the context of the *Rinau* case, but let's return to it now. Immediately after the changes to the Statute of the Court and its Rules of Procedure entered into force, our colleague Catherine Barnard published an article in the European Law Review asking what was perhaps a rhetorical question, whether the PPU was worth the candle.[1] With the benefit of hindsight, was it worth the candle indeed?

Eleanor: I think my first comment is that the Treaty of Lisbon, which was already signed but not yet in force, required us to create and put in place a special, much swifter, procedure to handle the categories of cases that the PPU covers. Article 267 TFEU received a new paragraph which obliged the Court to 'act with the minimum of delay' in cases of preliminary rulings dealing with people in custody. It was obvious that the new *modus operandi* would have to be radically different from the existing procedures because the cases had to move much faster. The existing accelerated procedure wasn't going to fit the bill: it was (still) too slow and too cumbersome. So we didn't have a choice. We had to invent a brand new procedure. My second comment is that in a sense, the PPU is a bit surreal. The CJEU is a court that normally relies heavily on written pleadings, and regards an oral procedure as being the optional icing on the cake. Yet we created a new procedure where, in order to achieve the required speed, a lot of the heavy lifting is done at the hearing. In a sense, that is just bizarre. The PPU works by telescoping translation time. So, after the order for reference is received, the first (urgent) decision is: does this new order for reference meet the requirements to be treated using the PPU? If so, the parties, the Member State from which the reference has arrived and the Commission are invited to lodge written observations – all of which will (of course) be in the same language as the order for reference. Meanwhile, the order for reference is being translated as a top priority and sent out to all other Member States. Unlike the normal reference procedure, those other Member States are *not* allowed to lodge written observations (which would then need translation). Instead, they are invited if they so wish to come to the hearing. That means that the hearing – which as usual has simultaneous interpretation – serves as the channel for getting the views of other Member States. That places an enormous weight on the hearing – and of course on the interpreters.

Adam: That was a big change of dynamics, indeed. It perhaps made the Member States more interested in making the best use of hearings, rather than merely reading out what is already in their written pleadings. (One hopes!) The pace at which the Court was due to proceed must have also affected the dynamics between the Advocates General and the chamber that is allocated a PPU case.

Eleanor: There is an inherent and uncomfortable tension. Time is running simultaneously for the Advocate General to give their Opinion and for the *juge rapporteur* to pull together the first draft of the judgment. When I say simultaneously, I do mean simultaneously. Both have 10 working days from the date of the hearing. Consequently, if as the AG you took – in a difficult case – five days working flat-out to produce your Opinion, you knew that while you were trying to get your views down on paper, the *juge rapporteur* was already drafting. In a sense, if you took time to think you were (inevitably) being side-lined. That is not a comfortable feeling. Another problem that is baked into the PPU is that cases that go through the PPU are cases in really sensitive and difficult areas of EU law. The Brussels IIa Regulation on judicial cooperation in matrimonial matters and the Framework Decision on the European Arrest Warrant are two obvious examples.[2] It is very easy to make the wrong call, and yet you are making those decisions at breakneck speed.

Having done a few PPUs, including the *Rinau* case (C-195/08 PPU),[3] in which we were putting the procedure through its paces for the first time and seeing if it worked, let me offer a couple of further comments. First, when we were doing a PPU, all other work in my *cabinet* was pretty much put on hold (including Grand Chamber cases). The PPU would throw a big spanner into the works. Effectively, it sabotaged the ordinary processing of cases in my *cabinet*. That spanner lasted as long as we were trying to get the PPU Opinion out. And for the PPU we would invariably write in French rather than in English, because we had to produce the Opinion in the language in which the Court could instantly make use of it. Second, whenever we were doing a PPU, I had my heart in my mouth. I lived with the constant worry that I might be about to say or do something absolutely daft which, in a case going through under an ordinary procedure, my team and I would have picked up and rectified. In a normal case it would always be possible to stand back and have a second think about what I was proposing to the Court. I would have had the time and space to reflect – and then perhaps say to myself: 'wait a minute, that can't possibly be the right place to get to'. With the PPU, we were going too fast for any of that. And so I really lived in fear that I was about to produce some monumental howler which I would fail to spot in time, and of which afterwards I would obviously be ashamed.

Adam: That is a very good point about the pressure that is on Advocates General, on the *juge rapporteur*, and on the designated Chamber dealing with the PPUs. When a PPU case lands on the table, everyone is in a pressure cooker, so to speak.

Eleanor: But, Adam: the Advocate General is still meant to provide the same quality service to the Court. You can't get away with a more superficial, less rigorous analysis because you are writing for the PPU. You are still there to assist the Court, to try to set out for the Court the different options that it has, to explore each of those options properly, to get any red herrings out of the way, and then to make a recommendation to the Court as to what the best way forward is. So the service you are meant to be providing is meant to be exactly the same. It is just that you are meant to be doing it at supersonic speed. I have perhaps a slightly graphic image to offer you.

Adam: I am all eyes and ears, Leo!

Eleanor: In Grand Prix racing there is a moment where each car comes into the pit to have its tyres changed. That tyre change is about split-second timing, about getting four tyres off and four new tyres on at lightning speed, and getting the car back on the road – ideally, in under 2 seconds! Nevertheless, the mechanics doing that tyre-change have to make sure that when they put the new tyres in position, everything is aligned and the central nuts are secured properly onto their axles. What the pit team has to do, conceptually, is just the same as what they would do if you took your car into the garage on a March morning to get its tyres changed from winter tyres to summer tyres. You know: you bring the car in, you leave it, you go and drink a coffee, and the mechanics chat to each other while they change the tyres. The process of changing over the tyres is the same process; but the Grand Prix version and the standard version are radically different.

Adam: I believe with *Rinau* there are two background stories which, perhaps, we should mention. The first has to do with your very kind *chauffeur*.

Eleanor: When we were doing the *Rinau* case, everyone was involved. That also meant getting in supplies so that we could keep working stupid hours. The hearing itself was a challenge. At the CJEU, a hearing will normally last a couple of hours. In *Rinau*, the hearing started at 2pm on Thursday 26 June 2008. It overran its scheduled finishing time that day by an hour – as I recall we ended just before 7pm. We gave the parties questions to think about overnight. We resumed the hearing on Friday morning at 9am and we ran till lunchtime. My team and I then worked straight through the weekend and at the beginning of the following week I presented my Opinion orally to the Chamber, as well as presenting it in writing. It was exactly the way it had been when I had had a crisis at the Bar. The whole team was going flat out with me and yes, our nice *chauffeur* Gilles Bracchetti was foraging for food as required.

Adam: The second story is about the *interpreters*. I remember you told us about it in Dubrovnik at one of the seminars. If I recall correctly, although the hearing overran on the first day, the air conditioning in the interpreters' booths was switched off automatically at the scheduled finishing time ….

Eleanor: Our poor interpreters! We – sitting on the bench – had no idea what had happened. Within the courtroom, everything was normal. We saw the interpreters fanning themselves, but we did not know what was going on. Of course if we had known, we would have stopped sooner and started the next day a bit earlier. Our interpreters were so devoted, so professional, so loyal that they just carried on without telling us that something was amiss. But I had lots of good friends amongst the interpreters, so I discovered (probably about 10 minutes after the hearing had finished) what had actually happened.

Adam: *Oy gevalt*, that does not sound good. Since then, however, the PPU has become a permanent feature of the Kirchberg landscape. I have one more question about PPUs, Leo. Initially, the advice of the Advocates General was provided in 'Views', not 'Opinions'. And then, quite out of the blue, the 'Views' became 'Opinions'. Why was that?

Eleanor: Ah, that's a very nice observation, Adam. It has a lot to do with the issue of publication. When we wrote Opinions for Opinions of the Court (for example, on trade agreements), what we wrote was also called a 'View' and it wasn't published. (We are talking here about the *ex ante* control of international agreements, as envisaged by Article 218(11) TFEU.) The change from View to Opinion in the PPU goes with the View becoming a published text. As the 'college' of Advocates General, we felt – I am going to say not unnaturally – that if we were putting considerable effort into setting out for the judges what the options were and suggesting what the Court should do in difficult and sensitive cases, the material which was informing the Court's thinking in reaching its judgment should also be available publicly. In the case of Article 218(11) TFEU Opinions, the change likewise came when we moved from a 'View' in which all the Advocates General participated to a single Opinion by a single Advocate General. (By the way: this was, above all, a resource-saving measure.) At that stage it was clear to the AGs – and our judge colleagues kindly concurred – that the resulting text should be published, just like any other Opinion. Remember, the Opinion of AG Sharpston on the Free Trade Agreement between the EU and Singapore was the longest text I ever wrote at the Court.[4]

Adam: I see. The fact that initially the Views of Advocates General in the PPU were not necessarily to be published caused quite an uproar in the academic community. In the same article that we have already mentioned, Catherine Barnard included a letter signed by several academics arguing that, for a host of reasons, the Views of AGs in PPU cases should be published. This has become a standard with, I believe, only a single PPU case not having the View of the AG made available to members of the public.

Eleanor: They are now called 'Opinions'; but – *unlike* the normal procedure – they may not be made public until well after the Court has delivered its judgment in the case.

Adam: Which makes me wonder if, even with the best intentions in the world, the judges are given a chance to make good use of the Opinion of the Advocate General in a PPU. By the time the Opinion is presented, the judgment must be in an advanced stage of drafting. So the judges will have only a few days to familiarise themselves with the Opinion's contents and reflect on it when putting the finishing touches to their judgment.

Eleanor: The system puts enormous pressure on the Advocate General to produce the Opinion at lightning speed and make it available to the judges as swiftly as possible. You are breaking your neck to get your views about the case across to the chamber before any serious drafting has happened. In contrast, in the Court's eyes getting an AG's Opinion in a PPU case translated and made publicly available is actually a relatively low priority. As I've said, often that will only happen some time after the judgment itself has been delivered.

Adam: The other important matter that you worked on, as a member of the Rules of Procedure Committee, was the mechanism for handling security sensitive information. This, I guess, became a major issue when the first challenges to sanctions imposed by the European Union on people allegedly engaged in terrorist activities reached the courtrooms on the Kirchberg plateau. They belong to those post 9/11 issues that frequently land in the docket of the General Court and, on appeal, of the Court of Justice.

Eleanor: Following *Kadi* (Joined Cases C-402/05 P and C-415/05 P)[5] and similar challenges to the legality of sanctions or asset freezes imposed by the EU, we had to work out a system for having sensitive security information put before the Court. This resulted in Decision of the Court 2016/2386 on the security rules applicable to information or material produced before the General Court.[6] We spent a very long time designing what became known as the 'Fiducia system'. I should add that we designed that system in parallel, and in cooperation, with the Rules of Procedure Committee of the General Court. Actions for annulment brought by individuals always land, in the first instance, in the General Court's docket. However, we – as the Court's Rules of Procedure Committee – were the ones who would be putting forward the proposed system to the Council. We spent a lot of very tender loving care trying to work out how to square the circle. It was something that was taken very seriously, and it was intellectually challenging.

Adam: I can imagine. The information that you would have access to could potentially land some people into a great deal of trouble.

Eleanor: These are desperately serious issues. If you have someone who is a terrorist, and you allow information to be disclosed to them which enables them to identify somebody who has infiltrated their organisation, that person may end up headless in a ditch. On the one hand, rights of the defence matter: they are an essential component of the rule of law. On the other hand, we had an obligation to protect the lives of people engaged in the shadow world of spying, information gathering, or reconnaissance. The underlying and fundamental issue was: do you reach a point in the procedure where you accept that the Court is going to see material from one party that the other party will not have seen, and will not be able to make submissions about? Is that conceptually acceptable? And, if so, how do you make sure that the fact that the other party (the applicant) hasn't had the chance to comment on it is duly reflected in the weight that the Court gives to that information in its judgment?

Adam: Could the UK model of the special advocate have been used in this instance?

Eleanor: The special advocate model is a peculiarity of the UK system and nobody at the Court wanted to go there. Having said that, I had a degree of usefulness on that committee, because I had, in fact, done cases for the UK Government in front of the Special Immigration Appeals Commissioners ('SIAC'). (Somehow I have a habit of being around, and therefore being the guinea pig, at the moment when we do the first case!) SIAC was no exception. I did *El Rehman*, which was the first case in front of that court involving the special advocate procedure. And a right mess it was, too!

Adam: The third big matter you worked on in the Rules of Procedure Committee was the filtering system for some of the appeals going from the General Court to the Court of Justice. Finding a balance between what should go through to the Court and what should not, must have been tricky. As you put it in your Opinion in *Bund für Umwelt und Naturschutz Deutschland* (Case C-115/09): '[…] like a Ferrari with its doors locked shut, an intensive system of review is of little practical help if the system itself is totally inaccessible for certain categories of action'.[7]

Eleanor: The filtering system was one of the last issues that I worked on in the Rules of Procedure Committee while I was still at the Court. It was a matter of trying to find a way, without reinventing the wheel, to reconcile various principles that do not reconcile very easily. First, some colleagues regarded the right to appeal a judgment of the General Court to the Court as an absolute right. If you took that view, you could not have any kind of a filtering system because – of course – you would have to let every appeal through. Once we managed to move on from there, the question became: which criterion (or criteria) were we going to apply in the filtering system? We were helped there by the fact that we had already, in the past, invented a procedure for staff cases which had gone on appeal from the Civil Service Tribunal to the General Court, where the First Advocate General then reviewed the resulting judgment of the General Court *ex officio* to see whether to recommend that the Court reexamine what the General Court had done. The criterion for a 'reexamen' was: did the judgment of the General Court create a serious risk to the unity and coherence of EU law? So we took the same basic criterion and massaged it a bit. We took over something that we were familiar with, that we had seen working well in practice, and we used that as the criterion for filtering certain categories of appeals from judgments of the General Court, namely those that (like the staff cases that served as the model) had already been through two layers of review.

Adam: Indeed, it is worth emphasising that the system – both the initial system and the current system, following the 2024 reform – was not meant to apply to all appeals but only to certain categories of appeal. To be more specific, only cases where the General Court was hearing actions for annulment of decisions of selected EU agencies, whose boards of appeal would have already heard the case. In other words, the challenges to legality would already – at the stage of potentially reaching the Court of Justice – have been looked into by two instances.

Eleanor: Let me add one gloss – something that was important to my thinking when helping to design the system. If you are going to have a filtering system, it is important that at least some cases do make it through the filter to be heard on appeal by the Court of Justice. As you have kindly quoted from my Opinion in Case C-115/09, what is the point of having a Ferrari if the doors are firmly shut? If every case gets knocked out by the filter, it becomes apparent to practitioners that actually the Court is going to block all appeals in those categories of cases. Whatever happened, however egregious the judgment of the General Court, you won't be allowed to appeal. That is not a good message to send. I don't know what the statistics look like now. I do know that when Judge Rosario Silva de la Puerta was the Vice President and therefore running the system, it was almost (I think) a matter of pride to her that no case got through the filter. Have any cases made it since, Adam?

Adam: If my memory serves me well, there was a trademark case called *KaiKai* (Case C-382/21) in which our mutual friend AG Ćapeta delivered an Opinion,[8] and the Grand Chamber ruled in 2024.[9]

Eleanor: Oh, I am glad to hear that. I think that for the overall credibility of the system, it is really important that from time to time, a case does make it through.

Adam: A side note, perhaps, but the filtering system was one of the topics of our dinner conversations during the annual seminars in Dubrovnik. That was at the time when the Committee was working on exactly this issue.

Eleanor: Ha! Dubrovnik seminars, we will talk about them at some point, right?

Adam: Oh yes, too good to be missed but a little later. For now let's carry on talking about the Court.

Eleanor: If you insist, if you insist …

Adam: In early autumn of 2024, we had quite a few personnel changes at the Court of Justice. Several Advocates General and judges retired and we have had a considerable number of new appointments to the bench. It is a good opportunity to reflect on fifteen years of having the Article 255 Committee. Do you think it was a good idea to establish it and has it made a difference in terms of the composition of the Court?

Eleanor: It was unquestionably a good idea. It has provided an important safety net in terms of guaranteeing basic competence and quality, in a world in which nomination to the 'Luxembourg bench' is at the complete discretion – sometimes, the rather political discretion – of the Member States. Without being invidious or naming names, I can perhaps think of one or two colleagues who were at the Court and the General Court when I joined in 2006 who might possibly have had slight difficulty getting through the Article 255 Committee, had it then existed. The Committee puts a sort of 'floor' in place, in terms of knowledge of EU law and the ability to express oneself in the language of the Court, which for better or worse is, as we already said, French. You have to be able to read and work in French effectively if you are going to contribute.

Adam: This was not an issue in your case, Leo.

Eleanor: Although I shall never be what I myself would call bilingual, let's say that I am at least very comfortable in French. I think that fact alone helped me to punch well above my weight as a newly-arrived Advocate General. I could always say what I wanted to say in meetings, without linguistic preparation, and indeed occasionally colleagues who trusted me would pass me a note in English saying: 'Eleanor, I want to intervene to say this ('XXX'): how do I do that in French?'

Adam: This is very interesting (and it must have been a tad frustrating for the person asking for help). Going back to the Article 255 Committee, over the years they have rejected quite a few candidates put forward by the Member States.

Eleanor: The way the Committee operated in the early years was extremely clever. According to Article 255 TFEU, the Committee's opinion on a candidate is not binding. Over time, the Committee turned down candidates including candidates from well-established Member States, and the Member States in question swallowed hard but then withdrew the candidate and selected someone else. That, therefore, created the present internal dynamic. If the Article 255 Committee turns down a candidate, the sponsoring Member State is *expected* to withdraw that candidate. If they demur, one (or more) of the Member States which has earlier had to put up with having its candidate turned down will say quietly to them: 'Listen, if you go on putting that candidate forward, we will veto them and, as you know, appointments to the Court have to be by the unanimous consent of all the Member States. So accept that they haven't got through the Article 255 Committee, and go and find someone else'. It is a very interesting example of soft power effectively becoming real power.

Adam: But the system does not come without limitations, does it?

Eleanor: The first limitation – and this is an important point that has been picked up by knowledgeable academic commentators such as Alberto Alemanno – is that the work of the Article 255 Committee is and remains shrouded in secrecy.[10] The Committee refuses adamantly to publish its reports on individual candidates, saying that these are 'confidential' and are to be disclosed only to the Member States who will then decide whether or not to make the appointment. That is not good for the legitimacy of the Committee or for those whom it endorses. It gives rise to all kinds of suspicions – which may or may not be well-founded – about what is going on behind the scenes, what criteria the Committee is really applying, and why particular candidates did or did not find favour. I know the counter-arguments, which are mainly about protecting unsuccessful candidates. However, the plain fact is that if someone has been put forward but rejected by the Committee, that is public knowledge anyway. It might be less damaging for an unsuccessful candidate if it were also public knowledge that (for example) the Committee had found them to be a person of integrity with appropriate knowledge of EU law, but had failed them on their knowledge of French. Personally, I think that the Committee should change its practice and be fully transparent with its recommendations.

Adam: That could, potentially, also deter potential candidates with dubious qualifications but strong political support from applying and, in turn, dissuade governments from gambling and putting forward people who may not survive grilling by the Committee.

Eleanor: The second limitation is that the Committee only looks at the candidate that is put forward by a Member State. They don't look at other candidates, because only a single candidate is put forward after the national part of the appointment procedure. (Unlike appointments to the European Court of Human Rights, where three candidates have to be put forward to the Parliamentary Assembly.)

The third limitation is not so much a limitation of the Committee as a generic limitation of the appointment system. Let's look at a national legal system. There, you try to have in your Supreme Court judges who between them cover all the main areas of law that the Supreme Court is going to have to deal with. So if, for example, you lose from the Supreme Court through retirement a couple of judges who represent everything the Supreme Court really knows about taxation and employment law, you would – probably – in making your new appointments to the Supreme Court try to make sure that your incoming justices have at least some competence in those areas. They might not be specialists, but you wouldn't want to leave the Supreme Court in a situation where there was no judge who had the slightest idea about taxation or employment law. You just would not do that.

Adam: And here is the problem, this is not how the system of appointments to the CJEU works.

Eleanor: There is no guarantee or equivalent procedure in terms of appointments to the CJEU. You can see the result if you look at the composition of the Court: at the list of Members and their backgrounds before appointment. For example, when I was in service at the Court, we were rather light in terms of expertise in criminal law. As we already mentioned, Judge Lars Bay Larsen and my much lamented and lovely colleague Advocate General Yves Bot were the two real experts on criminal law. The rest of us muddled through. On the basis of the very few criminal cases I did as a barrister in front of the English courts, I was deemed to have some sort of nodding competence.

Adam: And yet, it did not stop you from delivering excellent Opinions in cases on *ne bis in idem*, the European Arrest Warrant, or the Framework Decision on rights of victims.[11]

Eleanor: True, I wrote Opinions in such cases.

Adam: The other thing about the composition of the Court which, I think, merits attention is that it is still struggling for gender balance. Also, the composition of the bench does not reflect the social fabric of many Member States. I find it quite puzzling and uncomfortable.

Eleanor: As an empirical observation, that is completely accurate. In order to understand why that is so we need to look more closely at the appointment procedures in each Member State. Indeed, one of the interesting suggestions that have started to be made, for now primarily in relation to the European Parliament elections, is that maybe we should have slightly more standardised procedures for 'EU appointments'. Perhaps the same could, should be said of appointments to the Court of Justice. I think it would be difficult to impose uniformity in judicial appointments. You would need a willingness on the part of the Member States to see that that was a good idea. The Court is, in many ways, a very strange place. You do need to have a wider balance of members than might be candidates for a national supreme court. The Court has been well served by people who have been public servants, academics, practitioners, or national judges. How do you legislate for that to happen, when at the same time, every Member State should be at liberty to put forward the candidate whom they want to sponsor?

Adam: Now that is a one million Euro question, something that is not amenable to a quick and easy fix. At least some progress has been made to make the General Court and the Court of Justice more gender balanced.

Eleanor: It is noteworthy that, as a percentage, there are many more women in the General Court than in the Court of Justice. For a long time, Juliane Kokott and I were the only two female Advocates General. Then Verica Trstenjak was appointed for a six-year mandate. I am delighted that now there are more female Advocates General (albeit on single-mandate posts), and they are very good. But, just as an observation, if you look around the table during the *réunion générale*, those present are mainly elderly white men. If I think about the composition of *cabinet Sharpston* when I left the Court, I had a wonderful and stunningly good *chef de cabinet* – Doyin Lawunmi – who is a British woman of colour. (I can't think offhand of many other people of colour who were *référendaires* in either Court, though.) I had another female *référendaire*, Panagiota ('Penny') Katsorchi, who is Greek, and then I had two male *référendaires*: Matthias Lamberty (Belgian) and Muiris O'Connor (Irish). As it happened, my first and second assistants at that point, Johan Vekeman and Sam Wickens, were male rather than female – often, in the past, there was one female, one male in the secretariat. Overall, *team Sharpston* was usually a cocktail of nationalities and more or less balanced in terms of gender.

Adam: With your permission, Leo, I should like to steer our conversation now into the future of the Court of Justice. Perhaps we could use, as our starting point, a topic that is very close to your heart: the relationship between the Advocates General and the Court. We are used to the Court cryptically, if at all, referring to Opinions with generic sentences along the lines: 'as noted by the Advocate General in this or that section of the Opinion'. Do you think that the Court should, in the future, be more explicit whether it agrees or not with what the Advocate General advises it to do?

Eleanor: Well, when the Court cites you, you look up in keen expectation. ('They are citing me!') Then you look to see what (actually) they are citing. Often, you find that they have very courteously cited you saying, 'Two and two make four in most instances, and they make four here as well'. That's not really citing the Advocate General for something which was key and important to the reasoning of the judgment. I don't understand the logic or why they do it on those occasions, except that maybe somebody is feeling like being nice. I cannot recall often seeing an instance where the Advocate General is cited as having directed the Court to a pivotal point in its reasoning. My short answer is: I think it would be very helpful, in the interest of transparency, if the Court were to say, 'although the Advocate General recommended 'A', actually we, the Court, have decided that the answer should be 'B', for the following reason'. I think that would make life much easier for everyone to understand what exactly is going on. Instead, we all tend to play guessing games as to what in fact the Court is doing. As you may have noticed, Adam, a standard question to an Advocate General is: 'How often were you followed by the Court?'

Adam: And what would be your standard answer, Leo?

Eleanor: My standard answer would be: 'It depends how you would like to define 'follow'!' If the Court and I end up in the same place, but we get there by radically different routes, then – on an ordinary use of the verb 'to follow' – I wouldn't say the Court had 'followed' me, even though it reached the same conclusion. Conversely, suppose that you have a chain of legal reasoning with, let's say, 18 steps in it, and the Court faithfully reproduced the first 17 steps in the argument, and at the 18th step I turned left, and the Court turned right. Obviously, the answer will be different. Did the Court 'follow' me? Well, the judges didn't follow me in terms of result, but if I can see that they used all my reasoning, then I will feel that I probably did a useful job in terms of helping the Court to deliberate and reach an answer. I would add that fairly often, the final step in such a chain requires an assessment of proportionality. It is entirely possible to reach different appreciations of whether an EU measure or a national measure is proportionate, without having really disagreed about the substance of the case.

Adam: This is really interesting, Leo. I am sometimes surprised at the ease with which some commentators claim that the Advocate General was followed or not. Of course, you will have cases where it is obvious, but many a time there is a big question mark. As you said earlier on, in *Ruiz Zambrano* even you – the Advocate General who offered such a robust Opinion in the case – are not sure whether the Court followed you or not.

Eleanor: Exactly so!

Adam: Let me now ask you something different but of course related to the Court. We don't have *amicus curiae* briefs at the CJEU. Do you think that in the future this is an option to consider? Would it be a good idea to allow them?

Eleanor: I have never understood why the Court has set its face so firmly against having them. Except, I suppose, because anything which might potentially add to the length of proceedings is, in the Court's eyes, a Bad Thing by definition. Yet in *El Kott* (Case C-364/11), we did have, effectively, an *amicus curiae* brief.[12]

Adam: How come?

Eleanor: The UNHCR had got involved in the national proceedings in Hungary. It therefore had the right to lodge observations and be heard in Luxembourg as part of the Article 267 TFEU proceedings. So it was that the judges and I had the real benefit of having the UNHCR present, represented by the truly excellent Marie Demetriou KC as counsel. The UNHCR intervention was very valuable. The Court had the opportunity to ask a number of the underlying questions and received very sensible answers.

So, let me go back to your question. The recent partial transfer of jurisdiction to deal with preliminary rulings in six areas to the General Court may indicate that the Court of Justice wants to position itself to be more of a constitutional court, and less of a jack-of-all-trades court. If that is what is happening, then it seems to me that the argument for permitting an *amicus curiae* brief in an appropriate case becomes stronger. Why should you not want to be better informed?

Adam: Absolutely, if you have an *amicus curiae* brief in a case like *El Kott*, that will potentially show a completely different perspective on matters. The *amicus* may take a stance that will not necessarily be in lockstep with what the Member States plead at the Court of Justice.

Eleanor: What the UNHCR pleaded in *El Kott* was not what the Member States were saying to the Court and not what the European Commission was saying. Come to that, it was also not exactly what the applicant before the national court had been saying. It was genuinely useful to be able to ask Marie Demetriou KC about the institutional background leading up to the very particular arrangements for Palestinian refugees set out in the UN's 1951 Refugee Convention – or, to put that point a bit more colloquially, how everything got to be that way up, and why.

Adam: One of the themes reappearing in our conversations is the dynamics within the Court, in particular the fact that judges have to arrive at a unanimous judgment. In the case of Sir Gordon Slynn, that could result in huge frustration. It may also affect the quality of judgments. As we saw in *Ruiz Zambrano*, if you cannot agree on the text, you chop it and massage it, and sometimes the full reasoning gets lost.[13] Do you think that an option would be to reform the Court in the future and allow for dissenting opinions? Or, is perhaps the nature of the Court such that dissents would not work?

Eleanor: That is a really interesting question. I think that there are strong arguments both in favour and against. To the extent that removing the unanimity requirement might improve the clarity and focus of both the lead judgment and the dissent(s), that might be a very good thing. As against that, maybe it would lead to less clarity overall, in terms of what the Court was actually deciding. I recall something President Skouris said shortly after I joined the Court which did strike a chord with me. He was defending the system of having just a single judgment. And his argument essentially was this: suppose that the national court has made a reference on a question of EU law that is sensitive politically, where the national government wants a particular answer to that question. The Court looks at the question and decides it and it gives an answer that the government doesn't like. If that answer has been given in a single judgment, then at least the position is clear enough for the national judge. She or he knows what is the correct interpretation of EU law, therefore they know what they should do. But now suppose that you had a system where you had dissenting judgments, and let us suppose that the majority judgment produced the answer the government didn't like, but that there were two or three dissents (all of which were published) which reached the conclusion that the government wanted. That would put the national judge who had made the reference in a very awkward position. I didn't necessarily always agree with President Skouris but it did seem to me that he had a valid point here: dissents might create difficulties when the case returned before the national court.

Adam: It is a strong argument. I would add that in some instances having multiple texts could also create confusion among the national judges who often send references with a desire to receive a well-crafted and clear answer to their queries. Hearing a cacophony of views from the Court could make it rather challenging and, potentially, counterproductive. Are there any alternative solutions to this problem?

Eleanor: I have a different solution: let's work on avoiding ambiguities in the single judgment. So, let's make sure that – when necessary – there is a second *délibéré* and the loose ends are tidied up. During the fourteen and a half years that I served at the Court, there was a perpetual concern about the judicial statistics and how long the 'average' case spent in the pipeline. Year after year, every possible step was taken to try to reduce that time. As a result, many cases are decided on the basis of a single oral *délibéré*. Of course I can see the efficiency argument for that approach; but there is a counter argument. Suppose that you have one *délibéré*, and during that *délibéré* you run into serious disagreement. During the *délibéré*, without the help of their (reasonably Francophone) *référendaires*, the judges are chewing at the contentious text. They are cutting paragraphs out. They are drafting substitute text 'on the hoof'. And some of them may be working in their fourth language. Inevitably, you risk getting bridging passages in the judgment (*precisely* in the difficult places), which are not as good as they might be. Maybe it is a counsel of perfection (or perhaps it is my *naïveté*) but I wish that the Court had a better system for making sure that it reviews such judgments, has a sensible look at them, and cleans them up before it presses the 'go' button on translation and delivery. I think the Court might save itself a lot of work in the long run. It might make the process run a little slower for that particular case; but overall, I think it would be more efficient.

Adam: That is a very interesting suggestion, Leo. For it to materialise, you would require a change of mindset at the Court but at least it would not necessitate a revision of the Statute and the Rules of Procedure.

Eleanor: While I am about it, let me offer a second suggestion, something that I tried and signally failed to make progress with while I was at the Court. In cases which have Opinions of Advocates General, both the AG's Opinion and the judgment of the Court have sections setting out the facts, the relevant EU and national law, the procedural evolution of the case, and (in a reference for a preliminary ruling) the questions referred by the national court. That's a lot of duplication. The reporting judge's chambers and the Advocate General's chambers are doing the same drafting in parallel. It is also an immense waste of translation time. Remember that the European Union functions in 24 official languages and the translation time is something that should matter. In the Afterword I wrote for the book about the British Advocates General, I suggested that one could eliminate that double work without treading on the toes of either the Advocate General or the reporting judge.[14] I am sure the suggestion I put forward there could be improved on, but it is something which surely the Court could think about in terms of saving both valuable resources and valuable time.

Adam: This sounds like a very good idea to me. It is puzzling indeed that you would have the same kind of material in both the Opinion of Advocate General and in the judgment of the Court.

Eleanor: And here's something else that is available but has never – to my knowledge – been used in practice. Article 13 of the Statute, and the corresponding Article 17 of the Rules of Procedure, allow the Court to benefit from assistant *rapporteurs*.

Adam: Oh? I did not expect this to pop-up in this conversation. Just before Covid-19 hit in 2020, I wrote a chapter about the rules of procedure at the CJEU for an edited volume. I recall coming across assistant *rapporteurs*. I have to admit that I had never heard of them before. If my memory serves me well they may, in particular, participate in preparatory inquiries in cases pending before the Court, assist the President of the Court in interim proceedings and assist the judge *rapporteurs* in their work.

Eleanor: I have never known why that particular provision for having assistant *rapporteurs* has not been activated. In an appropriate case they could provide a useful backup for the judges. If you wanted to make sure that you had more quasi-judicial manpower available for case-handling, including the filtering of appeals, that might be the way to go.

Adam: Do you think, Leo, that assistant *rapporteurs* could be deployed also to help Advocates General?

Eleanor: I doubt the Court would want to have them doing that, even if the wording of the Statute and the Rules of Procedure could be stretched to allow it. The Court is worried about the throughput of cases and judgments, and the number of Advocates General has already been increased from eight to eleven. I would have thought it more likely that the Court might want to see assistant *rapporteurs* as a supplementary resource on the judges' side of the house. The Statute talks specifically about assisting the President in interim proceedings. However, the Court doesn't have that many applications for interim relief. They represent quite a small part of the Court's work in the judicial statistics. So, my sense is that the Court might perhaps wish to deploy assistant *rapporteurs* for Grand Chamber cases. The President is always going to sit in a Grand Chamber case, so it is an obvious way of assisting his/her cabinet.

Adam: If my reading of the Statute of the Court is correct, such assistant *rapporteurs* could not be appointed by internal decisions of the Court. While the Article 255 Committee would not be involved, still a decision of the Council of the European Union (albeit taken by simple majority) would be required.

Eleanor: And that may be the insuperable problem, Adam. As soon as the Council of the European Union is to decide (even by simple majority) about such appointments, there is going to be the usual scrabble about how many posts should be created and which Member States should get them. Perhaps I am being cynical here; but I lived through what happened when we proposed to the Council that there should be a modest increase in the number of judges at the General Court. Since the Court did not put forward a proposal to have one more judge from each Member State, the whole proposal went round in circles for years. Bluntly, the message that kept on coming back to the Court from the capitals of Member States was: 'Listen, no proposal that involves less than one more judge per Member State is going to fly'. So, it would be very difficult to create assistant *rapporteurs* and put them to use unless one could come up with some kind of a rotation system. To my mind one thing is certain: the Court would not enjoy being treated as a political football again, as it was when the number of Advocates General was being increased to the current eleven, and when the number of judges at the General Court was being doubled.

Adam: Perhaps this is one of the reasons why the Court has, so far, not requested appointment of assistant *rapporteurs*. But let's dig a little deeper. The Statute also lays down general preconditions that would have to be met by candidates: they would have to be 'persons whose independence is beyond doubt and who possess the necessary legal qualifications'. Who, do you think, would fit the bill, so to speak?

Eleanor: I don't think you would have to look very far. You could easily find them among the long-serving *référendaires* at the Court of Justice. It is true that some of the *référendaires* are bright-eyed, bushy-tailed, relatively young lawyers, or officials who are on (in principle, temporary) secondment from, for example, the translation service or the research and documentation division of the Court. But there are also some seriously long-service *référendaires*, who have got both the experience and the maturity of judgment to be made assistant *rapporteurs*. They would be of very high quality, reliable, and trustworthy. It would also be a lovely recognition for their years of devoted service to the institution. Above all, it would be good for the Court. It would be a way forward: a way of adding to the human resources necessary to run case management systems which involve filtering, checking, making sure that something hasn't gone wrong, and – if it looks as though it is going wrong or it might go wrong – then making sure that is stopped in time. It would be an intelligent way of using resources so as to work more efficiently.

Adam: This is really interesting; definitely something that should be explored and considered. It is, of course, a matter for the future. As for the present, the talk of the town is the partial transfer of jurisdiction to the General Court to deal with preliminary rulings. This reform materialised on 1 September 2024, so we do not know how it is going to work in practice. Still, however, it is worth talking about it. What is your take on it, Leo?

Eleanor: I'd say it was long overdue, in the sense that the Court for a long time resisted transferring any of those cases! I think the proof of the pudding will be in the eating again. How will the supervisory system work out? It was always said, when I was at the Court, that this wouldn't really work because there might be cases in one of the areas transferred to the General Court which raised key issues of principle. And it was said that we could never give the General Court references that involve money, particularly VAT.

Adam: And here we have it, all six areas deal directly or indirectly with money. They include: VAT; excise duty; the EU Customs Code; classification of goods for customs purposes; compensation and assistance to passengers in the event of denied boarding or of delay or cancellation of transport services; and the system for greenhouse gas emission allowance trading.

Eleanor: Well, my crystal-ball take on the new system is that the First Advocate General is going to have a lot of meticulous additional work riding shotgun on whether a particular case within one of those six areas should nevertheless be retained before the Court of Justice. With Maciej Szpunar as First Advocate General as the new system gets up and running, I think that task is in very safe hands.

ENDNOTES

* Cambridge, 2024.

[1] Catherine Barnard, 'The PPU: Is it Worth the Candle? An Early Assessment' (2009) 34 *European Law Review* 281.

[2] Council Regulation (EC) No 2201/2003 of 27 November 2003 concerning jurisdiction and the recognition and enforcement of judgments in matrimonial matters and the matters of parental responsibility, repealing Regulation (EC) No 1347/2000 [2003] OJ L 338/1; Council Framework Decision 2002/584/JHA of 13 June 2002 on the European arrest warrant and the surrender procedures between Member States [2002] L 190/1.

[3] Case C-195/08 *Inga Rinau* ECLI:EU:C:2008:377, View of AG Sharpston.

[4] *Opinion 2/15 (Free Trade Agreement with Singapore)* ECLI:EU:C:2016:992, Opinion of AG Sharpston.

[5] Joined Cases C-402/05 P and C-415/05 P *Yassin Abdullah Kadi and Al Barakaat International Foundation v Council of the European Union and Commission of the European Communities* ECLI:EU:C:2008:461.

[6] Decision (EU) 2016/2386 of the Court of Justice of 20 September 2016 concerning the security rules applicable to information or material produced before the General Court in accordance with Article 105 of its Rules of Procedure [2016] OJ L 355/5.

[7] Case C-115/09 *Bund für Umwelt und Naturschutz Deutschland, Landesverband Nordrhein-Westfalen eV v Bezirksregierung Arnsberg* ECLI:EU:C:2010:773, Opinion of AG Sharpston.

[8] Case C-382/21 *European Union Intellectual Property Office v The KaiKai Company Jaeger Wichmann GbR* ECLI:EU:C:2023:576, Opinion of AG Ćapeta.

[9] Case C-382/21 *European Union Intellectual Property Office v The KaiKai Company Jaeger Wichmann GbR* ECLI:EU:C:2024:172.

[10] Alberto Alemanno, 'Op-Ed: "Sunlight is the best Disinfectant for EU judicial Selection"' (EU Law Live, 25 September 2024) <https://eulawlive.com/op-ed-sunlight-is-the-best-disinfectant-for-eu-judicial-selection/> accessed 1 September 2025.

[11] *Inter alia*, Case C-367/05 *Criminal proceedings against Norma Kraaijenbrink* ECLI:EU:C:2006:760, Opinion of AG Sharpston; Case C-396/11 *Ciprian Vasile Radu* ECLI:EU:C:2012:648, Opinion of AG Sharpston; Case C-79/11 *Maurizio Giovanardi and Others* ECLI:EU:C:2012:297, Opinion of AG Sharpston.

[12] Case C-364/11 *Mostafa Abed El Karem El Kott and Others v Bevándorlási és Állampolgársági Hivatal* ECLI:EU:C:2012:826; Case C-364/11 *Mostafa Abed El Karem El Kott and Others v Bevándorlási és Állampolgársági Hivatal* ECLI:EU:C:2012:569, Opinion of AG Sharpston.

[13] Case C-34/09 *Gerardo Ruiz Zambrano v Office national de l'emploi (ONEm)* ECLI:EU:C:2011:124.

[14] Eleanor Sharpston, "Can't Those European Judges Think for Themselves?' An Afterword on Why the Court (Still) Needs its Advocates General' in Graham Butler and Adam Łazowski (eds), *Shaping EU Law the British Way. UK Advocates General at the Court of Justice of the European Union* (Hart, 2022).

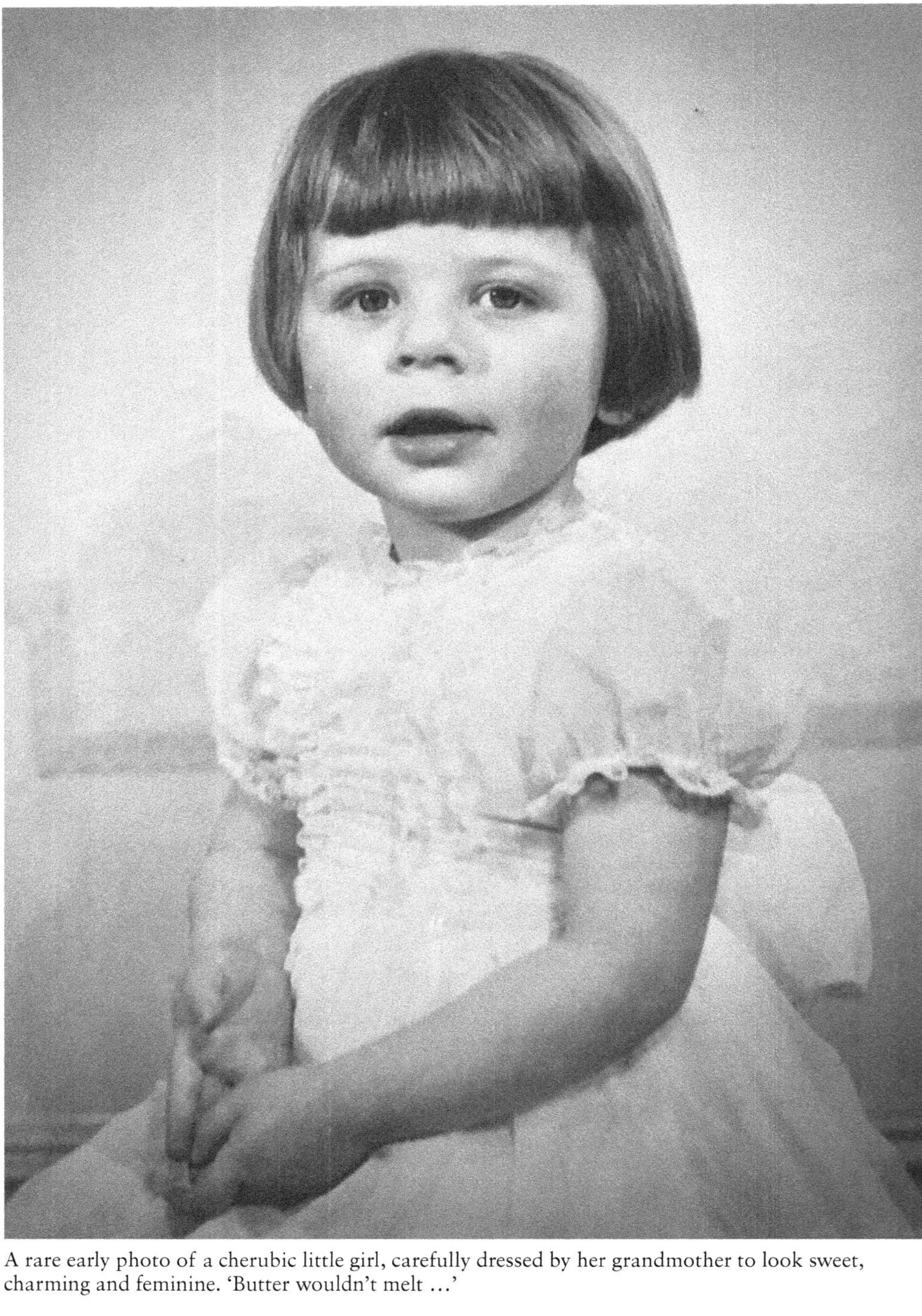

A rare early photo of a cherubic little girl, carefully dressed by her grandmother to look sweet, charming and feminine. 'Butter wouldn't melt …'

A small stocky tomboy dressed as a Brazilian Indian, proudly seated astride her big ex-Brazilian Army cavalry charger, Pegasus

Poised, glamourous and deeply loving – my mother Pauline

What a mensch – my father Charles

Family Sharpston at a joint UNIDO / IAEA ball in the Hofburg Palace, Vienna (from left: my father Charles, my mother Pauline, my brother Michael and myself), under the benevolent eye of Kaiser Franz Joseph II

The mistress and the apprentice – my dear mother showing me a dance move. From memory, we were visiting friends for lunch at the time …

A well brought up young Viennese girl in a *dirndl* (Austrian traditional dress) outside a student house in Cambridge

The photo that got me into so much trouble – the winning Oxford University Women's Boat Club (OUWBC) Blue Boat, Women's Boat Race, Henley on Thames, 1980 (courtesy of *The Times)*

The proud and happy OUWBC President, 1980

The latest recruit to the junior Bar of Ireland, Dublin, 1986

My marriage to David Lyon at the Temple Church, London, 1991. Following the excellent family tradition established by my dear mama, the bride wore red

Leo in her tall ships watch leader incarnation

LAW

THE TIMES
TUESDAYS

November 1, 2005 ■ "He is no lawyer who cannot take two sides" — Charles Lamb, 1833

ACCIDENT CLAIMS: Time to halt the gravy train 4-5

ALL FALL DOWN: Help for those who drink too much 4

CITY POWER: Can lawyers keep us warm this winter? 6

BRITAIN'S WOMAN AT THE EUROPEAN COURT

Eleanor Sharpston revs up for her new job as Advocate-General

A motorcycle-riding female QC was an absolute photographer's gift for this 2005 story (courtesy of *The Times*)

AG Sharpston joyfully subbing into King's College Boat Club ('KCBC') Women's Second Eight on the last day of the May Bumps in June 2013 – and we made the bump!

The 'school photo' – the annual official photo of the members of the Court of Justice of the European Union ('CJEU'), 2019 (courtesy of the CJEU)

eo with Boris-the-beloved-samoyed and Rudy-the-regal-hovawart at the Luxembourg European
mateur Theatre Summer School ('LEATSS'), Clairefontaine

The viola section of the *Orchestre de la Place de l'Europe* ('OPE'), 2024

Two friends at the College of Europe (Natolin, Poland, 2025)

7

Academic

In many respects, my work at the European Court of Justice,
my teaching, and my academic research are intertwined.
Legal education has always been, and continues to be,
immensely important to me.
*Talking with younger lawyers is a real pleasure.**
Honestly: I do not bite,
and I have never been known to eat a student
*alive, raw, and in public.***

Adam: Out of necessity, but also because of her passion for everything academic, when she returned to the United Kingdom after her three-year stint as a *référendaire* at the Court of Justice Eleanor Sharpston pursued two parallel careers: as a practising lawyer and as a scholar. Within a couple of years, she found her way back to the University of Cambridge and to her beloved King's College. For Eleanor Sharpston (the barrister), all roads lead to Luxembourg. For Eleanor Sharpston (the academic), all roads lead to Cambridge. Cambridge is not only her and her brother Michael's Alma Mater; Cambridge is where her parents studied and met, and – of course – King's College Cambridge is where her late husband David also studied. Having returned to Cambridge in 1992, she stayed there in various capacities beyond her appointment to the bench at the CJEU as an Advocate General in 2006. Initially, she was a University Lecturer in EC Law at the Faculty of Law (1992–1998). Between 1998 and 2005, she was an Affiliated Lecturer at the Faculty and a Senior Research Fellow at the Centre for European Legal Studies ('CELS'). At King's College she was a Fellow (1992–2010) and has been an Emeritus Fellow since 2011. She was also Director of Studies in Law and a Personal Tutor (1992–2003). After her untimely departure from the CJEU, she returned to Cambridge for the academic year 2023/2024 as the Arthur Goodhart Visiting Professor in Legal Science.

For decades, therefore, she has taught and inspired generations of lawyers. As Eleanor Spaventa, now herself the Professor of EU law at the Università Bocconi in Milan, reflected: 'Eleanor's intellectual finesse, as well as her passion for EU law (and for law more generally) taught me a great deal – but more to the point, discussing legal minutiae with her is great fun'.[1] But the job of academics is not only to teach. Many of us write relentlessly and travel around the world to speak at conferences and deliver guest lectures. Eleanor Sharpston definitely fits that broad description of the academic way of living. She has published extensively in academic journals and contributed to edited volumes, including a *Festschrift* for her former boss Sir Gordon Slynn. She also published an early monograph about interim relief and remedies in EC law: at the time, a pioneering work.[2] It goes without saying that conference appearances and guest lectures were her cup of tea. Interestingly, even during the busy fourteen and a half years working as an Advocate General, she stayed firmly on the guest lecture/conference circuit and continued publishing. All these contributions were her own work. Although she naturally asked her nice *référendaires* to do background research she never – unlike certain of her colleagues! – asked her *référendaires* to ghostwrite a speech or an academic article for her.

It was at one of such academic gatherings that our paths crossed for the first time. Neither of us cares to remember exactly how long ago that was, but it must have been in the late 2000s. It surely was in Dubrovnik during one of many seminars organised by the lovely Zagreb 'gang': Professors Tamara Ćapeta, Siniša Rodin, Tamara Perišin (now, respectively, an Advocate General and judges of the Court of Justice and the General Court) and Professor Iris Goldner Lang. Back then the Dubrovnik seminar was a wonderful one-week long retreat during which professors would deliver morning lectures and PhD students would present their work in progress during the afternoons. All of this in the presence of students from the University of Zagreb and other visitors. Every day would also involve an evening social programme. No wonder, together with a fellow Macedonian academic and friend Prof. Julija Brsakoska-Bazerkoska, I call these seminars 'the epicentre of academic tourism'. So, here is a story for you. After a day of academic discussions, we decided to take a short boat trip to *Lokrum*, a small island inhabited by peacocks which is a stone's throw from Dubrovnik. As colleagues were selecting snacks and wine in a tiny cramped local store, Alicia Hinarejos (back then a PhD student at Oxford, now a distinguished EU law professor at McGill University's Faculty of Law) and I were busy blocking traffic between the aisles by standing and passionately discussing the idiosyncrasies of the then special preliminary ruling regimes. Traffic was eventually unblocked, bills were paid. Loaded like donkeys with provisions for the rest of the day, we all proceeded to the harbour. There we bumped into Eleanor, who was wandering around the old town. Having learned what we were up to, she immediately asked us to let her join – just as a puppy would beg for a treat. She dashed back to her hotel to change and off we went for a late afternoon of adventures. We ended up sitting on some rocks by the sea, munching the supplies, drinking wine and, above all, chatting about EU law. I remember thinking to myself: 'This is what good academia is about. Here we are, young and aspiring academics, some more bushy-tailed than others, and we have AG Sharpston telling us inspirational stories about EU law and, in more general terms, about life'. She was so kind and gracious all the way. I am not sure about the others but for this young academic coming from Central Europe where – for years – we were told that we were not supposed to sing the blues where we came from (new Member States and all the rest), it was a moment of recognition and encouragement. Priceless.

*

Adam: Leo, so far we have talked a lot about you as a practitioner at the English Bar and at the Court of Justice. But, of course, you have also worn an academic hat. How did your academic career start?

Eleanor: It started with a failure, Adam.

Adam: Right, not the answer I was expecting at all.

Eleanor: Well, it started with my going to the University of Oxford to do a DPhil – and that came spectacularly off the rails. I left Oxford with multiple qualifications as a sportsman but nothing on paper to show an academic result for my three years there. The reason is simple enough to explain, although the sequence that led to that result was rather complicated. I was doing interdisciplinary work between law and economics, and I was registered for my DPhil with the Faculty of Economics, not with the Faculty of Law. The work that I was doing, inasmuch as it was truly interdisciplinary, was a continuation of the dissertation that I'd written in my final year at Cambridge. My research involved looking at how an ordinary company reacts to the law. I wanted to find out how much it knew about the various areas of law that affected its operations, how much effort it then made to comply with the law, and what it did if things went wrong. On the theoretical side, this drew on decision theory and a little bit of game theory. I hasten to add that I am not very mathematical, so the theoretical part was not about building a very big, brilliant, new mathematical model. Truth to tell, I was probably more interested in the empirical side. What was actually happening out there? And I ran into the obvious problem that if a company is not complying with the law, it probably doesn't want to tell a curious research student what it is (or is not) doing.

Adam: Fair enough. One would hardly expect companies to run around with megaphones trumpeting about their accidental or even deliberate failures to comply with the law. Having said that, did you manage to get them to talk?

Eleanor: I had two supervisors in succession for my DPhil. Both of them were very distinguished and busy men. They were getting on with their own research. They weren't particularly interested in what I was working on. I am going to use strong words here: I think the level of contact between the research student and the supervisor was woefully inadequate. My supervisor would see me once a term for 10 minutes ('How are you getting on?' 'OK, thanks: I am busy working on this …'. 'Jolly good, jolly good. Well, have a nice vacation. See you next term'.) In my book, that doesn't qualify as directing a PhD.

I had no guidance from either supervisor as to how to sort out the empirical side of my thesis. Crucially, we had not discussed with the Faculty Board how to handle any of the (very predictable) issues about confidentiality. At some point I started going out and talking to companies. I found that – of course – I could get some basic information about them, what they did and so on. But as soon as I started asking them questions which even began to border on 'do you actually change what you're doing in order to comply with the law?', the answer was (naturally) always: 'Yes, of course, we comply with everything to the letter'.

Adam: As one would … but that did not cause trouble. Did you manage to get them to talk under some version of the Chatham House rules?

Eleanor: I quickly realised that without some form of confidentiality agreement, I would never get to the bottom of what I was investigating. So, I started asking if it would make it easier for us to continue to talk, and whether there would be more information that they would feel able to share, if I were to give them an undertaking of confidentiality as to source. I would use the information that they were willing to give me, but I would make absolutely sure that it could not be traced back to their company or to my interviewee. Perhaps I have an honest face. Perhaps I transmit the idea that I am trustworthy (I do hope so!). Anyway: once I gave such an undertaking, a number of companies did unbutton and did explain what they actually did. They told me things that, as an economist, I found both really interesting and perfectly rational.

Adam: For example?

Eleanor: Well, I had been talking with one manufacturing company, and my interviewee had been swearing blind that there were never any problems with health and safety issues in their factory. Then, we had a coffee together and I gave him my confidentiality undertaking. He looked me up and down thoughtfully. Then he said:

> *Do you really want to know what we do? Okay, I'll tell you. First of all, the Factory Inspectorate is not a problem. Their people turn up maybe once every five years, and when they do, obviously, they come to the reception to show their ID. If that happens, the receptionist will phone me and ask me: 'Is Mr Maguire there?'*
>
> *That's our code for 'we have got a factory inspector at the door now'. It's my job to make sure that they are not going to see anything that would make them unhappy. So, let me show you what I mean.*

My interviewee then walked me across to a small additional workshop in a corner of the factory site. It was locked. When we got there, he unlocked it. He explained that the company only used it as an overflow workshop for manufacturing when their books were very full – otherwise, they did not need it. He walked me around that workshop and he showed me fourteen breaches of the Factories Act 1961. He pointed them out to me: oil dripping, a trip hazard, a cutting machine that wasn't properly fenced, and so on. He was perfectly aware of the defects – of the illegalities. However, he also knew what it would cost to put everything right. It made no sense for the company to do so. That particular workshop was not used that often. When it was in use, only experienced and reliable people were sent to work there. I thanked him very much indeed. He had provided me with a really valuable empirical example. From an economic point of view, spending a lot of money just to comply with the law would have been a ridiculous decision to make.

Adam: I can sense that the confidentiality undertakings you had given became a problem for the University. These days we have very tedious but overall helpful ethics procedures and committees, which review applications made by PhD students well in advance of them engaging in empirical research. I guess this was not the case back then.

Eleanor: I wrote up my DPhil. When I was – roughly speaking – a couple of months away from submission we *started* to have that discussion with the Faculty Board of the Sub-Faculty of Economics about the use of my empirical material. Their point of departure was that in order to ensure that my material was genuine, they needed full details about all the interviews. So, to take the example I have just given you, they would have wanted to know the full name and job title of the person I had talked to, the name of the company, their address, the exact location of the workshop I saw, and a detailed list of all 14 breaches of the Factories Act 1961. There was absolutely no way I could provide that. I had been given privileged access to sensitive information on the basis of my undertaking of confidentiality. I had given my word. I could not break it. I could not allow a detailed list containing all that (highly incriminating) information to float around for three months, God knows where. I offered to come along to the viva with all my notebooks, to allow them to check everything against the material I had written down at the time. However, I refused to supply a separate list that would leave my control and which would enable my informants to be identified. I was not going to break my word of honour. So, my DPhil ran into the sand. I tried to see if I could find some published material that I could use instead for the empirical side of my thesis, but it didn't work. For example, I tried looking at the 'Judicial Statistics', which gave information about cases brought before courts, but that data told only an incomplete (and skewed) version of the story. It just was not feasible to retrofit three years-worth of research and do it differently. So, I left Oxford with 'Blue's' for rowing and squash, and having been President of Oxford University Women's Boat Club for two consecutive years and won the Women's Boat Race, but I left without my DPhil. That would normally be the kiss of death to any academic career.

Adam: And yet, you restarted your academic career after your three years as a *référendaire* at the Court of Justice.

Eleanor: The reason I managed to get back into academia, I guess, is precisely that my re-entry point was immediately after my stint as a *référendaire*. I had been in practice for seven years, then at the Court for three years. I was a lawyer with 10 years' worth of experience. UCL advertised two teaching posts, one in EU law and one as the (grandly-named) Director of European Legal Studies, whose job would be to set up their three brand new programmes in Law with French Law, Law with German Law, and Law with Italian Law. They needed somebody who knew about EU law, who wasn't frightened at the idea of comparative law, and who was fairly practically inclined. I applied for both jobs. I went along to the interview, and it went very well. Towards the end of the interview, very gently they broke the news to me that in the meantime, additional budgetary constraints had arisen that they had not anticipated. In consequence, they didn't have funding for two posts. They had two posts but they could only offer one salary. Could I possibly do both jobs if appointed? I smiled sweetly and said 'yes'. I got the (two) jobs and that, of course, gave me an academic footing. I had a visiting card saying 'Director of European Legal Studies'. This created a presumption that I must be an (exceptionally well-qualified) academic, otherwise I would clearly not have been given that role. I spent two years at UCL. I confess that I was living hand to mouth. I had done some work in comparative law, but I had never studied it myself as an academic subject. You will remember that I had only done one academic year's worth of law at Cambridge; and that year had not included EU law as an academic subject either! I was teaching across the full spectrum of EU law. Well, that was all right, apart from the fact I was teaching in English and I had mainly been working on EU law in French for the previous two years, when Gordon had been a judge. As for the comparative law course, which also included legal history, I taught that in French. The idea was that we would prepare the students for their year abroad in France by starting to teach them in French while they were still in the UK. So, I taught them basic elements of French civil and administrative law, judicial structures, and also some legal history, so that they had some reference points. That was fine, except – of course – I didn't have the lecture course in my back pocket when I arrived. I spent that entire academic year just one jump ahead of my students. I would get up at four o'clock in the morning and work from four to seven to get some lecture notes ready. Then I'd have a shower, get on my motorbike, go into town, and give the lecture at nine o'clock. I did that three times a week for two and a half terms, and then ran some revision classes and marked the exams. That was my first academic year at UCL.

Adam: This sounds like one hell of a year, Leo. I do hope, however, it had some rewarding moments, too.

Eleanor: Well, it certainly had its excruciatingly funny moments. Probably the funniest was this one. I didn't ever have time to go back over anything as I was putting those lectures together. I was doing it all with one eye on the clock. My sole objective was getting enough material ready for the lecture I was about to give, in something that resembled a structured order. One morning I was hunting for an example of a feudal arrangement. I had been given a legal history book as a leaving present by a very nice Portuguese colleague from the Portuguese translation section of the Court. It was an excellent read: full of lovely, juicy examples. It was, of course, in Portuguese. At about five in the morning, hunting for my feudal example, I found a really good one to use. 'Great', I thought, grabbed a post-it note, and slapped it on the corner of the page, marking it '17' (or whatever, because my post-it notes were keyed in numerically with my manuscript lecture notes). The next thing I realise is: I am in the classroom, I am holding forth in French, and the time comes for my nice illustration of the point that I have just made about feudal arrangements. I reach for the book. I flip to the note. And then, just as I am opening my mouth, I realise I am about to read out Portuguese in the middle of a class that I am teaching in French. I produced a little more fluff about the forthcoming example as a filler for a few vital seconds ('it's a really interesting example … here's the background …'), while – in the back corner of my brain – I was thinking, 'OK, so now I am going to have to translate this from Portuguese into French *and* make it sound as though I am reading from the printed page in French'. I translated it on the hoof. What else was I going to do? That's probably a good indication of quite how hand-to-mouth that year was. The second year was easier. At least in the second year I knew in advance that that passage about feudal arrangements was in Portuguese.

Adam: And then destiny took you back to the University of Cambridge, didn't it?

Eleanor: A university lectureship came up in the Faculty of Law at Cambridge. Obviously, had I tried to go directly to Cambridge against the background of what had happened to my DPhil in Oxford, I would never have made the shortlist. Those two years at UCL were the springboard. I was shortlisted and interviewed. Naturally, the first question I was asked was, what happened to the DPhil in Oxford? I simply told them, very straightforwardly, what had happened. I added that part of the problem may have been that in Oxford I was registered as an economist. In one way, that was sensible enough because I had a first in economics from Cambridge. The Sub-Faculty of Economics was therefore a natural place to put me as a research student. However, the problem that shipwrecked my DPhil – the undertaking of confidentiality – was a problem that economists are much less familiar with than lawyers. Had I been trying to navigate the same problem with the Faculty of Law, we would at least have been talking roughly the same language, in terms of our understanding of confidentiality and its importance. When you say 'confidentiality' to a lawyer, it resonates in a particular way, because we all have to deal with confidentiality one way or another in our professional lives. Whereas the economists (in a sense, reasonably enough) saw the primary need as being to be able to verify the empirical data collected for the DPhil. They didn't really see what I was on about when I said that I had given my word and that I could not break it. I think if I'd said that to a faculty full of lawyers, at least they would have seen the problem. It would have been an easier place to start from in terms of explaining what it was that we needed to resolve. I said as much at the end of explaining to the Cambridge interview board what had happened. There was a sort of nod around the table; and then we went on to talk about other things. And I was offered the lectureship, which I accepted. Somehow, as it were, I managed finally to get over the fact that I didn't have a PhD. Of course, thanks primarily to having spent fourteen and a half years as an Advocate General, I have now been lucky enough to be honoured by four universities: the University of Glasgow (2010), Nottingham Trent University (2011), the University of Stockholm (2014), and the University of Edinburgh (2017). They have made an honest woman of me at last by giving me honorary doctorates.

Adam: After the relatively short (yet intense) UCL episode, your entire academic career has been linked to the University of Cambridge. (Even now, as we are talking, you are spending a year teaching back at Cambridge as the Arthur Goodhart Visiting Professor in Legal Science.) However, Leo being Leo, you were at least two-timing all the way. How did you manage to be, at the same time, an academic and a practitioner?

Eleanor: I tried very hard to make sure that what I was doing as an academic – what I was teaching, what I was researching – dovetailed with what I was doing as a practitioner. In a sense, that was easy enough. As a practitioner, I didn't have a specific subset of EU law that was my area of practice (for example: competition law, labour law, or whatever). If it was EU law, I did it. And indeed, because many people apparently were hazy about the difference between EU law and the ECHR, I did the ECHR as well – because it was 'European', wasn't it? So, I ran the two – my academic existence and my practice – in a way that meant there was the maximum synergy between the two. I am going to say (but it's surely almost self-evident!) that that was the only conceivable way of having two real, full time, parallel careers.

Adam: This sounds very sensible, indeed, though it must have been really hard, especially at the beginning.

Eleanor: Well, my slightly ruthless approach to making it all work somehow is perhaps sufficiently illustrated by the following. When I went to Cambridge, in my first year the Faculty of Law asked me to give eight lectures for the constitutional law paper in Law Tripos Part I (the first set of law examinations at the University of Cambridge), as well as lecturing in EU law. They handed me what was a bit of a hospital pass: the (frankly rather tedious) chunk of constitutional law that deals with delegated legislation and statutory instruments.

I deliberately kidnapped the topic. The way that I taught it was to look at how you would put an EU measure – a directive, or a regulation that needs further fleshing out – into English national law. What would you do by way of primary legislation? What might you do by way of delegated powers and making statutory instruments? How (technically) were those statutory instruments made? In other words, when I was asked to teach constitutional law, I deliberately picked it up, flipped it over, and turned it into 'how do you do EU law within the constitutional law system of this particular Member State'?

Adam: This sounds very familiar, like my early days of teaching UK public law.

Eleanor: Partly it's a matter of survival, partly it is that you do better teaching what you know about and understand, rather than what you don't know about or don't understand. For sure, you will be more interesting to the students if you talk about what you understand.

Adam: Absolutely. One of the worst living nightmares is teaching something brand new for the very first time. I find it rather uncomfortable to be literally a few metres ahead of my students.

Eleanor: On that note, let me share my Mishal Husain story with you.

Adam: Wait, THE Mishal Husain, whom – for years – we regularly saw on the BBC programmes and who recently published a most fascinating book about her roots?[3]

Eleanor: The very same. One of my proudest claims to fame is that while I was an academic at Cambridge, I taught Mishal Husain, for years a truly outstanding anchorwoman for the BBC and a household name in the United Kingdom. Mishal read law at New Hall (now Murray Edwards College, Cambridge). The first year that I taught her was when she was in her second year, and she was doing contract law. I supervised her in contract law for no better reason than that the normal supervisor in contract law for New Hall was on maternity leave that year. There was a general supervision agreement between three colleges, New Hall, Clare, and King's (my college). As well as supervising EU law for all three colleges (and quite a few others), I was therefore on standby (in a sense) to help out as required. So, when the normal contract law supervisor for New Hall went on maternity leave, New Hall asked me if I could possibly cover for contract law that year as well. Naturally, I agreed, both because one does and because contract law was a subject that I felt reasonably comfortable about. I had, after all, got a first in it as an undergraduate. It did require some work for me to 'get it up' to teach it, but I felt I could probably supervise contract law. So, I taught Mishal Husain and her New Hall colleagues contract law. They did their end of year exams, and they did fine. Then, in their third year, they came back to me for supervision in EU law. Of course, by this stage we all knew each other, indeed we were on very friendly terms. During the first EU law supervision

I said happily that we would really have fun together this year. Then I did everything from talking about the 'first' Treaty (establishing the European Coal and Steel Community: 'the ECSC') to explaining how to go about reading EU law so that you understand it. At the end of the supervision, Mishal and her colleagues were packing up their papers and preparing to depart. Suddenly, Mishal turned to me, and absolutely spontaneously and unprompted said: 'Leo, you are so different when you're supervising EU law. I mean, you really know what you are talking about'.

Adam: Brutal honesty but I guess it was very much true.

Eleanor: It was a wonderful, wonderful comment. It was sharp, perceptive, and spot on. She was absolutely right. There was an enormous difference between ES supervising contract law and ES teaching EU law. The first was adequate, competent, not setting the Thames on fire, but she would get you through what you needed to know. The second was ES on fire, communicating something she *was* passionate about to a group of really nice students whom she knew to be intelligent and interested. Mishal absolutely nailed it.

Adam: How did you react to Mishal's observation?

Eleanor: I howled with laughter; and I said: 'You've got it! It's going to be a good year'. I did not know Mishal was going to go on to forge a career at the BBC, but to me she had already demonstrated absolutely exceptional qualities of perception and analysis. She knew the difference between being taught a subject which I sort of knew reasonably well, and being taught a subject that I absolutely knew inside out and cared deeply about. By the way, Mishal remembers that story.

Adam: Oh that's very nice! The appointment to the Court of Justice meant that you had to part ways with more regular academic endeavours, but nevertheless you remained on the conference circuit and regularly published scholarly work. You were Advocate General Sharpston but you did not forget about the academic hat you used to wear.

Eleanor: It was important to stay in touch with academia, to know what was going on, what people were talking and writing about. Obviously, it could not get in the way of my main job, which was writing Opinions, but it seemed to me very important to be open and outgoing as a Member of the Court. And I am going to say that, within limits, the Court going out on tour really matters. The Court should not be perceived as being exclusively located in its nice, rather grand, ivory tower on the *Plateau de Kirchberg* in the fairytale Duchy of Luxembourg. It is really important that the Court as an institution and, in particular, the individual Members of the Court go out and interact with academics, practitioners, and national judges. There are ways and ways of doing that, of course. It always seemed to me as important to turn up and listen as it was to turn up and speak. Furthermore, if you did turn up to speak, you should not try to pretend that everything was automatically easy and self-evident, and that naturally the Court is infallible. You need to be accessible, open, available to listen to people and to engage with them. Going into the job of being an Advocate General, I made a kind of picture. I made a role description for myself of what an Advocate General is (or perhaps 'should be'), both in terms of the job they do for the Court and in terms of the job they do in accessibility, in transparency, in being in listening mode, understanding, engaging. I had to do that because, in some respects, I'm actually quite a shy person, particularly when faced with a large group of total strangers. I'm truly terrible at parties where I don't really know anyone. They make me curl up inside. I hate them! So, I needed to fashion – to structure – the AG's role that I was now, suddenly, going to be taking on. Having fleshed out the job description, in a sense I then played the role. (Remember, I do a lot of theatre!) I overcame my shyness and my nerves by assuming the necessary *persona* for the role that I had designed and created, and I tried to make sure that wherever I went and whatever I was doing, living up to that role was the central plank of what was going on. What I was aiming for was *not*: 'We are very honoured. We have a visit from the Advocate General, and we are going to spend the first five minutes before she ever speaks, explaining what a stellar career she has had' (that has always embarrassed me incredibly, by the way). What I very much preferred was: 'The Advocate General came to participate in our conference, we had a great discussion with her about a whole lot of things. She was really interested in what we had to say, she listened and she engaged. It was so nice to see that there are members of the Court who care about what it is like to be a national judge or a national academic looking at what the Court of Justice is saying'.

Adam: Being at the receiving end, I have to say that it was extremely beneficial for all of us who had a chance to listen to your public talks. When I met you, Leo, for the very first time I was full of trepidation as by then I already had met several judges and Advocates General, and that had not been a pleasant experience. This time it was different. You were so engaging and passionate about EU law. Within a minute you had the entire room in the palm of your hand.

Eleanor: Awww, thank you, Adam – that's very kind! What I have just said also explains why I have never, ever turned up at a conference with a speech written by my *référendaire*. I did always ask one of my nice *référendaires* for help in doing research, in checking to make sure that there wasn't some recent judgment of the Court that I was simply unaware of. But in fourteen and a half years I never asked one of my *référendaires* to write a conference speech or a an article for me. I always wrote my own notes and I spoke from them. Also, I never read out a full prepared text for a lecture. I always speak *extempore*. That is also why I was (and I am) always disconcerted when people say to me afterwards: 'Oh, you know, that was fantastic. Can we publish it?' My reaction is always: 'Well, er ... yes, but I am going to have to reconstruct it because, actually, that was not delivered from an oven-ready text'.

Before I give a public talk, I do know what I am going to do and say, more or less. But I'm not ready and organised to give you Hamlet verbatim:

To be, or not to be: that is the question:

Whether 'tis nobler in the mind to suffer

The slings and arrows of outrageous fortune ...

It's more that I know that Hamlet is coming on stage now. It's a pivotal moment in the play and he's going to say something really important to the audience. I have some bullet points as to what is going on in Hamlet's head, but the rest is all live. It plays off – one might almost say, it feeds off – the audience. It is all 'impro' (as we say in the theatre).

Adam: Such speeches and lectures are absolutely the best, I think. It reminds me of my inaugural professorial lecture at the University of Westminster in early 2016. One of my colleagues saw it on YouTube and asked when I was going to publish it. I was perplexed as I did not have a script, I spoke off the top of my head and scribbled bullet points.

Eleanor: Adam, most people read faster than they listen. If the speaker is going to read a text, the listener might as well read it whenever it best suits them: in the evening with music in the background, perhaps sitting on the train or flying somewhere high up in the sky. The whole difference between that and something that is live is that you can *hear* that it is live, you can hear it being hammered out on the anvil. It is like watching a smith making a horseshoe. You can watch him take the iron, turn it into the shape of the horseshoe, and make it fit the horse.

Adam: This, quite naturally, has taken our conversation to two aspects of academic work which I think both of us find the most attractive parts of the job – being a teacher/mentor and being a writer. (Truth be told, I have never met an academic who would have said – with hand on heart – that their favourite parts of the job were marking assessments and doing tedious administrative tasks.) We will get to writing shortly, but for now let's continue for a bit longer with teaching. With many years of teaching under your belt, what would be your advice, Leo, to young academics? Often when people start academic careers they are given a class full of students and they are just told to get going. How should one approach teaching?

Eleanor: That's a difficult question, Adam. To begin with, you do have to know your material and, as my Mishal Husain story shows, you should, if possible, teach what you are passionate about. However, you also have to understand that teaching is a two-way process of communication. The challenge of teaching is not fulfilled by standing up there with your set of lecture notes and declaiming them to the audience so that the squiggly marks on the pieces of paper in front of you can be transferred into a new set of squiggly marks (now, electronic squiggly marks) by the students. That is not teaching. Teaching is taking your listeners with you on a journey into a subject that you know well and that you think is interesting. And you want to take them with you. You want them to start to understand how that subject bolts together, and that maybe there are also places where it doesn't bolt together quite so well. You want to get them interested in thinking about the next steps, about how the next pieces in the mosaic should be laid. You don't have a full picture – a full 'cartoon' – of the mosaic. You know what has happened so far, including the bits which do not look as though they are laid out right. You want to try to give your students the understanding and the tools to help in the process of completing the mosaic. That is a long way away from saying: 'I need to make sure they know the following five basic things from my lecture'. Of course, somewhere in the process you do need to have made sure that you have transmitted those five basic things; but you need to do much more than that. Why were you bothering to get those five pieces of information across? Why do they matter in this context? Do they provide a complete solution to all possible problems and questions (spoiler alert: the answer is usually 'no')? All of that is something that is very much interactive.

Adam: I absolutely agree with you, Leo. The trouble is that there is only so much one can do to achieve the interaction. If your classroom is empty, or filled with students who express no desire to learn anything from you, then it can turn into a very frustrating experience. It frequently is even worse when we teach online.

Eleanor: I very much prefer teaching in person, Adam. I am prepared to teach virtually, obviously. That was what had to happen during the pandemic. But when it is not in person, I need to be able to see the people I am talking to. I need to be able to find out, in real time, whether the way I have just put something has worked. I may think that my original way of putting a particular point was perfectly clear and simple. But if I see people looking a little bit puzzled, if I cannot see the light bulb go on behind their eyes, I know that I need to try again. I need to approach whatever I just said in a slightly different way and see if I can make it clearer for my listeners. I need to have another go at it. If I do not have the feedback loop, if I cannot see with my own eyes whether a point has 'landed', then I cannot teach properly. I can deliver prepared material, but I cannot teach. This is partly why I found it rather disappointing, during my recent year in Cambridge, to discover that for the main teaching for the undergraduate course in the Faculty of Law, the lectures were all recorded and uploaded. Probably in consequence, about nine tenths of the students who were signed up to take the course I was lecturing for were not in the lecture theatre. Nor were they online at the same time as I was giving the lecture. Unlike (for example) the various seminars that I also did for the Centre for European Legal Studies, which worked much better, the Tripos lectures were not 'hybrid' (that is, partially in person and partially online). Presumably some (many? most?) of the students did log on to the server later to watch the lecture, a bit the way that one might watch catch up TV. I would say that this system diminishes what the lecturer can give and therefore what the audience – the students – will receive out of the transaction.

Adam: As I was listening to you, I could hear my own thoughts, we are absolutely on the same page. During the pandemic, one of the most frustrating things was screaming at the computer screen. All cameras were off and you were talking to yourself, basically not knowing if there was anyone at the other end. Of course, everything was recorded so even when not a single soul was listening to you live, you had to do it. Tutorials were a nightmare. As much as I hated all those Zoom/MS Teams classes by the time Covid-19 subsided, it became a blessing when Russia started its full-scale invasion of Ukraine. Suddenly, using those wonders of modern technology became the only way that young people could get any education in many Ukrainian schools and at universities. I absolutely agree with you that when teaching virtually it is very important to see peoples' faces. Although sometimes when I do my weekly online lectures at the University of Lviv, seeing what is happening at the receiving end may be challenging. My courses have found a home in Lviv, however they are open to students from all over Ukraine. In the last three years I have had students who were paramedics, who – during my classes – were sitting at the back of ambulances. I have had students who had to log off to run to shelters and then they would log back in again to listen to me for as long as they could do so from a place deemed to be safe. I often find myself lost for words, seeing these lovely young people staying online against all odds, wanting to listen to whatever I have to say. It gives me an enormous boost of energy to carry on doing it because they need it and they try to get as much from this experience as possible. Having said that, it makes me really sad where frequently these days we are faced with classrooms full of switched-off or uninterested students. I know that times are hard and we also have to navigate choppy waters, yet we live in a country which is not in the middle of a war. I wish many of our students understood that what they have is actually a blessing, that they can go to a class or they can listen to someone speaking live, engage in meaningful conversations, and then just go home without the risk of having bombs landing on their heads. Once you realise that this is priceless, you do see what is on offer in Cambridge or at Westminster, or elsewhere in the UK, from a completely different perspective.

Eleanor: That is an enormously powerful description, Adam. All respect to your Ukrainian students and you. Obviously, in those circumstances you will try your very, very best to teach well, to communicate well, because it matters so much to the people who are listening. Doing it live over a video link, under such extraordinary and surreal conditions, really matters. But if you are giving a lecture or a talk in a nice comfortable lecture theatre, in a heated building that people can turn up to with no threats of bombs, and the lecture is scheduled for 11am in the middle of the working week, there is no particularly good reason why most of the students shouldn't physically be in attendance. Obviously, I understand there are some people who may have difficulties or extra challenges with following the material. I have no problem at all about making a recording available (and indeed providing extra help) to students who have a genuine medical reason for needing a recording, or who perhaps have had to rush home suddenly because someone is sick. But I think the idea that the recording, instead of being a backup to what was done live, has become the only genuine article, is a serious mistake. I do remember the moment in Cambridge when I got an email from one of those invisible students on the undergraduate course, asking me to switch the captions on. Not only was that student not interested in coming in person to the lecture: he wanted the AI subtitles to be available with the recording as well. I had no desire to take the responsibility for the content of the captions. As we both know, they may or may not resemble what we actually said, and AI expecting to hear words in English is likely to do very strange things to EU law case names (how about *Rewe Zentrale v Bundesmonopolverwaltung für Branntwein* – otherwise known as '*Cassis de Dijon*')![4] I was not going to spend significant time (for which, read hours) after each lecture to go through and check the AI-generated captions and then to try to get somebody who was technically savvy to amend every caption that was wrong. The request (coming from someone who was *not* registered with the Faculty as having a medical condition) really did give me pause for thought. Most undergraduates in Cambridge need ten minutes, perhaps a quarter of an hour at most, to travel on a bike from where they live to the lecture hall. If you are there in person, who knows, you might even learn something extra. You might privately ask a follow-up question at the end of the lecture. The answer might be illuminating. And your question might help the lecturer to improve the quality of his next lecture, and that would be to everyone's benefit.

Adam: Well, as my personal story shows, coming over to a lecture may completely turn your world upside down and put you on a different railway track that you thought you would be travelling on. I read law for my undergraduate degree at the University of Warsaw and, honestly, I was sick and tired of the way the courses were organised and taught back then. The classrooms were packed with students to the point that we would have to jump through windows to get a spot. (Rest assured, to a ground floor classroom!) We did not even have proper tutorials. This was a mockery of legal education. In other respects, it was an interesting period of my life as I worked a lot with orchestras, conductors, soloists, and I was all ready to turn my side job as a music promoter into my lifelong professional activity. What kept me in the realms of the law was, first, the British Law Centre ('BLC' for short) which, back then, was run by the University of Cambridge. We had proper lectures and tutorials with fascinating teachers coming over to Warsaw from the UK. I was blessed to have, among others, Professor Jan Grodecki teaching contract law, Professor

Catherine Barnard doing EU law, and Professor Bill Cornish delivering IP law lectures. It just could not get better than that. Never in my dreams would I have thought that a few years later I would be one of the teachers at the BLC. Second, I went to an EU law lecture delivered by Professor Eugeniusz Piontek, who later became my mentor and PhD supervisor. I heard on the grapevine that there was this very interesting teacher who not only held the title of professor but who actually was a real professor. As he told me years later, with his usual and brutal honesty, these are not always two sides of the same coin. I remember his first class for us as if it were yesterday. He walked into the classroom, dressed very nicely wearing a striped suit and a bow tie. The latter and his pipe that he would smoke during classes were his staples. He was a very handsome man, in fact he looked like Sean Connery. Not surprisingly, male members of the student cohort always had to look for a free seat at the back of the lecture theatre. On this occasion, to break the ice before diving into free movement of goods (not the easiest of topics to commence your course with) he started the lecture with a joke. It was back in 1996, and I still remember it.

Eleanor: What was the joke Adam, do tell!

Adam: Alright Leo. We are in a courtroom where someone is being prosecuted. The scene looks like this:

> **The Bench:** *The Court is asking you to answer our question simply yes or no.*
>
> **The Defendant:** *I cannot, I am afraid.*
>
> **The Bench:** *This is the Court's order, you do not have much choice. Yes or no?*
>
> **The Defendant:** *My Lords, I really cannot answer your question yes or no.*
>
> **The Bench:** *But this is the Court's order! Yes or no?*
>
> **The Defendant:** *All right. If I ask your Lordships a question, would you answer it yes or no?*
>
> **The Bench:** *Of course. What is your question, then?*
>
> **The Defendant:** *Are your Lordships still accepting bribes?*

Eleanor: Fabulous!

Adam: Then the lecture commenced and after 10 minutes or so, I knew I wanted to be like him when I (eventually) grow up. If I had not attended that lecture, I would have been in a different place now. For sure, I would have not travelled on the academic trajectory. This was my equivalent of Marin Alsop's 'Leonard Bernstein moment'. In the interview you have mentioned earlier, she recalled the moment she saw Bernstein conduct a live concert and, by the end of it, she knew she wanted to be a conductor.[5]

Eleanor: What a great story, Adam.

Adam: I was very lucky. Eugeniusz became my mentor and, I dare to say, somehow also a friend, despite the age gap between us. Even when I left for the Hague and then moved to London, we stayed in touch. The last thing we did together was to advise the right-hand man of the then Polish Prime Minister, Donald Tusk, as to the constitutional feasibility of Poland joining the Eurozone. This was in January 2009. A month later, having delivered his last seminar at the University of Warsaw, he went to his law firm and died.

Talking about mentors, throughout our conversations you have mentioned John Temple Lang but there must have been others.

Eleanor: Yes, of course. As a young lawyer, I owed a lot to my wonderful mentor at King's College, Cambridge: Ken Polack. Ken's heart was absolutely in the right place for every good cause you can think of. But by training Ken was a company lawyer (and a very good company lawyer at that). Ken was meticulous to the point of obsession about getting everything – every last detail – nailed down correctly. If there was a gap in your logic, a gap just about big enough for a mouse to squeeze through, Ken would find it. He would point it out to you, and he would explain how and why it made all the difference. Because that little mouse-sized gap would have allowed the court to go the opposite way to the way that you were arguing for.

I should also, and unquestionably, speak about Sir David Edward, who has been a mentor to me for more years than I think either of us really quite wants to remember. I worked with him in Edinburgh when I was an academic. He was not only interested in EU law but also in computer databases. Those were the early days of CELEX and other software. I knew a little about it, not a lot, but still he wanted me to brief him how it all worked. He was absolutely instrumental starting from the time I was instructed with him and with Jeremy Lever QC: a very junior barrister and two QCs ('silks'). We were writing an advisory opinion for a commercial client about what was then Article 95 EEC Treaty (now Article 110 TFEU), prohibiting tax discrimination. This was an area of EU law that I truly knew nothing about. Jeremy and David were both in Paris because they were working together on the IBM case. I showed up in Paris too and, basically, I had five days to put together a first draft of our joint opinion. I went at it like a wild thing. I produced a horribly shaggy document, which was a starting point. I sent it to David for him to have a look at. Half an hour later the phone at my desk rang. David could speed-read very well indeed. He asked me if I had a moment, and if so, could I please come through. I put my jacket on and went in. There was David with his feet balanced on the desk. At the time he was still smoking his pipe. He instantly got to his feet and he invited me to take a chair. He said:

> *Eleanor, this is grand. This is exactly what we needed as the starting point. You have obviously been incredibly thorough, and we are going to need to work on it a bit together. But this is a super starting point. Thank you so much.*

After that, of course, we rewrote it entirely. We did an executive summary at the front so the clients could see and understand where it was going. We trimmed the shaggy locks of the narrative, we added all sorts of things. I had conducted a kind of napalm bombing of the field. Now it had to be turned into a document that was fit for consumption by our clients. I shall never forget the kindness in the way that David received it. He could so easily have said: 'what on earth do you think we – or the client – can do with this document?' But no. It was so nice of him to be so positive, to see the good elements about what I had done under a lot of pressure in a very short time. Then I learned so much from working with him, watching how this sow's ear was then turned into a beautiful silk purse.

Adam: This is precisely what a good mentor should be like. As my favourite yoga teacher, Leon Taylor, a former Olympic champion in diving, put it in his book about mentoring:

> *[s]upport isn't everything; it's only one side of the equation. It's unlikely anyone was ever comforted into high-performance. As a mentor, you are supporting people to encourage them to push their comfort zones, to strive, and grow. Support is essential, but it's not enough. You may also need to gently challenge to evoke determination, curiosity, motivation, obsessive focus and maybe even temporary frustration.*[6]

Eleanor: Well said, well said.

Adam: Mentoring or teaching is not confined to a standard university classroom. Leo, our paths have crossed many times, including the annual seminars organised in Dubrovnik by our friends from the Faculty of Law of Zagreb University. But somehow the latest one we both attended in 2023 stands out. Remember, we both spoke about solidarity. My turn came first and, I have to admit, it was a rough ride. It was the first time I had the stomach to speak about the war in Ukraine, not on Zoom or MS Teams from the comfort of my desk at home, but in front of a live audience. It was very emotional, not a typical Adam lecture filled with substance, occasional jokes, and self-deprecation sandwiched in between. There was a high risk that I would just burst into tears and walk out. You may not remember it, Leo, but you and Niamh Nic Shuibhne maintained constant eye contact with me as I was moving from one aspect of the war to the next. This was mentoring at its best, perhaps unintentional but such a strong tacit support. Having said that, you got me completely when you started your lecture, which came right after mine, with a very loud and powerful *Слава Україні! Героям слава!* (Glory to Ukraine! Glory to heroes!). Thank you.

Eleanor: What can I say? There are moments when you know, without any pre-planning, what needs to happen to support a friend. It is instinctive. Niamh and I never talked to each other about it, either before or after your lecture. It was obvious that what you were talking about was intensely personal and emotional for you. You were approaching it very professionally; and your friends had to be there for you to support you. We knew without conscious thought that we had to give you absolute, quality attention – because that is what best supports a speaker. A lot of the time, you know, we don't truly listen to people. We sort of listen to them but, at the same time, we are half-thinking about something else (probably, about the wonderfully clever and perceptive intervention that we are going to make as soon as the speaker finishes!). Knowing that people are really listening to you, not partially listening, but listening 100% to what you are saying is incredibly supportive. Those listening in that way know that what you are going to say is important to you, and they are sitting expectantly on the edge of their seat waiting for you to tell them. This doesn't just hold good for helping a colleague through a very stressful moment. A very, very good Swedish friend of mine from Cambridge days, Monica Schüldt, has done a lot of excellent work (following on the pioneering approach of Nancy Kline) based on the importance of giving someone your undivided, respectful attention as a way of helping them to express and develop their thoughts (and often to find their own solutions to apparently intractable problems). What she has taught me about that has been enormously useful.

Adam: Dubrovnik seminars bring a lot of nice memories, don't they? They are loved by many people because part of what happens is in the classroom; but then we go out, dine, have some wine – and the conversations continue. I wonder how many young academics came back home after a week of that never-ending conversation in sunny Croatia, full of new ideas and energy.

Eleanor: My recollection of Dubrovnik seminars is that they are a wonderful event that I look forward to every time one happens and I am invited. There are always nice younger colleagues who are just starting out on their journey, and who have their precious piece of work, which they've been persuaded to present with the assurance that there is no risk of being eaten alive. The whole point is to give them encouragement to carry on. It is really interesting to see what people have been working on and talk about it. The questions asked at those seminars were never condescending or negative. They were always questions that enabled the person making the presentation to do an even better job of treating their chosen subject. It is really nice to be able to give a younger colleague a helping hand. If you are a slightly older colleague, you probably turn up and tell some war stories. That is certainly what you do if you are a barrister. The discussions that happened over meals, or on a boat going to *Cavtat* or whatever other excursion destination we chose, are an integral part of Dubrovnik. An awful lot that matters, in terms of moving thinking forward, happens in such informal contexts, where everyone (irrespective of perceived hierarchy or status) is given time and space to bring their own contribution to the discussion. Some of that ties across very well to the work of Nancy Kline (whom I mentioned just now), who does a lot of teaching for management and for leadership teams about creating a 'thinking environment' and facilitating the process of thought.

Adam: I am sure we have both seen it all. People who have all the qualifications in the world, and they just can't teach, they can't speak in public, they're just not capable of delivering an interesting talk or a lecture. And then we have the other extreme: people who not only have great knowledge but are also passionate about what they do and are capable of sharing it with others.

Eleanor: Nobody taught me how to teach. For a start, I never did a teacher training course. Like you, Adam, I had a lot of experience both of being taught badly and of being taught well. Sometimes I was taught in environments which were positively antithetical to learning. I was taught in environments where what was being taught didn't align with what I needed to know or study. Occasionally I had already done both the work and the corresponding exam, but nevertheless (because it was 'tidy' for school administrative purposes?) I was locked into being in that class for an entire year. Fortunately, my teacher for one of those courses whilst I was at boarding school – Catherine Dwyer – was intelligent. She gave me a separate list of topics and books that I might be interested in looking at and I sat quietly and read. Then she and I had discussions about what I had been reading. That was so good and thoughtful. By the way, it was also very unconventional behaviour by that nice idealistic young teacher, and was not really approved of by the school authorities. My own education finished in a sort of late Edwardian way with me being taught different subjects one-on-one by different people. For example, my beloved mother taught me superlatively well about literature during many nice walks together in the *Wienerwald*. I suppose that along the way – whilst I was on the receiving end of the education process – I must have picked up some useful tips on good ways of getting people engaged, getting them interested. Teaching is about communication. It's not like having a row of little pitchers, into which you pour information up to some mark on the outside, and then that batch of pitchers gets moved along on the production line, and the next batch of empty pitchers turn up, and you start pitcher-filling again. That always seemed to me to be a completely useless way of teaching.

Adam: I absolutely agree, and by the way, nobody taught me how to teach either. For many people the word 'teaching' is associated only with organised tuition, but being a teacher is a vocation. We are prone to teach even when the other side does not realise that. Sometimes it can turn into an accidental one-on-one class for a Brexiteer in a gondola taking skiers up to the top of the slope.

Eleanor: Well, yes, that is a true story. Whilst it has a funny aspect to it, it was a real eye-opener for me, and it gave me a terrible sense of foreboding about what was going to happen in the Brexit referendum. We are talking here about February 2016. It was the *semaine blanche*, the week when we had no hearings at the Court. So I – like many other people – earmarked that week as an opportunity to go skiing: *une semaine blanche* in more ways than one. I was in *Kitzbühel*, getting into a small four-person gondola. Already installed is a young man wearing the red anorak of the *Kitzbühel* ski school, *Die Rote Teufel*.

As a politely brought up Viennese, I naturally greeted him – as one would in Austria – with '*Grüß Gott*', a perfectly standard Austrian opening gambit. (I mean, it would have been very rude to get into a part-occupied ski gondola in Austria without saying '*Grüß Gott*'!) He looked at me and said: 'Er … I don't speak German'. Coming from someone wearing a *Rote Teufel* anorak, this got me curious so I started to explore.

He was a very nice young man, born and bred in Essex. His acquaintance with skiing had begun with watching 'Ski Sunday' on TV. He got fascinated and joined a package holiday ('Discover skiing!') in *Kitzbühel*. Well, he was a complete natural. He wanted to continue; and the ski school saw a good business opportunity. The clientele in *Kitzbühel* is very international. Having a native English speaker on the ski school staff as one of their ski instructors would obviously be a plus. They encouraged this nice young man. They helped him a bit financially, and they signed him up for the right steps to take his career forward. So there he was, finishing off his Austrian qualifications as a ski instructor and teaching skiing for six months of the year at the *Kitzbühel* ski school.

Naturally I said, 'You lucky man, that sounds pretty damn good. If I may be curious, what do you do during the other half of the year?' In the meantime, of course, the EU lawyer had said to herself: 'Let me see: six months of the year … since he is an employee of the *Kitzbühel* ski school, that is free movement of workers. What about the summer, I wonder?'

'Oh', said he, 'that's no problem at all'. Back home in Essex he had trained as a chef, so in the summer months (he told me) he would pack his roll of knives and head south to the sun. There were always places that needed a spare chef, and everyone spoke English. He had worked on the Costa del Sol, the Costa Brava – also in France for a bit. ('Aha', says the EU lawyer to herself, 'so during the other six months of the year, that will be freedom to provide services as a self-employed person.') This led to the crucial part of the conversation.

> **Leo-the-EU-lawyer:** *Look, that sounds more than all right. You are obviously very well organised, and you just get up and go. Good on you, mate. But aren't you a bit worried about this referendum coming up in the summer? About, you know, the UK and whether to remain part of the European Union and all that?*
>
> **Ski instructor/chef:** *Oh yes … Well, I think we should leave.*

At this point I had trouble believing my ears. I asked myself: 'did I really hear what I think I heard? I just heard a turkey vote for Christmas. You know, Christmas is a lovely family festival; great parties with paper hats and streamers and confetti; lots of good food ….

Adam: I guess at this stage Leo-the-EU-lawyer quickly became also Leo-the-educator.

Eleanor: I did use the remaining couple of minutes on that gondola to communicate some really basic elements of EU law, the gist of which was that his entire economic existence was predicated upon UK membership of the EU.

Adam: One-on-one class with Advocate General Sharpston.

Eleanor: Well, he was a bit surprised. In fact, he asked me:

> *Are you sure about this, luv?*

I didn't tell him what my day job was. I just said that I had kind of worked in this area of law for a long time and, well, I knew a reasonable amount about it. As we parted at the top, he looked very thoughtful.

Adam: You probably saved one vote, Leo. I had my version of your skiing gondola story, though, I have to admit, I failed miserably in my efforts.

Eleanor: Aha? Do tell.

Adam: It had been way before the referendum was announced, though it had already been hanging like Damocles's sword over our heads. We had three English builders redecorating our flat and at some point I joined them on the mission to collect tiles and whatever else was needed to bring the flat back to service. On the windscreen of their van there was a copy of one of the tabloids, screaming from the cover about some wretched anti-British judgment of the CJEU (along the lines 'EU Court does not allow the UK …'). I spent a good twenty minutes trying to explain to these three nice chaps that it was not the EU Court but rather the European Court of Human Rights in Strasbourg, and that the judgment the article talked about was a way more nuanced affair than the newspaper suggested. Alas, we were not operating on the same wavelength. Their repeated reaction was: 'The paper says it, mate'. (We then switched to football and the roles swapped: they knew what they were talking about and I knew absolutely nothing.) I fear such people probably voted leave without knowing what the entire thing was about. The debate before the Brexit plebiscite was abysmal at so many levels that, years later, my blood still boils when I think about it.

Eleanor: Hmmm … I remember thinking to myself, as I went out to put on my skis and head down the next slope, that I may indeed have saved one vote, but I did wonder how many other people out there were thinking like him. I really, really want to emphasise that I am not being in any way disparaging about this young man. He was very nice, very motivated, pleasant, and hard-working. A decent member of society, a good bloke. It was just horrifying that he had no idea about what the EU was or that indeed, what he was doing was so crucially dependent on Britain's EU membership. Actually, I have thought of him since the referendum and the UK's exit from the EU. I hope he has managed to find some way of positioning himself because he deserved to succeed.

Adam: Indeed, it is such people that have been affected by Brexit most. I often look at generations of students I teach at Westminster that have been deprived of so many personal and professional opportunities in the name of wrongly perceived 'sovereignty'. We talk through some ideas how to fix the Brexit mess later in the book. For now I should like to return to Leo-the-academic. In the spring of 2024, when we were both in Prague, you delivered a very enriching keynote speech at a conference organised by the Charles University and the Czech Ministry of Foreign Affairs. When you arrived, you were extremely tired and, as you told me, this was because you had worked well into the previous night on a Bar related assignment. But the moment you started to speak, I could see you coming alive. I was thinking to myself, someone turned the switch on and Leo was back in her element.

Eleanor: You know me well, so I am sure that you noticed. When I turned up, I was exhausted. But then there is the adrenaline. It is like at the Bar, or on stage in the theatre, or anywhere else where you have to perform. It really was like somebody flicked the switch. You cannot go on stage and start by saying: 'I am so dog-tired, I don't think I can generate the voltage necessary to convey to you the character that I am playing'. I was genuinely happy to find myself back in Prague to do the keynote on that day, and to preside over the Central and Eastern Europe Moot Competition during the following two days. As to the keynote, I had had less time to think about it than ideally I would have wanted to have. But actually that was alright because – as always – I had the basic structure of what I wanted to say. The Greeks who wrote about oratory said that you need to know how you are starting and how you are ending. If you have both, and you have the adrenaline, speaking live is probably going to be fine. I am always nervous when I start. Actually, I would be really worried if I stood up to speak and I didn't have that little flutter of nerves. It would probably mean that I was about to produce a truly appalling performance.

Adam: That was one of the first things that I learned when, as a teenager, I did some amateur theatre. Our director told me that one has to be somehow a little bit stressed on stage. If you were not stressed, you would need to trigger it because otherwise you would just not perform. Having said that, you just cannot let the stress take you over and negatively impact your performance. Talking about it now brings back one occasion when that nearly happened and I was saved by a cat.

Eleanor: Adam, are you trying to tell me that you brought a cat with you to a conference venue?

Adam: Sadly no, although that would have been entertaining in itself. (Don't give me such ideas, Leo!) This happened some ten years ago at a conference in Istanbul. The atmosphere from the start was tense, to put it mildly. A big conference dedicated to two legal and political issues that, back then (and still now), were not on speaking terms with each other: freedom of expression and the independence of the media, on the one hand, and the Turkish judiciary, on the other hand. As I walked in, I quickly realised that I was not going to address a small group of *aficionados* but rather a crowd of 1500 people: ministers, representatives of the European Union, judges, journalists. As the day's proceedings were about to start with the Turkish national anthem, I was standing there thinking: 'What on earth did I get myself into? Where is the emergency exit?' With the first bars of the Turkish national anthem blasting from the speakers, a massively panicked cat jumped out from under a covered grand piano that was on the stage. The poor thing was running back and forth making her/his disapproval clear with loud 'miaows'. The whole thing was surprisingly amusing (though I obviously felt very sorry for the poor cat). A very solemn moment mixed with a truly comical twist. I spent a good few minutes pressing my thumbs really hard into my hands to stop myself from bursting out with a howl of laughter. It did the trick and that scene brought the stress levels to something more like what I normally have before speaking in public. A cat came to my rescue.

Eleanor: That is a wonderful story, Adam.

Adam: Over the years we give many lectures, conference speeches, or evidence to public institutions. I suppose, in your case, one of many highlights were the three Hamlyn Lectures you delivered in 2020.

Eleanor: First of all, I was extraordinarily surprised, pleased, and honoured to be invited to give the Hamlyn Lectures. In my mind, the Hamlyn Lectures are always given by outstanding legal figures, and I never really thought of myself in that category. So, of course, I was absolutely chuffed to be invited to give the 2020 lecture series. Secondly, when I was invited, the Covid-19 pandemic was not yet even a cloud on the horizon; and I planned very carefully and deliberately with Professor Avrom Sherr that I would give the lectures in different venues within the United Kingdom. So, the first lecture was meant to be at the Faculty of Advocates in Edinburgh in Scotland, the second lecture at Queen's University Belfast in Northern Ireland, and (since the third lecture is always in London) I wanted the third lecture to be at my Inn of Court – the Middle Temple. The planning was deliberate because what I wanted to say about EU law and the EU law story was not meant to be London-centric. It was meant to involve all parts of the United Kingdom. I wanted to try to tell the story of this great and extraordinary experiment, of trying to construct a modern day European entity: not an empire achieved by conquest, but sovereign states coming together under the rule of law, sharing a common purpose, a common vision, and surrounding that joint enterprise with legal parameters.

Adam: Makes me wonder which of the three Hamlyn lectures I enjoyed most. I think it was the third one, also because it was looking forward; you made so many good points about the future of European integration. We will come back to this later in the book and, of course, I look forward to seeing their written version due for publication by Cambridge University Press in 2026.

Eleanor: Now that – thanks to the courteous urgings of Avrom Sherr and Joshua Rozenberg – the lecturer has finally got her act together and cleaned up the rough speaking notes into a publishable text, that should indeed happen!

Adam: Readers, watch this space! So, now we have moved on to the other aspect of academic work: writing. A few weeks ago, I read a book dedicated to the memory of Victoria Amelina.[7] She was a promising young Ukrainian writer whose first book in English was published posthumously in 2025.[8] At the College of Europe she is *patron de promotion* 2025/2026. Victoria was killed in 2023 when a Russian missile purposely targeted a popular pizzeria in Krematorsk where she, together with a group of colleagues, was having dinner. From the book in her memory, I learned that she used to say: 'As long as a writer is read, he's alive'.[9] It did strike a chord. The more I think about it, the more I agree with her.

Eleanor: I remember seeing the information about her passing on Twitter (now X). I did not previously know her work but then I came across a little bit of what she had been writing and doing. I remember feeling desperately sad that among the many consequences of the Russian invasion of Ukraine was the wiping out of such a promising young life. I really like that quote from her that you found. It's a very good point that she makes. Truly, 'As long as a writer is read, he's alive'.

Adam: Thanks to the two hats you have been wearing as a lawyer (Leo-the-practitioner and Leo-the-academic) your writing is so versatile. Yes, we do have your academic contributions to ongoing debates but we also have the Opinions that you presented as an Advocate General. Yes, they were produced for the benefit of the Court of Justice but they radiate well beyond the courtrooms at Kirchberg. I will use the words of Professor Elizabeth Fisher who, in her contribution to the *Festschrift* for you, wrote:

> *My intellectual reflex in pointing to Sharpston's opinion was because over more than a decade I had seen how her opinions were particularly good at helping students and in so doing fostering their expertise.*[10]

I couldn't agree more and I do not have to look very far. Earlier this very week I delivered a lecture about the rule of law in the European Union, and guess what? The first ten minutes were about your Opinions in *Heinrich*,[11] *Sturgeon*,[12] and – of course – the *Reallocation* cases.[13] Sometimes it is also the invisible hand of Eleanor Sharpston. We talked in Cambridge in the spring of 2024 about the *Metric Martyr* case. The following day, I was running my weekly public law tutorials at Westminster. As I walked into the classroom, I burst into laughter. Right there on the whiteboard were the remains of graffiti from the previous class. What was it? Of course, '*Thoburn v Sunderland City Council*'.

Eleanor: That case casts a long shadow.

Adam: Throughout your academic career you have published many journal articles as well as many contributions to edited volumes. I have noticed that during your time as an Advocate General at the Court of Justice you frequently wrote academic contributions on topics similar to what was currently in your docket (rights of third country nationals, direct effect of international treaties, to name a few). This was not accidental, was it?

Eleanor: Of course not; and the explanation is exactly the same as the one that I gave you earlier about running the Bar and my academic existence in parallel. Maybe (just maybe) if you are a lawyer who is so tied up in being a lawyer that you eat, live, and breathe law 24/24 and 7/7, you can work professionally on refugee rights under EU law, and then publish a very thoughtful academic article about the law of trusts in English law. I can't do that. Sometimes I have spare intellectual ideas that haven't been able to find their way into what I am working on professionally, and I want to find a home for them before they vanish like will o' the wisps.

Adam: Back in 1993, you published a monograph on interim relief and remedies in EC law.[14] At the time it was a very novel topic, at least here in the UK, or the English-speaking world. Was the choice of topic determined by your experience at the Bar and at the Court or did you just think that there was a gap in the literature?

Eleanor: I think it was both, Adam. At that time, most people were writing copiously about EC substantive law. A few people were writing a little about EC procedural law. But nobody was writing about remedies. If you are a practising barrister, your client is going to ask you at some stage: 'if we win this, what can I get?' Because that's what clients ask. So, this was the academic and the practitioner speaking with one voice, as it were. There was no book out there at the time that addressed the question of remedies. That is why I thought it would be good to try to write something on interim and substantive relief in cases under EC law. I was rolling up everything together. The discussion went everywhere from direct effect for certain treaty provisions and vertical direct effect for directives as against the State or an emanation of the State (where the article in question is clear, precise and unconditional) to the important practitioner's question: if the national court makes a reference for a preliminary ruling because the interpretation of the relevant EC law is unclear and (as was true at the time) it takes 18 months to get an answer back, does the client need protection in the meantime? If so, what's on offer? That's a vital question for your poor client. Ending up triumphantly with the Court giving the interpretation of EC (EU) law that you wanted isn't going to help the client if they go bust in the meantime. So that is why I wrote what I wrote. It took me two years because, at the same time, I was teaching and arguing cases. The book was on top of that, and – I am afraid – I have nothing like your output productivity, Adam. What really depressed me was that having written this blessed book, it was then not marketed or publicised by the publishers, Butterworths, in any useful way. In total, I think, only 164, maybe 168, copies got sold. The rest were withdrawn and pulped. I gave two years of my life to getting that book out and it went nowhere at all. After that, a couple of years later, other people started to publish books on remedies. Mark Brealey KC comes to mind as one of the authors who got in there early. I am happy to say, because Mark is a friend of mine, that his book and later books on remedies were much more successful than mine.[15]

Adam: It is hardly surprising that it makes you sad, Leo. Always when we write, or we put a recording or an exhibition out, our job is done and the result of our work gets its own life. This is the point when we take a deep breath and see what is going to happen. If nothing happens, it simply hurts. You would have spent a lot of time and effort thinking, putting it all together, your family would have suffered.

Eleanor: Indeed, Adam.

Adam: By the way, Leo, I am happy to say that one of those 164 or 168 sold copies of your book is sitting proudly on the shelf at home in our library. I bought it second hand, but still. When we met in 2023, in Dubrovnik, you wrote a very touching inscription for me. Thank you.

Eleanor: You are more than welcome – it was my pleasure!

Adam: Let us now move to something slightly different. One of the things that I find fascinating in teaching EU law, or law more generally, is that our students at the other end of their university studies will have many options to choose from. Some will become judges, others may go to the civil service or step on the academic path. Finally, many will, hopefully, join the Bar. When they are still students, moot courts are a very good way of checking and improving their knowledge and advocacy skills. You are presiding over one of the top EU law moot courts: the Central and Eastern Europe Moot Competition.

Eleanor: That particular moot court started on the initiative of a far-sighted trio: Sir Gordon Slynn, Judge Jan Dobry, and Denise Ashmore. It was an offshoot of the British Law Centre in Warsaw, where you studied and taught, Adam. As a matter of historical fact, I wasn't involved when Gordon got that project up and running. Much later, shortly after I started as an AG, I got a phone call from Professor Bill Cornish from Cambridge, who was in charge of the British Law Centre at the time. He began by swearing me to secrecy ('Leo: this phone call never took place, because if Gordon finds out about it he will kill us both'). The non-existent call was prompted by the fact that, sadly, Gordon's cancer had returned. Gordon was adamant that he would be fit enough to preside over the CEEMC to be held that year in Kyiv, but (not unnaturally!) Bill Cornish wanted to have a backup plan. I assured Bill that the conversation had of course never happened, since like Bill I was sure that Gordon would indeed kill us both very slowly if he ever found out that we had spoken. I marked the dates for the CEEMC 2009 in invisible ink in my diary, and I ring-fenced that weekend in case I was needed in Kyiv. Sadly, Gordon passed away in April 2009, so I flew to Ukraine and presided over the CEEMC. Actually, I thought I was just covering for one year, whilst the organisers looked for a new permanent president. As often happens with temporary Cambridge solutions, it somehow became quasi-permanent. Let's just say that they haven't yet found a different successor to Gordon! I love presiding over the CEEMC and I would not willingly relinquish it.

Adam: I have had the honour of sharing the CEEMC bench with you for three years now, Leo, and I can see how much you enjoy it. It is very demanding, though, for the students. They have to be on their hind legs from the beginning till the end of every court sitting.

Eleanor: I love it. Truly, I am trying to help the students with my questions. Sometimes perhaps I may seem a little bit ferocious …

Adam: (interrupting and laughing) no, never in the world!

Eleanor: … ok, ok but a lot of the time I'm actually trying to throw a life belt in their direction, not fire a torpedo. That said, if they choose to bat the life belt out of the way and go on swimming resolutely out into the middle of the deep blue sea, I may not be able to mount a rescue mission.

Adam: Absolutely, Leo. There is only so much we can do. But talking about life belts and advice to future lawyers: what would be your key ideas that you would like to share with young generations of future lawyers, especially the ones who are (and should be) passionate about the rule of law?

Eleanor: I'd give you five principles to apply, which I first set out when I spoke to the 'Our Rule of Law Academy': the offshoot of a project set up by four wonderfully enterprising first year students at the University of Groningen under the mentorship of Professor John Morijn.

Adam: I am all ears!

Eleanor: First principle: do not accept the status quo without asking questions first. We are all taught to regard our own legal system as the natural way of doing things. Obviously it adds up, it makes sense. It is the embodiment of justice-meets-law. English lawyers are particularly prone to making this assumption, because we just know in our bones that the English legal system, based on the sacred common law, is naturally superior to any other legal system. More generally, however: we all have an instinctive respect for our own legal system. Of course it makes sense and of course it is impeccably fair.

Adam: I feel there is a trap ahead. Is fairness and the rule of law really guaranteed? Just look at the Safety of Rwanda (Asylum and Immigration) Act 2024. To me, it is an abhorrent breach of the rule of law.

Eleanor: Exactly. Let me give you a couple of other dubious examples from the English legal system: one from recent, the other from more ancient times.

The recent example comes from the middle of all the Brexit shenanigans. As is well known, the UK doesn't have a written constitution, but there are numerous 'constitutional conventions' which are meant to do the job instead because, naturally, they will be respected. One of those conventions is that, save for specified 'recesses' (breaks), Parliament is meant to be in session to deal with Parliamentary business. And yet, in September 2019, we suddenly saw a six-week prorogation of Parliament. (Please remember, Brexit was meant to be about Parliament taking back control.) Why? Well, Parliament had started asking tedious questions about what exactly was being negotiated and whether it was a sensible form of Brexit. So, how much better for the executive *not* to have Parliament meeting for six weeks during that crucial period. Then it could present Parliament with a *fait accompli* and rush the deal through before the (then) deadline for leaving the European Union on 31 October 2019. It took a trip to the Supreme Court financed by a very public-spirited (and wealthy) ordinary citizen, Gina Miller, to get that prorogation of Parliament declared unlawful.

Adam: Oh yes …. and the second example?

Eleanor: A much older example, one of the most notorious miscarriages of justice under the English legal system, was the case of the 'Birmingham Six'. For years already, in what were euphemistically known as 'the Troubles', there had been sectarian bombings and shootings in Northern Ireland. Atrocities were committed by armed groups on both sides. In 1974, the IRA extended their campaign into mainland Britain. On 21 November 1974, 21 people were killed and almost 200 injured when bombs exploded in two public houses in Birmingham. This was the deadliest attack on English soil during the thirty years of the Troubles. Six Irish immigrants (who became known later as 'the Birmingham Six') were arrested, charged with the bombings, convicted and sentenced (in 1975) to life imprisonment. In 1976, a first application for leave to appeal was dismissed. In 1988, a first full appeal was dismissed and the convictions were upheld as 'safe and satisfactory'. In 1991, on a second full appeal with additional fresh evidence, their convictions were finally quashed. The basis for quashing those convictions was police mishandling of the evidence and indications that the defendants' convictions had been coerced. Just to give you a flavour of what had been happening: I was told by the defendants' solicitor (my late cousin, Ivan Geffen – a wonderful and fearless defender of the rule of law) that a key piece of evidence for the prosecution at the original trial had been tests carried out on the defendants' hands, which were said to reveal the presence of nitro-glycerine, which was one of the components used in making the Birmingham pub bombs. The only problem is, the same test would also show a positive result if you had recently washed your hands with commonly available soap. The Birmingham Six spent fifteen years inside prison because the English legal system failed to recognise and take proper account of that possibility of a false positive. Everyone, except a few rule of law campaigners, was sure that the English criminal justice system was infallible. An atrocity had been committed and these Irish defendants must be guilty. The system is good, and we never convict the wrong person. Except when we do. So, Leo's first principle is *don't accept the status quo without asking (lots of) questions first*.

Adam: That's a very good point. I recall that you once became a victim of police officers getting their facts horribly wrong.

Eleanor: I told that story publicly when I was being made a bencher of my Inn of Court, Middle Temple. The way that process happens is that Master Reader announces at dinner in Hall that, with the compliments of the Benchers, you are invited to take your seat at the high table. Later, you are asked to 'give an account of yourself.' In other words, you are invited to tell something about yourself to the people who are there. I decided to tell this particular story because I think you can draw some really interesting conclusions from it about the criminal justice system and how things work (or come off the rails).

Adam: Could we have that story here as well, please?

Eleanor: But of course. It goes back to the university term when I was the student editor of the Cambridge university student newspaper, which was called *Stop Press with Varsity*. That paper essentially occupied my life. I spent upwards of 60 hours a week working on the paper whilst I was its editor. The way you edited *Stop Press* was that – as well as general stuff spread over the week – you did three all nighters in a row. You dealt with 'copy' (articles and news stories) on Tuesday night into Wednesday, and Wednesday night into Thursday. Then – faint but pursuing – on Thursday night into Friday, you went back for the final all nighter. That was the moment when you took your stories and you did the layout of the paper. In those days, you were literally glueing strips of typeset text onto large rectangles of paper representing each page, and marking where the photos would be. On Friday morning, a student would drive this precious creation (accompanied by appropriate instructions) in a hire van across to the printers in Bicester, near Oxford. The paper would be printed there and 10,000 printed copies would be brought back to Cambridge where they would be distributed (by a different student driver and helper) on Friday evening to colleges and selected retail outlets. Between Friday evening and Saturday lunchtime, you slept the sleep of the just, convinced that you had just produced the most marvellous edition of a newspaper in the whole history of journalism. Then on Saturday at lunchtime, there was a bread and cheese lunch where anyone who had worked on the paper in the previous week came along. They ate lunch and they ripped your work to shreds. They pointed out everything that was wrong with it, from content ('weak'; 'shallow') to miscalculated photo instructions to the printers that had resulted in the Varsity sports picture on page 15 wearing a mourning band of black around its border. Then we discussed what was going to go into the paper for the next week. The cycle recommenced with gathering in material on Saturday, Sunday, and Monday, writing it up on Tuesday and Wednesday, doing the layout for the next edition on Thursday, and so on.

Now, at this time Cambridge was going through a very unpleasant period, because there was a sexual predator on the loose, who quickly became known by the self-explanatory nickname of the 'Cambridge rapist'. He preyed upon women students who were living in bedsits outside the colleges, in 'digs' in the town. By the time my story happened, he had already scored about seven rapes and counting. He was clearly mentally sick. Among various accoutrements he had a black balaclava-style face mask, which he used to wear, with the word 'RAPIST' across the forehead. Cambridge Police was, obviously, on full alert to stop any suspicious character so as to find and arrest this man. I had just finished my second all-night stint at the paper. We are about 4:30am – 5.00am on a Thursday morning. Very, very wearily, I cycled back from the offices of the paper in Round Church Street to my college, King's – fortunately, no great distance. I parked my bicycle outside. Of course, now I needed to get into College, crawl back to my room, and get a little sleep before my 10am supervision (for which, naturally, I had done no work). In those days, students did not have keys or electronic cards to open front gates, or indeed any gate, to a college; and it wasn't good form to wake the porters. After all, you were not meant to be outside College at that time of night. For every College, there were therefore a number of well-known and well-accepted routes (handed down from one year to the next) enabling students to get in and out quietly without disturbing the porters. For King's, one of these routes was just by the big tree at the eastern end of Chapel. That tree is very close to the iron railings dividing the Front Court from the more public area and King's Parade, and one of the vertical bars in the railings behind the tree was missing. So if you were reasonably slim and turned sidewards, you could, in fact, get through the railings, walk back to your room in College and go to bed. I had parked my bike outside the Porters Lodge and I was walking along the strip of grass that belongs to King's College between the railings and the public road, King's Parade, when I became aware that I was being shadowed by a 'panda car'. (We called them 'panda cars' because they were black and white; they were police cars.) I carried on walking. The panda car carried on shadowing me. Eventually, of course, I reached the point near the tree where I had to make up my mind. Was I going to go through the railings and climb into College? Or was I going to go the long way round: down Senate House Passage, along to the 'Clare gate' into King's, and climb over that gate (which is much more difficult)? I was tired. I turned left towards the tree, to take the easy way into College. Then all hell broke loose. Two very tall and burly policemen leapt out of the panda car. They rushed across the grass, and they rugby tackled me to the ground. I wasn't offering any resistance but they got me down very flat, very quickly, and very hard. Then they picked me up and dragged me over to stand in front of the headlights of the panda car. One of them started asking me questions. The other one took the army surplus khaki kit bag that was slung over my shoulder, and started burrowing through it like a terrier looking for a rat. Meanwhile, his colleague was asking me all sorts of questions which I would have got wrong at midday when I was rested, and which I was certainly going to get wrong in the early hours of the morning, with two nights of practically no sleep.

Adam: What were the questions then?

Eleanor: For example, 'what is the college registration number for your bike?' I have never been able to remember that! Anyway, the policeman looking through my army surplus kit bag didn't manage to find a black mask with the word 'RAPIST' on it. What he did find were lots of membership cards for societies, envelopes, and things like that, all of which had my nickname 'Leo' rather than my full name 'Eleanor'. I was dressed as a student in those days would have been. I was wearing a rather shapeless donkey jacket and jeans, and I had short hair. Apparently I looked reasonably like the identikit picture of the rapist that the various victims had helped the police to piece together, and which was what they were working from. The description accompanying that picture was that the suspect was 'short, about five foot five, stocky, shifty looking'. The police put two and two together and they made five.

Adam: So, you got arrested, didn't you?

Eleanor: Yes, they arrested me and they cautioned me. They had radioed in to the central command at Parkside: 'We think we've got him. We think we have the rapist'. So, they had already started the process of getting the arrested suspect into the system. Having cautioned me, they produced the standard phrase: 'Do you wish to make a statement? If you do, it will be taken down: anything you say will be taken down in writing and may be used in evidence against you'. With the benefit of hindsight, I should have played along and let them take me into Parkside because it would have been funnier. But I was so very tired. I badly wanted to go to sleep. I also thought there would be a credibility gap here. That academic year, I had already tested the patience of my long-suffering economic theory supervisor to near breaking point. I didn't think that he was (plausibly) going to buy the idea that I had skipped my impending supervision at 10am that morning because I had been arrested as the Cambridge rapist and was languishing in a cell in the police station at Parkside. So when I was offered the opportunity of making a statement following arrest and caution, I said: 'Yes, I do want to make a statement'. The policeman got out his notebook and his pencil. He licked the pencil and he waited.

> **Leo:** *As I have told you, I have a good reason for being out in the early morning. I am the editor of the student newspaper – Stop Press with Varsity.*
>
> [Then I waited for him to catch up]
>
> *Normally, Thursday morning is a bit late for news* [pause], *but if we have something that our readers will really want to know about* [pause], *we type it out on an electric typewriter* [pause] *and we stick it on the front page.* [pause] *I am sure our readers are going to love to discover on Saturday morning* [pause] *that you have just arrested a woman as the Cambridge rapist.*

The policeman started writing down those final words. Then, realisation dawned. He looked me up and down. I stood up very straight and I stuck out my chest. There was a very long pause. Then the two policemen looked at each other and they said 'oh'. I thought I'd better seize the initiative at this point and – if possible – also be generous in victory.

> **Leo:** *Gentlemen, listen, I am really delighted, speaking as a woman, that you are trying to catch the Cambridge rapist. I am right behind you, but you haven't yet got the Cambridge rapist. You have got me. Now, would you please de-arrest me and let me get into College and go to bed?*

They un-handcuffed me, and de-arrested me. That was fine, but they were not keen on letting me climb through the hole in the railings. They marched me up to the front door of King's College and they rang the bell, which, of course, got the night porter out. The night porter took one look at me in the arms of the law (you must imagine, two very tall policemen with all five foot three inches of me in between them), and in a really resigned voice he said, 'Oh, Leo, and what have you been up to now, then?' Brief explanations followed, and I was released. The night porter duly vouched for me as a (female) undergraduate member of College. So I got in and headed off to bed. Naturally, the story was all over College by breakfast. Within the College community, I have never really lived it down.

Adam: (laughing out loud) Has it haunted you since?

Eleanor: Well, one afternoon shortly after I got back to King's as a law fellow, I walked into the Porter's Lodge to find Reg Prentice, one of our lovely porters, busy confirming what had happened to a student who was asking about this.

> **Student:** *I heard that one of the King's fellows was once arrested as the Cambridge rapist.*

> **Reg:** *Why yes, that was our law fellow, Leo Sharpston* [seeing ES] *Oh, hello, Leo. How are you?* [continuing] *It was Leo here. I know the story cos' I was the desk sergeant on duty at Parkside police station when that young idiot of a copper radioed in to say he'd got the Cambridge rapist, and then 10 minutes later, he radioed in again and said:*

> *'Sarge, we made a bit of a mistake there. Seems like we got a woman. Can we let her go?'*

So that was the story that I told, to the delight – it has to be said – of the assembled company in Middle Temple Hall, and I then proceeded to draw various lawyerly conclusions about (for example) the importance of not jumping to conclusions, and respecting the rights of the defence.

Adam: It proves so well Leo's first principle: do not accept the status quo without asking questions first. Obviously, now I am eager to learn what is Leo's second principle?

Eleanor: *Do not expect an opportunity to knock at a convenient moment because it never does. Just take the opportunity when it comes – and remember that you can also go out there and look for that opportunity.* From the perspective of some four decades in the profession, allow me to share with you an unpalatable truth. Opportunity never, by any chance, arises at the right moment.

Adam: Meaning?

Eleanor: Opportunity doesn't come along when you are just sitting there peacefully and you have got plenty of time, at 10 o'clock on a Wednesday morning when there's nothing much else in your diary for the rest of the week. Opportunity will always turn up at a moment when you are harassed and overworked. It will turn up at 10pm on a Sunday evening (I know, I know). It will turn up late on a Friday afternoon before a holiday weekend. It will turn up when you cannot imagine how on earth you are going to fit this additional demand into your day along with everything else that is already happening. And the news is: you have got to fit it in. The news is: if this is something that needs doing, somehow you have to make the space to do it. And if you really care about being a rule of law defender and an opportunity hasn't knocked at your door for a while – well, you know, you can go out and look for it. There is an awful lot happening. There is an awful lot of *pro bono* work that needs doing. There are many tribunals which make decisions that matter to people, but where those concerned cannot get legal aid to pay for representation. There is an awful lot that can be done, and you can do the work applying the principle of cross-financing. If I think back over my practising time at the Bar, the cases that come immediately to mind, the ones that I found most fulfilling and that really gave me most satisfaction, the ones that I still have a warm glow about – all of them were cases that I did *pro bono*. We talked about some of them earlier on.

Adam: Indeed. We have talked about *Brown and others* and *SS Storaa* but I am sure that is just the tip of the iceberg. What is the third principle, Leo?

Eleanor: *Actively consider whether this small, insignificant, unimportant case that you are currently doing is maybe the case that is going to break new ground if pleaded in a new way.* Of course, it is very easy to see some interesting new points of law after the event. Once a point has been picked up and has been pleaded, of course it is obvious. We all understand that under the surface, just waiting to be brought out, there was, for instance, a really interesting human rights point. There was a point that could be run under the ECHR. There was a breach of fundamental rights under the constitution. There was a breach of due process. Yes, we can all spot the point with hindsight, once a bright lawyer has got up and said 'hang on, wait a minute, I am not sure that was okay'. Always ask yourself that question.

Adam: Excellent. How about the fourth principle?

Eleanor: Every case matters; and most of them are about individuals – about human beings. To you, it may be yet another case in a long and possibly boring series: 'Oh yes (yawn), this is the 15th bylaw application I am doing this week'. To your client, it is THE case (definite article). It is the only case that matters.

It is her/his case; it is her/his entire future. And for that reason, it deserves your best, every single time. You cannot say as an actor, 'I am sorry but I am feeling rather 'off' this evening. I'll I'll do my best with playing Hamlet but you will have to cut me a bit of slack if I don't really do "To be or not to be …" quite as well as you might expect me to'. As we say in Ireland, 'it's the same difference' with being a lawyer. If you are representing a client, the client doesn't care how good you were last week; and the client doesn't care how good you may be next week. The client needs you to be at the top of your game today, because today is when you are representing him.

Adam: Last but not least: may we have the fifth principle, please?

Eleanor: The fifth and most important principle: *having your heart in the right place isn't actually enough. You have to be technically better than your opponents*, than the lawyers earning the fat fee notes who are instructed by the big corporations or acting on behalf of the State. I owe this last principle to my director of studies at King's College, Ken Polack, whom I've already mentioned. Sometimes a point may sound a bit technical. Perhaps it is some fiddly little procedural or evidential rule that you learnt at law school but never seriously thought would matter in real life. And yet the day may come when that little procedural or evidential rule may be the key to getting a result that is in accordance with the rule of law.

Adam: Fair enough, but I guess that sometimes it also helps to be somewhere higher in the legal hierarchy.

Eleanor: Oh yes, in the British context, there's the importance of 'silk'. If I look back at *SS Storaa*, the fact that Eleanor Sharpston QC said: 'I'll do it for free' helped to launch the proceedings on a positive note. There are some advantages to having those two letters after your name. Another advantage, as we discovered on day two of the hearing in *SS Storaa*, is that if you are a silk you can make really cheeky applications, like 'Here is some evidence I was unaware of and could not have known about until yesterday evening that may help the court to understand what was really happening on those wartime convoys; I have an affidavit that was sworn last night; I know that this is a very unusual application but can I introduce it please?' You definitely stand a better chance of being listened to as a silk than if you are a junior member of the Bar making the same application. (Remember, I got permission to introduce the affidavit evidence.) This may not sound terribly fair but it is the reality of the way that practice works. It's also true of legal propositions. As a King's Counsel, you can advance something that may seem a bit far-fetched and – whilst you may or may not win the point – you will be listened to with more respect and attention than if you were a junior advancing the same argument.

Adam: That's for sure but to get there you need to put in a lot of effort, tears, and sweat. Law students who think that there is an easy way into the legal profession, not filled with bumps and potholes, are very much mistaken. Over the past few years I have noticed an ever growing propensity among the student population to use shortcuts and, these days, it seems to be becoming even acceptable to submit essays largely or even entirely generated by AI. I do wonder how AI will affect the legal profession (and others, for that matter). Are you scared of or intrigued by AI?

Eleanor: I am intrigued. I can see ways that it could save a lot of time on very routine stuff. I think that we need, first of all, to stop pretending that AI is somehow not there. Manifestly it does exist and it is here to stay. I think we need to be intelligent about artificial intelligence. We need to work out what it does well, and how it can be harnessed to help us in our work. I also believe that we need to ask ourselves, 'what are the things that a human does better?' That partly links through to questions of law and morality, law and decisions of principle. What direction do we want the law to take? Can it be steered in the desired direction? How do we want to present this case, and how are we going to suggest that it fits into the overall mosaic? I would like to have a human mind focussing on those big underlying questions, fresh and liberated from ploughing through all the tedious stuff that AI does faster and better. I don't really want AI telling me that X 'must' be the answer and that this piece 'must' fit into the mosaic in this way and no other. AI would often be a useful reference point, though. Imagine that you are working on a case, or preparing a piece of academic analysis. Imagine there were three authorities pointing the other way to your preferred line of argument that you'd forgotten about. It would be really nice if the AI popped up and said: 'Excuse me. You may have a slight problem, as you seem to have missed these three cases or at least not engaged with them'. It would alert you to their existence. What about you, Adam? Are you scared of or intrigued by AI?

Adam: I have to admit that I am, in equal measure, intrigued, annoyed, and worried. I think it is primarily based on my experience with students, who tend to over rely on AI.

Eleanor: Of course they do, because it is a really time-efficient way of doing your case law research and getting your essay written.

Adam: True, but one thing is to use it like we use internet search engines, quite another is to use it as the only source of information and submit whatever it has generated as your own work. This way one switches off critical thinking and, more generally, the brain. Both are fundamental for good lawyering (and this applies, of course, to many other professions).

Eleanor: This is why we need to find ways of getting people to use AI knowledgeably, including (incidentally) spotting if AI has just invented material – decided authorities, for example – that simply doesn't exist. If we want to have good lawyers, we need to train and refine their legal thinking. By the way, we (still) spend a lot of time teaching lawyers how to do things which (actually) good AI can probably do better. So we need to shift – perhaps to some degree – the focus of what we think is important in terms of training our lawyers.

Adam: I gather you have had a go at AI generated material, Leo. What was your experience?

Eleanor: Out of curiosity, I tried the experiment of using AI to generate case summaries. Sometimes they were how I would have summarized the case, but sometimes they weren't. I think we need to make people aware of the fact that, because AI works the way it does, by harvesting massive quantities of existing data, it is likely to come up with a summary with a particular direction of travel. That's because of how it is created and how it operates.

Adam: Let's do a little experiment and ask ChatGPT to give us a summary of *Associação Sindical dos Juízes Portugueses* (Case C-64/16).[16]

Eleanor: Why not? Let's do that.

Adam: Here we go then:

> *The Case C-64/16 is a significant decision by the Court of Justice of the European Union (CJEU), involving the Associação Sindical dos Juízes Portugueses (ASJP), the Portuguese Association of Judges. The case revolves around the interpretation of European Union law concerning judicial independence and the protection of judicial officers in relation to national legislative changes.*
>
> *Background:*
>
> *The case began when the ASJP challenged Portuguese legislation that altered the judicial retirement system, specifically provisions that reduced judicial pension entitlements. The changes were perceived to undermine judicial independence, particularly as they targeted judges' salaries and retirement benefits. The ASJP argued that the legislation violated EU law, particularly the principle of judicial independence guaranteed under both EU law and the European Convention on Human Rights.*
>
> *The case was referred to the CJEU, which was asked to interpret whether the national legislation complied with EU law, including the requirement for judicial independence under Article 19(1) TEU (Treaty on European Union) and Article 47 of the EU Charter of Fundamental Rights. Judicial independence is essential to ensure that judges can decide cases impartially and without influence from other branches of government.*
>
> *The Key Legal Issues:*
>
> *Judicial Independence: The central issue was whether national measures that affected the remuneration and pension systems of judges could compromise judicial independence.*
>
> *EU Law and National Law: The case questioned the interaction between national measures (in this case, Portuguese pension reforms) and EU principles, particularly in relation to the protection of judicial independence.*

CJEU Ruling:

The CJEU ruled that national measures that alter judicial remuneration in a way that affects judges' independence may violate EU law. In its judgment, the Court emphasized that judicial independence is a fundamental principle of EU law and that any measure that undermines this independence, including changes to the financial conditions of judges, must be carefully scrutinized.

The Court clarified that the financial status of judges must be such that they are free from external pressure that could influence their decisions. This is an essential element of the rule of law and the protection of fundamental rights within the EU.

Implications:

This ruling reaffirmed the importance of judicial independence and the role of the CJEU in ensuring that national laws comply with EU principles. It also served as a warning to Member States that attempts to undermine judicial independence through legislative changes could be scrutinized by EU institutions.

The case highlighted the tension that can sometimes arise between national sovereignty and the protection of fundamental EU values, such as the rule of law and judicial independence.

In sum, Case C-64/16 Associação Sindical dos Juízes Portugueses was a pivotal judgment that reinforced the EU's commitment to safeguarding the independence of the judiciary as a cornerstone of democratic governance within the Union.

Eleanor: Well, it is reasonably competent but to some degree it misses the big picture. You and I, like many lawyers (academics and practitioners alike) read that judgment as being a blockbuster judgment, laying the foundations for important statements about the rule of law, the independence of the judiciary, and highlighting the possibility of using Article 19(1) TEU in a very teleological and creative way going forwards.

Adam: Which is something we will talk about in depth in the closing chapter of this book. All of the nuances are missing here. AI used a telescope and a microscope but not the wide angle lens.

Eleanor: It does not surprise me, though. I was expecting pretty much what we got from the AI-generated summary: a description of the nuts and bolts of the case and a passing reference (or two) saying something like 'along the way, the Court made a number of statements about judicial independence'. What we need to do is to make our law students understand the limitations of reading the case law exclusively through AI.

Adam: I think we can also use our experience of using otter.ai to generate transcripts of these conversations. I find some of those 'Otterisms' rather funny, clearly showing the limits of AI.

Eleanor: Oh, some of them have been exquisite. Let's have an annex, then, of the best 'Otterisms'!

Annex

The best Otterisms

Exhibit # 1

Otter said:

> *And a week before it's opened in the House of Lords, the team there were five defendants than eight barristers already for socks for juniors.*

We meant:

> *A week before it opened in the House of Lords, we had five defendants and eight barristers, four silks and four juniors.*

Exhibit # 2

Otter said:

> *I think I was that was fortunate because given the relentless assault, on salary from the chair, it was nice to be able to have a civilised discussion with one of the members of the panel and Lord mustard was obviously was also very interested ask very good questions, and was very civilised.*

We meant:

> *I think I was fortunate. Given the relentless assault, the artillery fire from the chair, it was nice to be able to have a civilised discussion with one of the members of the panel. And Lord Mustill was obviously very interested, asked good questions, and was very civilised.*

Exhibit # 3

Otter said:

> *It was just an opinion of the African general. It went to my colleague a very nice French colleague advocate tool bought.*

We meant:

> *It was an Opinion of the Advocate General. It went to my colleague, a very nice French colleague, Advocate General Yves Bot.*

Exhibit # 4

Otter said:

> *Orchestra de la plaster new hop.*

We meant:

> *Orchestre de la Place de l'Europe.*

Exhibit # 5

Otter said:

> *She leant forward, and she punched the button on her microphone with a certain richness and in the voice so cold that it was about 30 degrees below absolute zero. She said in Uganda that contain bloggers should love ally he has just made a joke about poultry.*

We meant:

> *She leant forward. She punched the button on her microphone with a certain viciousness; and in a voice so cold that it was about 30 degrees below absolute zero, she said: 'Il vient de raconter une blague sur la volaille' ('He has just made a joke about poultry').*

Exhibit # 6

Otter said:

> *For some reason, until I managed to win the women's bloke race in 1980 everything I did for Cambridge. I've been a second team, or it wasn't yet a blue sport.*

We meant:

> *For some reason, until I managed to win the women's boat race [for Oxford] in 1980, everything I did for Cambridge was either in a second team or it wasn't yet a Blue's sport.*

ENDNOTES

* As quoted in Joshua Rozenberg, 'Injustice put right. Eleanor Sharpston KC appointed DCMG' (*A Lawyer Writes*, 1 January 2025) <https://rozenberg.substack.com/> accessed 1 September 2025.

** Eleanor Sharpston, "Can't Those European Judges Think for Themselves?' An Afterword on Why the Court (Still) Needs its Advocates General' in Graham Butler and Adam Łazowski (eds), *Shaping EU Law the British Way. UK Advocates General at the Court of Justice of the European Union* (Hart, 2022) 591.

[1] Eleanor Spaventa, 'Some Reflections on the European Commission's Changing Roles' in Catherine Barnard, Adam Łazowski, Daniel Sarmiento (eds), *Pursuit of Harmony in a Turbulent Europe. Essays in Honour of Eleanor Sharpston* (Hart, 2024) 137.

[2] Here is a non-exhaustive list of Leo's publications. Book: Eleanor Sharpston, *Interim and Substantive Relief in Claims under Community Law* (Butterworths, 1993). Articles in peer-reviewed journals: Eleanor Sharpston, 'Further EU enlargement – a 'brave new world', or more like 'back to the future'?' (2024) 25 *ERA Forum* 275; Eleanor Sharpston, 'From "Do Trees Have Rights?" to Wondering About Ecocide: Some Legal Reflections' (2022) 52 *Environmental Policy and Law* 117; Eleanor Sharpston, 'Making the Court of Justice of the European Union More Productive' 21 (2014) *Maastricht Journal of European and Comparative Law* 763; Eleanor Sharpston, 'Effective Judicial Protection through Adequate Judicial Scrutiny – Some Reflections' (2013) 4 *Journal of European Competition Law & Practice* 453; Eleanor Sharpston, 'Transparency and Clear Legal Language in the European Union: Ambiguous Legislative Texts, Laconic Pronouncements and the Credibility of the Judicial System' (2010) 12 *Cambridge Yearbook of European Legal Studies* 409; Eleanor Sharpston and José Maria Fernández-Martín, 'Some Reflections on Schengen Free Movement Rights and the Principle of Ne Bis in Idem' (2007–2008) 10 *Cambridge Yearbook of European Legal*

Studies 413; Catherine Barnard and Eleanor Sharpston, 'The Changing Face of Article 177 References' (1997) 34 *Common Market Law Review* 1113; Allan Dashwood, Angela Ward, Albertina Albors-Llorens, N Bamforth, Catherine Barnard, Philip Moser, Siofra O'Leary, Eleanor Sharpston, Takis Tridimas, 'CELS: E.C. Treaty Project' (1997) 22 *European Law Review* 395; Clifford Jones, Eleanor Sharpston, 'Beyond Delimitis: pluralism, illusions, and narrow constructionism in Community antitrust litigation' (1996/97) 3 *The Columbia Journal of European Law* 85; Eleanor Sharpston, 'When is an agreement anti-competitive?' (1991) 135 *Solicitors' Journal* 1186; Eleanor Sharpston, 'Legitimate Expectations and Economic Reality' (1990) 15 *European Law Review* 103; Eleanor Sharpston 'European Community law and the doctrine of legitimate expectations: how legitimate, and for whom?' (1990) 11 *Northwestern Journal of International Law & Business* 87. Chapters in edited volumes: Eleanor Sharpston, 'Twenty five years of the European Arrest Warrant – an odyssey in mutual trust towards an unknown destination?' in Adam Łazowski and Valsamis Mitsilegas (eds), Coming of Age? The European Arrest Warrant at Twenty Five (Hart, 2027) forthcoming; Eleanor Sharpston, 'Comparative Legal Reasoning (Overt and Covert) in the Work of the Advocate General' in Daniele Gallo, Roberto Mastroianni, Fernanda G. Nicola, Lorenzo Cecchetti (eds), *The Italian Influence on European Law Judges and Advocates General (1952–2000)* (Hart, 2024); Eleanor Sharpston, 'Thinking About Solidarity and EU Law' in Eva Kassoti and Narin Idriz (eds), *The Principle of Solidarity. International and EU Law Perspectives* (Asser Press/Springer, 2023); Eleanor Sharpston, ''Can't Those European Judges Think for Themselves?' An Afterword on Why the Court (Still) Needs its Advocates General' in Graham Butler and Adam Łazowski (eds), *Shaping EU Law the British Way. UK Advocates General at the Court of Justice of the European Union* (Hart Publishing, 2022); Eleanor Sharpston, 'Legislating and Adjudicating: Where and How to Strike the Balance' in Elizabeth Fisher, Jeff King, and Alison Young (eds), *The Foundations and Future of Public Law. Essays in Honour of Paul Craig* (OUP, 2020); Eleanor Sharpston, 'About that Sunday Trading Mess …' in Fabian Amtenbrink, Gareth Davies, Dimitry Kochenov, Justin Lindeboom (eds), *The Internal Market and the Future of European Integration: Essays in Honour of Laurence W. Gormley* (CUP, 2019); Eleanor Sharpston, 'Religion in the Workplace: When is Enforcing of Religious Ethos Acceptable? and When is Neutrality Discrimination?' in Koen Lenaerts, Jean-Claude Bonichot, Heikki Kanninen, Caroline Naômé, Pekka Pohjankoski (eds), *An Ever-Changing Union? Perspectives on the Future of EU Law in Honour of Allan Rosas* (Hart Publishing, 2019); Daniel Sarmiento, Eleanor Sharpston, 'European Citizenship and its New Union: Time to Move On?' in Dimitry Kochenov (ed), *EU Citizenship and Federalism: The Role of Rights* (CUP, 2017); Eleanor Sharpston, 'Protection concepts associated with both refugee status and complementary or subsidiary forms of protection' in Matthew Happold, Maria Pichou (eds), *The protection of persons fleeing armed conflict and other situations of violence/La protection des personnes fuyant un conflit armé et d'autres situations de violence* (Larcier, 2016); Eleanor Sharpston, 'European citizenship and social rights?: the views of the Advocates General and the Court' in Christian Calliess (ed), *Europäische Solidarität und nationale Identität: Überlegungen im Kontext der Krise im Euroraum* (Mohr Siebeck, 2013); Eleanor Sharpston and Michael-James Clifton, 'The two EEA courts: unequal balance or fruitful partnership?' in *EFTA Court, Judicial protection in the European Economic Area* (German Law Publishers, 2012); Eleanor Sharpston, 'Citizenship and fundamental rights: Pandora's box or a natural step towards maturity?' in Pascal Cardonnel, Allan Rosas, Nils Wahl (eds), *Constitutionalising the EU judicial system: essays in honour of Pernilla Lindh* (Hart, 2012); Eleanor Sharpston, Geert De Baere, 'The Court of Justice as a Constitutional Adjudicator' in Anthony Arnull, Catherine Barnard, Michael Dougan, Eleanor Spaventa (eds), *A Constitutional Order of States? Essays in EU Law in Honour of Alan Dashwood* (Hart,2011); Eleanor Sharpston, 'The Changing Role of the Advocate General' in Anthony Arnull, Piet Eeckhout, Takis Tridimas (eds), *Continuity and Change in EU Law: Essays in Honour of Sir Francis Jacobs* (OUP, 2008); Eleanor Sharpston, 'Different but (Almost) Equal – The Development of Free Movement Rights Under EU Association, Co-operation and Accession Agreements' in Mark Hoskins, William Robinson (eds), *A True European: Essays for Judge David Edward* (Hart Publishing, 2003); Eleanor Sharpston, 'Common Agriculture Policy' in Cheryl Saunders and Gillian D Triggs (eds), *Trade and Cooperation with the European Union in the New Millenium* (Brill, 2002); Eleanor Sharpston, 'Milk Lakes, SLOMs, and Legitimate Expectations – a Paradigm in Judicial Review' in David O'Keeffe, Antonio Bavasso (eds), *Liber Amicorum in Honour of Lord Slynn of Hadley. Judicial Review in European Union Law* (Kluwer, 2000); Eleanor Sharpston, 'Interim relief in the national courts' in Julian Lonbay and Andrea Biondi (eds), *Remedies for breach of EC law* (Wiley, 1997).

[3] Mishal Husain, *Broken Threads: My Family from Empire to Independence* (Fourth Estate, 2024).
[4] Case 120/78 *Rewe-Zentral AG v Bundesmonopolverwaltung für Branntwein* ECLI:EU:C:1979:42.
[5] This cultural life (BBC Podcast) <https://www.bbc.co.uk/programmes/m00274xz> accessed 1 September 2025.
[6] Leon Taylor, *Mentor. The most important role you were never trained for* (Noggin, 2010) 21.
[7] Askold Melnyczuk (ed), *Nothing Bad Has Ever Happened: A Bouquet for Victoria Amelina* (Arrowsmith Press, 2023).
[8] Victoria Amelina, *Looking at Women, Looking at War: A War and Justice Diary from Ukraine* (William Collins, 2025).
[9] Melnyczuk (n 7) 21.
[10] Elizabeth Fisher, 'EU Environmental Law and the Importance of Active Legal Work' in Catherine Barnard, Adam Łazowski, Daniel Sarmiento (eds), *Pursuit of Harmony in a Turbulent Europe. Essays in Honour of Eleanor Sharpston* (Hart, 2024) 521, 530.
[11] Case C-345/06 *Gottfried Heinrich* ECLI:EU:C:2008:212, Opinion of AG Sharpston.
[12] Joined Cases C-402/07 & C-432/07 *Christopher Sturgeon, Gabriel Sturgeon and Alana Sturgeon v Condor Flugdienst GmbH (C-402/07) and Stefan Böck and Cornelia Lepuschitz v Air France SA (C-432/07)* ECLI:EU:C:2009:416, Opinion of AG Sharpston.
[13] Joined Cases C-715/17, C-718/17, and C-719/17 *European Commission v Republic of Poland and Others* ECLI:EU:C:2019:917, Opinion of AG Sharpston.
[14] Eleanor Sharpston, *Interim and Substantive Relief in Claims under Community Law* (Butterworths, 1993).
[15] For instance, Mark Brealey QC, Mark Hoskins, David Vaughan QC, *Remedies in EC Law: Law and Practice in the English and EC Courts* (2nd ed, Sweet & Maxwell, 1998).
[16] Case C-64/16 *Associação Sindical dos Juízes Portugueses v Tribunal de Contas* ECLI:EU:C:2018:117.

8

'And' Instead of 'Or' – A Polymath

*I stretched the system to the point where the seams were nearly bursting in terms of, yes, doing my academic work, but I went off and tried everything. I tried student journalism. I ended up editing the student newspaper and then being collected from the offices of the newspaper at six o'clock in the morning, having had two hours sleep [...] we'd go down to the river and we'd have the early morning outing before the 9 o'clock lecture. And so it went on.**

Adam: It all started early in Eleanor's family home, where her parents, her brother Michael and she pursued various passions and interests. Yes, there were daily jobs and tasks but that did not stop members of the family from being engaged in extracurricular activities. In Eleanor's life, this is how it has stayed since. As the opening quote suggests, already at the time of her academic studies in Cambridge and Oxford, she was very skilled at stretching the system or, in other words, she excelled at filling every minute of the day with a wide variety of activities. There were various sports, including rowing and squash (both among her favourite disciplines). There was, but of course, music. It has always had a special place in Eleanor's heart. If there was no time for something, that must have been procrastination. As her life and professional career progressed, not only did she continue with what she had been doing earlier (albeit sometimes with a lesser intensity) but she did not shy away from entering new unchartered territories. On came sailing and karate, not to mention several new musical instruments she mastered along the way. Even now, whilst we have been working on this book, she has been pursuing her new musical passion – an old string instrument, the *viola da gamba*. As attested by her former *chef de cabinet*, Doyin Lawunmi in her contribution to the *Festschrift* for Eleanor, paraphernalia from those various walks of life filled her office at the Court of Justice of the European Union.[1] She also kept various musical instruments there though, to my disappointment, there was no drum kit. (Or perhaps it was well kept out of sight? One never knows.) Even during those busy fourteen and a half years on the bench in Luxembourg, Eleanor kept herself entertained with extracurriculars. We already know that she continued to play an active role on the international conference circuit and carried on publishing scholarly work in academic journals and books. At the Court itself, there was also time to participate in sport competitions, to train herself and others in karate, or to become a fire warden. Rumour has it that at the annual staff parties at the Court, Eleanor Sharpston would be the first gyrating on the dance floor – usually, in the company of the Court's interpreters. Larger than life, you ask? Yes, here is your archetype in the flesh. In various languages we can find good descriptors for such people. A 'Renaissance (wo)man' is rather common. Greeks would call such a person a polymath (η πολυμαθής). In the two Slavic languages which are close to my heart, we call them 'a human being – an orchestra' ('*człowiek orkiestra*' in Polish and '*людина-оркестр*' in Ukrainian). Aptly, we will start with music before moving on to – spoiler alert – rowing, sailing, karate, squash, skiing, and football referee qualifications.

*

Adam: We already know that, from the very early days, music has been an important part of your life and it continues to be the case now. As it happens, it has also been a part of my DNA from very early days, even though – for a host of reasons – I do not play any musical instrument. In your case, Leo, music came very early, too. Didn't it?

Eleanor: My father, naturally, saw to it that I learned to read music as soon as I learned to read text. In his eyes, I couldn't possibly read books and not read music. As I make that statement to you, I am aware of how extraordinary it sounds. But genuinely, it never occurred to him (or to me) that I wouldn't, simultaneously with my ABC, learn to read music. I remember him teaching me to read an orchestral score and to follow it. I was going to be an educated, civilised human being, so naturally I should be able to read an orchestral score. You could pick up and read a novel by Charles Dickens, so why could you not do the same with an orchestral score by Brahms? What is the difference? I suppose I never thought there was a difference either. I always found it very interesting listening to something without a score, and then getting hold of the score and starting to trace through what was happening. My father taught me the knack of focussing on one part and following it through. You would start off by saying: 'well, okay, if this is a flute concerto, what's the solo flute doing?' Then you would say: 'wait a minute, what is the interplay between the solo flute and the celli who have picked up the theme in the meantime – oh, and now the oboe is doing extra twiddles, that's interesting'. That quickly became a natural thing to do.

Adam: Earlier on we spoke a lot about listening to the music and how enriching your time in Vienna was. But listening is one thing, making music is quite another indeed.

Eleanor: There's a big difference between music I have only listened to and music I have played. When I play in an orchestra, I am on the building site, I know how it all bolts together, and it is just different. I was amusing myself by asking what would be the works I would list if I were ever to be invited onto 'Desert Island Discs'. It is a spread that goes everywhere, from Beethoven's Ninth Symphony through Shostakovich Jazz Suite No 2 to *Danzón* by Arturo Márquez. I love the latter because it has got such energy. I possibly also love it because we played it last Saturday in Luxembourg (20 January 2024), and the audience wouldn't let us go without playing it again.

Adam: Wonderful. It's quite an extraordinary piece of music. Having to play something twice, by popular demand, is the best reward for a musician. But let's travel back to Vienna for a moment. We already know that your father bought that *Ehrbar* piano. I guess that meant that music was played at home, much to your delight and to annoyance, as you said, of the concierge (and perhaps your neighbours, *sic!*).

Eleanor: In Vienna, it was natural – I mean, not natural to annoy concierges and neighbours, but natural to play music, live, at home! I know, it sounds terribly old fashioned and anachronistic, but that's how it was.

Adam: Let it be old fashioned and anachronistic, I could not give a toss! It must have been lovely.

Eleanor: Oh yes, we just called it '*Hausmusik*'. A group of friends would be together, and they happened to play musical instruments. Sooner or later someone would say: 'Hey, why don't we play something? What have we got? Aha, two violins, a cello … of course you play the piano, you play the flute, let's make good use of that.' We didn't always insist on trying to do difficult stuff. For instance, before Christmas, we would play some carols and different instruments would take different parts.

Adam: For people who like Christmas, and all the razzmatazz that comes with it, this sounds idyllic.

Eleanor: One of the most lovely moments of *Hausmusik* that I can remember was when two very dear friends of my parents came over to spend Christmas Day with us. My father's best man, Bill Garfield, who was an excellent amateur pianist, was our house guest at the time. Visiting for the day were two delightful Australians, John and Cynthia Rames. John is a lawyer, who was the head of the International Atomic Energy Agency's legal team by the time he retired. His wife Cynthia is a very fine Baroque violinist. We'd eaten and we were sitting in the music room, chatting about one thing or another. (Of course we had a music room, which the *Ehrbar* shared with my violin and classical guitar, and stacks and stacks of sheet music.) Cynthia and Bill started talking about duets – specifically, about sonatas for violin and piano. At some point Cynthia said to me 'Leo, can I borrow your violin?' 'Of course you can, Cynthia', was my eager answer. 'So [Cynthia continued], what do you have here for violin and piano? Oh, good, Beethoven's Spring Sonata: how do you feel about that, Bill?' 'Well, I've played it several times,' Bill said, 'OK, why don't we give it a go?' The next thing we knew we were sitting there, at an ordinary small house party in Vienna, with Cynthia and Bill playing the Spring Sonata. It was the most wonderful Christmas present. Sometimes you put two musicians together and it's as though they have played and rehearsed together for years. With those two, it really did click. It was gorgeous. I got up quietly and turned the pages for Cynthia or Bill, as required. It was great.

Adam: You'd not be surprised Leo that I had the Spring Sonata in the background when working on this part of the chapter. In fact, as we have already mentioned in the introduction, one of my fondest memories from our conversations is the dinner, followed by a late-night walk, in Budapest in 2022. I remember we were jumping from Beethoven to Brahms, Mozart to Mendelson, and back to Beethoven. It took me back to very memorable conversations I was honoured to have with the great violinist Shlomo Mintz, whose concert I co-organised in the late 1990s in Białystok, an eastern Polish town where his father had come from. As we were travelling there from Warsaw I asked him perhaps a silly question: 'What is music?' He came back with a profound answer which has been at the back of my head since. He said: 'It is the truth never found'.

Eleanor: Oh, that is very good. I don't think I can do better than that. Though, if I were trying to answer your question, I might say, 'music is the oxygen that the soul breathes when you give it a chance to do so'.

Adam: Equally profound. Over the years I have interpreted Shlomo's words in different ways. In fact, what he said very often comes back to me. The way I look at it now is that you can have the same score, the same music, but it will sound different depending on who plays and what kind of emotions someone is capable of sharing and wants to share. So, you never really have the true version that the composer had in mind. In this sense, it is the truth never found.

Eleanor: Well, that is true, but that is also like the saying that 'no person steps twice into the same river' because it is not the same river and she/he is not the same woman/man. I think the same is true of music. I am not a particularly good pianist but the piano is the first instrument I was taught. If I play today one of Muzio Clementi's little sonatinas that I first played when I was six, the notes are the same but I am not the same person I was back then. Actually, I can play them with pleasure (not least because I can still get my fingers around them!) and I can hear things in them, things I want to bring out in them which I didn't hear when I was six. Having said that, I am still ever so proud of the fact that I can get to the end playing the right notes.

Adam: Do you know that the piano is also the first instrument I witnessed you play?

Eleanor: Oh? When and where was that?

Adam: Again, Budapest, in our CEEMC judges' room in the building of the Hungarian Supreme Court.

Eleanor: Well, it was very civilised of the Hungarian Supreme Court to have a piano in their judges' break-out room! Actually, I had forgotten that embarrassing incident. I saw there was a piano there, we were between moots, and I felt like playing. I needed to chill out a bit.

Adam: I do not remember 'embarrassing', not by any stretch of the imagination. I remember you sitting there, with people walking in and out, as usually happens during breaks between moots. I was standing there watching you, it was magical. You just created a space for yourself and I thought: 'right, let's not disturb Leo, she clearly wants to relax a bit'.

Eleanor: Indeed, I needed a bit of space. I had just been sitting on the bench for a very long and complicated moot. I needed to clear my head before I went back into being the President of the Moot Court. And, there was a piano …

Adam: Just like at your office at the Court of Justice, correct?

Eleanor: Well, yes Adam, I used to have a digital piano in my office at the Court, imperfectly concealed behind the big bookcase. It was reasonably well hidden, but if you looked carefully, that is if you were observant, you could see there was a horizontal bit sticking out, which obviously wasn't part of the bookcase. I often played that piano before I was about to go into what I knew was likely to be a stressful meeting or hearing. And sometimes I played it in the space at the end of the day, before I walked over, or was chauffeured over, to the Luxembourg Philharmonic Hall for the evening concert. I mean: let's suppose that it is now about ten past seven and the concert starts at eight. I am obviously not going to go anywhere else: for example, I haven't got time to go home before I go to the concert. On the other hand, I don't want to go on working. So why not play the piano for a bit? And thankfully, because it was a digital piano I could play it with headphones on, so no one could hear whether I was making a pig's ear of my sight reading (as was probably the case).

Adam: So, your first instrument was the piano.

Eleanor: That was the first instrument, because it was the obvious springboard for anything else. I mean, it went with being able to read music, and it went with being able … You know, if somebody showed you a score or a voice part, you could pick it out if you couldn't picture it totally correctly already in your head. I think being able to play the piano came into the 'basic musical literacy' category. I didn't object to that, but the piano (at least when I was a child) wasn't truly my instrument of choice. I really, really wanted to be allowed to play the violin. My parents, who were otherwise rather tolerant people, demurred a bit at that. A child learning to play the violin is a bit painful for anyone nearby.

Adam: Oh yes, my maternal grandparents did years of empirical research in this respect. You need good noise isolating headphones, which – back then – had yet to be invented.

Eleanor: They weren't being made in the 1960s. So, my mother tried saying: 'maybe the cello, darling'. But at that stage I wasn't interested in the cello. This was a sort of recurrent discussion. From time to time I would say I wanted to play the violin, and my parents would try to head me off at the pass. Obviously, I played the recorder, because there was a recorder class at school, and that was fine. Then, in 1967, my father was invited to Moscow as part of the celebrations to mark the 50th anniversary of the Revolution. At that time, he was the Secretary General of the International Standards Organization, and for that reason he was part of the jamboree. He wondered about taking me out of school but he didn't feel he should do that (unfortunately!). So, he went off to Moscow with my mother, and I stayed with some friends and carried on at school. Being a good father, he felt he should bring back a present for me. He wondered about a balalaika but that seemed rather exotic, so he returned with a mandolin. I am tolerably certain that he thought that I would hang a ribbon round its neck and suspend it from a hook in my bedroom. ('What a pretty thing!'). Instead of which, naturally, I rushed out with my accumulated pocket money clutched in my hot little hand and bought myself 'Teach Yourself To Play The Mandolin'.

Adam: As a twelve year old child does!

Eleanor: As one does! I discovered that I have a reasonable affinity for stringed instruments. I was okay with wind instruments but I don't have particularly good breath control and that is essential. A stringed instrument seemed to be much more friendly to the performer. I leapt onto the mandolin and started playing it, and I even made fairly quick progress. Soon I was massacring the start of a Vivaldi mandolin concerto that I didn't have the music for (a catchy little first theme … but how exactly did it go after that?). I decided I needed to acquire the score. So I went to *Musikhaus Doblinger*, walked in and said: 'I am looking for a mandolin concerto that I heard on the radio, it starts like this'. And I sang it for them. 'Oh yes, *Fräulein Sharpston*', they said and they quickly found the score for me. This is Vienna, right? So I had the score, and I was busy trying to get my fingers around the whole concerto, all three movements. At that stage, my father said: 'gosh, you do seem to have a bit of a knack for stringed instruments'. And I said, for about the thousandth time: 'Daddy, *please* may I learn to play the violin?' and I added the absolute killer point, 'it is tuned exactly like the mandolin, so I know all the notes already'. There was a pause, as my father realised he had been checkmated.

Adam: I suppose you got it your way, at last.

Eleanor: Yes, he gave way with grace, and I started playing the violin. I mean, obviously I was starting much too late to be any particular use as a violinist professionally. In parallel with that, my mother was still trying to keep me away from my obsession with the violin. She said, rather desperately: 'How about the classical guitar, darling?' My reply was: 'Oh, *yes please*, both classical guitar *and* the violin!'

Adam: *Touché!* So, this way the guitar was added to the mix.

Eleanor: At that point, I moved away from piano, and across to the classical guitar and the violin. The idea wasn't that I would be a soloist as a violinist, no. The violin would be my orchestral instrument. During my three years at boarding school in the UK, I had a very nice guitar teacher – David Channon – who was bored stiff with teaching lots of people who were really very bad at music but wanted to play the guitar because it was cool. David rejoiced at finding that he had got someone to teach who was moderately musical and genuinely wanted to play classical guitar. So the good thing about that was we played a whole heap of stuff, we played lots of duets, and it was fabulous. The silly thing about it was that he refused to teach me from normal notation. He taught me from tablature instead.

Adam: That's strange, especially given that you could already read music very well.

Eleanor: Well, it makes a sort of bizarre sense inasmuch as guitar tablature uses six lines to represent the six strings. You write a zero for an open string, the numeral one for the first fret, two for the second fret, and so on. You can see very clearly and intuitively the pattern of where something is to be played on the fingerboard. That is very useful, because many notes on the guitar can be played in three different positions. The trouble is, using guitar tablature produces a total disconnect between where you are placing your finger and the realisation that you are playing (say) G sharp. There's literally no link. There's an additional issue because, since you've used numbers to indicate where you are on the fingerboard, you can't use numbers to indicate which finger you should be playing that particular note with (whereas, if you use classical musical notation, numbers are available to be used to indicate the fingering). Guitar tablature is an adaptation of lute tablature, which also had six lines to represent the six strings, but then used A to denote an open string, B for the first fret, and so on. I don't know how good you are at assigning 'numbers minus one' to the letters in the alphabet. I have to think about it, but after a while it becomes more automatic – you know that E (the fifth letter) means the *fourth* fret, and then there's no problem. When I went to the *Konservatorium der Stadt Wien* to study classical guitar ('*Sie spielen gern, aber bitte nicht gut*') (non-literal translation: 'OK, you're musical but, dear God, your technique!'), this was one of the many things that

I had to sort out. Then they tried to remake my entire technique, which was not a particular success. Much worse than that, though, was the fact that I started going deaf.

Adam: That's horrible in all circumstances, but particularly when someone is as young as you were and wishes to pursue a career in music.

Eleanor: At the time I was – yes, pretty upset. But I would like to make clear that I am not putting out the begging bowl for sympathy. I think you have to be both remarkably good and very lucky to make a career as a solo classical musician. I am not at all sure that, on the evidence, I was going to be that good and you can never guarantee being that lucky. Having the additional problem of a hearing handicap made it fairly obvious that I wasn't going to go down that path. There are, of course, the Evelyn Glennie's of this world. I honour and respect them. I admire them deeply. But if you are a percussionist, you are not trying to play an instrument which has a pitch which you are meant to control. The trouble with something like the violin is that it is nearly impossible to guarantee that every finger will land in precisely the right place, always, every single time. But the point is that – of course – a good professional hears what is wrong before anyone else does and they correct it. I couldn't guarantee that on the violin with the higher frequency notes. The viola was a good fall-back choice because it is tuned in fifths, starting a fifth down from the violin, so three of the four strings have the same notes as a violin (and you 'just' have to add the bottom string, which is tuned to a C). What's more, save with more modern composers, you are usually not required to play very high on the top string (the A string). In reality, therefore, you are normally playing a part which is pitched about an octave down from what you might expect to be playing as a violinist. That makes it much, much easier for me to hear what I am up to.

Adam: So that is how the viola became your orchestral instrument. In both the *Luxembourg Philharmonia* and the *Orchestre de la Place de l'Europe* you play in the viola section.

Eleanor: Yes, I'm normally a viola player these days. Sometimes I have played second or third violin in a small chamber group – usually, that would be a lower part. But you know how it is: both viola players and tenors should be protected species. There aren't enough of us around to satisfy demand! If you can sing tenor (as I also do) and if you play the viola, you can sometimes cheekily get in through a door which wouldn't be open to you if you were a soprano or an alto, or if you were a violinist.

Adam: Have you experienced that first hand?

Eleanor: I think I probably did when I auditioned for the newer second orchestra that I play in – the *Orchestre de la Place de l'Europe*. I did a virtual audition online, which was stressful in itself (we were still in the fall-out zone from

Covid-19) and according to me I played pretty badly, but to my surprise I got in. Obviously, since then I have been trying to improve my viola playing (and actually the overall musical standard is probably rather higher than in my beloved *Luxembourg Philharmonia*). I don't think I would have got in as a violinist, but as a viola player …

Adam: I listened to the live recording which you sent the other day and it is a really good orchestra. Funny enough, the concert started with Beethoven's Coriolan Overture, which is one of my favourites. As things stand now, it is no 2 on my charts, right after Egmont (also a Beethoven overture). As I was looking at the orchestra I could see very well how you were in your element, clearly enjoying making the music.

Eleanor: We are very lucky in that orchestra. Our conductor is Benjamin Schäfer – the timpanist from the professional 'OPL' (*Orchestre philharmonique du Luxembourg*). He is fabulously good on his own instrument but he is also a very good conductor. He is excellent at striking the right balance. Conducting an amateur orchestra requires tact: it is a delicate business. We take ourselves seriously as musicians, but actually we are amateurs – we have all got day jobs somewhere else. So, you can and should be exigent in terms of what you want out of the orchestra, but you have to be reasonably nice to your musicians as well. If you scream at them and demotivate them, they are going to walk. If you are ever in Luxembourg on a Monday evening, you are welcome to attend a rehearsal and then you will see why I am so fond of playing under him. You can't help being carried along with this kind of infectious enthusiasm for making it sound better.

> **Benjamin:** *Friends, I think here, four before 'H', we need it to be a bit more crisp, really detached. Do you agree?*
>
> *Let's try it like that. Yes – that's better. Again – and please, even more!*
>
> *Now here, at 'J': horns! I need more horns.*
>
> *Do you like this passage? It is a wonderful moment, yes? But the violins will eat you alive if you play it like that. Everyone who has come to the concert – they are waiting to hear YOU at this moment. Come on horns!*

By the time Benjamin started conducting he was already a professional timpanist. He has played under many conductors, and now, standing on the conductor's stand, he knows what it looks like from the back. He was probably the youngest professional to join the OPL, almost a *wunderkind*. Since he is such a nice guy to play for, you want to do your best for Benjamin. He inspires that feeling. (Thus, ES to self: 'Leo, get that viola out and practise those sixteen bars in the wretched second movement that you never quite get your damn fingers around. Maybe if you were to play it in second position rather than third and first position, would that be any better? Or second and fourth? Let's try it. Maybe that would run more smoothly? You've got to get it straight.')

Adam: One of my favourite instruments, the one I actually tried to learn how to play (and miserably failed) is the cello. *Jacqueline du Pré*, who is one of my favourite cellists ever …

Eleanor: … Oh, please, the same …

Adam: She said 'the cello is my voice, my medium for expressing my deepest emotions'.[2] It makes me wonder which of the instruments that you play you would pick if you were to express your emotions?

Eleanor: Funnily enough, I think right now it might be the *viola da gamba*. I am not yet technically good enough to be able to play it effortlessly, with a degree of assurance that what I am trying to generate is what is going to come out. In some respects, perhaps my 'go-to' instrument is still the guitar. I have played the guitar in so many guises. If you have a guitar at boarding school, the price of being allowed to practise scales is that you play folk tunes for your dorm. You play chords and you play accompaniment to whatever they want. I haven't done that for years, and then on Monday, two days ago, I was at a retirement party for a friend of mine. It was a party in their house, and they started playing music and singing Irish songs. My friend said to me: 'Hang on, you play the guitar, don't you?' I said: 'Yes'. The next thing I knew, I was part of the band. I hadn't done that for at least 20 years, but actually it was kind of fun, doing it again. The guitar has that degree of familiarity to it for me. And for chamber music it's definitely the viola – despite all the bad jokes (mainly from violinists), it's a noble instrument. There's some beautiful duets for violin and viola: Mozart, Stamitz, Pleyel … And Mozart, though of course a fine violinist, often played the viola in string quartets. Being 'in the middle' gives such a nice perspective. And the Sinfonia concertante in E flat for violin and viola (K. 364) has a remarkable partnership and equality between the two soloists.

I am giving you a kind of chameleon answer because, truth be told, the answer is probably 'any instrument that happens to be in my hands at this given moment'. The choice would also be conditioned by the context and what I am trying to do. If we're talking about orchestral playing, then I need to have a viola in my hands, because that is how I am going to fit in and be useful as part of an orchestra. Playing in a quartet, I used to play second violin but nowadays it would probably be the viola. I have also started to play the bass *viola da gamba* from time to time in a *viol consort* with friends, and it is a fun place to be. The *viola da gamba* is a bit like the cello, except that it has gut strings, not metal strings. At places, you can get the expressiveness of the human voice out of the bass *viola da gamba*. And I was 'borrowed' recently by another amateur Luxembourg group, 'Pirate Productions', because they were staging 'The Sound of Music' and needed a mandolin soloist. I found myself swapping back and forth between mandolin and viola, providing reinforcement for the viola section of the band in between the four mandolin solo numbers.

Adam: Do you think you can express as much with an instrument as you can with the human voice?

Eleanor: If I were a better singer, the answer probably would be a 'no'. But I am not sure. Singing is a combination of things. Almost by definition, there are (usually) words which are an integral part of the message. Although some of my attention, perhaps even most of my attention, is probably on the beautiful musical sequences, part of my attention inevitably switches across to following the text – assuming I can truly hear the text, because not all words are capable of being sung very clearly by all voices. (Notoriously, a female soprano voice loses the clear differences between the various vowels as it goes up into the higher registers, whereas a man's voice will tend to keep those differences between the vowels, making it correspondingly easier to detect what the word is that's being sung.) When I am listening to singing, I am listening to both the music and the words. Whereas when I am listening to a musical instrument, I am listening to the music and only the music. Probably, I come down in favour of the instrumental.

Adam: Sometimes the lyrics and the music cannot be separated from one another. From the top of my head I have two examples, one of which borders on classical music and rock, and the other that can be classified as prog rock.

Eleanor: Your musical choices, Adam, are quite eclectic.

Adam: Absolutely so, but this reflects the environment I was raised and lived in, it is a mix of different genres of music. To the mix created by my parents and grandparents, my wife Anna added other genres of music: jazz and world music, to mention a few.

Eleanor: So, give me the first example.

Adam: The first example I have for you is a unique collaboration between Freddie Mercury of *Queen* and an opera diva, Montserrat Caballé. This extraordinary duet released an album called *Barcelona*. The story started with a vocalise that Freddie recorded and gave to Montserrat Caballé after her concert in Covent Garden. It was called *Exercises in Free Love*. Fast forward, they recorded an entire album, but to make sure that the entire project was financially viable there was no orchestra, just synthesisers. During the recording sessions Freddie was diagnosed with HIV/AIDS, which – back then – was a slow but inevitable death sentence. He sang in the studio knowing that he was dying. Many years after Freddie passed away, the remaining members of *Queen* arranged for proper orchestration and this divine music was finally given justice. I remember listening to it in its new reincarnation on the plane to Vienna and tears were running down my cheeks. The symbiosis of those two beautiful voices and the orchestra are a match made in heaven. This is particularly the case in a song titled *How Can I Go On*. By the way, *Exercises in Free Love* made it to this version of the album, and I have no clue which one of the two is singing (or perhaps both?).

Eleanor: And what is the second example that you have for me, Adam?

Adam: The second example is all about the guitar. It is a stellar exemplar how much you can express with the guitar, be it an electric or acoustic. What I am talking about is a song by David Gilmour (ex *Pink Floyd*) and his live performance in Pompeii. You will find there a song titled *Faces of Stone*. The studio recording is okay, but the live version takes it to completely new levels. Listening to it for the first time, I could not resist the temptation to switch on the 'deconstruction' mode. First comes the piano and I immediately thought of Zbigniew Preisner, a Polish composer famous for, among others, writing soundtracks to movies of the late Oscar nominee Krzysztof Kieślowski. I was right. Then came the lyrics. You can easily figure out that David Gilmour is singing about someone that was close to him, but the relationship must have been strained. Then comes his guitar and hell breaks loose. At the beginning, it is very mellow, then he is screaming with anger and, in turn, crying with that guitar. You have all ranges of emotions going up and down until the song ends. When I got to the end, my curiosity prevailed. I wanted to be that fly on the wall. I really wanted to know what this was all about, and if my ear for the music was taking me in the right direction. What I discovered was that this was a song about his late mother, who died of dementia. That explained the melancholy, the anger, the tears. The song is magical; to express so many emotions on a guitar in literally six minutes is beyond my comprehension. So here is a piece of homework for you, Leo. Please listen to both songs and tell me what you think.

Eleanor: (later) Well, Adam – those two songs were a revelation for me. To begin with Gilmour: a beautifully simple classical piano opening, an exposition with imaginative use of instrumentation to add colour as the song develops; and then truly virtuoso solo guitar to drive home the edgy lyrics. The Freddie Mercury / Monserrat Caballé collaboration is really amazing: as you say, initially there are places where it's not immediately obvious which of the two is singing which part; and then the wonderful coloratura soprano of Monserrat Caballé weaves over and around Freddie Mercury's voice carrying the narrative.

Adam: As we continue talking about music, I should like to return to the theme from the first chapter where we spoke about the role that particular compositions have played in our lives. I am currently reading a very interesting book called *Beethoven in the Bunker*. It is about how music was used for good and bad reasons during the Second World War. I found a very poignant sentence, which is so very true: 'During periods of conflict, church attendance grows, and music often assumes a healing, comforting, or uplifting role'. You may remember that in the summer of 2024, I was lucky enough to attend a performance at St Paul's Cathedral by the *Ukrainian Freedom Orchestra* of Beethoven's Ninth Symphony. Around that time the conductor – Keri-Lynn Wilson – wrote an article for *The Guardian*. She said something that really struck me about the

Russian invasion of Ukraine: 'While I could not take up arms, I could take up my baton as my weapon instead'.[3] I got hold of a copy of the official programme for the Polish part of the tour and there was one more comment that made my eyes sweat. 'They have come here to defeat the occupying forces with sensitivity. With the power of their talent and the might of their souls. They have come to prove, yet again, that beauty, goodness, music, and poetry are our power, not our weakness'.[4]

Eleanor: There are occasions – some very special occasions – where the significance of the event gives the music an extra set of wings. One of my absolute favourite recordings is of combined orchestras from all over Europe under Leonard Bernstein at their Christmas 1989 concert, celebrating the fall of the Berlin Wall – yes, of course – by playing Beethoven's Ninth. You also mentioned it earlier in the book. As you said, Bernstein deliberately tweaked the words of Schiller's Ode to Joy, in the fourth (choral) movement, from 'Freude' (Joy) to 'Freiheit' (Freedom). Or think of the young Yehudi Menuhin's wonderful interpretation of the Brahms Violin Concerto with the BBC Symphony Orchestra under Adrian Boult – a recording for the BBC Home Service modestly made in 'Studio 1, Maida Vale, on 5 April 1943'. Menuhin was touring and giving concerts to help the war effort. I fell across it joyfully when the BBC Music Magazine reissued it as an archive recording in 1997.

Adam: It shows that music can be used for a lot of good causes, for instance, to express solidarity. I treasure the little poster of the 2022 tour of the *Luxembourg Philharmonia* you gave me as a gift. You played, among others, *Melodia* by Myroslav Skoryk. It is a part of the Ukrainian DNA, an unwritten anthem. What did the orchestra feel about it, performing it, and especially under the circumstances?

Eleanor: We firmly intended to play it everywhere, it was an integral part of our performance, because it expressed our solidarity with Ukraine. But there was one venue that refused to let us play it. They said they felt it was a rather political statement. We were truly angry – some of us even said we should refuse to play the concert. We were absolutely behind making that statement. It is a lovely tune, Adam. Wherever we played it, the audiences reacted very well. They applauded, sometimes they stood up and applauded.

Adam: How did you personally feel about playing that particular tune? Prior to that, had you experienced playing something similar, playing an orchestral piece as a sign of solidarity?

Eleanor: No, it is not something that I have done before. We don't often have events as dramatic as that. When the Berlin Wall came down in Germany and when the Velvet Revolution happened in Czechoslovakia, I was passive: I was looking at what other people were doing, listening to what they were playing. Leonard Bernstein gave that performance we have already mentioned, a wonderful performance because of the electricity behind it. So I have listened to such events, but I haven't played in them. Playing Skoryk's *Melodia* was my opportunity to be active as a musician, to play something very important at such a moment of history.

Adam: At this juncture, there is one thing that I find very interesting. When we talked about you being at the Court, considering whether to try to move across to being a judge, and then shredding the first draft of your 'motivation letter' (which had said, basically, that you were totally happy being the Advocate General!), we get the picture of 'Eleanor Sharpston the soloist'. Of course, you worked with your team; but, at the end of the day, you were the one who was signing the Opinions. You fretted about being a part of the collegiate Court, with its single judgments adopted by consensus. But then, as a musician, you seem to be happy as a part of the collective: an orchestra or a smaller ensemble.

Eleanor: I think that's because it's about teamwork, balance, and creating something together. But it depends on the instrument. The piano, I play solo, I don't tend to play it with other people. The classical guitar, I also tend to play solo, though I have played guitar duets and obviously I have used the guitar to accompany songs. But there is relatively little solo music for the viola. When you think about the repertoire, it is big on violin, not for the viola. The violin literature is so vast. You have beautiful unaccompanied Bach, you have all that wonderful material for violin and piano, the quartets, the compositions for violin and orchestra. Whereas as a viola player – apart from the chamber music and the orchestral music, what really do you have? Well, you can play (for example) the Bach suites for solo cello, transposed for viola. Actually, they work rather well, because the viola is tuned an octave above the cello, and both instruments are tuned in fifths, so the pieces 'fall under the fingers' in exactly the same way on the viola as they do on the original instrument.

Adam: Absolutely, all the classic violin concertos spring to my mind: Mozart, Beethoven, Sibelius, Mendelson, Brahms. Though, there is Mozart's *Sinfonia Concertante*, written for violin, viola, and orchestra – which you've already mentioned. But I reckon that your latest passion is the *viola da gamba*.

Eleanor: I am indeed very attracted to the *viola da gamba*. That is precisely because there is a lovely solo repertoire, and also lots of material for two *violas da gamba*, and for viol consorts. There's so much to explore. I have an excellent and enthusiastic *viola da gamba* teacher at the *Conservatoire du Nord* in Ettelbruck, Stéphanie Houillon. Although I am really still only a (false) beginner, we already play duets, as well as my working on solo pieces. Playing together – paradoxically – is in some ways easier for me as somebody with a hearing impairment than playing solo, because automatically I tune to and fit in with the other instrument(s).

Adam: Was there any time in your life when music, at least making it, just stopped?

Eleanor: Yes. The only time in my life that I have not been able to play music was during the three years after my husband David died and before my father Charles died. During those three miserable years I could not manage – I literally could not manage – to play music. I would sit down to try to play. But David's death had been so brutally sudden, so unexpected, and so cataclysmic in its impact, that I could not find the emotional energy, strength, and light within myself to play music. I could not do it. And I felt utterly, utterly bereft. Weirdly, after my father died, I started gradually to be able to play again. I cannot tell you why my father's death should have operated to make that possible, to remove the gag from my musician's soul, except perhaps that my way of lamenting and marking *his* passing could only be through making music. I have never really worked this one out. But I was and am profoundly grateful that I was given my music back.

Adam: Since then you have regularly played in the *Orchestre de la Place de l'Europe* and in the *Luxembourg Philharmonia*. You have also toured, which is always a nice experience, a bit of an extra adrenaline kick but, as my experience tells me, it can be loads of fun, too. I've had my share in my younger years and I have to say that touring a symphonic or even a chamber orchestra is always a great source of shaggy dog stories (missing instruments, lost passports, musicians on wrong coaches and trains, and things like that). Do you have any to share from your life with the orchestras?

Eleanor: Well, the question is not if I have them but which one to choose! Let's try this one but under one condition: I give you one, and you give me one in return.

Adam: Deal! Off we go.

Eleanor: It was Beethoven's anniversary year and the *Luxembourg Philharmonia* had gone on a tour in northern Italy. We pride ourselves on being an international touring orchestra. By the way, the *Orchestre de la Place de l'Europe* is now also in on that act. The *OPE* is going to join another amateur orchestra in Berlin in June 2025 for a big joint concert and part of the programme is Shostakovich's Fifth Symphony. The dates are ring-fenced, written in red in my diary. I need to do some serious work to get on top of the viola part properly, but I am very excited!

Anyway, here we were in Italy – the *Lux Phil* on tour – and our final concert was to be in *Massa Marittima*. The programme was, obviously, all Beethoven: we opened with the Emperor Piano Concerto (No 5 in E flat major, Op 73), and were to follow with the Seventh Symphony. This was an outdoor concert that we were playing in *Piazza Garibaldi*, otherwise known as *Piazza del Duomo*. We were perched in the elevated triangular space between the *Duomo* and the bishop's palace. It's a wonderful, natural theatrical stage set. As you know, outdoor concerts are always a bit of a lottery. But of course it is going to be fine, because we all know that it never rains in Italy in the summer. That's an article of faith. We were playing with a very nice, very good Italian pianist, Pietro Bonfilio, who is a local son. We had already played three concerts with Pietro and he had been doing an excellent job with the Emperor Concerto. The *Piazza del Duomo* was packed. We started the Emperor Concerto. Shortly before we reached the cadenza towards the end of the first movement, our pianist, who was – as is usual – playing from memory, suddenly had a complete blank as to where he had got to in the piece. (This could happen to anyone – we all just pray that it never happens to us!) Pietro kept his head admirably. He kept himself busy miming stuff, he did little twiddles here and there. If you didn't know the Emperor Concerto really well, you wouldn't probably have guessed that he had gone off script. (He was not playing Gershwin jazz in the middle of the Emperor, right?). But what he was playing was definitely not the Emperor Concerto as set down by Beethoven. Of course, our conductor Martin Elmquist – an experienced professional – kept on conducting and the orchestra carried on playing. Inside, we were all praying hard: please, Pietro, please get back inside your head somehow and work out where you are in the script. The problem was that the cadenza was coming up in about thirty two bars' time. At that point, the orchestra would fall silent and Pietro would be on his own. The cadenza is the moment when the soloist shows his brilliance; and it was approaching like fate. We were twenty four bars out from the 'fermata' where the orchestra would hold the final long note before the cadenza and then, collectively, shut up and listen to the soloist … now we were twenty bars out … sixteen bars out … twelve bars out … eight bars out …

Adam: My palms are starting to sweat, it feels like you were heading for a total car crash.

Eleanor: Miraculously, Pietro snapped back in with about four bars to go. Suddenly, he was again playing what we all knew to be the right notes leading up to the cadenza. There was a collective gasp of relief from the orchestra. We shut up and (at least in my case) went on praying. Pietro gave us a beautiful cadenza, and we came in triumphantly to finish the first movement. The slow movement followed ('Thank God, all is well …') and we went straight into the third (and final) movement. Part way through, we began to wonder whether something was now wrong with the timpani (the kettledrums). Could our timpanist – normally so reliable – have gone off the rails and be playing in the wrong places? There was definitely no entry for the timpani there, and yet we could hear long, loud, menacing drum rolls. What was going on had nothing to do with the timpanist and our set of kettledrums. The sky swiftly turned black and the summer storm raced in. Our conductor Martin could see it. The first violins and the cellos could see it. I could see nothing, because sitting in the viola section I had my back to the storm arriving from behind the bell tower. The woodwinds and the brass section, like me, couldn't see what was happening – but we could all hear and feel it, and see our violinist and cellist colleagues shooting anxious glances over our heads. Martin picked up the tempo and our nice *Konzertmeister* Sally Cooper swept the string sections with an urgent look: come on, follow! Move it, together! Then Martin picked it up some more, and the speed dial went to *accelerando … presto … prestissimo*. We had to get to the end of the piano concerto before it started to rain. We finished the last chord and the heavens opened. Two people managed to grab the protective cover and drag it over the top of the piano. Everyone who had a string instrument cuddled it in their arms and fled for the nearest shelter, because string instruments do not like getting wet.

Adam: But you had the *Duomo* right behind you, couldn't you just go inside?

Eleanor: We could have, except that the *Duomo* was locked shut, We had no back-up plan. We had never thought through, still less negotiated, using the *Duomo* for the concert if it should happen to rain. So, unfortunately, the final concert of our tour stopped dead after the first half of the programme. We never made it to the second half to play the Seventh Symphony. That was a damn shame as we had spent the morning rehearsal tidying up a few little rough edges from the previous performance, and we were about to give the performance of our lives: *the definitive performance of Beethoven's Seventh*. But, given the amount of high drama that we had already survived in the first half of the programme, perhaps it was just as well. That is my most immediate response to your question 'Do you have a shaggy dog story from touring?' Your turn, Adam.

Adam: I need to travel back in time. We were in the late 1990s and I was managing a summer tour of the *Kammerorchester Hannover* which was conducted from the first violin by my Mum's brother, Adam. One of the stops was a town near Marseille. It was the middle of summer so, of course, it was blistering hot but also quite windy. It was an outdoor concert, one that we were desperate to play as it was keeping the budget of the entire tour together. Just as in your case, Leo, there was no plan B, no alternative venue was envisaged by the local promoter. The concert was scheduled for very late in the evening. That had nothing to do with the habits of the locals but rather with the daily cycle of very loud crickets which go to sleep when the sky turns dark. To my horror, as I was arranging the stage, making sure that the correct music scores were on the correct stands, I realised that the wind was picking up and, to make it worse, that ash was falling down from the skies. A local forest on a nearby mountain was on fire and the wind was blowing the ash our way. I was prepared and dressed for the occasion. I am not sure how it is these days, but back then a standard way of attaching music sheets to the music stands for an outdoor concert was by using laundry clips that one would otherwise use for hanging wet clothes in the garden. That, of course, does the trick when the winds are mild; but the stronger they are, the more likely you are going to have kites flying around. Quite desperate, but adamant that we needed to play the concert, we all got on stage. So, there we were. The orchestra sat after the opening applause and we – two Adams – were standing at the very front of the stage to explain to the audience, in several languages, that if our music stands were to turn into kites, we would have to stop. I would then run around to put all back into position, and then the orchestra would start playing again. As I was standing there explaining the rules of the game in English, I could see that the audience (and it was a sold-out concert) was not paying attention to what I had to say but rather they were staring at my jacket and, with limited success, fighting back the howls of laughter. At this point Adam looked at me and whispered: 'You silly man, everyone is laughing at your laundry clips'. There I was in my jacket, both lapels looking like rainbows made of laundry clips. Now it was Adam's turn to address the audience in German. The same thing, everyone was staring at him and, out of respect, trying not to giggle (with limited success, I have to admit). For me, it was payback time. I turned to Adam and whispered: 'You silly man, everyone is laughing at you. You may be wearing a nice penguin suit but look down, you forgot to put proper shoes on, you are still wearing your espadrilles'.

Eleanor: Delicious.

Adam: That's all not all, Leo. That was just the beginning. After the clothing debacle we settled down, with me at the very back of the stage to help the double bass player to turn the pages. Even before we started, I noticed that musicians were making strange and rapid moves with their legs and feet. Not only did we have ash falling on the stage, we also had king size cockroaches running around. I don't remember the full programme but we definitely started with Vivaldi's Four Seasons. What I did know at that stage was that the double bass player was a joker. I did not expect, though, what would happen next. Picture this. The double bass player is a really big guy (let's put it this way, there was no way he could hide behind his double bass) and he was playing standing. We were going through the first movement (Spring) and after one of those sections where the solo violin plays there is a nanosecond tacet. He twirled his double bass round as one would do on the stage in the Cotton Club in New York or at Ronny Scott's in London, and shouted from the top of his lungs 'Hurray!' And then the orchestra came. At this point my acting training proved beneficial. Miraculously, I managed to stop myself from laughing like there was no tomorrow.

Eleanor: Did you actually manage to perform and finish?

Adam: Yes, we made it through to the end, though the concert was way longer than anyone could have anticipated. It took ages as those portable light music stands were flying all over the place and I was running around like a headless chicken putting everything back in place again. We even received a standing ovation. With the benefit of hindsight, I am inclined to think that was not for the quality of performance but for perseverance.

Eleanor: Perhaps it was for both?

Adam: One should hope so! Classical music is not the only form of art that you are passionate about, Leo. Earlier in the book we have already spoken briefly about the amateur theatre summer school. But, knowing you, there is much more than meets the eye. Your parents did amateur theatre, too, so I guess this is where the inspiration has come from.

Eleanor: My mother both acted and wrote one act plays, tailored to the available casts. When we were in Brazil and she found out more about the (rather complicated) relations between Portugal and its big former colony, she wrote an excellent play called *The Emigrant* which was for my father, my brother Michael, and herself. I was a bit too young to 'tread the boards' at that stage. A little later, when we were in Vienna, she wrote another one-acter – I think, even better – called *The Homecoming*. This offered a slightly different 'take' from Homer on Odysseus's return to Ithaca. This time the play was written for my father, my mother and myself, and there were gorgeous acting parts for all three of us. *The Homecoming* had Odysseus returning to find that Penelope – who was, indeed, having trouble with the suitors – had engaged a young graduate in business management called *Polysofia* to help her with an *Ithaca Urban Development Plan*. It was lovely. We gave several performances of that to appreciative friends. She also wrote an extremely fine post-Nativity play called *The Flight to Egypt*. I have got the script and I'd love to get that put on: partly in her memory, but also because it is a really good play which deserves to be aired.

Adam: This sounds very creative and absolutely delicious. As you said in the First 100 Years Biography interview, you 'came from a family background which was unashamedly card-carrying intellectual'.[5] This is yet another evidence (if one were needed) of that. So, theatre, just like music, was an inherent part of your upbringing. Any interesting roles you have played since?

Eleanor: Well, I have done bits of this and that in different places. I was once painted green all over to be 'Craig, the leader of the moon dwellers' in a rubbish playlet at my school in Brazil. I am not quite sure how I got myself into that one, but I remember it took ages to get the green makeup on and even longer to get it off again. Then I played *Kvashnya* – a vendor of meat-pies – in Gorky's *The Lower Depths*: a King's–Newnham production whilst I was at Cambridge. I was also one of those useful extras who rushes around doing everything in sight in an under-resourced production of *Henry V* by the same company. Someone not on nodding terms with intelligence (or common sense) had the idea of trying to stage the (many) fight scenes under strobe lighting. That was seriously stupid. You cannot judge distances with a strobe, because you are temporarily blinded. For amateur theatre fights, that's a recipe for disaster. A number of people got hurt, including me. As you have mentioned, much more recently, I have been indulging in the Luxembourg European Amateur Theatre Summer School ('LEATSS' to its friends). I got into that because my lovely *chef de cabinet*, Doyin Lawunmi, had participated in LEATSS in the previous year and said to me: 'Leo, you may like it'. So I went along and obviously I got hooked. I have been doing that probably for eight or nine years now. There was, of course, a hiatus during the pandemic, but we did some stuff online. LEATSS is a very firm fixture in my diary. Every year I spend a lovely week *not* being '(former) Advocate General Sharpston', but stepping into completely different characters, doing mime and impro … One year we had the chance to do *commedia dell'arte* – of course with proper masks – with a splendid tutor, Mitch Mitchelson, and that was fabulously good fun. I suppose you could say that some of what I do at LEATSS cross-fertilizes, inasmuch as I perform when I teach and give speeches. What I work on every year at LEATSS helps my sense of timing and improves my ability to have a stage presence. None of that actually hurts me professionally. But that is not why I do it!

Adam: Our touring and theatre shaggy dog stories have quite a few things in common, including real or figurative stormy weathers and how we battled them. I reckon that you had a fair share of those as you have been pursuing your other great passion – sailing. How did that come into the picture?

Eleanor: I have had a fascination with boats and ships and the sea from the early days. I have spent an awful lot of my time sailing square riggers. Actually, I guess this is a big part of who I am and how I function. Having said that, I should make it clear that I have a rather peculiar relationship with water: I like to have something between myself and that element. Sailing, rowing, kayaking are all fine, and so is being underneath the water. But swimming? Forget it. I *can* swim, but I am extremely bad at it.

Adam: This I can (partly) associate myself with. My preference is to be on the water, but in (or under) the water – well … my swimming style is very idiosyncratic, it has been referred to by a really elderly lady in my local swimming pool as a 'wounded turtle style'. I guess it says it all.

Eleanor: That's a good one, Adam. In my case the passion for sailing started really early. As a child, I read everything. I read *Swallows and Amazons* (and everything else) by Arthur Ransome,[6] and I read C.S. Forrester: all the *Hornblower* novels set in the Royal Navy during the Napoleonic Wars.[7] Decades later, of course, I devoured every book that appeared in Patrick O'Brian's *roman fleuve* of Jack Aubrey and Stephen Maturin.[8] I started sailing because – unbelievable though it sounds – I won a small and very impractical sailing dinghy (an 'Avi Onda') in my school raffle just before we left Brazil. (The school chaplain had been told by his religious superiors that it was not seemly for Father to disport himself on this flimsy craft in swimming trunks, so he raffled it for charity – I bought four tickets and one of them was the lucky number.) And I yearned to sail on big 'tall ships'. But, at the same time, I am not naturally that sociable. I had spent three years at a boarding school and that had been a disaster. So, there was a bit of me that passionately wanted to go sailing on square riggers.

But, at the same time, there was another bit of me that said: 'Yeah, but you know, it is a closed environment. You can't get off easily. Once you are on, you are on. This could also be absolutely horrible, just like boarding school was horrible'.

Adam: But somehow you must have persuaded yourself that it was a good and plausible idea, after all. When and how did that start?

Eleanor: I had developed the habit of going along to the London Boat Show. Among the many stands there was always a stand from the Sail Training Association ('STA'). I am not sure what their successors, the Tall Ships Youth Trust, do now; but in those early days the STA were very innovative. They had a video recorder with a video cassette playing of their two schooners at sea: the *Winston Churchill* and the *Malcolm Miller*. You would drool watching it. They were beautiful sailing vessels and they were cracking along 'with a bone in their teeth' as one says. The white foam was flying back from the bows as they cut through the waves: they were heeling over in the stiff breeze; and you could hear the creak of the rigging. I used to stand there and watch that video cassette go round and round and round. I would then, of course, go and get the brochure and the application form before, reluctantly, I wandered away. Then, at some point, I would get cold feet. I would start wondering about how it would work out. Somehow, I wouldn't put in that application form after all. I did this year after year. From the moment that I left university until I was slightly older than the top limit for the youth voyages, it was the same scenario every year: the London Boat Show – watch the video – get the paperwork – get cold feet. Rinse and repeat.

Adam: What made you change your mind and throw your hat in the ring, Leo?

Eleanor: I think it happened in the seventh year of my merry-go-round, which sounds very biblical. I did exactly the same routine, except that at some point – having collected the paperwork – I bumped into an old rowing mate of mine: Jenny Mitchell. Jenny and I had rowed together in a coxless pair at national championships. If you row in a pair with somebody, believe me, you know them well. A pair is a very small boat. There's one of you rowing on either side – bow and stroke. You literally rely on each other (if one of you does something stupid, the boat may well capsize) and you know each other inside out. Jenny and I fell into each other's arms and then, of course, we repaired to a nearby bar so that we could have a pint (or maybe two pints) and we could talk about stuff. Somewhere along the line (whether it was the first or second pint, I do not remember) she asked me what stands I had been visiting at the boat show. I told her that I had been looking at the Sailing Training Association stuff. I pulled out all the paperwork and put it on the table. We looked at it together and then there were probably other things – other brochures – that I also put on the table. At some point I got up to get the next round of drinks. In due course I collected my belongings and put them back in my bag. When I got home, I couldn't find the paperwork about the Sailing Training Association. I thought I must have left it behind and, anyway, it made no difference as I never put in my application form anyway. Three days later, back came a letter from the STA offering me a berth on the last voyage of the year. My good friend Jenny had quietly purloined the paperwork, filled in the application form, forged my signature and posted it. She knew me very well. She knew that, left to my own devices, I might again do nothing; but that if I were actually offered a berth, I would of course go. So, she decided to solve the problem in a very direct way. Actually, I owe her big time.

Adam: This is what friends are for, huh? I guess you took the offer and joined the last voyage of the season.

Eleanor: I did go on that last voyage and it was extraordinary. It was the end of November. It was very cold, and there was a lot of wind. I even managed to be seasick, which had never happened to me before. But the conditions were such that everyone was seasick. Despite which, by the end of the voyage I was totally hooked. When we finished the voyage at Shoreham-on-Sea, the schooner was booked to go into the drydock there immediately to get some repair work done. I stayed on for an extra couple of days working on board, because I was absolutely immersed in what was happening. I booked immediately to go back as a trainee again the following year. By the time I had done three voyages as a trainee, I got a letter from the STA asking if I would like to sail as a watch leader. I phoned them up and we had a friendly conversation along roughly the following lines:

> **Leo:** *Are you guys nuts? I don't know that much, I have only done three voyages with you.*
>
> **STA:** *Yes but you have had a strong recommendation from the watch officers and watch leaders on all three voyages. If you don't mind stepping up, we will tell you what you need to know to do the job. And we will shout at you if you are about to kill somebody so that that doesn't happen.*
>
> **Leo:** *Oh* [pause]. *Well, all right then!*

So I started sailing with them as a watch leader and the story goes on from there. All of that has made an enormous difference to who I am and how I function. It really has. My transatlantic voyage as watchleader on board *Stavros Niarchos*, the epic 75th anniversary voyage on *Stadsraad Lehmkuhl* from Bergen up to Svalbard (Spitsbergen) and back; working flat out as crew on board *Christian Radich* when she won Class A in the Tall Ship Races in the North Sea and the Baltic (not once, but on several occasions!) – all these are unforgettable and deeply important. I have learned so much sailing tall ships, and I don't mean just the interesting technical side of how you sail a square rigger. Some of the rougher corners have been knocked off me over the course of those voyages as working crew.

Adam: I have to admit, Leo, that I have never been on a square rigger, let alone sailed. So, do forgive me if my next questions show profound ignorance. I guess, though, that the fact that you took that opportunity and have sailed since has cemented your leadership skills. And you do have such skills, no question about it.

Eleanor: Funny you mention that, Adam. During my interview for the job of Advocate General I was asked whether I had any experience of team management. I simply said: 'Well, I have sailed as a watch leader on square riggers on multiple occasions, and I am one of a rather small group of people – perhaps about twenty of us at the moment – who hold a 'RYA watch leader – square rig' 'ticket'.' I added an illustration:

> *So, for example: you have got six people available to work with you. They're all more or less afraid. We are standing spread out along a footrope well above the deck, with our harnesses clipped onto the safety line. We are having a fight with the sail. The wind is blowing awkwardly and we are trying to gather the sail in and get it safely stowed. You have to get the job done. You also have to make sure that nobody loses their nerve or has a really bad nightmare working up there and also, preferably, that nobody falls off the yard and ends up dangling in midair in their harness! To run that show, you need team management skills.*

That shut them up.

Adam: I bet it did. I have my own version of such a shutting up line, though it has nothing to do with sailing but rather with classical music.

Eleanor: Do tell, Adam.

Adam: Well, when I am asked if I ever managed a team, I truthfully say: 'Yes, many times and the first time I was in charge of a big team was in 1995, and I was twenty'. This usually raises an eyebrow or two. Once that happens, I just continue: 'Yes … you know … I managed a sixty-piece symphonic orchestra on their US tour, and by the way, the first three concerts were in New York's Carnegie Hall. (And yes, if you were wondering, no mobile phones or internet were at hand, just pagers and public phones in case of emergencies.)'

Eleanor: Now, that is what you call a showstopper!

Adam: Not sure it is one but I really like to look at people's faces when I say these things (and they are all true). I get in return a good dollop of disbelief mixed with 'what the hell is he talking about'. (He is a law professor, right?)

Anyhow, back to square riggers. I guess that it has not always been hunky dory and you must have had some scary voyages, too.

Eleanor: Oh yes … I have done about 18,000 miles in square riggers. It's had its worrying moments (another British understatement). Here's one of the worst. On that particular occasion I wasn't sailing as a watch leader but rather as an ordinary crew member, as a trainee, on board *TS Astrid*. I'd not sailed on her before. We were only a couple of hours out of port, and (stupidly) we hadn't done the safety briefings properly before departure. To make matters worse, experienced sailors or not so experienced, none of us knew the precise layout of the pinrails where all the lines to handle the various sails and hoisting yards were belayed. These are always slightly different on every ship. Even though the basic ideas are the same, and obviously a particular line (for example: a halyard, a clewline, a sheet) will always do a particular known job, they may not always be belayed in exactly the same places. That's up to the bosun: he's in charge of all the standing and running rigging and what goes where is his call. As we got further out into the open [English] Channel and the wind freshened, the officer of the watch decided that we had too much sail set. One of the higher sails couldn't be furled because the clewline was jamming in a block at the yardarm. So a bosun's mate was told to go up and clear it. She went up the ratlines – and she didn't clip her harness onto the safety line before stepping onto the footrope and making her way out to the yardarm. (I think, to be honest, many of us have probably done the same as we have become more comfortable working aloft – I know that, before this voyage, I had sometimes omitted to 'clip on' when I'd been in a hurry and wanted to get on with an urgent job at hand.) We had a wind of force seven or eight on the Beaufort scale blowing crosswise over the stern quarter of the ship, from diagonally behind us, from our tail. Obviously, *Astrid* was moving back and forth, and corkscrewing unpredictably. And the combination of wind and tide had kicked up a real swell coming up the Channel. The bosun's mate was using both hands to try to unjam the clewline inside the block. (Not 'one hand for yourself and one for the ship', but then again, many (many) of us have broken that old rule when we have needed both hands for the job!) She lost her grip and came off.

Fortunately, she bounced off the main shrouds on the way down, so she didn't land on the deck. Had she landed on the deck, she would assuredly have been killed. She bounced off the shrouds, breaking her arm in the process, and ended up in the Channel. Now, a well drilled crew would immediately have furled all the sails, checked for trailing lines, started the engine, and motored around to execute our man overboard ('MOB') routine and pick her up. There is a procedure for rescuing someone in the water, right? The problem was that none of us knew where the hell anything was. People were running around hunting for the right belaying pin and the right line to pull. We made a complete pig's ear of getting the sails in quickly, and ended up with lots of loose ropes trailing in the water. That means that you can't immediately start the engine because one of those loose ropes might get around the prop. You have to get all the ropes out of the water and back on board before you can start the engine. In the meantime, of course, you are drifting further and further away from the casualty. About the only thing that did work correctly was that the lookouts were pointing continuously at the casualty so that we didn't lose her. You can lose sight of a MOB very, very quickly as all you can see of them is their head on the surface of the water, in between the waves. Eventually we got all the lines out of the water and started the engine. We motored around. Then the second mate said: 'I'll go into the water and help her out'. He tied a rope around his waist. In his haste, instead of tying a bowline he tied a slip knot. He jumped into the water and the rope duly came loose. So then we had two casualties, not one, and we were drifting away again. When we came around for the second time, we put a scrambling net down the side. A number of us, including myself, went down the scrambling net to help. At that stage, we no longer cared whether we hurt her broken arm getting her out. She had been in the water for 25 minutes, meaning that hypothermia was rapidly setting in (this is the English Channel in May). We got her (and our intrepid second mate) out on that second circuit round. Thank God, in the meantime the RNLI lifeboat had launched from Weymouth and they joined us very shortly afterwards with a paramedic on board. It turned out alright in the end. Our bosun's mate was wrapped up warm and taken ashore for medical treatment. After that over-exciting start, we got ourselves a bit better organised for the rest of the trip – although, having said that, we also managed to get ourselves knocked down flat by a line squall towards the end of it. We went briefly almost fully over sideways, but fortunately then came straight back up. So in the end it was quite a lively cruise.

Adam: Now that was one hell of a voyage. Good that it ended well; you seemed to have been very lucky. Sailing is not the only water related activity that you have excelled at, rowing also came early into the picture. We already know that it put you in a great deal of trouble when you were doing the Bar course, but let's go back to where your passion for rowing started and how it has evolved over the years.

Eleanor: Well, that's easy. I have always messed about in boats. When I was growing up, if you went to somewhere that was on a river or on a lake, and they were renting out boats, those would most likely be rowing boats (less frequently sailing boats). These days perhaps you get a pedalo or a small motorboat. My family liked being on the water, looking at things, but neither of my parents, and certainly not my brother Michael, particularly enjoyed rowing the boat.

Adam: Who rowed the boat then? You were very young back then.

Eleanor: I was always the one who rowed the boat. So, when I was ten or eleven, I would often be rowing a boat that contained three adults and our dog, *Viking*. And, of course, it would not be a racing rowing boat with moving seats, just a standard rowing boat for leisurely weekend rides. So I was rowing mainly using my back muscles and using my legs to brace. If you have done that for years, you already have a pretty clear idea of how rowing boats operate and manoeuvre on water. Then I went up to Cambridge.

Adam: Right, that's when rowing, among other extracurricular activities, kept you busy.

Eleanor: But of course, naturally. As we have already mentioned, I went to King's College, which had only just started taking women. When I arrived the pioneer women in the year above me – the first year of women at King's – had already founded the women's section of King's College Boat Club ('KCBC'), which had a proudly separate name and existence: it was called Queen Margaret of Anjou Boat Club ('QMABC'), to commemorate the wife of Henry VI, the founder of King's College. Perhaps inevitably, I ended up taking over as captain. Back then the bumps races in Cambridge (the 'Lent Bumps' and the 'May Bumps') were held in fours for the women, not in eights. That was helpful for us because we didn't have that many people to put into a first or a second crew. I rowed with QMABC, and then, in due course, when I was in my third year, I tried out for the University squad (the Cambridge University Women's Boat Club: 'CUWBC'). Rachael Scarth – an unbelievably talented QMABC novice! – and I managed to get into the CUWBC second eight (the women's second crew is called 'Blondie', while the Cambridge men's reserve crew is 'Goldie'). We beat our opposite numbers in the Oxford University Women's Boat Club ('OUWBC') second eight 'Osiris' (the Oxford men's reserves are called 'Isis'). Rachael then became CUWBC President. QMABC was so proud of her! I tried again for the CUWBC squad in my fourth and final year, when I was pretending to be devoting myself – finally – to learning something about the law. But I didn't make it into the Blue Boat. I raced again, and won again, in Blondie: that year, with another friend from QMABC, Louise Forward.

Adam: Then came Oxford, didn't it?

Eleanor: Yes, I then transferred my allegiance to the Dark Blues. My Cambridge friends were uncharacteristically unkind about whether I was really serious about becoming an academic. When I explained that I had a fine idea for a research project in Oxford which was between economics and law, they said: 'Yes Leo, your research project will be the river'.

Adam: Were they correct? In other words, did their prediction materialise?

Eleanor: Well, it is true that within 48 hours of arriving in Oxford, I had found out when and where they were holding the trialists' meeting for OUWBC. And I had been greeted at the gate of my College, Corpus Christi, with a distressed cry from none other than Boris Rankov, who was already by that stage a legendary figure in Oxford rowing. He was rowing again in the men's Blue Boat but had also been coaching the Oxford women's crew. Corpus Christi is a lair of classicists. Boris, a fine classicist, had been at Corpus as an undergraduate and was now a research student there too. As I went into the Porters Lodge, Boris happened to be collecting his post. He turned around and saw me: 'Oh, my God, it's bow from Blondie'. That was my welcome to Oxford.

Adam: So, they were right, one of your research projects in Oxford was indeed the river.

Eleanor: Anyway, bow from Blondie duly became part of the Oxford Women's Blue Boat. In the Boat Race against Cambridge we got annihilated, though. We were beaten by such a margin that it was embarrassing. Let's just say that the Cambridge Blue Boat crossed the finish line, wound down from racing speed to a light paddle, stopped, spun (that is, turned their boat around) AND then put their tracksuit tops on before we managed to cross the finish line. It was particularly embarrassing because I had rowed in crews at Cambridge with seven out of eight of the members of the Cambridge Blue Boat. I mean, these were all my old mates. I had trained with them and rowed with them and we had just been wiped off the river by them. That scale of defeat would not do. OUWBC made me president for the following year. (I should add that in between, I had started the women's boat club at Corpus; and that we had a very successful 'Summer Eights' as a very fast new crew on the river, getting our 'blades' and a free Bumps Supper laid on by our generous College.)

Adam: So, that was your first year in Oxford. I suppose rowing continued in the second year, leading up to the final year when you won the Cambridge–Oxford race.

Eleanor: In my second year in Oxford I really concentrated on OUWBC. That year I did not even play squash seriously, as opposed to the first year when I did both. I had also lost to Cambridge on the squash court in the Varsity match (so, two 'full Blues' and two defeats). In that second year I was stroking the Blue Boat. We lost again, but by a much smaller margin than in the previous year. So, there was definite progress. In my third year, of course, I really should have not been rowing at all, because I was meant to be writing up my DPhil and doing the Bar finals in London. But then, well, I was re-elected as President of OUWBC for a further year (which is not that usual). So, I ran the Boat Club again in 1979/80, and I rowed 'six' in the Blue Boat: in the 'engine room', notwithstanding that I was the shortest person in the crew. And that year, as you already know, we won the Women's Boat Race – by 2 ¼ lengths.

Adam: And that, together with the cover photo of the winning Oxford crew in *The Times* newspaper, put you into a bit of trouble with the authorities for your Bar course. But we have been there already earlier in our conversations. With all this in place, the picture of your University years is rather clear. Leo was two-, or perhaps even three-timing, all the way.

Eleanor: Let's say, I concentrated on the academic work and the rowing, or maybe, I should say, the rowing and the academic work. My passion for rowing never really stopped. It certainly continued after my university years; and I tried to move up a gear. At one stage I was stroking a four that was training for the national squad. But the other three people in the four were all four or five inches taller than me. The national squad selector, Daniel 'Dan' Topolski, made it abundantly clear to one of my colleagues (but not to me!) that he was happy to have me there to make up the numbers so that the four went on training and performing well, but that there was no way he was interested in allowing into one of his GB crews somebody who, on a good day might – just about – measure five foot four inches (1m 62.5cm). He infuriated those of us who were small rowers with his poster recruitment campaign for British women's rowing, which literally said 'Five foot eight or over, and not quite making it in your chosen sport? Try rowing.' Those of us who were under five foot eight but had spent a lot of time learning how to row reasonably well were really unimpressed by that advertising campaign, as you can imagine.

Adam: I bet it did not fly terribly well. If I remember correctly, you also rowed at various championships, nationally and internationally.

Eleanor: I did; and a Thames Rowing Club four that I stroked managed to win one of those events (Ghent International) in the tightest race of my rowing life: we won by 0.29 of a second! It is just as well we did win, because if we had not won, I think my crew would have killed me. I took the final rating up to about 43 [strokes a minute] for the final sprint and we just managed to get our bow ball across the finish line first on the photo finish. None of us had any air left in our lungs, and the others were cursing me in between gasps before the good news came over the tannoy. Probably my best performance, though, was in a composite Thames-Rowing-Club-and-friends eight, at the World Veterans Championships at Bled (then, in Yugoslavia), when we took gold.

Adam: Wait a minute, veterans championships? Or is it, perhaps, like in running events? (I remember seeing the word 'veteran' next to my name when I ran one of my first half marathons when I was still on the right side of my forties and I felt it was particularly inconsiderate, bordering on rude, of the organisers!)

Eleanor: Well, you become a veteran quite early as a rower. The term 'master' has now replaced the word 'veteran'. Perhaps it's deemed more polite. Under the current World Rowing Rules on Racing, you can compete in masters rowing events from the beginning of the year in which you reach the age of twenty-seven. But I should say that the real honour that has been paid to me in my life is that both my Cambridge and Oxford Colleges have named boats after me. For a rower, believe me, that is a big deal. In Oxford I subbed in as an honorary member of the First VIII and we took the new boat out and put it through its paces. In Cambridge? Well, I had gone back for the May Bumps to do the official christening ceremony for the new eight, the 'Leo Sharpston'. I had just poured the ritual offering of champagne over the bow (and was preparing to drink a small glass myself) when I became aware there was some commotion happening offstage. One of the women's second eight rowers had unfortunately fallen off her bike on the way down to the boathouse. She was injured and couldn't row. The trouble was that the second eight was meant to be boating in ten minutes time on that last day of the May Bumps …

Adam: Just looking at the twinkle in your eyes, Leo, I think I know very well where we are heading now ….

Eleanor: You know, I kind of heard the trumpets calling me. Trying not to sound as desperately eager as I was, I said to the worried second eight rowers: 'Well, of course, you may already have a substitute all organised and ready to jump in – but if you don't, I have some kit in the back of my car'. The next thing I knew, I was in the 'two' seat of the boat, we were paddling down to get into position for the start of the race, and I was enquiring gently, 'Could somebody just tell me which version of a start you are doing, before we go and do it for real?' You need to know, Adam, there are various different ways of doing a racing start in an eight. Everyone has their pet theory about what will best overcome inertia and get the boat up to racing speed most efficiently, smoothly, and reliably. Some coaches like a very quick little jab, followed by lengthening rapidly. Some swear by three three-quarter length strokes, followed by lengthening over five. Yet others prefer a sitting-bolt-upright full first stroke, followed by a half-stroke, followed by two (or three) three-quarters strokes and then a full stroke … There are almost as many versions as there are coaches. And once you are at full length, how many strokes do you sprint for (10? 15?) before you settle into a (slightly) lower racing rhythm in the 'stride'? What you need above all to know is which version you are doing. Fortunately, I was let into the secret before the starting cannon was fired and we shot off to try to catch the boat in front. Bumps are crazy. The boats are lined up along the bank, with each cox hanging on to a bung line attached to a peg driven into the ground. The boats are at a length and a half distance from each other. There are warning guns at five minutes and one minute. Your bank party counts you down from the one-minute gun. At about 25 seconds to go the boatman pushes you out from the bank, aiming to have you all ready to go, with the bung line tight, at zero seconds. Then the starting cannon is fired, the cox jettisons the bung they've been holding as though it were red-hot, and you all row like blazes. Your job is to hit (literally, hit) the boat in front of you (to 'make a bump') before the crew behind can catch you and hit your boat. And we made our bump! There is lovely photographic evidence of a new Advocate General in Luxembourg looking exceedingly happy as one of the triumphant King's College women's second eight on that May morning. I think the next oldest person in that crew was probably under half my age, but we had a very fine time racing together.

Adam: This is such a Leo story. Wonderful indeed. Do we have an Oxford equivalent?

Eleanor: I suppose so, in a way. As I've said, I started the women's rowing club at Corpus and for two years we did very well. But our problem was that we only had women postgraduate students – there were as yet no women undergraduates. In my third year at Oxford, we no longer had an eight. We had a seven. Literally, we couldn't find another able-bodied woman whom we could teach to row and put into the boat. So, we had to come off the river, which was horrible. When that happened, I went to Corpus men's boat club and offered my services. For one outing, they put me into the third eight. That was really stupid, because the boat wouldn't go around corners against me. I mean, when we started rowing 'firm' the boat just went straight into the river bank on the opposite side to the side that I was rowing. (I made sure of that.) Then they put me in the stroke seat of the second eight, and that was fine. But then the lad who was rowing bow in the first eight decided that he had better concentrate on 'Schools' (his final examinations, coming up at the end of term). So, there was a spare seat in the men's first eight. They tried out three of us from the second eight for that seat, and I got it fairly. I fought for it and I got it (technique plus fitness plus strength plus, I guess, bloody-mindedness). That created an interesting situation because – of course – we were not meant to have a mixed crew. So I was treated to the wonderful spectacle of Boris Rankov (in full Blues regalia), standing up at the Oxford University Boat Club ('OUBC') captains' meeting and saying: 'I never thought I was going to have to make a request like this … [pause] … but can Corpus have permission for Leo Sharpston to row bow in the men's first eight, because it goes slower if she isn't in the boat?' There was a really interesting dynamic at that meeting. I was there because I was still the President of OUWBC. The women's boat club captains thought this was amazing and they were going to back it. Luckily, just enough of the men's boat club captains thought that it was ok too. It was quite a close vote, but Corpus got permission to have a woman rowing bow in the men's first eight. We couldn't row outside Oxford because under Amateur Rowing Association ('ARA') rules, this was absolutely forbidden. You could have a cox of the opposite sex, but you couldn't have a rower. In consequence, every time Corpus men's first eight went to an outside event, for example Wallingford Regatta, they dropped me and put the runner-up in the bow seat – and they duly got knocked out and came home growling. Then we got to Summer Eights. We were rowing at the top of the Second Division, rowing into the First Division. On the last day of Summer Eights, which was my last day at Oxford, we were chasing Queen's College first eight. By the way, Summer Eights was also overlapping with my Bar final exams but you can imagine that I wasn't about to pass up the chance of rowing bow in a men's first eight. I just rushed back as necessary from doing my exams in London to row in the races in Oxford.

Adam: As one does!

Eleanor: As one does, indeed. (C'mon, these chances only come to you once.) The final stretch of the Summer Eights course in Oxford passes in front of the boathouses. You row into a complete wall of sound. Everyone is screaming their heads off. We were chasing Queen's and getting closer to them. By the time we were outside the boathouses, we were a quarter of a length off them and we were gaining on them every stroke. The Queen's cox was sitting there, fishtailing desperately with his rudder, trying to move the stern of his boat across so that we would miss them when we decided that we had enough overlap and swung inwards to try to make the bump. He was looking back over his shoulder at Armageddon arriving, forwards at his own crew, back again … forwards again … and he was shouting: 'Row, you buggers, row, you're not going to get bumped by a f***ing woman'. Three strokes later, he had my oar in his back.

Adam: Brilliant on all counts, Leo. Again, you have twinkles in your eyes when you say it.

Eleanor: I have been quite lucky in some of the things that I have been able to do in my life. That was a very, very sweet moment. I mean, I didn't hurt him of course, but I made sure that my oar made solid contact with his back.

Adam: Well, he was asking for trouble, so he got what he deserved. As simple as that. At this stage, our readers may be asking themselves a fairly reasonable question: what else is Eleanor Sharpston capable of? Knowing you, Leo, my immediate answer to them would be: brace yourself, she is capable of quite a lot. Give her a sport discipline (or, as we have already discussed, a new musical instrument) and she will have a go at it.

Eleanor: The trouble about me is that I am not the kind of person that will do just one sport and be content to stick with it. Much too simple! Essentially, whatever sport is around and looks fun, I'm going to have a go at it. I've always been reasonably coordinated, reasonably fit, reasonably bloody-minded, and I can usually get some distance with a new sport whether I am officially meant to be doing it or not. Take modern pentathlon, which I tried at one stage in Oxford. The modern pentathlon combination of sports brings together three disciplines I am naturally quite good at, and two that I am hopeless at. It was invented as the tale of an imaginary soldier.

Adam: Oh? Is that so? (says he, whose father did the decathlon, thus he should know his basics!)

Eleanor: I probably won't get the five disciplines in the right order now, but here it goes. First our hero fights a duel (with an épée, not with foil or sable) against an opponent on foot. Then he turns and plunges into the nearby river and swims across. He finds a horse, conveniently saddled, standing by on the other bank and rides away on it, hotly pursued by more of the enemy. Fortunately there's a pistol in a holster by the saddle. The horse is injured, so he dismounts (with the pistol) and fires at those pursuing him. Having seen them off, he runs to complete his escape and rejoin his comrades.

If you treat it as a checklist and apply to me, then we have the following. I used to ride a horse as a child in Brazil, so the riding part was like breathing.

Adam: His name was Pegasus, wasn't it?

Eleanor: Yes, a beautiful horse called Pegasus. He was a one year old Brazilian Army cavalry charger, sold off because he was surplus to requirements. He was a ridiculously large horse for a compactly built small girl like me. Let's be clear: Pegasus was not a pony. He was eighteen hands (that's 72 inches, or 183 cm of horse). Pegasus' back was a long way up from the ground, so once I had mounted him, I had every incentive to stay on board. I was taught to ride by a retired colonel from the Brazilian Army Cavalry Division. Since the Brazilian Army was also the source of the horse, the whole thing was, in a sense, a package. I learned to ride well and securely on a really big horse. Consequently, finding myself riding whatever horse I was allocated when doing modern pentathlon was simply not an issue. Here is a horse, so I can ride it.

Adam: What about the other four disciplines that make the modern pentathlon?

Eleanor: I am a reasonably good shot and I can fence. That makes three out of five. The other two are a different story. Put simply, I am not very fast at middle distance running (as distinct from football pitch sprinting) and as for swimming, well, I have already told you, I am extremely bad at it. The only reasonably athletic person on record who, when they add a leg beat to the arm movement in the crawl, manages to travel backwards. I hasten to add that I was not officially part of the squad and that they were probably quite right not to encourage me to do modern pentathlon seriously.

Adam: The plot thickens, Leo. Shooting and fencing, which you have just mentioned, take us fast forward to another passion of yours – martial arts. Earlier on we spoke about you playing the piano in the judges room at the CEEMC in Budapest. I am not sure if you remember but during a break between the moots at the CEEMC in Prague (in 2024), you showed us your other side, you started doing karate. Are you aware that we, your fellow-judges at the moot court, have seen you doing both music in Budapest and karate in Prague?

Eleanor: I was trying to de-stress and chill, but there was no musical instrument available in Prague so naturally I turned to karate!

Adam: Right. Of course. Poor Dr. Steve Terrett, our good common friend and these days also the mastermind behind the CEEMC, was lying on the floor on his back pretending to be a little baby pleading for mercy. I kept my distance, just in case. But seriously, I find it fascinating that a person with such sensitivity as you, Leo, and a musician, would turn to martial arts.

Eleanor: I'd better explain how it started. Chronologically, I began with judo when I was a child at boarding school. I absolutely hated boarding school. I have a quick Irish temper, which – as a child – I struggled to keep. At the time, I was also not very verbal. This may perhaps surprise you, but it's true nevertheless. So if (or rather, when) I lost my temper, I started fighting. Normally, boys do that.

Girls call names or pull hair. Leo used a different technique – she punched. Very fortunately for me, one of the rare teachers with whom I was on good terms (there were a lot of teachers whom I was not on good terms with) suggested that I should take up judo. It would be good for me if I found a way of using that physical aggression productively, but it would also teach me how to keep my temper under control. In hindsight, that was an extremely good idea.

Adam: Have you ever lost your temper on the judo mat?

Eleanor: Once! The black belt who was taking the session noticed this and suggested I should come over and practice with him for a bit. So I did. Obviously, I took hold and got thrown. So, I got up off the mat, took hold again, and got thrown again. Since I am extremely pig-headed, I went on getting up off the mat and coming back in. Finally, when I had probably been thrown about 20 times and was seeing stars but still getting up and heading back in, he brought our bout to an end and said: 'Look, I like your spirit, but please, please understand you don't lose your temper in the dojo. OK?' I just replied: 'Yes, sensei.'

Adam: Then, at some point, it was judo no more – you switched to karate.

Eleanor: Karate came in much later in the story. When I arrived in Luxembourg to work as a *référendaire*, I looked around for a judo club. There was the national squad, of course; but I couldn't find much in the way of an ordinary club to join. However, there was a karate club, which grouped together people from the various EU institutions. I turned up to a session, had a look and thought: 'I'll give it a try. Why not?' That is how I started doing karate.

Adam: And you excelled in it, you now have a black belt.

Eleanor: Well, I do Adam – but that did not happen in an instant. Initially, thanks perhaps to my judo background, I moved forward reasonably fast. At the end of my three years as a *référendaire*, I had a blue belt in Shotokan karate.

Adam: This sounds very good. If I understand the rules correctly, there are nine 'learner' belts in karate before the coveted black belt?

Eleanor: Correct. But then after my stint at the Court, I returned to the UK and started – as we discussed – two parallel careers in academia and in practice. I tried to carry on with my karate but it was absolutely impossible. I was here, there, and everywhere: what one calls in Belgian French '*une vie de bâton de chaise*' [literally, 'the life of a chair leg']. I would turn up twice for training one week, then disappear for three weeks, then get back for one session before heading off somewhere else again. So, I took an unscheduled seventeen year break from karate, between 1990 and part way through my second year as an Advocate General. During my first year back at the Court, my beloved mother was still with me and any spare time I had we spent very happily doing things together. She was 89 when we moved to Luxembourg and we didn't know how long she had. Sadly, it was only one year. After she passed, I had to sort out what I would do with myself when I wasn't being a lawyer (apart from re-joining the *Luxembourg Philharmonia*, of course, which I did almost immediately). Playing squash and practising karate were the answers.

Adam: Two disciplines, not one. But of course, Leo.

Eleanor: Ah, well … Karate was interesting. I found out when and where the club's training sessions were happening and re-joined. I thought it would probably be both stupid and presumptuous to put a blue belt around my waist and go back in like that, so I put on a white belt again. Three weeks after I came back, we had our two-monthly visit from our very lovely *sensei*, Dirk Heene. At the beginning of the session, as is standard practice, we all lined up along the edge of the training area in descending order of grade: the black belts on the far right, then all the way down through the various coloured belts, and at the far left all the white belts. I was the newest of the white belts so I was at the very end of the line. *Sensei* Dirk looked along the line, and then he got to me and said: 'I know you'. '*Oss, sensei*', I replied with a suitable bow. 'I know you – and you are not a white belt. Let me see (pause) … I graded you as first blue belt [5th *kyu*].'

Adam: It is quite astonishing that he remembered such a detail as the belt you had been graded with 17 years earlier. What was your reply to his comment?

Eleanor: 'Yes *sensei*, but I have had 17 years when I haven't been doing karate, I am coming back to it now'. At the end of the session, he beckoned me over and said to me, 'I remember you well. And you have not changed! Well, you had better do the grading in June, please'. I started practising (obviously) very diligently. I thought to myself: 'Well, let's go for broke. It is probably a bit cheeky of me, but let's see if I can re-grade back to the first blue belt that I held before, rather than working my way back through each of the intermediate grades (proper white, then yellow, orange, and green). So, that was my target. Now, for each grade there is a different fixed sequence of moves – defensive blocks followed by counter-attacks against a series of imaginary opponents – called a *kata*.

Adam: How many moves are we talking about here?

Eleanor: For a basic sequence, anything between 20 and 27, but the most advanced *kata* can have 60 moves. When properly performed, a *kata* is full of intensity and focused aggression and power – and actually also very beautiful and rhythmical. A bit like ballet without the music: but you are of course performing to the inner music for that *kata* that is playing inside your head. Each grade has its specific *kata*. For the first blue belt in Shotokan karate, the set kata is *heian yondan*. So, I was diligently practising *heian yondan*, with my eye on trying to re-grade to first blue belt. *Sensei* Dirk turned up a month before the grading, and checked what everyone was up to. When it was my turn, the exchange looked like this:

> **Sensei Dirk**: What are you doing?
>
> **Leo:** *Sensei*, I am preparing *heian yondan*.
>
> **Sensei Dirk:** Why on earth are you preparing *heian yondan*?
>
> **Leo:** (subtext: oh dear, he thinks I am being presumptuous) *Sensei*, if you feel it is more appropriate, I could prepare *heian sandan*: the *kata* for the green belt.
>
> **Sensei Dirk:** I am expecting to see you present *tekki shodan*.

Now, *tekki shodan* is not even the kata for the *second* blue belt (for that grade, the kata is *heian godan*). *Tekki shodan* is the kata required to grade *from* the second blue belt (4th *kyu*) to the first brown belt (3rd *kyu*): the first of the three brown belts that lead to … attempting to get your black belt and become first *dan* (*shodan*). So what *sensei* Dirk was saying was, I want you to present yourself to grade two grades above the grade that you used to hold seventeen years ago. And obviously, with the full accompanying syllabus of blocks and attacks for that grade, not just the *kata*.

Adam: He upped the ante, no pressure whatsoever ….

Eleanor: When a *sensei*, a black belt, your teacher, says something to you, you repond '*Oss, sensei*' and you bow. That is of course what I did. But there was a little wheel going around and around inside my head:

> *He just said tekki shodan. Hang on a minute. Why did he say tekki shodan, when the kata for the first blue belt is heian yondan, and then for the second blue belt you do heian godan. Tekki shodan is the kata for the first … brown belt?! He cannot possibly mean that he is thinking about grading me to that level! But he has just told me to get tekki shodan ready. Well, if that is what sensei Dirk wants …*

I ended up doing a six-week crash course in a kata I had never seen, let alone practised, before. Please understand: it really takes time (as well as lots of practice) to get yourself into the spirit of a given *kata* and to present it well! I dug out the teaching manuals with their little line diagrams, and I begged for help from the black belts in the club. They rolled their eyes a little at first, and asked: 'Is that what *sensei* Dirk said to you?' 'Yes'. Very generously, they at once started teaching me *tekki shodan* and the rest of the 3rd kyu syllabus one-on-one. I presented myself for the grading, praying that I had managed to do enough. *Sensei* Dirk watched me with his usual eagle eye. I was so conscious of every little slip, every move that was sort of right but not really properly polished and diamond hard. At the end of the examination he said, 'I'm grading you 3rd *Kyu*. Now justify it.'

Sensei Dirk is an excellent judge of character. After that, of course, there was no way that anything was going to get between me and that black belt. Actually, karate helped me immensely when I had my first little encounter with bilateral kidney cancer. That was when I was just about to grade to 1st *Kyu*: the final brown belt before the black belt. I remember lying there in hospital after the second of the two big open surgery operations, as weak as the proverbial kitten. It was taking me 20 minutes to manage to get a glass of water off the table beside me, have a drink, get the glass safely back onto the table, and then get myself 'comfortable' again in bed. This was January 2012. I recall thinking: 'This is absolute rubbish. I should have been doing my 1st *Kyu* grading last month, instead of getting just well enough after the first operation in November to have them cut holes in me all over again.' (Two months between operations, not the six months originally scheduled. It helps if you start off fit.) And then I said to myself, 'Well – there are two *kyu* gradings a year. What about the June grading, Leo? Do you think that you can make that? You could give it a damn good try, anyway.' So I pulled myself together and I got back to being fit and operational with (ahem) indecent haste, because I wanted to be able to grade to 1st *kyu* in June and start my year-and-a-half's preparation for the black belt *shodan* examination.

Adam: I feel the urge to add that as all of this was happening you were, of course, producing Opinions as an Advocate General at the Court of Justice and playing music. One thing puzzles me, Leo. How did you marry karate with the simple, yet important fact, that as a musician, you needed your fingers and hands to be in pristine order. In other words, being a musician and doing martial arts aren't mutually exclusive activities?

Eleanor: Well, karate is admittedly a strange addiction for a musician. The way you reconcile the two is that you do not do stupid things like going around smashing bricks with your bare hands. You have other, important uses for those hands and if you want to smash a brick – well, use a sledgehammer! You organise the way that you spar, so that in *kumite* (fights), you use the physical weapons that make sense. It is no handicap, actually. It just means you need to think more carefully about what you are doing and have alternative strategies. Remember, in karate you are never meant to throw the first punch, unless it is obvious you have got somebody really big about to attack you and you might want to make a pre-emptive strike (a *deai* strike). It is very rare that you do that, though. You choose your weapons. I tend to use a lot of back-of-the-hand punches (*uraken*), which keep my fingers safe, and *empi* (close quarter elbow strikes). Likewise, given my height, I do *not* try to land *jodan* (head-height) kicks – particularly not now that my right hip is bionic rather than the original model provided by nature. My opponents are always taller than me and it would be a daft tactic. So I kick *chudan* below the ribcage, or *gedan* against an unwarily placed leading knee …

Adam: Karate was not the only sport you actively pursued when sitting on the bench in Luxembourg. I saw you have at home a rather big trophy which, when I saw it for the first time, made me think of Formula 1. But, in fact, you won it at the Court of Justice in a squash competition.

Eleanor: Ah, yes. It is indeed a ridiculously large trophy. Squash goes back a long way. My father played squash as well as tennis, and he was definitely good at squash. Although we were a tennis-playing family throughout my childhood, he kept saying to me that squash was a fun game and I should try it. So I did try it when I went up to Cambridge, got hooked, and played in (yet another) university second team. Then I went to Oxford, played in the first team and got beaten in the Varsity match. When I moved to Brussels and I started practising law there, I went back to playing squash reasonably competitively in the local league. Then life got in the way of many things that I could have wished to continue doing. I was busy trying to make a career, getting married, and losing my husband David. When I reappeared in Luxembourg as an Advocate General, rowing was not a serious option. The Luxembourg International Rowing Club was very embryonic at that stage. But there was a sports centre at the Court, including two squash courts. So naturally I picked up my squash racket again. I played a little bit, worked myself back into reasonable shape, and then the Court of Justice staff sports committee decided to hold two squash tournaments: women's squash and men's squash. I thought to myself: 'Well, my mates will have a laugh but why not? I will put my name down for the women's squash tournament'.

Adam: Judging by the trophy on your shelf, you won.

Eleanor: I am truly embarrassed to tell you, I liquidated the opposition. Of course, it shouldn't have been like that at all. By this stage, I was in my early fifties. Squash is a pretty ruthless game that demands fitness and flexibility. But that's not all. It also demands a certain knowledge of tactics, skills, and positioning. In short, it's high-speed physical chess. I was playing against all these nice young women who were in their 20s, but they weren't as fit as I was *and* they had very little idea how to play squash. I am a competitive beast. If we are playing a match, I play to win.

Adam: Is this how the football referee qualification came into the picture?

Eleanor: Oh, *that*! I was a rather effective defender in the newly-formed women's football team in Cambridge. (By the way: my grandfather on my mother's side played as a defender – left half, I believe – for England in the first ever England v France on May 25th 1911, at Roubaix Stadium – England won 2:1.) Attacking forwards (um) usually didn't get past me, any more than they usually got past him. But, initially at least, I was a brutally dirty player. My teammates signed me up for the refereeing course so that I could finally learn the detailed rules of football and pick up fewer yellow cards! But – to go back to the squash tournament at the Court of Justice – yes, a mixture of fitness and decades of low cunning meant that I ended up winning the trophy you mentioned. It is totally, ridiculously enormous. It does indeed look as if I had won a Formula 1 race. I also got a very nice padded sports bag to carry my rackets and stuff in. The best bit – the funny bit – was that when they presented me with my loot the organisers very, very sweetly and gently said, 'Um, would you mind playing in the men's competition next year, please?' So I did, and I got knocked out in the quarterfinals – which was fine. I felt that was honourable.

Adam: Looking at where – geographically – you spent a big part of your childhood (and remembering 'the EU law lecture in a gondola' story), I guess skiing is also a part of your *repertoire*.

Eleanor: Well, skiing was the core feature of growing up where I grew up – in Geneva and Vienna. It would have been amazing if I hadn't skied. Probably the bizarre highlight of my competitive skiing career was turning out for Cambridge against the Army for a parallel slalom held at Bassingbourn Barracks (near Royston, which is a little south of Cambridge). The competition took place on a very horrid artificial slope made of plastic lozenges that looked like upturned hairbrushes. They are really unpleasant and very painful to fall on. Our captain Dougie Lowe went first, fell, and was stretchered off with blood pouring from a nasty cut on his face. That put the fear of God (and plastic hairbrushes) into the rest of us. We stopped being dashing: indeed, we more closely resembled nervous grannies. Luckily for me, the soldier that I was skiing against was much less experienced as a skier, and even more frightened than I was of the damn slope. I managed to win my parallel slalom against him, but it was not a display of finesse. I am glad that there is no known photographic record of the way I skied through the gates of that particular race. Let's just say that I got to the bottom before he did. I remember that we shook hands with heartfelt relief that we had both made it down in one piece. I really felt for him because I had so many more years of experience on skis than he did, and I felt really worried about staying upright. It was very brave of him to be doing the race at all. The bottom line is, he didn't feel secure and I didn't feel secure either.

Adam: I can imagine. I did ski on an artificial slope when I was at school here in England and it is not something that I remember particularly fondly. Putting it mildly, not my cup of tea. Not by any stretch of imagination.

Eleanor: It was absolutely horrible. The skis do not behave like skis on snow – it was more like solid, treacherous ice. Oh, and a side note – it was a typical Leo day. I did the ski race immediately after finishing the Fairbairns – the main Michaelmas Term distance rowing race for college crews. I cycled in my damp rowing kit to the meeting point where my friends picked me up in the CU Ski Club minivan – with my skiing equipment already on board – and we nipped along to Bassingbourn Barracks.

Adam: Gosh, Leo, when did you actually study?

Eleanor: Oh, in the interstices, in all the little gaps between different activities. A lot of books visited a lot of places with me in the course of being read. Those books of mine acquired lots of air miles, except these weren't air miles. They were more like train miles, bus miles, walking miles. In the odd minutes here and there, the book came out and I went on reading. If you add up all the bits of the week, there are quite a lot of loose scraps of time. If you have a book with you, you flip the book open as you are standing waiting for a bus and you read another four pages. Then the bus comes. So you get on the bus, pay your fare, sit down and pick up on your reading again. You develop rather good powers of concentration, which is an added bonus. That said, it is true that the various extracurricular activities kept me busy as well, and that is how it has been ever since.

When I met my husband, David, we made a pact that he and I would each try the other's favourite sport. I definitely lucked out, because David had trained doing sub-aqua in the Royal Naval Reserve, so he loved being underwater with a scuba set. I had looked at so many films of flotillas of fish darting in and out of coral reefs, and thought that it all looked fabulous and I would really like to try that. Thanks to my pact with David, I got to try scuba diving, and it was wonderful. David was less fortunate because he had to try my favourite sport, skiing: not something that he had ever yearned to sign up for. I thought I would try to make things less awkward for him by opting to learn snowboarding whilst he was learning to ski. That way he would get to see me rolling around in the snow too. The idea of wifely solidarity was fine in itself, but we hadn't really factored in that if you take somebody who has skied since they were ten, and you put them on a snowboard, they are probably going to learn how to snowboard faster than somebody in their fifties is going to learn how to ski. After a week during which he very nobly tried to take to skiing, we agreed that he had honoured our pact and that it would be just fine for him to sit down by the fire with a nice book while I went off skiing or snowboarding.

ENDNOTES

[*] Eleanor Sharpston QC, *First 100 Years Biography*, 2019 (available on YouTube).

[1] Doyin Lawunmi, 'Behind the Scenes at the CJEU in Cabinet Sharpston: Extracts from Letters Home' in Catherine Barnard, Adam Łazowski, Daniel Sarmiento (eds), *Pursuit of Harmony in a Turbulent Europe. Essays in Honour of Eleanor Sharpston* (Hart, 2024) 29, 29–30.

[2] Piers Du Pre and Hilary Du Pre, *A Genius in the Family: Intimate Memoir of Jacqueline du Pre* (Minerva, 1998).

[3] Keri-Lynn Wilson, 'When Putin invaded my country, I couldn't take up arms – I raised my conductor's baton instead' (*The Guardian*, 29 July 2024) < https://www.theguardian.com/commentisfree/article/2024/jul/29/culture-ukrainian-freedom-orchestra-russia-putin-keri-lynn-wilson> accessed 1 September 2025.

[4] W Szabłowski, 'The power of sensitivity' in Ukraine Freedom Orchestra Tour Programme 2024, at page 22.

[5] Eleanor Sharpston QC, *First 100 Years Biography*, 2019 (available on YouTube).

[6] Arthur Ransome, *Swallows and Amazons* (Jonathan Cape, 1930).

[7] CS Forester, *The Happy Return* (Cassel, 1937); CS Forester, *A Ship of the Line* (Michael Joseph, 1938); CS Forester, Flying Colours (Michael Joseph, 1938); CS Forester, The Commodore (Michael Joseph, 1945); CS Forester, *Lord Hornblower* (Michael Joseph, 1946); CS Forester, *Mr Midshipman*

Hornblower (Michael Joseph, 1950); CS Forester, *Lieutenant Hornblower* (Michael Joseph, 1952); CS Forester, *Hornblower and the Atropos* (Michael Joseph, 1953); CS Forester, *Hornblower in the West Indies* (Michael Joseph, 1958); CS Forester, *Hornblower and the Hotspur* (Michael Joseph, 1962); CS Forester, *Hornblower and the Crisis* (Michael Joseph, 1967).

[8] Patrick O'Brian, *Master and Commander* (Collins, 1969); Patrick O'Brian, *Post Captain* (Collins, 1972); Patrick O''Brian, *HMS Surprise* (Collins, 1973); Patrick O'Brian, *The Mauritius Command* (Collins, 1977); Patrick O'Brian, *Desolation Island* (Collins, 1978); Patrick O'Brian, *The Fortune of War* (Collins, 1979); Patrick O'Brian, *The Surgeon's Mate* (Collins, 1980); Patrick O'Brian, *The Ionian Mission* (Collins, 1981); Patrick O'Brian, *Treason's Harbour* (Collins, 1983); Patrick O'Brian, *The Far Side of the World* (1984); Patrick O'Brian, *The Reverse of the Medal* (Collins, 1986); Patrick O'Brian, *The Letter of Marque* (Collins, 1988); Patrick O'Brian, *The Thirteen-Gun Salute* (Collins, 1989); Patrick O'Brian, *The Nutmeg of Consolation* (HarperCollins, 1991); Patrick O'Brian, *Clarissa Oakes* (HarperCollins, 1992); Patrick O'Brian, *The Wine-Dark Sea* (HarperCollins, 1993); Patrick O'Brian, *The Commodore* (HarperCollins, 1995); Patrick O'Brian, *The Yellow Admiral* (HarperCollins, 1996); Patrick O'Brian, *The Hundred Days* (HarperCollins, 1998); Patrick O'Brian, *Blue at the Mizzen* (HarperCollins, 1999); Patrick O'Brian, *The Final Unfinished Voyage of Jack Aubrey* (HarperCollins, 2004).

9

The Challenges and Future of European Integration

*The extraordinary adventure that is the European project has a challenging future ahead of it. However, history has shown time and again that it has always made most progress in times of crisis. It remains a noble and exciting endeavour.**

Adam: As we continued with our conversations throughout 2024, the European Union, its neighbourhood to the East and South, and the world more generally, were being torn apart by wars, multiple crises, climate change, and a plethora of other phenomena making one seriously worried where this was all heading. For two people who are passionate about European integration, it was inevitable that we would use the closing chapter of this book to reflect together on how the European Union has been addressing these challenges and what the future holds. Some would perhaps say that facing adverse phenomena has been at the heart of European integration from the very start. After all, its initial incarnation as the three separate European Communities (ECSC, Euratom, and EEC) was born in the 1950s out of the ashes of the Second World War. Those Communities were designed as platforms for deeper economic cooperation between the founding six countries, some of which had been at each other's throats for centuries. But the economic integration was not only meant to bring tangible benefits in the post-war recovery. Above all, it was designed to deliver the peace dividend. Many vintages later, the 'European project' is no longer a purely economic endeavour. EU competences, policies, and laws cover many areas going well beyond trade: environment, consumer protection, judicial cooperation, criminal law, immigration, data protection, to name just a few. As a result of seven consecutive enlargement rounds (and one withdrawal, *sic!*) – the EU is presently composed of twenty-seven Member States which, for better or worse, are united in diversity. This is not the end of the process. Several other countries have expressed their desire to join the European Union and their *rapprochement* has been progressing (however slowly at times). In December 2024, when we were making what we fondly imagined were our final recordings, the Israeli–Palestinian conflict unleashed by the horrendous Hamas attack on Israel on '10/7' continued. The brutal Assad regime in Syria collapsed, and Syrians were then proceeding on unchartered waters. Ukraine was fighting with the Russian aggressor to secure its place in the European family and, by the same token, also protecting the EU and its values from the so-called '*ruski mir*' (a Russian vision of the world). At the same time, thousands of Georgians, waving their national, EU, and Ukrainian flags, were protesting on the streets of Tbilisi and many other cities against the rigged elections, the government's U-turn towards Russia, and the brutality of police senselessly beating the protesters. And yet, all this stood in stark contrast to the European Union, whose millions of citizens continued to benefit from the dividends of EU membership without actually realising how much they owed to European integration (perhaps, not even knowing that they were European Union citizens to begin with). Surely, though, there were many others who, to use the words of Eleanor's predecessor at the Court, Sir Francis Jacobs, were proudly saying: '*civis europeus sum*'.[1] This, of course, is not to say that the EU, its institutions, and the system that was established are perfect. Nothing could be further from the truth. It is, after all, a fallible, man-made creation. For over seventy years now the European project has been 'work in progress'; and it continues to be just that. The meta question remains as to the *finalité*. To this, neither of us has the answer; nor do we have a beautifully polished crystal ball into whose depths we can gaze together. Nor do others. So, in this final chapter, we will talk about what we perceive to be the main challenges and crises that the European Union is currently facing and how one could go about meeting them.

*

Adam: I should like to use the leitmotif of this chapter as the starting point, Leo. You spent a large part of your career, both as practising lawyer and an academic, on all matters European. In your eyes and mine the European project is – as you have put it – 'a noble and exciting endeavour'. However, it has not always been a smooth ride. As we look at over seven decades of European integration, we see that the road has been full of potholes and diversions; and that the journey has been undertaken in – occasionally – very uncertain weather. But, as you said earlier, the paradox is that the old European Communities and later the European Union, have always made progress when a crisis hit. We have already mentioned the impact, for instance, that the terrorist attacks on New York and Washington ('9/11') had, triggering unexpected advances in European integration such as the European Arrest Warrant. But it is not just that. In recent times, look at how the Covid-19 pandemic has changed the European Union or how, right in front of our eyes, the Russian invasion of Ukraine is – again – changing the EU as we know it.

The list of challenges the European Union is currently facing is, of course, way longer. To name a few: rise of populism, rule of law vandalism, misinformation, misuse of artificial intelligence, lack of political leadership, solidarity crisis, wars in Ukraine and in the Middle East, future enlargements, climate change. That is a heavyweight catalogue, I am afraid. And above all, something that we cannot afford inadvertently to ignore or lose sight of: the dividends of European integration, especially peace.

Eleanor: Alright, let's look at the first few items on your list. I suggest we might begin by replacing those commas with forward strokes: so, the rise of populism/rule of law vandalism/misinformation/misuse of artificial intelligence. It all cross-fertilises, Adam. Just look at misinformation and AI. Misinformation is an old tool, AI is a new tool, and it is not the first time that populist leaders have used misinformation. I am sure if Adolf Hitler were alive today, he would be straight on to AI and its usefulness. Not to mention Joseph Goebbels, who even without the technical tools which AI would now make available, was the classic example of a spin doctor before the term was even invented.

Adam: It is a scary thought. As I mentioned earlier, while I appreciate that AI may bring some benefits, I am also mindful that an overuse of AI switches off thinking and curiosity. As soon as we take at face value what AI gives us, we are stepping onto very thin ice.

Eleanor: I know. The question is whether the person listening, watching or reading thinks they should engage their critical faculties or not. Let's travel back in time to the 4th century BC: Thucydides, the war between Athens and Sparta, and Pericles' speech over the Athenian dead. Put succinctly, that speech was wonderful propaganda for Athenian democracy as the system to be preferred over Spartan oligarchy. Now, I have just made a very rude statement about a fabulous piece of writing. It doesn't diminish the writing in my eyes that I know that there was a purpose behind putting those words into Pericles' mouth. So I can continue to appreciate the peerless quality of the prose. But I can also see that after the first year of the Peloponnesian war – this was the big, public funeral oration for the Athenian dead – it was vitally important to get those various messages across. Back to AI and fake news. I think the issue is not with AI per se, but rather whether people are willing to switch their brains on when they are listening to something or reading something. Do they instinctively ask themselves fundamental questions? Who is telling me this? Where did they go for the information? What am I being told? Am I also hearing the other side of the story? Why am I being told this: what is the purpose in giving me this perception of reality? If you ask those questions and do so consistently and impartially (that is, whether you like what you're getting or vehemently disagree with it), you are making an excellent start. Nothing is guaranteed, nothing is perfect, but you are probably moderately well inoculated against falling for pure misinformation.

Adam: The trouble starts when the instinct to ask questions goes awol and people without questioning accept whatever is thrown at them. This is an ideal ground for populists, autocrats, dictators.

Eleanor: This is why rule of law vandalism is linked to the previous two. The more interesting underlying questions are: why? and why now? For decades, we have thought that having a stable legal system and respect for the rule of law was, on the whole, a Good Thing. It might not be entertaining, it might perhaps even be quite boring, but it was good. Why have many now moved from there to thinking that we are all a bit tired of experts and lawyers and independent judges?

Adam: Sadly, this trend is not only confined to the European Union and its Member States. Frequently when people in the EU think about the rule of law crisis, that immediately takes them to discussing Hungary, Poland, Romania, and Bulgaria. But the problem is not limited to these four countries. It has spread also to other parts of the democratic world.

Eleanor: Within the EU, you can point the finger at certain states. But I wonder if it would be right to point the finger exclusively at those states. You might find examples elsewhere where you felt a little bit iffy about what had gone on. But yes, you are right that rule of law issues within the EU are happening within a wider context. We seem to have moved away from the idea of a rules-based international order and towards the notion that even in a democratic country, somehow the rule of law is an optional extra. It is not. It is one of the big roots of the constitutional tree that you hack out at your peril.

Adam: I was astonished earlier this year when our UK Parliament, in my humble opinion, abused the principle of parliamentary sovereignty by adopting the Safety of Rwanda (Asylum and Immigration) Act 2024. It is in flagrant breach of rule of law principles and international law at so many levels that I would not know where to start. Just look at this, not only was it meant to deactivate parts of the Human Rights Act 1998, but also to overrule the Supreme Court. Both are fundamentally dangerous in a country that claims to have democratic credentials. First, the Supreme Court had ruled that Rwanda was not a safe country. The Parliament 'just' says: the Supreme Court is wrong, and since we think Rwanda is a safe country, it must be one. We say so, because we are sovereign.

Eleanor: It was all very, very bizarre to say the least. Meanwhile almost every respectable lawyer who knows about public international law and UK constitutional law was saying:

> *Excuse me, if Parliament says that the moon is made of blue cheese, does that as a matter of reality mean that the moon is really composed of Stilton or Gorgonzola?'*
>
> *Do we think that Parliament is so sovereign that if Parliament says the moon is made of blue cheese, that requires all the astrophysicists to go down on their knees and beat their breasts and say:*
>
> *'Forgive me. I have sinned. I never realized before that the moon was made of blue cheese. I thought it was made of various types of rock but clearly I was wrong, because Parliament has just told me it is made of blue cheese and Parliament is sovereign. How stupid I was.'*

The rule of law should be in the DNA of every lawyer working in a liberal democracy. Remember, democracy is not a given. Nor are the values it incorporates. Democracy is something that we need to fight for every day. As lawyers, we are privileged to be able to do that through striving to uphold the rule of law, wherever we practice, whatever precisely we are doing.

Adam: Well, exactly. Luckily, after the General Election of 4 July 2024, that particular constitutional monstrosity will not enter into force. But if we go back to the European Union and its rule of law crisis, the additional question – apart from 'why ?' and 'why now ?' – is whether the reaction of the EU was adequate. The rule of law crisis had been brewing for a while. First the premature accessions of Bulgaria and Romania, which meant that both of these countries imported their pre-existing rule of law troubles into the European Union. Then it was Hungary, and finally Poland with its government and president who, as of 2015, commenced their blitzkrieg to dismantle the rule of law. Do you think that the EU was too slow to react? Was it too cautious in testing the tools that could have been employed to tackle constitutional vandalism? For instance, the infringement procedures?

Eleanor: The trouble with the infringement procedures is that they are within the exclusive discretion of the European Commission. There have been cases in the past where somebody has tried to get the Commission to bring proceedings, and the Court has been adamant that it is the Commission's choice whether to make that call. It cannot be forced to do so. When the rule of law crisis erupted with its full force, the Commission was distracted. A lot of bandwidth was being occupied by something called Brexit; and that was a vast distraction. Having a Member State decide to leave, and then be quite as tedious about leaving as the UK was, was truly a distraction from other very important matters that the EU could and should have been focusing on as a greater priority.

Adam: What would your list of priorities include, Leo?

Eleanor: Well, for starters: climate change, rule of law, regaining proper and effective stability after the financial crisis and getting back to employment and growth, being ready to deal with an emergency like the Covid-19 pandemic. When Brexit was happening, there really were other things going on that required attention.

Adam: Not to mention the Western Balkan countries, which – when Brexit happened – had been knocking on the EU's doors for many years.

Eleanor: Of course, by 2020 there was the group of former Yugoslav countries (plus Albania) which were aiming to join the EU. Perhaps more attention should have been being paid to people who wanted to join than to people who weren't happy with the club and wanted to leave.

Adam: Alas, that was not the case. We will come back to this later, but still, I should like to talk a bit more about the rule of law crisis. I suspect that one of the main legal issues for the Commission was whether, in infringement proceedings, it could rely on Articles 2 and 19 TEU. In other words, the meta question was whether those Treaty articles were justiciable.

Eleanor: Absolutely. But you are only going to find that out by asking the Court of Justice. You won't discover the answer by sitting in a solemn circle and contemplating the text of Article 2 TEU or Article 19 TEU, or both – right? You need to have the '*cojones*' to take the political decision. Either you are going to use Article 2 and/or Article 19 TEU and see whether they stick; or you decide, however sad this may be, that you cannot use them as legal weapons. Then again, doing nothing is itself a choice. It is a choice to kick the can down the road in the hope that maybe times will improve, people will start to behave better, and the problem will go away. Or that by then the problem will be in somebody else's in-tray, so you won't have to deal with it. These are not very glorious explanations, but they do take us across to one of your other questions, which is the lack of political leadership.

Adam: You are absolutely right here, Leo, that the Commission was not doing what they should have done, but they were waiting for some national court to take the initiative and make a reference for a preliminary ruling. That eventually arrived in *Associação Sindical dos Juízes Portugueses* (Case C-64/16).[2]

Eleanor: This is the history of EU law. For those of us who are sufficient nerds that we have been following it all our professional lives: all the really big moves forward that have happened in EU law have come through the preliminary ruling procedure. Whether you are looking at *Van Gend en Loos* (Case 26/62),[3] *Costa v ENEL* (Case 6/64),[4] *Francovich & Bonifaci* (Joined Cases C-6/90 and C-9/90)[5] or *Brasserie du Pêcheur & Factortame* (Joined Cases C-46/93 and C-48/93)[6] it is the same story every time. You could easily add to that list.

Adam: So very true. This is one of many reasons why the preliminary ruling procedure is so important for everyday application of EU law.

Eleanor: Yes, indeed. Big moves forward in European integration do not generically happen because the Commission has the political will to push the boat out and see whether it will work. The moves forward come because a national judge has a case before her/him brought by an enterprising lawyer, usually a moderately young lawyer, who is looking at an EU law text and wondering if it will help the client. A sensible national judge, faced with a bold argument on behalf of the applicant and the predictable counter-argument from the Member State ('Good Lord, no! Naturally, EU law couldn't possibly confer that type of right'), will stay the proceedings and make a reference. When that happens, all bets are off. As we've already mentioned, unlike the US Supreme Court the Court of Justice does not have docket control. Provided that the reference satisfies some pretty basic conditions as to admissibility, the CJEU judges (and Advocates General) are then faced with a case that is sitting there, smiling evilly, with a flashing yellow light oscillating over the top and a siren howling, saying: 'Look out. I am dangerous. I am very dangerous – but you have got to deal with me'.

Adam: *Associação Sindical dos Juízes Portugueses* is a very good example in this respect. When the judgment came out, I read it immediately on the same day in one sitting. I've still got that copy saved somewhere at home with my green fountain pen graffiti all over it. At some point, I underlined the text and added a comment: 'this is no longer about Portugal, this is about future rule of law cases'. It is a classic case of an invitation to sue, a message encouraging the European Commission to give the rule of law cases a go. Of course, with the judges bound by secrecy we do not know exactly what happened behind the closed doors of the deliberation room. Yet, in early May 2024, when I was moderating a panel at the conference organised by the Court of Justice to commemorate twenty years of the big bang enlargement, I threw this idea up into the air. President Lenaerts was sitting in the first row and he was nodding approvingly. (Hopefully I am a good judge of body language!)

Eleanor: Not, of course, that he would say or do anything to reveal the secret of the *délibéré*.

Adam: But of course not. I had to control myself not to start laughing. In that particular case, it is so obvious what the Court was doing and why. Using standard Court lingo, in reality they were passing a clear message along the lines of: 'For heaven's sake, do something. We are opening the door for you, can't you see?'

Eleanor: 'We are giving you all the quotes you need to copy-paste into the application. Now get on with it'.

Adam: It was all very nice, but the trouble was that by then the train had already departed. And (as a bonus) it was moving really fast, especially in Poland. The rush of legal vandalism reached such high levels that even the penalties imposed by the Court of Justice didn't work because the Polish government felt secure and comfortable enough simply not to pay them. The European Commission had, in turn, to figure out how to deduct them from financial transfers going from Brussels to Warsaw. *Associação Sindical dos Juízes Portugueses* came too late, the damage was done.

Eleanor: Lots of damage had already been done …

Adam: Trying to turn the tide is very, very difficult, I am afraid. I do wonder about what you have said earlier, Leo. Why has this happened?

Eleanor: Do you mean the rule of law crisis or the rise of populism? Or perhaps both, as they go hand in hand?

Adam: Both as indeed, conveniently for those supporting and using these phenomena to meet their political ends, they go hand in hand.

Eleanor: As we have really already said, the rule of law problem is a much wider one than Poland and Hungary (or Bulgaria and Romania for that matter), and does not necessarily have anything to do with the terms and conditions of those States' accession to the European Union. Just have a look at the far right ('*Rassemblement National*') in France or AfD in Germany, or the current Prime Minister of Italy. I believe this takes us in the direction of a bigger, deeper and very important question. How do we find a way for European citizens to understand that their citizenship of the Union is not merely a sound bite? That the European Union is *not* a project for the elite, not just something for the mandarins to talk about in Brussels? On the contrary: the European Union brings real and tangible benefits to European citizens in all sorts of areas. Yet bringing home the benefits of the European Union to the ordinary European citizen is a challenge on which, I think, the institutions and the politicians alike have so far signally failed to deliver.

Adam: I couldn't agree more, I am afraid.

Eleanor: Part of it has to do with education.

Adam: It does but I reckon that this has to do, more generally, with the way young generations are raised. That goes back to what our conversations started with, when you explained how your home, Leo, worked. In your own words, 'The standard way that the family spent time was talking about things, discussing issues. We didn't sit down with a TV dinner and while away the evening. We tended to start talking about something that was topical or something that was a philosophical problem'. This is how the home I come from worked, too. I spent my formative years in Warsaw, with occasional extended stays in London, and we witnessed history unfolding in front of our eyes: the fall of communism, the economic and societal disaster that first the communist system itself and then its subsequent collapse have brought upon people, and so on. This is what my parents and my grandparents talked with me about. But, perhaps, the (relative) welfare and peace that we enjoy mean that such things do not occupy households any more these days. It seems that what a particular celebrity / influencer wore (or more likely, the bit of garment she or he did not wear) the previous evening is more worthy of attention. It is easier to digest. ('Oh, I have so had enough of this or that war or crisis or disaster: I need to switch my mind to something more pleasant.') It also makes me think that never in the history of the world have people had access to so much information and used that information so little.

Eleanor: I think that is true, but I also believe that what occupies households is partly a reflection of the quality of what is being served in the media airwaves. If the news is about sound bites and particular messages, but contains relatively little substance, that is surely a contributing factor. So often a politician gets on the news and produces a real 'switch your mind off message' along these lines: 'We are putting in place a world-beating programme that will deliver A and B at pace'. Many will fall for that message. There will – I hope! – be some part of the population that will think to themselves: 'I don't necessarily need the programme to be world-beating. You just need to convince me that you've thought it through and that it might stand a chance of working'. My trouble is that, given how I grew up and given my family background, I find it very difficult to imagine becoming an adult and taking my place in society as a European without an awareness of European history, and therefore without that awareness of why this great experiment of a European project is so crucial and so necessary. That is a reflection on how I grew up. I just cannot imagine reaching adulthood without that awareness and, indeed, without a desire to play some part in that project.

Adam: And you played such an important role, indeed, Leo. A long serving Advocate General at the Court of Justice, an academic who taught and mentored thousands of students, a widely read contributor to the academic discourse. I could go on for quite a while.

Eleanor: Please don't!

Adam: What you have just said about your upbringing is very familiar territory to me and, I guess, to many people of my generation in the part of the world that I come from. Being raised behind the Iron Curtain, many of us knew how the other, the Western world smelled and what it looked like. When it came our way, many things nevertheless stayed at the back of our heads. I remember going through passport control at Gatwick Airport in early May 2004. Once on the other side, my eyes started to sweat and I texted my parents to tell them how it feels to enter the United Kingdom without interrogation and without a stamp in the passport. It just felt so surreal. Similarly, I will never forget having an unplanned overnight stop in Vienna, when my connecting flight was heavily delayed into the wee hours of the morning. Facing a prospect of spending the night on the bench at the Schwechat Airport, following the prudent advice of my wife Anna, I quickly re-booked the ticket and opted to stay in a hotel in central Vienna. By sheer luck I ended up in the Bristol Hotel, just next to the Opera building and, thanks to a very kind receptionist, in the Giacomo Puccini suite. When I found out that Puccini actually stayed there whenever visiting Vienna, not only did I not sleep for most of the night but I also opened the windows wide and listened to *Tosca* on repeat. My heart is always full of gratitude that I can carry my passport with me, that I can just change plans, get off the plane and just walk out into Vienna (or any other city, for that matter) without asking someone in a uniform for permission.

Eleanor: That was a very lovely landing zone. It is a very beautiful and very 'Adam' story.

Adam: (*chuckles*) I see a big difference with the younger generations who were born in the EU and have always had the benefits of the EU. You name it: cheap flights, no roaming charges for your mobile, Erasmus student exchange, and many other very tangible benefits. But somehow many young people take them for granted and do not appreciate what they owe to EU membership. A bit like your companion in the ski gondola in Kitzbühel or my builders in Richmond upon Thames.

Eleanor: The question is perhaps whether they have forgotten, or whether they simply do not realize it.

Adam: I think it is both. Then again, what of the role of parents, of teachers, but also of those who are in charge of our countries? This takes us to the leadership crisis we are facing. What we need in times like ours are true leaders, not people in particular positions of power that have the word 'leadership' in their job description, but who are too mediocre to lead in anything. Holding a leadership position and being a leader are not always two sides of the same coin. Looking around makes me worried.

Eleanor: Well, it is worrying because I don't hear either of us immediately stepping forward to the microphone, as it were, with a long list of people who we think would fit the bill as outstanding true leaders. Conversely, we can probably readily think of people who don't fit the bill and that would be a long list. We might even have a considerable overlap between the list that each of us put forward.

Adam: And the list of real democratic leaders would be very short, instead. The crux of the issue is that we live in very volatile times where the underlying beat of the music is determined by war criminals, bandits or populists who want to make this or that country 'great again'.

Eleanor: Precisely. But then, in democratic countries it also boils down to whom the voters elect. What does the engaged citizen do about this, Adam? What is the committed academic supposed to do? What is our public duty?

Adam: Well, call me old fashioned, but I think we have a major role to play in our academic microworld before we let the young generations walk out into this wild, wild world. I always start my UK public law classes with a pep talk. I say that this is the module which they should excel at, because it is about the foundations of their country or the country in which they reside. I also stress that they should vote in elections, that it is their utmost duty to do so and to set an example. (Of course, I would never tell them whom to vote for, but I do advise them not to make their choice lightly.) Sadly, frequently the reaction I get back is smiles and laughter. When that happens, I deliver my usual punchline: 'This is not a laughing matter. You should appreciate how lucky you are because elsewhere people die to have that right to vote. Or sometimes, even if they do have the right to vote, it is illusory as elections are rigged, merely a facade and a mockery'.

I should add that I haven't skipped a single election in which I had the right to vote.

Eleanor: I made a point of getting myself back on the electoral register in Cambridge when I was there for the academic year 2023–2024, so that I got back my right to vote as a UK national.

Adam: Ah, of course. You had been disenfranchised in the United Kingdom after fifteen years of living in Luxembourg.

Eleanor: Indeed, and I very carefully arranged to be in Cambridge in order to vote in the general election on 4 July 2024. I did the same with the elections to the European Parliament on 9 June 2024, when I voted in Luxembourg. Having said that, as a Luxembourger I would like to wave a little flag for the wonderfully sophisticated voting system that we have in Luxembourg. You can probably only have our system in a very small country where people are reasonably well educated. The system is designed so that I can express real nuance in the party (or parties) and the individual politicians whom I wish to vote for. That gives me the democratic assurance that, if I want to express a particular balance of political views, the government that I get may have some vague or faint resemblance to the views which I and other citizens expressed. It is the diametric opposite to the 'first past the post' system for elections to the House of Commons.

Adam: The trouble is that 'first past the post' did save us in 2024 from having a large UKIP representation in the Commons (under the label of the Reform Party). On the one hand, that gave the current Labour administration more room for manoeuvre with their handsome majority. On the other hand, many of those who voted for the Reform Party may feel disappointed at not being properly represented (which would have been the case, if we had a proportionate system).

Eleanor: The reach of the voting system goes beyond that, of course. You do campaigning differently. Political parties go into the electoral campaign in a different way if they know that they are in a system where they may very well end up having to negotiate a coalition. It is no longer a zero-sum game. And with participation in a coalition government comes shared responsibility. You cannot generate perpetual streams of hot air, fake news and downright lies without ever being called to account …

Adam: It starts with the selection of candidates. Under 'first past the post', in the areas where you stand no chance as a political party, you put forward a candidate for the sake of having a candidate, even though you know that that person stands no chance of being elected. In my constituency, where we traditionally have either Liberal Democrats or Conservatives, those two parties offered the voters a choice between two strong candidates, while the Labour Party could not care less.

Eleanor: And that brings us on to tactical voting. As far as I understand, there was a lot more tactical voting in the UK at the 2024 election than there has tended to be in the past. But the 'first past the post' system also means that if you are running in a seat where you know you are not going to get elected, you can say literally whatever you want. And you can make the wildest, most irresponsible of populist promises. You are never going to have to deliver on them.

Adam: Do you think there is a way of persuading young generations that democracy is good for them and they should treat the right to vote with real respect? And, in the EU context, is there a way of bringing EU citizenship back to life through educating younger generations?

Eleanor: Yes, there are lots of ways, starting with education at very early stages. Let me mention Kris Grimonprez, an unsung heroine of EU law, and a book she authored which is based on her PhD thesis titled: *The European Union and Education for Democratic Citizenship. Legal Foundations for EU Learning at School.*[7] I was there at the viva when she defended her thesis – partly out of solidarity with her and her husband, Koen Lenaerts (the President of the Court of Justice of the European Union), but principally because I was really very much interested in the area she had been working on and in her ideas. I think she has been extremely perceptive in identifying the reality on the ground; and she has really done her fieldwork work carefully. If you want to know how much information there is about the European Union in curricula and how matters European are handled, that book is the place to go.

Adam: You inspired me to read her book and, indeed, it is a very interesting read that we can draw on. It looks like education has to treat some absolute basics as points of departure.

Eleanor: I think you need to begin with the underlying ideas of what citizenship means and what belonging to a community means. I don't think you can tackle EU (or national) citizenship as being about living in a particular, special box. I think you need to go back as far as the Greek *polis*. It was really clear there that if you were a citizen, that gave you rights, but it also gave you obligations. The idea that citizenship is only about rights – about what you can *get out* of the community to which you belong – is a very extraordinary and distorted picture of citizenship.

Adam: It is very self-centred and feeds into the contemporary world where many people think that everything circles around them, that they are not part of a community.

Eleanor: But whose fault is that? Who has created the narrative and allowed the narrative to spread, in which the only question you ask is: 'What can I get out of this?' rather than 'What can I put into it?'

Adam: Which was exactly the powerful point you made as the Advocate General in your Opinion in *Reallocation* cases.[8]

Eleanor: It looked as though that would be the only opportunity I was going to have to make a point about which I cared deeply. I knew that the Court was unlikely to go there because it didn't have to. The Court was not going, in the judgment, to write in a whole lengthy section on solidarity because strictly speaking it didn't have to address that issue. But the Advocate General could and did. There I was really speaking from the heart, saying: 'Listen, if we want to make the European project work, we have got to do better than running a cost-benefit analysis on exactly what I can get out in return for every penny, pound, or euro that I put in'.

Adam: My sentiments exactly. But the question is how we can help solidarity and EU citizenship to spread their wings.

Eleanor: Again, education, Adam. It has to do with explaining to children, as they come through school, what has happened, why the European Union came into being, what are the sort of impacts that it has had in your life. Even simple examples may make a difference. You and your mobile phone are going to go on holiday. Well, the fact you are not paying roaming charges is not because the big phone companies were feeling nice. It is because European Union law was used to stop them from ripping you off by charging exorbitant roaming fees (as happened in the past).

Adam: I would add to this the Air Passenger Regulation. People travel in millions and as we have both experienced, flights, train or coach journeys get severely delayed or cancelled (or overbooked). What I find really interesting with all these examples, Leo, is that such rights have only been around for the past two decades and yet many people take them completely for granted. But then, not everyone can see, or even wants to understand, the benefits of integration. As Owen Matthews put it so splendidly in his book *Overreach*, 'The truth doesn't make you free if you don't want to hear it'.[9]

Eleanor: Well said. Still, I have a lot of sympathy for somebody who was in a job in a failing industry and then became unemployed. They have been on benefits for a while. They themselves have never travelled abroad. They see no prospect of a new job, and they live in an economically deprived region of their own country. Then they see that there is some new industry starting up, but they also see that immigrants are coming in who have different skills from them, and that the immigrants are hoovering up the new jobs. The immigrants are also, of course, occupying the housing, and sending their children to the local schools, and if they fall sick – well, they use the health service. Admittedly, the immigrants are there legally and they are also paying taxes into the national and local budgets; but that bit does not tend to get highlighted. It doesn't really require a big leap of the imagination to see that my hypothetical disappointed – even fearful – ex-worker will feel that he has been left behind, and that the people in government have simply forgotten about him and his mates. I can see the appeal of populism here. Into that fertile space comes a charismatic person who produces some good sound bites, and who cheerfully promises the moon if you will only vote for them. If part of promising the moon involves pulling on the levers of fear and envy in order to pin the blame on the foreigners who have been let in because there is EU free movement, I can see how you get to the anti-EU populist vote.

Adam: Absolutely. You need to add to the mix something I saw once glued to the phone booth around the corner from the Westminster Law School. It said: 'Good news has the worst shipping method'. It is so true and, in this context, it is very difficult to counter populism with reasonable and substantive arguments because populism relies so much on those sound bites that appeal to basic emotions.

Eleanor: True, but populism also often relies on nostalgia. And so somebody, or more than one person who has communication skills, urgently needs to get out there and communicate the balancing counter-message. The counter-message to nostalgia for the 'good old days' is:

> *Who were those 'good old days' so good for?*
>
> *Have you forgotten that …*
>
> [Here comes a list of things which weren't so great in the good old days, right?]

Adam: In other words, there were certainly good old days but they were for a very small minority.

Eleanor: They were probably very good old days if you happened to be in the English upper class. I really doubt that they were such wonderful good old days if you were a Welsh miner or a Welsh miner's family. To be sure, you did have the solidarity of your village, the village pub and the rugby team. That takes us through to the crisis of solidarity. This is a big topic of its own. Why do we have solidarity? Why does solidarity matter? How do you create solidarity? In the EU context, if you go back to the Schuman Declaration, what was proposed were concrete measures which would create a *de facto* solidarity. It was not: 'Let's sit down and design an abstract concept which only ENAP (*École nationale d'administration publique*) and Oxford graduates with postdoctoral qualifications can understand. That wasn't where Schuman was going.

Adam: Perhaps I am just a naïve idealist but I see solidarity as a virtue that should travel up from the very basic level of the local community to the highest level. For instance, solidarity within the European Union, between the Member States.

Eleanor: I don't think you are a naïve idealist, Adam. I am wondering though how much local solidarity you find. If there's a local problem, do you find local solidarity? Or do you find people turning to the microphone of the eager reporter from the main news station, who has rushed to the scene, saying that the government should be here doing something? Here we come back to education. Solidarity is a concept, like EU citizenship, that you have to teach people to understand while they are school children. You have to teach them to understand why these things matter.

Adam: At least you should try.

Eleanor: You should, because it is essential to get people to understand, at that early stage, that there may be a communal good which can only be created if people are prepared to chip in and do their bit. Opponents will say that you are brainwashing the young. But is it brainwashing to tell an animal that it is a social animal? That (actually) you have to be a social animal, otherwise, society as such is not going to work?

Adam: I never thought about it this way.

Eleanor: Within a wolf pack, would you call it brainwashing if Mama Wolf explains to the cubs why the wolf pack matters as something separate from the sum of the individual wolves?

Adam: No, but I think it is in human nature that when times are good, people turn to look inwards, but when times become rough, they start looking around.

Eleanor: When times are good, people look at how their neighbours are doing and they want some of that. The target becomes my individual gratification. Since times are good I can, probably, concentrate on being selfish and doing stuff just for myself and then get a decent chunk of the resulting benefit. If times are bad, you realise that looking after yourself is fine but if you don't *also* spend some time looking after each other, you may not be able to avert disaster. And if there is a disaster, then at that point looking after only yourself is not going to work. If you have a river bursting its bank, you need people to get out there filling sandbags, trying to erect flood defences, evacuating people who are frail or old (or both) to higher ground. You know you need collective action. Everyone retreating into their house and putting a couple of sandbags against their own front door is not going to get you where you need to be as a community.

Adam: That would not take you far at all. It starts with very small things that may lead to really big things. I have three examples for you.

Eleanor: I am all ears.

Adam: The first one is something that I saw on Facebook yesterday. As you probably know, as we are speaking in December 2024 things have become extremely rough in Georgia. Thousands of people are protesting against the rigged elections and the new government's pro-Russia U-turn. I saw a very touching photo of a cab driver sitting in his car. He put a note on his door saying: 'Protesters, if you are cold just get inside, I will turn the heating on so you can warm up a bit'. Someone made a comment under that photo: 'Nothing beats the power of solidarity'. And I thought, that is solidarity in a nutshell.

Eleanor: That is very simple and very effective solidarity. Touching … It has the feel of my own story when I fell asleep on my parked motorbike at Dover docks and was kindly offered a cup of tea. We spoke about it earlier.

Adam: Oh yes, indeed. It has the same feel to it. The second example is from Kyiv. A few months ago, a residential building where one of my acquaintances lives was hit by a Russian drone. Her flat was not affected too much, but her neighbours lost pretty much everything. My immediate reaction was: 'Tell me, tell me: what can I ship from the UK or Poland to help them? Plates, utensils, a kettle?' The reply was: 'You probably won't believe it, but we are so in this together that we have already sorted everything out'.

Eleanor: I have no words that I need to add.

Adam: There is in fact a system in place in the high-rise residential buildings in Kyiv and elsewhere: residents make sure that there is always food and water in the elevators. If the electricity gets cut off, someone may be stuck inside for hours. Neighbours basically look after each other. The third example is from my corner of London. When the full-scale invasion started, we immediately started helping out in a local Ukrainian restaurant called *Prosperity*. Overnight it became a humanitarian aid hub. Most of us working there were volunteering for 10–12 hours a day, packing aid, and loading trucks. We were mostly from the area but the whole community got together. I have to say that I was shocked and touched in equal measure. Yes, you had Ukrainians or people with a Central European background (or Polish–Ukrainian mixtures with a British twist, like myself); but most of those volunteering were British through and through. Many of them were just dropping off their donations and immediately joining the human chain to help loading a truck. We were all painfully aware that there was a humanitarian crisis of immense proportions. The supply chains were broken, millions of people were heading to Western Ukraine and to the borders with neighbouring countries. The aid had to get there before the Russian army bombed the main roads and the railway tracks. Time was of the essence and we were all mindful of the urgency of our actions. Every can of food, every bag of nappies mattered. We have just carried on since then. All of this in a leafy south-west suburb of London. The sad thing, though, is that such levels of solidarity only kick in when something so dramatic happens.

Eleanor: This is a rhetorical question, unless you happen to know the answer, Adam. Why is it that when you have such wonderful examples of real and spontaneous solidarity, the political leaders cannot take courage from that and – at a political level – lead: take decisions, point in directions which are not just sound bites about solidarity, but which are very clear, very immediate, and address what is needed? If the Ukrainian army had effective artillery for every time a Western politician has said: 'We'll stand with Ukraine for as long as it takes', it would make life a whole lot easier for them.

Adam: Unfortunately, that did not happen. There has been a lot of solidarity at the human level. But at the state level and in real terms, it has been largely a part-time endeavour. Ultimately, history will be the judge. The way I see it, it looks like the civilised world did not want Ukraine to lose – but not to win either. Ukraine was asked to defend the rules-based world against barbarians with one hand tied.

Eleanor: I am not a spokesperson for President Zelenskyy, whom I admire very much. I guess that from his point of view, there has been too little solidarity and such solidarity as has been shown has happened months after it was asked for. Various things are being allowed (and supplied) now at the end of 2024. That is fine; but they were asked for a while ago and could have been supplied earlier. Meanwhile, the landscape has moved on and Ukraine has lost an awful lot of soldiers. We need to remember that the population of Ukraine is smaller than the population of Russia, which is now also drawing on its North Korean friends.

Adam: Sadly, you are absolutely right. This is all happening at our doorstep and the European Union will have to stand up to the challenges it all brings. In the autumn of 2024 we had a very interesting high-level lecture to mark the opening of the new academic season at the College of Europe in Natolin. Our speaker was Luc Frieden, the Prime Minister of Luxembourg. He made a number of really good points, and one of them stuck in my head. He said: 'History did not just happen. It was made. The future does not just happen either. We make it happen. Now is our time to act. To dare. To be bold'.[10]

Eleanor: I am glad to hear that the Prime Minister of Luxembourg made such a valid point. I see three main strands emerging here: the next EU enlargement(s), internal EU reform, and, from the UK perspective, the future of bilateral relations between the European Union and its former Member State.

Adam: Enlargement is again the talk of the town. For a host of reasons it has been sitting idle for a good part of the last two decades, with short intervals for the accession of Bulgaria and Romania in 2007 and then Croatia in 2013. Even in the world of legal scholarship, not many colleagues have dealt with enlargement (unless they were from one of the candidate states). With the Russian full-scale invasion of Ukraine, and Ukraine's application for membership submitted by President Zelenskyy, shortly followed by the authorities in Chişinău (Moldova) and Tbilisi (Georgia), EU enlargement has become a geostrategic issue again. To think that it is partly 'thanks' to someone wanted for war crimes by the International Criminal Court in Den Haag is mind-blowing.

Eleanor: But then, so is the fact that Finland and Sweden, after decades of neutrality, opted for NATO membership as a direct result of the Russian invasion of Ukraine. Not, perhaps, the result that President Putin wanted to see … Clearly, we have to deal with the geostrategic issue, just as we had a major geostrategic issue when the Berlin Wall came down and the Soviet Union collapsed. Even those of us who were fairly hard of hearing, those who were sleeping, woke up and thought: 'This is happening and it's *big*!' A whole swathe of former Soviet satellite states soon expressed a desire to join the European Union. Do we *want* them in with us? Can we afford *not* to welcome them in and to have them instead as loose balls rolling around on the table? I know that I am putting it in very crude terms. Fast forward: the issues with the Soviet Union have not gone away. They have come back labelled as issues with Russia. Essentially, President Putin would like to go back to the Soviet Union and extend Russian post-imperial, but nevertheless imperialistic, control over the former satellite states all around the edges of Russia's territory. If we're being charitable, this is reminiscent of earlier points in the history and geography of Europe: controlling people who are between you and your potential enemy where geography hasn't put a mountain range in place to protect you. I am thinking of the European plain. In a strange sense, we have hit the replay loop, except that Russia now, instead of having just collapsed, is trying very hard and very single-mindedly to reassert itself. And, simultaneously, there are a number of neighbouring countries to the east and to the south that are knocking on our doors. If we don't want them under one guise or another to be client states of Russia, we'd better work out a good way of bringing them into the EU sheepfold.

Adam: Especially given that they all have applied for EU membership voluntarily and that the support for EU integration among the members of the public in each candidate state is strong – indeed, in some instances it is overwhelmingly high. The Revolution of Dignity in Ukraine in 2014 (referred to often as Maidan 2.0) and the even more recent protests against the pro-Russian government in Georgia are very good examples. The events of 21 December 2024 in Tbilisi are very telling. It will be hard to erase from memory the videos of the pro-EU rally with the two hundred thousand strong crowd proceeding on Rustaveli Avenue in dance steps of Khorumi (ხორუმი) – a traditional warrior dance – with EU, Georgian, and even Ukrainian flags being waved all around.

Eleanor: Cast your mind back to Greece after the colonels, to Spain after Franco, to Portugal after Salazar: the badge of newly-acquired (or regained) democracy is to join the European project. Or think of the enthusiasm for accession in many of the states that joined as part of the Big Bang enlargement in 2004. I am not saying that history always repeats itself, but there are very striking similarities. There are also differences, of course. Right now, we have the biggest military conflict in Europe since 1945. Previous accessions to the EU took place under the comfort of a military umbrella, with the world's policeman – America – picking up the tab. Everyone really knew that NATO was, in fact, bankrolled and guaranteed by the USA. Western Europe had enjoyed decades spending rather little money on defence because it could afford not to. The money was spent instead on promoting economic prosperity. It does now look as though we are going to have to work out how to look after ourselves rather more.

Adam: In the light of what we already said about the lack of leadership, it is very worrying indeed. Even when it comes to EU enlargement, I have a feeling that there is a bit of kabuki theatre going on. Yes, the EU is talking about enlargement and institutional reforms, and some of them are either long overdue or/and badly needed. Having said that, I am missing the energy that there was in the EU in the late 1990s, when it seemed that EU leaders actually meant what they were saying. I fear now that, because the situation is so shaky, there is a big difference between the mask and what is behind it. We don't know what Ukraine will look like a year from now, what is going to happen in Bosnia and Herzegovina, whether the separatist movements will gain force. How will the standoff in Georgia end?

Eleanor: For sure, no one has a crystal ball; and all these questions seem not to be getting the anxious study and attention that they deserve.

Adam: That is my fear.

Eleanor: How much of all this is because the Franco–German engine, which has always been the crucial motor for forward movement in the EU, has stalled?

Adam: Indeed. As we were finishing our conversations in December 2024, both countries were without governments with the general elections in Germany looming on the horizon. But that does not change the fact that the EU, however slowly, is now moving in the direction of some serious reform. Where do you think those reforms should go? Which issues should we tackle?

Eleanor: Well, there are certain issues we are going to *have* to tackle if we are not going to get arteriosclerosis when adding in more Member States. The original design for the European Economic Community worked very well for six Member States. Over the following decades, we have gradually added more (and more) Member States. Without throwing out the baby with the bath water, we do need to think seriously about how to shape, modify, amend some bits of the institutional structure so that the EU can still manage to function effectively with thirty plus Member States. Part of that restructuring may be the idea of having concentric circles. It is not new by any stretch of imagination (I seem to recall that, in an earlier incarnation, it was called 'variable geometry'). The idea resurfaced in the Report of the Group of Twelve a bit over a year ago.[11] If it were to be followed, you would have an innermost circle consisting of those who want to be closer than present: to share more power and decision-making. The second circle would be 'standard' EU membership. The third circle would lie outside the EU, but would nevertheless still be quite close in terms both of economics and shared values. Some idealistic and optimistic people feel that maybe it would be possible for the UK to fit into that third circle. The fourth and final circle would be the European Political Community, which would not be within the main EU structures, but which would still be heading down the road in roughly speaking the same direction. If you think that that is a plausible model, restructuring becomes easier. Having said that, you need to work out how you would change the institutional arrangements. If everyone has got to be in everything and accept everything, it becomes correspondingly more difficult to change the institutional arrangements, because Member States will be very reluctant to give up power, to give up their veto rights, or to pass up having their man or woman in whatever position it is.

Adam: In all likelihood, though, the current candidates for EU membership will not want to hear about the outer circles of the European Union (just as Poland and others refused on the spot the option of joining the European Economic Area as a stepping-stone to EU membership). This leaves us with possible rearrangements of the European Parliament, the European Commission, some of the voting rules, or even the number of judges and Advocates General at the Court of Justice. What about other reforms that the EU needs anyway? I think if Covid-19 taught us one thing, it is that the EU needs to have a bigger share of powers in the area of health protection.

Eleanor: We could probably put together a list of things if we apply the principle of subsidiarity. After all, that principle makes its appearance every time that the EU legislator produces a piece of secondary legislation in an area of shared competences. There is always a recital somewhere which explains that the issue covered by the legislation has been analysed and that, by reason of what is required, action needs to be taken at EU level (and therefore the principle of subsidiarity is satisfied).

I would be inclined to say, how about looking through the other end of the telescope? How about saying, what are the things which we have seen we really need to deal with on a trans-border basis – be that dealing with threats to youth on the internet, health protection, or – my favourite – obviously, climate change. And then we would say: 'OK, if we can see that we really have to deal with this, and individual states trying to deal with it simply will not work, then *an intelligent exercise of sovereignty* requires us to agree that we're going to deal with this at EU level'.

Adam: A stellar example is Covid-19. When the pandemic started, many people in the European Union were screaming and shouting, 'What is the EU doing and why is it doing so little?' The answer was simple: the EU has very limited competences in the realm of health protection, and therefore it lacked expertise and manpower to deal with it. The same is true of defence policy, including procurement of weaponry. A lot of clever legal minds had to look into both issues to come up with solutions which would be both effective and legally sound.

Eleanor: I think that what we are saying requires the EU to give itself permission to reflect more deeply on the next steps. There is always a risk here, because the key question is: are you going to have the EU as a thinking project for the elite, or are you going to bring the citizens with you? It is not beyond the wit of man to do the necessary 'blue sky thinking', but it may not be something which is at the top of everyone's agenda. And it is so important, so fundamental to bring the citizens with us on the future road. We had such an exercise a few years back – the Conference on the Future of Europe. Having said that, holding a big one-off listening exercise is only the starting point. We need to continue listening to the citizens. They may have things to tell us about what should go onto the shopping list: what needs to be done at EU level, what ordinary citizens are concerned about, and where they think that, if we got our collective act together, we might be able to do something more effectively at EU level than if each Member State tries to act individually. Very useful ideas may come forward from the citizens. But as a minimum, we really, really have to involve them, and we have to take them with us. Otherwise, we merely exacerbate past trends. There have been a number of occasions when the European project has moved on and those who were part of the inner circle rejoiced and patted each other on the back. The typical pattern? The insiders repeat to each other how fabulous it is that EU competencies have been extended to new areas, and that we have this and that new initiative. ('Gosh, aren't we happy we're all working on this?') Meanwhile, Joe Citizen is sitting there outside his pub, *Stube*, or *brasserie* and he says to his mate: 'I don't know what that lot in Brussels are doing, but I don't really trust them. And why are they doing it anyway? Why is it they, rather than our government, for whom we vote, who are taking action on this?'

Adam: That's a very fair point, Leo. The recent elections to the European Parliament, just like the previous ones, are very telling in showing that we are a long way away from having a pan-European political sphere and pan-European debates.

Eleanor: I would so like European elections to be about things that matter for the European Union. I would love there to be such European elections. Alas, what we have is usually a kind of mockery: a type of national election with domestic topics, but with an MEP label. I am struggling to think of any European electoral campaign that I've seen up close, where policies for the EU occupied a plausibly large part of what the candidates were saying by way of message. The turnout figures also reflect that phenomenon. That's a bit 'chicken and egg'. Those of us who were originally worried that there seemed to be a democratic deficit in the EU point to the fact that the European Parliament is now democratically elected rather than being an appointed Assembly. The procedures for adopting EU legislation now involve the European Parliament much more than they used to. We can pat ourselves on the back and say, 'this is better than it used to be'. That's true as far as it goes, but it really doesn't answer the question, 'Why are we not managing to get more people, more citizens, interested in the European Union's direction of travel?'

Adam: Well, I still hope that the European Union has a future. Sometimes I question myself but I do not see any alternative. It reminds me of the FIDE (*Fédération Internationale pour le Droit Européen*) Congress in Budapest in 2016. I was walking along the Danube with a fellow academic, a German colleague, who said: 'The EU is not perfect but give me a model that is better and that guarantees that we don't start killing each other again, I am all for it'. Brutal, but very accurate, I think.

Eleanor: I believe passionately that a model that consists of, 'We are not killing each other and we are trying to get on and help each other towards greater prosperity' is the right one. It is the model that we should all, almost instinctively, prefer to the other model. My concern is that people seem to have forgotten history. They seem to have forgotten how Europe was in the past. We were nationalist, we were populist, and we ended up shooting each other.

Adam: I tend to add into such conversations that the peace dividend is too important to be lost. What do you think the EU will look like 10 years from now?

Eleanor: I would rather hope it will consist of those concentric circles. That would take the brake off those Member States that want to get closer together. It would mean that the first two circles – the more federalist circle, and the circle comprising the rest of the EU Member States – had pretty strong connections. Other states could become a part of the two outer circles. I think it would make logical sense, for instance, for the United Kingdom to be part of that third circle.

Adam: Would you see yourself as an active contributor to the debate about the future that the European Union will have in the coming years?

Eleanor: I would dearly love to be a part of the process of thinking about it. The trouble with me is that I fall between two stools. For the Brits, I am apparently irredeemably suspect because I smell too European. For the European side of the story: sad to say, it seems that despite my dual nationality – despite being a Luxembourger – I am automatically classified as a Brit and so suspect for that reason alone. But if I could have my desire, it would be to be part of the thinking and the discussion and the exploration of ideas as to how we take the European project forward. I would be so proud and happy to be part of that.

Adam: I sincerely hope that an opportunity will arise. Having said that, we have worked on this book for over a year and I am in position to attest that Dame Eleanor Sharpston KC is super active in many fields. You are constantly on the academic circuit, involved in the Aarhus Committee, performing in two orchestras, shuttling between Luxembourg and Italy. As we saw on 4 February 2025, you have also been back pleading before the Court of Justice of the European Union (Case C-679/23P).[12]

Eleanor: Part of recovery from being at the Court is working out what you do after your term ends. To some extent the choices are constrained by the Code of Conduct for former members, which has restrictions in it. Those restrictions make perfectly good sense from the Court's perspective; and they are no impediment if one is going back to be a member of the Supreme Court in one's Member State, or if one is going into peaceful retirement in the Tuscan hills. If you are not doing either of those, respecting the Code of Conduct is – in fact – like operating inside a straitjacket. First of all, you cannot appear in front of the Court of Justice and the General Court for three years. Well, fair enough. Much more importantly: there is a general prohibition on doing anything that would be embarrassing or might cause eyebrows to be raised. You also have a more specific obligation: you are not meant to advise or otherwise work on anything that is close to what you did when you were a Member of the Court. I delivered Opinions in about 350 cases, and of course, I also looked in detail at lots of other cases where I ended up not giving an Opinion. Finding an area of EU law which doesn't have a Sharpston footprint on it is actually quite difficult!

Adam: Indeed, good luck trying to find one!

Eleanor: The combination of the provisions in the Code of Conduct makes it very difficult for me to practice: to accept instructions as a barrister. But then, a few days after my three year period for no appearances expired, and to the disgust of the academic community, the General Court sitting as a three judge chamber handed down judgment in Case T-600/21 *WS v Frontex* (the EU Border Agency).[13] The case concerns a family of six Syrian Kurds: the parents and their four young children. They had paid for passage on a boat to get out of Syria and travel to a Greek island. They were on the island for about six days, and then they were put onto a plane. They thought they were being flown to Athens, but in fact, the flight was a 'return flight' and the plane landed in southeast Turkey. They maintained this was totally illegal. They wanted to apply for asylum in Greece and they had already indicated this. Crucially, there was no evidence that a 'return decision' had been taken against them by the Greek authorities. In the absence of a return decision, it was unlawful to put them onto a return flight. It really is as simple as that. They argued that Frontex, which was jointly responsible for the return operation, should have checked whether there was indeed a return decision (which it had not done) and they lodged a damages claim against Frontex before the General Court.

Adam: And that's when things went even more south …

Eleanor: Sadly, yes. The General Court managed to mischaracterise what was very clearly a claim for damages against Frontex for failing to check whether there was a return decision as being instead a challenge to the return decision itself (or rather, on the facts, the non-existent return decision). Return decisions are the responsibility of a Member State, not of Frontex. If you say (wrongly) that the claim was a challenge to the return decision, you can then say that there was no causal link such as would be required to make Frontex liable in damages. That is exactly what the General Court did. There was a howl from the academic commentators. As I recall, Steve Peers wrote an incandescent blog within about 48 hours of the judgment saying, more or less, 'good God, what have they done?' Shortly after that, the very nice firm of Dutch human rights lawyers who had been representing the Kurdish claimants reached out to me.

They had got my contact details via a mutual friend in London. They wanted to appeal the judgment but did not have much money. Still, they enquired if I might conceivably be prepared to help. I nearly bit their hands off! I was like a dog with three tails ('I am in! I am in!') and of course they didn't need to worry about the funding, because I was happy to do it *pro bono*. I hasten to add, any self-respecting member of the Bar would have had the same reaction. I mean, the General Court's decision was outrageous. It clearly needed to be appealed, and by an absolute miracle, I *could* take the case. It arose just after the end of the three year period, and among all the Opinions that I had written during my fourteen and a half years at the Court, I had never been opinionated about Frontex.

Adam: What are the chances … Never?

Eleanor: The most I had ever said about Frontex was to record, in a footnote in an asylum Opinion, that there was an EU agency called 'Frontex' set up by Regulation 2007/2004.[14] Full stop. However restrictively you interpreted the Code of Conduct, there was no impediment to my taking the case.

Adam: Right, but – as a Brexit 'dividend' – you could not do it as an English barrister (even one who had taken silk).

Eleanor: Quite right. After Brexit, my membership of the English Bar no longer gave me rights of audience on the Kirchberg. I needed to resuscitate my membership of the Irish Bar. Remember, I had been called to the Irish Bar way back in 1986 and there was a paper trail. So it was now a matter of getting back in touch with King's Inns (where, in the meantime, I happened to have become an honorary bencher), getting in touch with the Legal Services Regulatory Authority, collecting all the necessary certificates, and paying my registration fee so that I could be on the roll of practising barristers. The registry of the Court of Justice checked every scrap of paper to see whether it was really true that I had a right of audience as an Irish barrister. Fair enough, they were doing their job.

Adam: It must have felt good to be back to practice and be a member of a team.

Eleanor: I had the real pleasure of working with a lovely team. They were such good fun to work with, and they were so committed. And we had a good cause, and we were all absolutely invested in it. After we had dealt, in our Reply, with the rather strange propositions that Frontex was advancing in its Defence, and had received their Rejoinder, the written pleadings closed. We waited. And then we heard that the case was being referred to the Grand Chamber.

Adam: Leo, that's the way to return to the Court.

Eleanor: Well, the final gorgeous touch to this (and it really is a gorgeous touch) is that at the Irish Bar, I am not a silk. In other words, I am not the Irish equivalent of a King's Counsel (an 'SC', or 'Senior Counsel'). I am just a junior barrister.

So I went from being Advocate General Sharpston to being Eleanor Sharpston, barrister at law of the Irish Bar. I enjoyed that. It appeals to my sense of humour.

Adam: I watched the recorded stream of the hearing several times and I shared the link with many of my friends and colleagues. Leo, as I wrote in my WhatsApp message to you on the day of the hearing, it was a masterclass in advocacy.

Eleanor: That's truly kind, Adam. But once again, I want to emphasise the teamwork. As a barrister, you tend to get the glory. After all, you are up there on your hind legs arguing the case. If you do it well, there is a lot of (in the best sense) good performance art. But I think that being a barrister is really like being the steel tip on a javelin. Of course it matters that the steel tip is very sharp and that it's properly fixed onto the shaft. But without the shaft, you don't have a javelin. Truly, it was about teamwork when I was at the Court as an Advocate General and I had the privilege of having Team Sharpston with me. What was so lovely about doing this appeal was that I was again working with an excellent and committed team in a shared endeavour to do the very best that we could for our Syrian family.

Adam: Looking at this case, I cannot stop from thinking about *tikkum olam*, the Jewish tradition of repairing the world injected in you by your parents.

Eleanor: In a way it bookends my time at the Court. My last case in practice at the English Bar before going onto the bench in Luxembourg was *SS Storaa* (a *pro bono* case).[15] And now, the only case I have done since leaving the Court [*Adam* (aside): thus far] is a *pro bono* case.

Adam: I hasten to add that your opening line was brilliant.

Eleanor: Well, it helps if you can find an attractive way of framing the case right from the beginning, and the opening actually wrote itself. I was able to say, with perfect sincerity, that I was grateful to the Court for sending the case to the Grand Chamber.

Adam: Not every case gets that Rolls-Royce treatment. The Grand Chamber is reserved for judgments that are going to serve as major precedents.

Eleanor: Referral to the Grand Chamber showed that the Court had realized what was at stake. The central question was, how do you want to read the Frontex Regulation?[16] Is it essentially a Regulation that imposes reporting duties and allows recommendations to be made as to how things could be done better, perhaps, on another occasion? Or does the Frontex Regulation put Frontex out there as the guardian of those fundamental rights and values that are so crucial to the European Union; and does it therefore impose on Frontex positive duties to make sure that fundamental rights are respected during the course of the joint operations that it is coordinating? It wasn't difficult to write the opening three paragraphs of the speech. If you lay out the case on the table like that, by the time you have got to the end of the first minute of your pleading, everyone should be sitting up and listening.

Adam: And everyone was. When you finished your opening statement, I said to myself: 'Good God. I would not like to be in the shoes of the opposing counsel'. Having said that, this case is symbolic at so many levels. Your family on the paternal side were Lithuanian–Jewish refugees who fled the persecution in Eastern Europe. One of your last cases as an Advocate General at the Court gave you an opportunity to speak about solidarity and refugees coming from the war-torn countries in the EU's vicinity, and your first case before the CJEU after leaving the Court is standing up for Syrian refugees. It strikes a chord and reminds me of the book written by Eva Evans, 'Once a Refugee – Always a Refugee'.[17] Generations pass but sensitivity to particular issues remains.

Eleanor: As an Advocate General, I was lucky enough to have some cases where I could speak from the heart as well as propose appropriate legal solutions to messy problems. As a barrister, you give your time *pro bono* because you believe that a particular case *should* be brought and you have the skills to do that job. It was an honour to represent the merchant seamen in *SS Storaa*. It was likewise an honour to represent that Syrian family.[18]

ENDNOTES

* Eleanor Sharpston, *'Further EU enlargement–a 'brave new world',or more like 'back to the future'?'* (2024) 25 *ERA Forum* 275, 280.

[1] Case C-168/91 *Christos Konstantinidis v Stadt Altensteig – Standesamt and Landratsamt Calw – Ordnungsamt* ECLI:EU:C:1992:504, Opinion of AG Jacobs, para 46.

[2] Case C-64/16 *Associação Sindical dos Juízes Portugueses v Tribunal de Contas* ECLI:EU:C:2018:117.

[3] Case 26/62 *Van Gend en Loos v Nederlandse Administratie der Belastingen* ECLI:EU:C:1963:1.

[4] Case 6/64 *Costa v ENEL* ECLI:EU:C:1964:66.

[5] Joined Cases C-6/90 and C-9/90 *Francovich and Bonifaci v Italy* ECLI:EU:C:1991:428.

[6] Joined Cases C-46/93 and C-48/93 *Brasserie du Pêcheur SA v Germany and R v Secretary of State for Transport, ex p Factortame Ltd* ECLI:EU:C:1996:79.

[7] Kris Grimonprez, *The European Union and Education for Democratic Citizenship: Legal Foundations for EU Learning at School* (Nomos Verlag, 2020).

[8] Joined Cases C-715/17, C-718/17, and C-719/17 *European Commission v Republic of Poland and Others* ECLI:EU:C:2019:917, Opinion of AG Sharpston.

[9] Owen Matthews, *Overreach. The Inside Story of Putin's War Against Ukraine* (HarperCollins, 2023) 255.

[10] Luc Frieden, 'Europe. A necessity. An ambition.' (4 November 2024) <https://gouvernement.lu/en/actualites/toutes_actualites/communiques/2024/11-novembre/04-frieden-discours-college-europe.html> accessed 1 September 2025.

[11] Report of the Group of Twelve, *Sailing on High Seas: Reforming and Enlarging the EU for the 21st Century* <https://www.diplomatie.gouv.fr/IMG/pdf/20230919_group_of_twelve_report_updated14.12.2023_cle88fb88.pdf> accessed 1 September 2025.

[12] Case C-679/23P *WS and Others v Frontex (Joint Return Operation)*, ECLI:EU:C:2025:976.

[13] Case T-600/21 *WS and Others v Frontex* ECLI:EU:T:2023:492.

[14] Council Regulation (EC) No 2007/2004 of 26 October 2004 establishing a European Agency for the Management of Operational Cooperation at the External Borders of the Member States of the European Union [2004] OJ 349/1.

[15] *Fogg & Anor, R (on the application of) v The Secretary Of State For Defence & Anor* [2005] EWHC 2888 (Admin).

[16] Regulation (EU) 2016/1624 of the European Parliament and of the Council of 14 September 2016 on the European Border and Coast Guard and amending Regulation (EU) 2016/399 of the European Parliament and of the Council and repealing Regulation (EC) No 863/2007 of the European Parliament and of the Council, Council Regulation (EC) No 2007/2004 and Council Decision 2005/267/EC [2016] OJ L 251/1.

[17] Eva Evans, *Once a Refugee – Always a Refugee* (Words by Design, 2023).

[18] On 18 December 2025, as this book was going to press, the Grand Chamber handed down judgment in Case C-679/23P *WS and others v Frontex* (*Joint Returns Operation*). In a landmark ruling, the Court allowed the appeal and referred the case back to the General Court for further consideration. See also the fine Opinion by AG Ćapeta, ECLI:EU:C:2025:427.

Epilogue

ON CHARLES BRIDGE[1]

After the seminar[2] was over
(The thanks; the handshakes) and the team dispersed,
I slipped away into the cold December night.

Standing in silence in the metro's crowds
Of cheerful students, homebound travellers,
I made my way into the Old Town, and my past.

Outside, under the soft velvet of the evening sky,
The bulk of Prague Castle marked the way;
Unhesitatingly I found myself upon Charles Bridge.

After the greyness of the Communist years,
The hope of Dubček's spring;[3] then shattering fear
In August sixty-eight, when the Soviets came,
And tanks patrolled on Václavské Náměstí.[4]

Twenty more frozen years; until the time
We did not believe we'd live ever to see.
The Velvet Revolution;[5] the Berlin Wall destroyed.

I came back then to Prague, and walked again
In disbelieving joy – and tears – across Charles Bridge
Where, sat between the statues, a cellist played.

Prague opened out, while my own path
Took me away from Middle Europe and my roots,
And stranded me in London at the Bar.

A chance initiative for the 'Accession States' -
A programme teaching judges EU law -
Had brought me back now, finally, at last.
Under the bridge, the water swirled and flowed.

Time faded; vanished; and I stood
At once all ages, overwhelmed
By such quiet peace, content, and grace.

I knew again with utter certainty
Where I belonged – that I am part
Of this uncertain yet compelling tale;

Knew why, and how, I too am called to play
My own small part towards 'tikkun olam':[6]
To build this Europe from whose heart I come.[7]

And so I made my vow; then
Walked away – content
To be a feather on the breath of God.[8]
A lucky feather, when all's said and done.

---

[1] Written in outline December 2004 / February 2005; revised when back in Prague in February 2009, representing the Court as First Advocate General at a conference on EU family policy organised by the Czech Presidency.

[2] TAIEX seminar on Article 234 EC references, organised by the European Commission, Prague, December 2004.

[3] The short-lived experiment under Alexander Dubček to have 'communism with a human face'.

[4] Wenceslas Square.

[5] Leading to the presidency of Václav Havel.

[6] Repairing the world.

[7] The geographical centre of Europe is said (at least by Lithuanians!) to be in Lithuania, not far from my family's home at *Vilkomir* (now *Ukmergė*), about 60 kilometres from Vilnius. It would be fair to add that similar claims (mutatis mutandis) can be heard in other Eastern European Member States.

[8] Hildegard of Bingen.

Index

www.ingramcontent.com/pod-product-compliance
Ingram Content Group UK Ltd.
Pitfield, Milton Keynes, MK11 3LW, UK
UKHW021148250926
475688UK00012B/149

9 781509 992324